40 Days

THE DAILY OFFICE FOR LENT

Compiled and edited by
Frank L. Tedeschi

CHURCH PUBLISHING
New York

Church Publishing Incorporated
445 Fifth Avenue
New York, NY 10016
www.churchpublishing.org

5 4 3 2 1

Contents

Psalms for the Holy Days

Some Explanations and Help for the Reader

The Daily Office—that is, the daily public prayer of the Church—has its roots in the ancient Jewish practice of marking the rhythm of the day with prayers at fixed hours. We know from the Acts of the Apostles that the earliest Christians continued this practice. In the ensuing centuries, with the development of monasticism, the daily round of Christian prayer grew in structure to include psalm-singing, hymn-singing, and readings from Scripture several times a day.

In 1549, the first Book of Common Prayer of the Church of England was published and included services of Morning Prayer and Evening Prayer—in English rather than Latin—with elements from the monastic rites. These services were no longer primarily the province of monks, nuns, and members of the clergy, but were intended for use by the entire community in parish churches throughout the land. Since that time, these services have provided treasured spiritual nourishment not only for groups praying together but also for individuals praying by themselves.

The services of Morning Prayer, Noonday Prayer, Evening Prayer, and Compline (end of day) in this book are adapted from the contemporary (rite two) versions found in the 1979 Book of Common Prayer of the Episcopal Church in the United States. The usages and forms of address are in modern English.

The Shape of the Offices

The Offices of Morning and Evening Prayer have a common shape:

- A seasonal opening sentence of Scripture and confession of sin (optional)
- An invitatory psalm or other song, used as a "call to worship"
- The psalm or psalms appointed for the day
- Readings from the Bible appointed for the day, with each reading followed by a canticle (song of praise)
- The Apostles' Creed
- The Lord's Prayer and other prayers (often called "collects")
- Optional concluding prayers

The shorter Offices of Noonday and Compline follow a similar pattern, omitting certain elements.

Praying Alone

This book has been designed for use by individuals as well as groups. There are ceremonial directions about standing, kneeling, and sitting. There are also texts that indicate dialogue between the leader of worship and the assembly. For example, the leader says, "The Lord be with you," and the people respond, "And also with you." However, when praying the Office alone, the individual reader should not be distracted or intimidated by these features. Rather, it is important and useful to remember that when each of us prays "alone," we are in fact part of a stream of prayer that is going on at all times and in all places here on earth and in heaven. When we pray alone, we are in fact joined and supported by a great cloud of witnesses—whom we in turn support and nurture by our offering of prayer.

Amid the realities of busy modern life, the Daily Office can be prayed on a bus or subway, on a commuter train or an airplane, or in a special corner of a room at home. Some pilgrims of the faith have even been known to start the day in a favorite chair, reading Morning Prayer and having a cup of coffee with God!

Whatever your situation, if you are praying the Office alone—and if you are taking on this spiritual discipline for the first time—it may be helpful to note the following:

- Set a realistic personal regimen. If you have time to pray only one Office a day, do not try to take on more. Failed attempts can lead to unnecessary feelings of frustration and inadequacy.
- Before you begin the Office, take a moment to focus. Even if you are in a public place, be aware of your breathing; center yourself.
- When praying alone, many find it helpful to omit the opening sentences and confession of sin in Morning and Evening Prayer and begin the Office with "Lord, open our lips" (morning) or "O God, make speed to save us" (evening), an ancient and classic opening for these services.
- Keep bookmarks in the daily readings section and in the daily psalms, so that you can turn to those pages easily. The major sections of this book are separated by black ink tab markers on the page edges.
- Do not recite salutations and responses such as "The Lord be with you. And also with you. Let us pray." Instead, go directly to the prayer in question.

- However, *do* recite both parts of other dialogues, such as "O God, make speed to save us. O Lord, make haste to help us," and the versicles and responses that follow the Lord's Prayer. These texts, while designed for corporate use between leader and assembly, can also make great spiritual sense when prayed alone.
- With a few variations, three lessons from Scripture are provided for each day of the week. With the exception of some of the Sunday lessons, most of these are "course readings"—that is, they follow a narrative line from one day to the next. Stay with the same biblical book or books every day to receive the full effect of the story.
- If time permits, take a moment to be quiet after each reading before praying a canticle. Remember that the canticles, like the psalms, are songs—and they can be prayed beautifully without music.
- If you wish to use different canticles after the readings on different days of the week, the tables on pages 49-50 offer a helpful guide.
- If you find it possible to pray two complete Offices a day, each with two readings from Scripture, take your fourth reading from the lectionary of the alternate year. For example, if you are in lectionary Year One, use the three lessons appointed for that day, and take the fourth reading from the same day in the lectionary for Year Two.
- After the Lord's Prayer and the other appointed prayers, take a moment to offer your own concerns and thanksgivings. Personal prayer, not bound by texts, is a fitting way to finish this special time with God before concluding with "Let us bless the Lord. Thanks be to God," and, if desired, one of the concluding sentences of Scripture.

Which Year? One or Two?

The Daily Office Lectionary of the Book of Common Prayer is arranged in a two-year cycle. Year One begins on the First Sunday of Advent (four weeks before Christmas) preceding odd-numbered years, and Year Two begins on the First Sunday of Advent preceding even-numbered years. Therefore, if you are praying the Office in Lent, follow the guide below. (*Note:* The Psalms appointed for each day are *the same in both years.*)

2006 Year Two
2007 Year One
2008 Year Two
2009 Year One
2010 Year Two
2011 Year One
2012 Year Two

A Word about Noonday and Compline

The shorter Offices for midday and close of day have psalms and brief passages of Scripture "built in," and do not follow a lengthy schedule of readings. However, if you find that one of these hours is the most suitable part of your day for praying an Office, both services can be easily adapted to include the readings from the Daily Office Lectionary.

A Note about St. Joseph (March 19) and the Annunciation (March 25)

The feasts of St. Joseph and the Annunciation fall often in Lent and sometimes during the Easter season. During these two holy seasons, special precedence is given to all Sundays, as well as to the days of Holy Week and Easter Week. When these feasts fall on any of these special Lenten or Easter days, they are normally transferred to the next open weekday. The Annunciation, because of its importance as a major feast of Our Lord, may also be celebrated and anticipated with Evening Prayer on the night before (March 24). Complete readings, prayers, and psalms for St. Joseph and the Annunciation have been included in this book. If you choose not to observe either feast with a complete Office, you may want to include the collect for the feast among the prayers at the conclusion of the Office.

A Note about Omitted Passages

From time to time, the lectionary indicates that certain passages of Scripture and certain psalms or parts of psalms may be omitted if desired. For example, in some of the psalms there are passages that refer to plotting ruin or murder for one's enemies. These passages do not always make sense to modern ears or spiritual sensibilities, and may therefore be omitted. Psalms or portions of psalms that may be omitted are indicated with brackets [ ], and optional biblical passages are indicated with indentations from the left and right margins.

Keeping a Holy Lent

Many people follow the laudable practice of making dietary or other sacrifices in Lent. Praying the Daily Office is a fine example of "taking on" a discipline during this season of renewal and self-examination, as we reflect on the mysteries of Christ's passion and of God's mighty acts in human history. The publishers hope that you will find this book a valuable companion on your Lenten journey.

Daily Morning Prayer:
Rite Two

The Officiant begins the service with one or more of these sentences of Scripture, or with the versicle "Lord, open our lips" on page 3.

Lent

If we say we have no sin, we deceive ourselves, and the truth is not in us, but if we confess our sins, God, who is faithful and just, will forgive our sins and cleanse us from all unrighteousness.   *I John 1:8, 9*

Rend your hearts and not your garments. Return to the Lord your God, for he is gracious and merciful, slow to anger and abounding in steadfast love, and repents of evil.   *Joel 2:13*

I will arise and go to my father, and I will say to him, "Father, I have sinned against heaven and before you; I am no longer worthy to be called your son."   *Luke 15:18, 19*

To the Lord our God belong mercy and forgiveness, because we have rebelled against him and have not obeyed the voice of the Lord our God by following his laws which he set before us. *Daniel 9:9, 10*

Jesus said, "If anyone would come after me, let him deny himself and take up his cross and follow me."   *Mark 8:34*

Holy Week

All we like sheep have gone astray; we have turned every one to his own way; and the Lord has laid on him the iniquity of us all. *Isaiah 53:6*

Is it nothing to you, all you who pass by? Look and see if there is any sorrow like my sorrow which was brought upon me, whom the Lord has afflicted. *Lamentations 1:12*

The following Confession of Sin may then be said; or the Office may continue at once with "Lord, open our lips."

Confession of Sin

The Officiant says to the people

Dearly beloved, we have come together in the presence of Almighty God our heavenly Father, to set forth his praise, to hear his holy Word, and to ask, for ourselves and on behalf of others, those things that are necessary for our life and our salvation. And so that we may prepare ourselves in heart and mind to worship him, let us kneel in silence, and with penitent and obedient hearts confess our sins, that we may obtain forgiveness by his infinite goodness and mercy.

or this

Let us confess our sins against God and our neighbor.

Silence may be kept.

Officiant and People together, all kneeling

Most merciful God,
we confess that we have sinned against you
in thought, word, and deed,
by what we have done,
and by what we have left undone.
We have not loved you with our whole heart;
we have not loved our neighbors as ourselves.
We are truly sorry and we humbly repent.
For the sake of your Son Jesus Christ,
have mercy on us and forgive us;
that we may delight in your will,
and walk in your ways,
to the glory of your Name. Amen.

The Priest alone stands and says

Almighty God have mercy on you, forgive you all your sins through our Lord Jesus Christ, strengthen you in all goodness, and by the power of the Holy Spirit keep you in eternal life. Amen.

A deacon or lay person using the preceding form remains kneeling, and substitutes "us" for "you" and "our" for "your."

The Invitatory and Psalter

All stand

Officiant	Lord, open our lips.
People	And our mouth shall proclaim your praise.

Officiant and People

Glory to the Father, and to the Son, and to the Holy Spirit: as it was in the beginning, is now, and will be for ever. Amen.

Then follows one of the Invitatory Psalms, Venite or Jubilate.

The following Antiphons may be sung or said with the Invitatory Psalm

In Lent

The Lord is full of compassion and mercy: Come let us adore him.

On the Feast of Saint Joseph (March 19)

The Lord is glorious in his saints: Come let us adore him.

On the Feast of the Annunciation (March 25)

The Word was made flesh and dwelt among us: Come let us adore him.

Venite   *Psalm 95:1-7*

Come, let us sing to the Lord; *
  let us shout for joy to the Rock of our salvation.
Let us come before his presence with thanksgiving *
  and raise a loud shout to him with psalms.

For the Lord is a great God, *
  and a great King above all gods.
In his hand are the caverns of the earth, *
  and the heights of the hills are his also.
The sea is his, for he made it, *
  and his hands have molded the dry land.

Come, let us bow down, and bend the knee, *
  and kneel before the Lord our Maker.
For he is our God,
and we are the people of his pasture and the sheep of his hand.*
  Oh, that today you would hearken to his voice!

or Psalm 95, as indicated in the Psalms section

Jubilate   *Psalm 100*

Be joyful in the Lord, all you lands; *
  serve the Lord with gladness
  and come before his presence with a song.

Know this: The Lord himself is God; *
  he himself has made us, and we are his;
  we are his people and the sheep of his pasture.

Enter his gates with thanksgiving;
go into his courts with praise; *
  give thanks to him and call upon his Name.

For the Lord is good;
his mercy is everlasting; *
  and his faithfulness endures from age to age.

Then follows

The Psalm or Psalms Appointed

At the end of the Psalms is sung or said

Glory to the Father, and to the Son, and to the Holy Spirit: *
as it was in the beginning, is now, and will be for ever. Amen.

The Psalms for Lent begin on page 229.

The Lessons

One or two Lessons, as appointed, are read, the Reader first saying

A Reading (Lesson) from _____.

A citation giving chapter and verse may be added.

After each Lesson the Reader may say

The Word of the Lord.
Answer   Thanks be to God.

Or the Reader may say Here ends the Lesson (Reading).

Silence may be kept after each Reading. One of the following Canticles is sung or said after each Reading. If three Lessons are used, the Lesson from the Gospel is read after the second Canticle.

8   The Song of Moses   *Cantemus Domino*
Exodus 15:1-6, 11-13, 17-18

I will sing to the Lord, for he is lofty and uplifted; *
the horse and its rider has he hurled into the sea.
The Lord is my strength and my refuge; *
the Lord has become my Savior.
This is my God and I will praise him, *
the God of my people and I will exalt him.

The Lord is a mighty warrior; *
 Yahweh is his Name.
The chariots of Pharaoh and his army has he hurled into the sea; *
 the finest of those who bear armor have been drowned in
    the Red Sea.
The fathomless deep has overwhelmed them; *
 they sank into the depths like a stone.
Your right hand, O Lord, is glorious in might; *
 your right hand, O Lord, has overthrown the enemy.
Who can be compared with you, O Lord, among the gods? *
 who is like you, glorious in holiness,
 awesome in renown, and worker of wonders?
You stretched forth your right hand; *
 the earth swallowed them up.
With your constant love you led the people you redeemed; *
 with your might you brought them in safety to your
    holy dwelling.
You will bring them in and plant them *
 on the mount of your possession,
The resting-place you have made for yourself, O Lord, *
 the sanctuary, O Lord, that your hand has established.
The Lord shall reign *
 for ever and for ever.

Glory to the Father, and to the Son, and to the Holy Spirit: *
as it was in the beginning, is now, and will be for ever. Amen.

9 The First Song of Isaiah *Ecce, Deus*
Isaiah 12:2-6

Surely, it is God who saves me; *
 I will trust in him and not be afraid.
For the Lord is my stronghold and my sure defense, *
 and he will be my Savior.
Therefore you shall draw water with rejoicing *
 from the springs of salvation.
And on that day you shall say, *
 Give thanks to the Lord and call upon his Name;
Make his deeds known among the peoples; *
 see that they remember that his Name is exalted.
Sing the praises of the Lord, for he has done great things, *
 and this is known in all the world.
Cry aloud, inhabitants of Zion, ring out your joy, *
 for the great one in the midst of you is the Holy One of Israel.

Glory to the Father, and to the Son, and to the Holy Spirit: *
  as it was in the beginning, is now, and will be for ever. Amen.

10 The Second Song of Isaiah *Quaerite Dominum*
Isaiah 55:6-11

Seek the Lord while he wills to be found; *
  call upon him when he draws near.
Let the wicked forsake their ways *
  and the evil ones their thoughts;
And let them turn to the Lord, and he will have compassion, *
  and to our God, for he will richly pardon.
For my thoughts are not your thoughts, *
  nor your ways my ways, says the Lord.
For as the heavens are higher than the earth, *
  so are my ways higher than your ways,
  and my thoughts than your thoughts.
For as rain and snow fall from the heavens *
  and return not again, but water the earth,
Bringing forth life and giving growth, *
  seed for sowing and bread for eating,
So is my word that goes forth from my mouth; *
  it will not return to me empty;
But it will accomplish that which I have purposed, *
  and prosper in that for which I sent it.

Glory to the Father, and to the Son, and to the Holy Spirit: *
  as it was in the beginning, is now, and will be for ever. Amen.

11 The Third Song of Isaiah *Surge, illuminare*
Isaiah 60:1-3, 11a, 14c, 18-19

Arise, shine, for your light has come, *
  and the glory of the Lord has dawned upon you.
For behold, darkness covers the land; *
  deep gloom enshrouds the peoples.
But over you the Lord will rise, *
  and his glory will appear upon you.
Nations will stream to your light, *
  and kings to the brightness of your dawning.
Your gates will always be open; *
  by day or night they will never be shut.

They will call you, The City of the Lord, *
  The Zion of the Holy One of Israel.
Violence will no more be heard in your land, *
  ruin or destruction within your borders.
You will call your walls, Salvation, *
  and all your portals, Praise.
The sun will no more be your light by day; *
  by night you will not need the brightness of the moon.
The Lord will be your everlasting light, *
  and your God will be your glory.

Glory to the Father, and to the Son, and to the Holy Spirit: *
  as it was in the beginning, is now, and will be for ever. Amen.

12 A Song of Creation *Benedicite, omnia opera Domini*
Song of the Three Young Men, 35-65

One or more sections of this Canticle may be used. Whatever the selection, it begins with the Invocation and concludes with the Doxology.

Invocation

Glorify the Lord, all you works of the Lord, *
  praise him and highly exalt him for ever.
In the firmament of his power, glorify the Lord, *
  praise him and highly exalt him for ever.

I The Cosmic Order

Glorify the Lord, you angels and all powers of the Lord, *
  O heavens and all waters above the heavens.
  Sun and moon and stars of the sky, glorify the Lord, *
praise him and highly exalt him for ever.

Glorify the Lord, every shower of rain and fall of dew, *
  all winds and fire and heat.
  Winter and summer, glorify the Lord, *
praise him and highly exalt him for ever.

Glorify the Lord, O chill and cold, *
  drops of dew and flakes of snow.
  Frost and cold, ice and sleet, glorify the Lord, *
praise him and highly exalt him for ever.

Glorify the Lord, O nights and days, *
  O shining light and enfolding dark.
Storm clouds and thunderbolts, glorify the Lord, *
praise him and highly exalt him for ever.

II   The Earth and its Creatures

Let the earth glorify the Lord, *
  praise him and highly exalt him for ever.
Glorify the Lord, O mountains and hills,
and all that grows upon the earth, *
  praise him and highly exalt him for ever.

Glorify the Lord, O springs of water, seas, and streams, *
  O whales and all that move in the waters.
All birds of the air, glorify the Lord, *
  praise him and highly exalt him for ever.

Glorify the Lord, O beasts of the wild, *
  and all you flocks and herds.
O men and women everywhere, glorify the Lord, *
  praise him and highly exalt him for ever.

III The People of God

Let the people of God glorify the Lord, *
  praise him and highly exalt him for ever.
Glorify the Lord, O priests and servants of the Lord, *
  praise him and highly exalt him for ever.

Glorify the Lord, O spirits and souls of the righteous, *
  praise him and highly exalt him for ever.
You that are holy and humble of heart, glorify the Lord, *
  praise him and highly exalt him for ever.

Doxology

Let us glorify the Lord: Father, Son, and Holy Spirit; *
  praise him and highly exalt him for ever.
In the firmament of his power, glorify the Lord, *
  praise him and highly exalt him for ever.

13 A Song of Praise *Benedictus es, Domine*
Song of the Three Young Men, 29-34

Glory to you, Lord God of our fathers; *
  you are worthy of praise; glory to you.
Glory to you for the radiance of your holy Name; *
  we will praise you and highly exalt you for ever.

Glory to you in the splendor of your temple; *
  on the throne of your majesty, glory to you.
Glory to you, seated between the Cherubim; *
  we will praise you and highly exalt you for ever.

Glory to you, beholding the depths; *
  in the high vault of heaven, glory to you.
Glory to you, Father, Son, and Holy Spirit; *
  we will praise you and highly exalt you for ever.

14 A Song of Penitence *Kyrie Pantokrator*
Prayer of Manasseh, 1-2, 4, 6-7, 11-15

Especially suitable in Lent, and on other penitential occasions

O Lord and Ruler of the hosts of heaven, *
  God of Abraham, Isaac, and Jacob,
  and of all their righteous offspring:
You made the heavens and the earth, *
  with all their vast array.
All things quake with fear at your presence; *
  they tremble because of your power.
But your merciful promise is beyond all measure; *
  it surpasses all that our minds can fathom.
O Lord, you are full of compassion, *
  long-suffering, and abounding in mercy.
You hold back your hand; *
  you do not punish as we deserve.
In your great goodness, Lord,
you have promised forgiveness to sinners, *
  that they may repent of their sin and be saved.
And now, O Lord, I bend the knee of my heart, *
  and make my appeal, sure of your gracious goodness.
I have sinned, O Lord, I have sinned, *
  and I know my wickedness only too well.

Therefore I make this prayer to you: *
  Forgive me, Lord, forgive me.
Do not let me perish in my sin, *
  nor condemn me to the depths of the earth.
For you, O Lord, are the God of those who repent, *
  and in me you will show forth your goodness.
Unworthy as I am, you will save me,
in accordance with your great mercy, *
  and I will praise you without ceasing all the days of my life.
For all the powers of heaven sing your praises, *
  and yours is the glory to ages of ages. Amen.

15 The Song of Mary *Magnificat*
Luke 1:46-55

My soul proclaims the greatness of the Lord,
my spirit rejoices in God my Savior; *
  for he has looked with favor on his lowly servant.
From this day all generations will call me blessed: *
  the Almighty has done great things for me,
  and holy is his Name.
He has mercy on those who fear him *
  in every generation.
He has shown the strength of his arm, *
  he has scattered the proud in their conceit.
He has cast down the mighty from their thrones, *
  and has lifted up the lowly.
He has filled the hungry with good things, *
  and the rich he has sent away empty.
He has come to the help of his servant Israel, *
  for he has remembered his promise of mercy,
The promise he made to our fathers, *
  to Abraham and his children for ever.

Glory to the Father, and to the Son, and to the Holy Spirit: *
  as it was in the beginning, is now, and will be for ever. Amen.

16 The Song of Zechariah *Benedictus Dominus Deus*
Luke 1:68-79

Blessed be the Lord, the God of Israel; *
  he has come to his people and set them free.

He has raised up for us a mighty savior, *
  born of the house of his servant David.
Through his holy prophets he promised of old,
that he would save us from our enemies, *
  from the hands of all who hate us.
He promised to show mercy to our fathers *
  and to remember his holy covenant.
This was the oath he swore to our father Abraham, *
  to set us free from the hands of our enemies,
Free to worship him without fear, *
  holy and righteous in his sight
  all the days of our life.
You, my child, shall be called the prophet of the Most High, *
  for you will go before the Lord to prepare his way,
To give his people knowledge of salvation *
  by the forgiveness of their sins.
In the tender compassion of our God *
  the dawn from on high shall break upon us,
To shine on those who dwell in darkness and the
                shadow of death, *
  and to guide our feet into the way of peace.

Glory to the Father, and to the Son, and to the Holy Spirit: *
  as it was in the beginning, is now, and will be for ever. Amen.

17   The Song of Simeon   *Nunc dimittis*
   Luke 2:29-32

Lord, you now have set your servant free *
  to go in peace as you have promised;
For these eyes of mine have seen the Savior, *
  whom you have prepared for all the world to see:

A Light to enlighten the nations, *
  and the glory of your people Israel.

Glory to the Father, and to the Son, and to the Holy Spirit: *
  as it was in the beginning, is now, and will be for ever. Amen.

18   A Song to the Lamb   *Dignus es*
   Revelation 4:11; 5:9-10, 13

Splendor and honor and kingly power *
  are yours by right, O Lord our God,

For you created everything that is, *
  and by your will they were created and have their being;
And yours by right, O Lamb that was slain, *
  for with your blood you have redeemed for God,
From every family, language, people, and nation, *
  a kingdom of priests to serve our God.

And so, to him who sits upon the throne, *
  and to Christ the Lamb,
Be worship and praise, dominion and splendor, *
  for ever and for evermore.

19 The Song of the Redeemed *Magna et mirabilia*
Revelation 15:3-4

O ruler of the universe, Lord God,
great deeds are they that you have done, *
  surpassing human understanding.
Your ways are ways of righteousness and truth, *
  O King of all the ages.

Who can fail to do you homage, Lord,
and sing the praises of your Name? *
  for you only are the Holy One.
All nations will draw near and fall down before you, *
  because your just and holy works have been revealed.

Glory to the Father, and to the Son, and to the Holy Spirit: *
  as it was in the beginning, is now, and will be for ever. Amen.

20 Glory to God *Gloria in excelsis*

Glory to God in the highest,
  and peace to his people on earth.

Lord God, heavenly King,
almighty God and Father,
  we worship you, we give you thanks,
  we praise you for your glory.

Lord Jesus Christ, only Son of the Father,
Lord God, Lamb of God,
you take away the sin of the world;
  have mercy on us;

you are seated at the right hand of the Father;
   receive our prayer.

For you alone are the Holy One,
you alone are the Lord,
you alone are the Most High,
   Jesus Christ,
   with the Holy Spirit,
   in the glory of God the Father. Amen.

21   You are God   *Te Deum laudamus*

You are God: we praise you;
You are the Lord: we acclaim you;
You are the eternal Father:
All creation worships you.
To you all angels, all the powers of heaven,
Cherubim and Seraphim, sing in endless praise:
   Holy, holy, holy Lord, God of power and might,
   heaven and earth are full of your glory.
The glorious company of apostles praise you.
The noble fellowship of prophets praise you.
The white-robed army of martyrs praise you.
Throughout the world the holy Church acclaims you;
   Father, of majesty unbounded,
   your true and only Son, worthy of all worship,
   and the Holy Spirit, advocate and guide.
You, Christ, are the king of glory,
the eternal Son of the Father.
When you became man to set us free
you did not shun the Virgin's womb.
You overcame the sting of death
and opened the kingdom of heaven to all believers.
You are seated at God's right hand in glory.
We believe that you will come and be our judge.
   Come then, Lord, and help your people,
   bought with the price of your own blood,
   and bring us with your saints
   to glory everlasting.

The Apostles' Creed

Officiant and People together, all standing

> I believe in God, the Father almighty,
>> creator of heaven and earth.
> I believe in Jesus Christ, his only Son, our Lord.
>> He was conceived by the power of the Holy Spirit
>>> and born of the Virgin Mary.
>> He suffered under Pontius Pilate,
>>> was crucified, died, and was buried.
>> He descended to the dead.
>> On the third day he rose again.
>> He ascended into heaven,
>>> and is seated at the right hand of the Father.
>> He will come again to judge the living and the dead.
> I believe in the Holy Spirit,
>> the holy catholic Church,
>> the communion of saints,
>> the forgiveness of sins,
>> the resurrection of the body,
>> and the life everlasting. Amen.

The Prayers

The people stand or kneel

Officiant	The Lord be with you.
People	And also with you.
Officiant	Let us pray.

Officiant and People

Our Father, who art in heaven,
  hallowed be thy Name,
  thy kingdom come,
  thy will be done,
on earth as it is in heaven.
Give us this day our daily bread.
And forgive us our trespasses,
  as we forgive those

Our Father in heaven,
  hallowed be your Name,
  your kingdom come,
  your will be done,
  on earth as in heaven.
Give us today our daily bread.
Forgive us our sins
  as we forgive those

who trespass against us.
And lead us not into temptation,
    but deliver us from evil.
For thine is the kingdom,
    and the power, and the glory,
for ever and ever. Amen.

who sin against us.
Save us from the time of trial,
    and deliver us from evil.
For the kingdom, the power,
    and the glory are yours,
now and for ever. Amen.

Then follows one of these sets of Suffrages

A

V. Show us your mercy, O Lord;
R. And grant us your salvation.
V. Clothe your ministers with righteousness;
R. Let your people sing with joy.
V. Give peace, O Lord, in all the world;
R. For only in you can we live in safety.
V. Lord, keep this nation under your care;
R. And guide us in the way of justice and truth.
V. Let your way be known upon earth;
R. Your saving health among all nations.
V. Let not the needy, O Lord, be forgotten;
R. Nor the hope of the poor be taken away.
V. Create in us clean hearts, O God;
R. And sustain us with your Holy Spirit.

B

V. Save your people, Lord, and bless your inheritance;
R. Govern and uphold them, now and always.
V. Day by day we bless you;
R. We praise your Name for ever.
V. Lord, keep us from all sin today;
R. Have mercy on us, Lord, have mercy.
V. Lord, show us your love and mercy;
R. For we put our trust in you.
V. In you, Lord, is our hope;
R. And we shall never hope in vain.

The Collect of the Day

The Officiant then says one or more of the following Collects

Ash Wednesday and the three days following

Almighty and everlasting God, you hate nothing you have made and forgive the sins of all who are penitent: Create and make in us new and contrite hearts, that we, worthily lamenting our sins and acknowledging our wretchedness, may obtain of you, the God of all mercy, perfect remission and forgiveness; through Jesus Christ our Lord, who lives and reigns with you and the Holy Spirit, one God, for ever and ever. *Amen.*

Week of 1 Lent

Almighty God, whose blessed Son was led by the Spirit to be tempted by Satan: Come quickly to help us who are assaulted by many temptations; and, as you know the weaknesses of each of us, let each one find you mighty to save; through Jesus Christ your Son our Lord, who lives and reigns with you and the Holy Spirit, one God, now and for ever. *Amen.*

Week of 2 Lent

O God, whose glory it is always to have mercy: Be gracious to all who have gone astray from your ways, and bring them again with penitent hearts and steadfast faith to embrace and hold fast the unchangeable truth of your Word, Jesus Christ your Son; who with you and the Holy Spirit lives and reigns, one God, for ever and ever. *Amen.*

Week of 3 Lent

Almighty God, you know that we have no power in ourselves to help ourselves: Keep us both outwardly in our bodies and inwardly in our souls, that we may be defended from all adversities which may happen to the body, and from all evil thoughts which may assault and hurt the soul; through Jesus Christ our Lord, who lives and reigns with you and the Holy Spirit, one God, for ever and ever. *Amen.*

Week of 4 Lent

Gracious Father, whose blessed Son Jesus Christ came down from heaven to be the true bread which gives life to the world: Evermore give us this bread, that he may live in us, and we in him; who lives and reigns with you and the Holy Spirit, one God, now and for ever. *Amen.*

Week of 5 Lent

Almighty God, you alone can bring into order the unruly wills and affections of sinners: Grant your people grace to love what you command and desire what you promise; that, among the swift and varied changes of the world, our hearts may surely there be fixed where true joys are to be found; through Jesus Christ our Lord, who lives and reigns with you and the Holy Spirit, one God, now and for ever. *Amen.*

The Sunday of the Passion: Palm Sunday

Almighty and everliving God, in your tender love for the human race you sent your Son our Savior Jesus Christ to take upon him our nature, and to suffer death upon the cross, giving us the example of his great humility: Mercifully grant that we may walk in the way of his suffering, and also share in his resurrection; through Jesus Christ our Lord, who lives and reigns with you and the Holy Spirit, one God, for ever and ever. *Amen.*

Monday in Holy Week

Almighty God, whose most dear Son went not up to joy but first he suffered pain, and entered not into glory before he was crucified: Mercifully grant that we, walking in the way of the cross, may find it none other than the way of life and peace; through Jesus Christ your Son our Lord, who lives and reigns with you and the Holy Spirit, one God, for ever and ever. *Amen.*

Tuesday in Holy Week

O God, by the passion of your blessed Son you made an instrument of shameful death to be for us the means of life: Grant us so to glory in the cross of Christ, that we may gladly suffer shame and loss for the sake of your Son our Savior Jesus Christ; who lives and reigns with you and the Holy Spirit, one God, for ever and ever. *Amen.*

Wednesday in Holy Week

Lord God, whose blessed Son our Savior gave his body to be whipped and his face to be spit upon: Give us grace to accept joyfully the sufferings of the present time, confident of the glory that shall be revealed; through Jesus Christ your Son our Lord, who lives and reigns with you and the Holy Spirit, one God, for ever and ever. *Amen.*

Maundy Thursday

Almighty Father, whose dear Son, on the night before he suffered, instituted the Sacrament of his Body and Blood: Mercifully grant that we may receive it thankfully in remembrance of Jesus Christ our Lord, who in these holy mysteries gives us a pledge of eternal life; and who now lives and reigns with you and the Holy Spirit, one God, for ever and ever. *Amen.*

Good Friday

Almighty God, we pray you graciously to behold this your family, for whom our Lord Jesus Christ was willing to be betrayed, and given into the hands of sinners, and to suffer death upon the cross; who now lives and reigns with you and the Holy Spirit, one God, for ever and ever. *Amen.*

Holy Saturday

O God, Creator of heaven and earth: Grant that, as the crucified body of your dear Son was laid in the tomb and rested on this holy Sabbath, so we may await with him the coming of the third day, and rise with him to newness of life; who now lives and reigns with you and the Holy Spirit, one God, for ever and ever. *Amen.*

Saint Joseph (March 19)

O God, who from the family of your servant David raised up Joseph to be the guardian of your incarnate Son and the spouse of his virgin mother: Give us grace to imitate his uprightness of life and his obedience to your commands; through Jesus Christ our Lord, who lives and reigns with you and the Holy Spirit, one God, for ever and ever. *Amen.*

The Annunciation (March 25)

Pour your grace into our hearts, O Lord, that we who have known the incarnation of your Son Jesus Christ, announced by an angel to the Virgin Mary, may by his cross and passion be brought to the glory of his resurrection; who lives and reigns with you, in the unity of the Holy Spirit, one God, now and for ever. *Amen.*

A Collect for Sundays

O God, you make us glad with the weekly remembrance of the glorious resurrection of your Son our Lord: Give us this day such blessing through our worship of you, that the week to come may be spent in your favor; through Jesus Christ our Lord. *Amen.*

A Collect for Fridays

Almighty God, whose most dear Son went not up to joy but first he suffered pain, and entered not into glory before he was crucified: Mercifully grant that we, walking in the way of the cross, may find it none other than the way of life and peace; through Jesus Christ your Son our Lord. *Amen.*

A Collect for Saturdays

Almighty God, who after the creation of the world rested from all your works and sanctified a day of rest for all your creatures: Grant that we, putting away all earthly anxieties, may be duly prepared for the service of your sanctuary, and that our rest here upon earth may be a preparation for the eternal rest promised to your people in heaven; through Jesus Christ our Lord. *Amen.*

A Collect for the Renewal of Life (Mondays)

O God, the King eternal, whose light divides the day from the night and turns the shadow of death into the morning: Drive far from us all wrong desires, incline our hearts to keep your law, and guide our feet into the way of peace; that, having done your will with cheerfulness during the day, we may, when night comes, rejoice to give you thanks; through Jesus Christ our Lord. *Amen.*

A Collect for Peace (Tuesdays)

O God, the author of peace and lover of concord, to know you is eternal life and to serve you is perfect freedom: Defend us, your humble servants, in all assaults of our enemies; that we, surely trusting in your defense, may not fear the power of any adversaries; through the might of Jesus Christ our Lord. *Amen.*

A Collect for Grace (Wednesdays)

Lord God, almighty and everlasting Father, you have brought us in safety to this new day: Preserve us with your mighty power, that we may not fall into sin, nor be overcome by adversity; and in all we do, direct us to the fulfilling of your purpose; through Jesus Christ our Lord. *Amen.*

A Collect for Guidance (Thursdays)

Heavenly Father, in you we live and move and have our being: We humbly pray you so to guide and govern us by your Holy Spirit, that in all the cares and occupations of our life we may not forget you, but may remember that we are ever walking in your sight; through Jesus Christ our Lord. *Amen.*

One of these prayers for mission is added

Almighty and everlasting God, by whose Spirit the whole body of your faithful people is governed and sanctified: Receive our supplications and prayers which we offer before you for all members of your holy Church, that in their vocation and ministry they may truly and devoutly serve you; through our Lord and Savior Jesus Christ. *Amen.*

or this

O God, you have made of one blood all the peoples of the earth, and sent your blessed Son to preach peace to those who are far off and to those who are near: Grant that people everywhere may seek after you and find you; bring the nations into your fold; pour out your Spirit upon all flesh; and hasten the coming of your kingdom; through Jesus Christ our Lord. *Amen.*

or the following

Lord Jesus Christ, you stretched out your arms of love on the hard wood of the cross that everyone might come within the reach of your saving embrace: So clothe us in your Spirit that we, reaching forth our hands in love, may bring those who do not know you to the knowledge and love of you; for the honor of your Name. *Amen.*

Here may be sung a hymn or anthem.

Intercessions and thanksgivings may follow.

Before the close of the Office one or both of the following may be used

The General Thanksgiving

Officiant and People

Almighty God, Father of all mercies,
we your unworthy servants give you humble thanks
for all your goodness and loving-kindness
to us and to all whom you have made.
We bless you for our creation, preservation,
and all the blessings of this life;
but above all for your immeasurable love
in the redemption of the world by our Lord Jesus Christ;
for the means of grace, and for the hope of glory.
And, we pray, give us such an awareness of your mercies,
that with truly thankful hearts we may show forth your praise,
not only with our lips, but in our lives,
by giving up our selves to your service,
and by walking before you
in holiness and righteousness all our days;
through Jesus Christ our Lord,
to whom, with you and the Holy Spirit,
be honor and glory throughout all ages. Amen.

A Prayer of St. Chrysostom

Almighty God, you have given us grace at this time with one accord to make our common supplication to you; and you have promised through your well-beloved Son that when two or three are gathered together in his Name you will be in the midst of them: Fulfill now, O Lord, our desires and petitions as may be best for us; granting us in this world knowledge of your truth, and in the age to come life everlasting. *Amen.*

Then may be said

Let us bless the Lord.
Thanks be to God.

The Officiant may then conclude with one of the following

The grace of our Lord Jesus Christ, and the love of God, and the fellowship of the Holy Spirit, be with us all evermore. *Amen.*
2 Corinthians 13:14

May the God of hope fill us with all joy and peace in believing through the power of the Holy Spirit. *Amen.*   *Romans 15:13*

Glory to God whose power, working in us, can do infinitely more than we can ask or imagine: Glory to him from generation to generation in the Church, and in Christ Jesus for ever and ever. *Amen.*
Ephesians 3:20, 21

An Order of Service for Noonday

Officiant   O God, make speed to save us.
People   O Lord, make haste to help us.

Officiant and People

Glory to the Father, and to the Son, and to the Holy Spirit: as it was in the beginning, is now, and will be for ever. Amen.

A suitable hymn may be sung.

One or more of the following Psalms is sung or said.

Psalm 119   *Lucerna pedibus meis*

105 Your word is a lantern to my feet *
       and a light upon my path.

106 I have sworn and am determined *
       to keep your righteous judgments.

107 I am deeply troubled; *
       preserve my life, O Lord, according to your word.

108 Accept, O Lord, the willing tribute of my lips, *
       and teach me your judgments.

109 My life is always in my hand, *
       yet I do not forget your law.

110 The wicked have set a trap for me, *
       but I have not strayed from your commandments.

111 Your decrees are my inheritance for ever; *
       truly, they are the joy of my heart.

112 I have applied my heart to fulfill your statutes *
       for ever and to the end.

Psalm 121 *Levavi oculos*

1 I lift up my eyes to the hills; *
  from where is my help to come?

2 My help comes from the Lord, *
  the maker of heaven and earth.

3 He will not let your foot be moved *
  and he who watches over you will not fall asleep.

4 Behold, he who keeps watch over Israel *
  shall neither slumber nor sleep;

5 The Lord himself watches over you; *
  the Lord is your shade at your right hand,

6 So that the sun shall not strike you by day, *
  nor the moon by night.

7 The Lord shall preserve you from all evil; *
  it is he who shall keep you safe.

8 The Lord shall watch over your going out and
                      your coming in, *
  from this time forth for evermore.

Psalm 126 *In convertendo*

1 When the Lord restored the fortunes of Zion, *
  then were we like those who dream.

2 Then was our mouth filled with laughter, *
  and our tongue with shouts of joy.

3 Then they said among the nations, *
  "The Lord has done great things for them."

4 The Lord has done great things for us, *
  and we are glad indeed.

5 Restore our fortunes, O Lord, *
  like the watercourses of the Negev.

6 Those who sowed with tears *
  will reap with songs of joy.

7 Those who go out weeping, carrying the seed, *
  will come again with joy, shouldering their sheaves.

Glory to the Father, and to the Son, and to the Holy Spirit: *
as it was in the beginning, is now, and will be for ever. Amen.

*One of the following, or some other suitable passage of Scripture,
is read*

The love of God has been poured into our hearts through the Holy
Spirit that has been given to us.   *Romans 5:5*

People   Thanks be to God.

or the following

If anyone is in Christ he is a new creation; the old has passed away,
behold the new has come. All this is from God, who through Christ
reconciled us to himself and gave us the ministry of reconciliation.
2 Corinthians 5:17-18

People   Thanks be to God.

or this

From the rising of the sun to its setting my Name shall be great among
the nations, and in every place incense shall be offered to my Name,
and a pure offering; for my Name shall be great among the nations,
says the Lord of Hosts.   *Malachi 1:11*

People   Thanks be to God.

A meditation, silent or spoken, may follow.

The Officiant then begins the Prayers

Lord, have mercy.
Christ, have mercy.
Lord, have mercy.

Officiant and People

Our Father, who art in heaven,   Our Father in heaven,
    hallowed be thy Name,   hallowed be your Name,

thy kingdom come,	your kingdom come,
thy will be done,	your will be done,
on earth as it is in heaven.	on earth as in heaven.
Give us this day our daily bread.	Give us today our daily bread.
And forgive us our trespasses,	Forgive us our sins
as we forgive those	as we forgive those
who trespass against us.	who sin against us.
And lead us not into temptation,	Save us from the time of trial,
but deliver us from evil.	and deliver us from evil.

Officiant   Lord, hear our prayer;
People   And let our cry come to you.
Officiant   Let us pray.

The Officiant then says one of the following Collects. If desired, the Collect of the Day may be used.

Heavenly Father, send your Holy Spirit into our hearts, to direct and rule us according to your will, to comfort us in all our afflictions, to defend us from all error, and to lead us into all truth; through Jesus Christ our Lord. *Amen.*

Blessed Savior, at this hour you hung upon the cross, stretching out your loving arms: Grant that all the peoples of the earth may look to you and be saved; for your tender mercies' sake. *Amen.*

Almighty Savior, who at noonday called your servant Saint Paul to be an apostle to the Gentiles: We pray you to illumine the world with the radiance of your glory, that all nations may come and worship you; for you live and reign for ever and ever. *Amen.*

Lord Jesus Christ, you said to your apostles, "Peace I give to you; my own peace I leave with you:" Regard not our sins, but the faith of your Church, and give to us the peace and unity of that heavenly City, where with the Father and the Holy Spirit you live and reign, now and for ever. *Amen.*

Free intercessions may be offered.

The service concludes as follows

Officiant   Let us bless the Lord.
People   Thanks be to God.

Daily Evening Prayer:
Rite Two

The Officiant begins the service with one or more of the following sentences of Scripture, or with the versicle "O God, make speed to save us" on page 30

Let my prayer be set forth in your sight as incense, the lifting up of my hands as the evening sacrifice.   *Psalm 141:2*

Grace to you and peace from God our Father and from the Lord Jesus Christ.   *Philippians 1:2*

Worship the Lord in the beauty of holiness; let the whole earth tremble before him.   *Psalm 96:9*

Yours is the day, O God, yours also the night; you established the moon and the sun. You fixed all the boundaries of the earth; you made both summer and winter.   *Psalm 74:15, 16*

I will bless the Lord who gives me counsel; my heart teaches me, night after night. I have set the Lord always before me; because he is at my right hand, I shall not fall.   *Psalm 16:7, 8*

Seek him who made the Pleiades and Orion, and turns deep darkness into the morning, and darkens the day into night; who calls for the waters of the sea and pours them out upon the surface of the earth: The Lord is his name.   *Amos 5:8*

If I say, "Surely the darkness will cover me, and the light around me turn to night," darkness is not dark to you, O Lord; the night is as bright as the day; darkness and light to you are both alike.   *Psalm 139:10, 11*

Jesus said, "I am the light of the world; whoever follows me will not walk in darkness, but will have the light of life." *John 8:12*

The following Confession of Sin may then be said; or the Office may continue at once with "O God make speed to save us."

Confession of Sin

The Officiant says to the people

Dear friends in Christ, here in the presence of Almighty God, let us kneel in silence, and with penitent and obedient hearts confess our sins, so that we may obtain forgiveness by his infinite goodness and mercy.

or this

Let us confess our sins against God and our neighbor.

Silence may be kept.

Officiant and People together, all kneeling

Most merciful God,
we confess that we have sinned against you
in thought, word, and deed,
by what we have done,
and by what we have left undone.
We have not loved you with our whole heart;
we have not loved our neighbors as ourselves.
We are truly sorry and we humbly repent.
For the sake of your Son Jesus Christ,
have mercy on us and forgive us;
that we may delight in your will,
and walk in your ways,
to the glory of your Name. Amen.

The Priest alone stands and says

Almighty God have mercy on you, forgive you all your sins through our Lord Jesus Christ, strengthen you in all goodness, and by the power of the Holy Spirit keep you in eternal life. *Amen.*

A deacon or lay person using the preceding form remains kneeling, and substitutes "us" for "you" and "our" for "your."

The Invitatory and Psalter

All stand

Officiant	O God, make speed to save us.
People	O Lord, make haste to help us.

Officiant and People

Glory to the Father, and to the Son, and to the Holy Spirit: as it was in
the beginning, is now, and will be for ever. Amen.

*The following, or some other suitable hymn, or an Invitatory Psalm,
maybe sung or said*

O Gracious Light   *Phos hilaron*

O gracious Light,
pure brightness of the everliving Father in heaven,
O Jesus Christ, holy and blessed!

Now as we come to the setting of the sun,
and our eyes behold the vesper light,
we sing your praises, O God: Father, Son, and Holy Spirit.

You are worthy at all times to be praised by happy voices,
O Son of God, O Giver of life,
and to be glorified through all the worlds.

Then follows

The Psalm or Psalms Appointed

At the end of the Psalms is sung or said

Glory to the Father, and to the Son, and to the Holy Spirit: *
as it was in the beginning, is now, and will be for ever. Amen.

The Psalms for Lent begin on page 229.

The Lessons

One or two Lessons, as appointed, are read, the Reader first saying

A Reading (Lesson) from _____.

A citation giving chapter and verse may be added.

After each Lesson the Reader may say

       The Word of the Lord.
Answer   Thanks be to God.

Or the Reader may say   Here ends the Lesson (Reading).

Silence may be kept after each Reading. One of the following Canticles, or one of those on pages 5-14, is sung or said after each Reading. If three Lessons are used, the Lesson from the Gospel is read after the second Canticle.

The Song of Mary   *Magnificat*
Luke 1:46-55

My soul proclaims the greatness of the Lord,
my spirit rejoices in God my Savior; *
  for he has looked with favor on his lowly servant
From this day all generations will call me blessed: *
  the Almighty has done great things for me,
  and holy is his Name.
He has mercy on those who fear him *
  in every generation.
He has shown the strength of his arm, *
  he has scattered the proud in their conceit.
He has cast down the mighty from their thrones, *
  and has lifted up the lowly.
He has filled the hungry with good things, *
  and the rich he has sent away empty.
He has come to the help of his servant Israel, *
  for he has remembered his promise of mercy,
The promise he made to our fathers, *
  to Abraham and his children for ever.

Glory to the Father, and to the Son, and to the Holy Spirit: *
as It was in the beginning, is now, and will be for ever. Amen.

The Song of Simeon *Nunc dimittis*
Luke 2:29-32

Lord, you now have set your servant free *
to go in peace as you have promised;
For these eyes of mine have seen the Savior, *
whom you have prepared for all the world to see:
A Light to enlighten the nations, *
and the glory of your people Israel.

Glory to the Father, and to the Son, and to the Holy Spirit: *
as it was in the beginning, is now, and will be for ever. Amen.

The Apostles' Creed

Officiant and People together, all standing

I believe in God, the Father almighty,
creator of heaven and earth.
I believe in Jesus Christ, his only Son, our Lord.
He was conceived by the power of the Holy Spirit
and born of the Virgin Mary.
He suffered under Pontius Pilate,
was crucified, died, and was buried.
He descended to the dead.
On the third day he rose again.
He ascended into heaven,
and is seated at the right hand of the Father.
He will come again to judge the living and the dead.
I believe in the Holy Spirit,
the holy catholic Church,
the communion of saints,
the forgiveness of sins,
the resurrection of the body,
and the life everlasting. Amen.

The Prayers

The people stand or kneel

Officiant   The Lord be with you.
People   And also with you.
Officiant   Let us pray.

Officiant and People

Our Father, who art in heaven,
    hallowed be thy Name,
    thy kingdom come,
    thy will be done,
on earth as it is in heaven.
Give us this day our daily bread.
And forgive us our trespasses,
    as we forgive those
who trespass against us.
And lead us not into temptation,
    but deliver us from evil.
For thine is the kingdom,
    and the power, and the glory,
for ever and ever. Amen.

Our Father in heaven,
    hallowed be your Name,
    your kingdom come,
    your will be done,
        on earth as in heaven.
Give us today our daily bread.
Forgive us our sins
    as we forgive those
        who sin against us.
Save us from the time of trial,
    and deliver us from evil.
For the kingdom, the power,
    and the glory are yours,
    now and for ever. Amen.

Then follows one of these sets of Suffrages

A

V.   Show us your mercy, O Lord;
R.   And grant us your salvation.
V.   Clothe your ministers with righteousness;
R.   Let your people sing with joy.
V.   Give peace, O Lord, in all the world;
R.   For only in you can we live in safety.
V.   Lord, keep this nation under your care;
R.   And guide us in the way of justice and truth.

V.	Let your way be known upon earth;
R.	Your saving health among all nations.
V.	Let not the needy, O Lord, be forgotten;
R.	Nor the hope of the poor be taken away.
V.	Create in us clean hearts, O God;
R.	And sustain us with your Holy Spirit.

B

That this evening may be holy, good, and peaceful,
We entreat you, O Lord.

That your holy angels may lead us in paths of peace and goodwill,
We entreat you, O Lord.

That we may be pardoned and forgiven for our sins and offenses,
We entreat you, O Lord.

That there may be peace to your Church and to the whole world,
We entreat you, O Lord.

That we may depart this life in your faith and fear, and not be condemned before the great judgment seat of Christ,
We entreat you, O Lord.

That we may be bound together by your Holy Spirit in the communion of [_____ and] all your saints, entrusting one another and all our life to Christ,
We entreat you, O Lord.

The Officiant then says one or more of the following Collects

The Collect of the Day

Ash Wednesday and the three days following

Almighty and everlasting God, you hate nothing you have made and forgive the sins of all who are penitent: Create and make in us new and contrite hearts, that we, worthily lamenting our sins and acknowledging our wretchedness, may obtain of you, the God of all mercy, perfect remission and forgiveness; through Jesus Christ our Lord, who lives and reigns with you and the Holy Spirit, one God, for ever and ever. *Amen.*

Week of 1 Lent

Almighty God, whose blessed Son was led by the Spirit to be tempted by Satan: Come quickly to help us who are assaulted by many temptations; and, as you know the weaknesses of each of us, let each one find you mighty to save; through Jesus Christ your Son our Lord, who lives and reigns with you and the Holy Spirit, one God, now and for ever. *Amen.*

Week of 2 Lent

O God, whose glory it is always to have mercy: Be gracious to all who have gone astray from your ways, and bring them again with penitent hearts and steadfast faith to embrace and hold fast the unchangeable truth of your Word, Jesus Christ your Son; who with you and the Holy Spirit lives and reigns, one God, for ever and ever. *Amen.*

Week of 3 Lent

Almighty God, you know that we have no power in ourselves to help ourselves: Keep us both outwardly in our bodies and inwardly in our souls, that we may be defended from all adversities which may happen to the body, and from all evil thoughts which may assault and hurt the soul; through Jesus Christ our Lord, who lives and reigns with you and the Holy Spirit, one God, for ever and ever. *Amen.*

Week of 4 Lent

Gracious Father, whose blessed Son Jesus Christ came down from heaven to be the true bread which gives life to the world: Evermore give us this bread, that he may live in us, and we in him; who lives and reigns with you and the Holy Spirit, one God, now and for ever. *Amen.*

Week of 5 Lent

Almighty God, you alone can bring into order the unruly wills and affections of sinners: Grant your people grace to love what you command and desire what you promise; that, among the swift and varied changes of the world, our hearts may surely there be fixed where true joys are to be found; through Jesus Christ our Lord, who lives and reigns with you and the Holy Spirit, one God, now and for ever. *Amen.*

The Sunday of the Passion: Palm Sunday

Almighty and everliving God, in your tender love for the human race
you sent your Son our Savior Jesus Christ to take upon him our nature,
and to suffer death upon the cross, giving us the example of his great
humility: Mercifully grant that we may walk in the way of his suffering, and also share in his resurrection; through Jesus Christ our Lord,
who lives and reigns with you and the Holy Spirit, one God, for ever
and ever. *Amen.*

Monday in Holy Week

Almighty God, whose most dear Son went not up to joy but first he
suffered pain, and entered not into glory before he was crucified:
Mercifully grant that we, walking in the way of the cross, may find it
none other than the way of life and peace; through Jesus Christ your
Son our Lord, who lives and reigns with you and the Holy Spirit, one
God, for ever and ever. *Amen.*

Tuesday in Holy Week

O God, by the passion of your blessed Son you made an instrument of
shameful death to be for us the means of life: Grant us so to glory in
the cross of Christ, that we may gladly suffer shame and loss for the
sake of your Son our Savior Jesus Christ; who lives and reigns with you
and the Holy Spirit, one God, for ever and ever. *Amen.*

Wednesday in Holy Week

Lord God, whose blessed Son our Savior gave his body to be whipped
and his face to be spit upon: Give us grace to accept joyfully the sufferings of the present time, confident of the glory that shall be revealed;
through Jesus Christ your Son our Lord, who lives and reigns with you
and the Holy Spirit, one God, for ever and ever. *Amen.*

Maundy Thursday

Almighty Father, whose dear Son, on the night before he suffered, instituted the Sacrament of his Body and Blood: Mercifully grant that we

may receive it thankfully in remembrance of Jesus Christ our Lord, who in these holy mysteries gives us a pledge of eternal life; and who now lives and reigns with you and the Holy Spirit, one God, for ever and ever. *Amen.*

Good Friday

Almighty God, we pray you graciously to behold this your family, for whom our Lord Jesus Christ was willing to be betrayed, and given into the hands of sinners, and to suffer death upon the cross; who now lives and reigns with you and the Holy Spirit, one God, for ever and ever. *Amen.*

Holy Saturday

O God, Creator of heaven and earth: Grant that, as the crucified body of your dear Son was laid in the tomb and rested on this holy Sabbath, so we may await with him the coming of the third day, and rise with him to newness of life; who now lives and reigns with you and the Holy Spirit, one God, for ever and ever. *Amen.*

Saint Joseph (March 19)

O God, who from the family of your servant David raised up Joseph to be the guardian of your incarnate Son and the spouse of his virgin mother: Give us grace to imitate his uprightness of life and his obedience to your commands; through Jesus Christ our Lord, who lives and reigns with you and the Holy Spirit, one God, for ever and ever. *Amen.*

The Annunciation (March 25)

Pour your grace into our hearts, O Lord, that we who have known the incarnation of your Son Jesus Christ, announced by an angel to the Virgin Mary, may by his cross and passion be brought to the glory of his resurrection; who lives and reigns with you, in the unity of the Holy Spirit, one God, now and for ever. *Amen.*

A Collect for Sundays

Lord God, whose Son our Savior Jesus Christ triumphed over the powers of death and prepared for us our place in the new Jerusalem: Grant that we, who have this day given thanks for his resurrection, may praise you in that City of which he is the light, and where he lives and reigns for ever and ever. *Amen.*

A Collect for Fridays

Lord Jesus Christ, by your death you took away the sting of death: Grant to us your servants so to follow in faith where you have led the way, that we may at length fall asleep peacefully in you and wake up in your likeness; for your tender mercies' sake. *Amen.*

A Collect for Saturdays

O God, the source of eternal light: Shed forth your unending day upon us who watch for you, that our lips may praise you, our lives may bless you, and our worship on the morrow give you glory; through Jesus Christ our Lord. *Amen.*

A Collect for Peace (Mondays)

Most holy God, the source of all good desires, all right judgments, and all just works: Give to us, your servants, that peace which the world cannot give, so that our minds may be fixed on the doing of your will, and that we, being delivered from the fear of all enemies, may live in peace and quietness; through the mercies of Christ Jesus our Savior. *Amen.*

A Collect for Aid against Perils (Tuesdays)

Be our light in the darkness, O Lord, and in your great mercy defend us from all perils and dangers of this night; for the love of your only Son, our Savior Jesus Christ. *Amen.*

A Collect for Protection (Wednesdays)

O God, the life of all who live, the light of the faithful, the strength of those who labor, and the repose of the dead: We thank you for the blessings of the day that is past, and humbly ask for your protection through the coming night. Bring us in safety to the morning hours; through him who died and rose again for us, your Son our Savior Jesus Christ. *Amen.*

A Collect for the Presence of Christ (Thursdays)

Lord Jesus, stay with us, for evening is at hand and the day is past; be our companion in the way, kindle our hearts, and awaken hope, that we may know you as you are revealed in Scripture and the breaking of bread. Grant this for the sake of your love. *Amen.*

One of these prayers for mission is added

O God and Father of all, whom the whole heavens adore: Let the whole earth also worship you, all nations obey you, all tongues confess and bless you, and men and women everywhere love you and serve you in peace; through Jesus Christ our Lord. *Amen.*

or this

Keep watch, dear Lord, with those who work, or watch, or weep this night, and give your angels charge over those who sleep. Tend the sick, Lord Christ; give rest to the weary, bless the dying, soothe the suffering, pity the afflicted, shield the joyous; and all for your love's sake. *Amen.*

or the following

O God, you manifest in your servants the signs of your presence: Send forth upon us the Spirit of love, that in companionship with one another your abounding grace may increase among us; through Jesus Christ our Lord. *Amen.*

Here may be sung a hymn or anthem.

Intercessions and thanksgivings may follow.

Before the close of the Office one or both of the following may be used

The General Thanksgiving

Officiant and People

Almighty God, Father of all mercies,
we your unworthy servants give you humble thanks
for all your goodness and loving-kindness
to us and to all whom you have made.
We bless you for our creation, preservation,
and all the blessings of this life;
but above all for your immeasurable love
in the redemption of the world by our Lord Jesus Christ;
for the means of grace, and for the hope of glory.
And, we pray, give us such an awareness of your mercies,
that with truly thankful hearts we may show forth your praise,
not only with our lips, but in our lives,
by giving up our selves to your service,
and by walking before you
in holiness and righteousness all our days;
through Jesus Christ our Lord,
to whom, with you and the Holy Spirit,
be honor and glory throughout all ages. Amen.

A Prayer of St. Chrysostom

Almighty God, you have given us grace at this time with one accord to
make our common supplication to you; and you have promised
through your well-beloved Son that when two or three are gathered
together in his Name you will be in the midst of them: Fulfill now, O
Lord, our desires and petitions as may be best for us; granting us in
this world knowledge of your truth, and in the age to come life everlasting. *Amen.*

Then may be said

Let us bless the Lord.
Thanks be to God.

The Officiant may then conclude with one of the following

The grace of our Lord Jesus Christ, and the love of God, and the fellowship of the Holy Spirit, be with us all evermore.
Amen.   *2 Corinthians 13:14*

May the God of hope fill us with all joy and peace in believing through the power of the Holy Spirit.
Amen.   Romans 15:13

Glory to God whose power, working in us, can do infinitely more than we can ask or imagine: Glory to him from generation to generation in the Church, and in Christ Jesus for ever and ever.
Amen.   Ephesians 3:20, 21

An Order for Compline

The Officiant begins

The Lord Almighty grant us a peaceful night and a perfect end. *Amen.*

Officiant	Our help is in the Name of the Lord;
People	The maker of heaven and earth.

The Officiant may then say

Let us confess our sins to God.

Silence may be kept.

Officiant and People

Almighty God, our heavenly Father:
We have sinned against you,
through our own fault,
in thought, and word, and deed,
and in what we have left undone.
For the sake of your Son our Lord Jesus Christ,
forgive us all our offenses;
and grant that we may serve you
in newness of life,
to the glory of your Name. Amen.

Officiant
May the Almighty God grant us forgiveness of all our sins, and the
grace and comfort of the Holy Spirit. *Amen.*

The Officiant then says
         O God, make speed to save us.
People   O Lord, make haste to help us.

Officiant and People
Glory to the Father, and to the Son, and to the Holy Spirit: as it was in the beginning, is now, and will be for ever. Amen.

One or more of the following Psalms are sung or said. Other suitable selections may be substituted.

Psalm 4   *Cum invocarem*

1   Answer me when I call, O God, defender of my cause; *
       you set me free when I am hard-pressed;
       have mercy on me and hear my prayer.

2   "You mortals, how long will you dishonor my glory? *
       how long will you worship dumb idols
       and run after false gods?"

3   Know that the Lord does wonders for the faithful; *
       when I call upon the Lord, he will hear me.

4   Tremble, then, and do not sin; *
       speak to your heart in silence upon your bed.

5   Offer the appointed sacrifices *
       and put your trust in the Lord.

6   Many are saying,
    "Oh, that we might see better times!" *
       Lift up the light of your countenance upon us, O Lord.

7   You have put gladness in my heart, *
       more than when grain and wine and oil increase.

8   I lie down in peace; at once I fall asleep; *
       for only you, Lord, make me dwell in safety.

Psalm 31   *In te, Domine, speravi*

1   In you, O Lord, have I taken refuge;
    let me never be put to shame: *
       deliver me in your righteousness.

2   Incline your ear to me; *
       make haste to deliver me.

3   Be my strong rock, a castle to keep me safe,
for you are my crag and my stronghold; *
   for the sake of your Name, lead me and guide me.

4   Take me out of the net that they have secretly set for me, *
   for you are my tower of strength.

5   Into your hands I commend my spirit, *
   for you have redeemed me,
   O Lord, O God of truth.

Psalm 91   *Qui habitat*

1   He who dwells in the shelter of the Most High *
   abides under the shadow of the Almighty.

2   He shall say to the Lord,
"You are my refuge and my stronghold, *
   my God in whom I put my trust."

3   He shall deliver you from the snare of the hunter *
   and from the deadly pestilence.

4   He shall cover you with his pinions,
and you shall find refuge under his wings; *
   his faithfulness shall be a shield and buckler.

5   You shall not be afraid of any terror by night, *
   nor of the arrow that flies by day;

6   Of the plague that stalks in the darkness, *
   nor of the sickness that lays waste at mid-day.

7   A thousand shall fall at your side
and ten thousand at your right hand, *
   but it shall not come near you.

8   Your eyes have only to behold *
   to see the reward of the wicked.

9   Because you have made the Lord your refuge, *
   and the Most High your habitation,

10   There shall no evil happen to you, *
   neither shall any plague come near your dwelling.

11   For he shall give his angels charge over you, *
   to keep you in all your ways.

12 They shall bear you in their hands, *
    lest you dash your foot against a stone.

13 You shall tread upon the lion and adder; *
    you shall trample the young lion and the serpent
        under your feet.

14 Because he is bound to me in love,
    therefore will I deliver him; *
    I will protect him, because he knows my Name.

15 He shall call upon me, and I will answer him; *
    I am with him in trouble;
    I will rescue him and bring him to honor.

16 With long life will I satisfy him, *
    and show him my salvation.

Psalm 134 *Ecce nunc*

1 Behold now, bless the Lord, all you servants of the Lord, *
    you that stand by night in the house of the Lord.

2 Lift up your hands in the holy place and bless the Lord; *
    the Lord who made heaven and earth bless you out of Zion.

At the end of the Psalms is sung or said

> Glory to the Father, and to the Son, and to the Holy Spirit: *
> as it was in the beginning, is now, and will be for ever. Amen.

One of the following, or some other suitable passage of Scripture,
is read

Lord, you are in the midst of us, and we are called by your Name: Do
not forsake us, O Lord our God. *Jeremiah 14:9, 22*

People   Thanks be to God.

or this

Come to me, all who labor and are heavy-laden, and I will give you rest.
Take my yoke upon you, and learn from me; for I am gentle and lowly in
heart, and you will find rest for your souls. For my yoke is easy, and my
burden is light.   *Matthew 11:28-30*

People   Thanks be to God.

or the following

May the God of peace, who brought again from the dead our Lord Jesus, the great shepherd of the sheep, by the blood of the eternal covenant, equip you with everything good that you may do his will, working in you that which is pleasing in his sight, through Jesus Christ; to whom be glory for ever and ever.   *Hebrews 13:20-21*

People   Thanks be to God.

or this

Be sober, be watchful. Your adversary the devil prowls around like a roaring lion, seeking someone to devour. Resist him, firm in your faith. *I Peter 5:8-9a*

People   Thanks be to God.

A hymn suitable for the evening may be sung.

Then follows

V.   Into your hands, O Lord, I commend my spirit;
R.   For you have redeemed me, O Lord, O God of truth.
V.   Keep us, O Lord, as the apple of your eye;
R.   Hide us under the shadow of your wings.

Lord, have mercy.
Christ, have mercy.
Lord, have mercy.

Officiant and People

Our Father, who art in heaven,
    hallowed be thy Name,
        thy kingdom come,
        thy will be done,
on earth as it is in heaven.
Give us this day our daily bread.
And forgive us our trespasses,
    as we forgive those
who trespass against us.
And lead us not into temptation,
    but deliver us from evil.
	Our Father in heaven,
	    hallowed be your Name,
	        your kingdom come,
	        your will be done,
	        on earth as in heaven.
	Give us today our daily bread.
	Forgive us our sins
	    as we forgive those
	        who sin against us.
	Save us from the time of trial,
	    and deliver us from evil.

Officiant	Lord, hear our prayer;
People	And let our cry come to you.
Officiant	Let us pray.

The Officiant then says one of the following Collects

Be our light in the darkness, O Lord, and in your great mercy defend us from all perils and dangers of this night; for the love of your only Son, our Savior Jesus Christ. *Amen.*

Be present, O merciful God, and protect us through the hours of this night, so that we who are wearied by the changes and chances of this life may rest in your eternal changelessness; through Jesus Christ our Lord. *Amen.*

Look down, O Lord, from your heavenly throne, and illumine this night with your celestial brightness; that by night as by day your people may glorify your holy Name; through Jesus Christ our Lord. *Amen.*

Visit this place, O Lord, and drive far from it all snares of the enemy; let your holy angels dwell with us to preserve us in peace; and let your blessing be upon us always; through Jesus Christ our Lord. *Amen.*

A Collect for Saturdays

We give you thanks, O God, for revealing your Son Jesus Christ to us by the light of his resurrection: Grant that as we sing your glory at the close of this day, our joy may abound in the morning as we celebrate the Paschal mystery; through Jesus Christ our Lord. *Amen.*

One of the following prayers may be added

Keep watch, dear Lord, with those who work, or watch, or weep this night, and give your angels charge over those who sleep. Tend the sick, Lord Christ; give rest to the weary, bless the dying, soothe the suffering, pity the afflicted, shield the joyous; and all for your love's sake. *Amen.*

or this

O God, your unfailing providence sustains the world we live in and the life we live: Watch over those, both night and day, who work while others sleep, and grant that we may never forget that our common life depends upon each other's toil; through Jesus Christ our Lord. *Amen.*

Silence may be kept, and free intercessions and thanksgivings may be offered.

The service concludes with the Song of Simeon with this Antiphon, which is sung or said by all

Guide us waking, O Lord, and guard us sleeping; that awake we may watch with Christ, and asleep we may rest in peace.

Lord, you now have set your servant free *
to go in peace as you have promised;

For these eyes of mine have seen the Savior, *
whom you have prepared for all the world to see:

A Light to enlighten the nations, *
and the glory of your people Israel.

Glory to the Father, and to the Son, and to the Holy Spirit: *
as it was in the beginning, is now, and will be for ever. Amen.

All repeat the Antiphon

Guide us waking, O Lord, and guard us sleeping; that awake we may watch with Christ, and asleep we may rest in peace.

Officiant   Let us bless the Lord.
People   Thanks be to God.

The Officiant concludes

The almighty and merciful Lord, Father, Son, and Holy Spirit, bless us and keep us. *Amen.*

Suggested Canticles
at Morning Prayer in Lent

	After the *Old Testament Reading*		*After the* *New Testament Reading*
Sun.	14. Kyrie Pantokrator	16.	Benedictus Dominus
Mon.	9. Ecce, Deus	19.	Magna et mirabilia
Tue.	13. Benedictus es	18.	Dignus es
Wed.	14. Kyrie Pantokrator	16.	Benedictus Dominus
Thu.	8. Cantemus Domino	19.	Magna et mirabilia
Fri.	14. Kyrie Pantokrator	18.	Dignus es
Sat.	12. Benedicite	19.	Magna et mirabilia

On the Feasts of St. Joseph and the Annunciation

16. Benedictus Dominus   21. Te Deum laudamus

Suggested Canticles
at Evening Prayer in Lent

		After the *Old Testament Reading*	*After the* *New Testament Reading*
Sun.		Magnificat	Nunc dimittis*
Mon.	14.	Kyrie Pantokrator	Nunc dimittis
Tue.	10.	Quærite Dominum	Magnificat
Wed.	12.	Benedicite	Nunc dimittis
Thu.	11.	Surge, illuminare	Magnificat
Fri.	13.	Benedictus es	Nunc dimittis
Sat.	9.	Ecce, Deus	Magnificat

On the Feasts of St. Joseph and the Annunciation

        Magnificat   Nunc Dimittis*

* *If only one Reading is used, the suggested Canticle is the Magnificat.*

Year One

Ash Wednesday

A Reading (Lesson) from the Book of Jonah [3:1–4:11]

The word of the LORD came to Jonah a second time, saying, "Get up, go to Nineveh, that great city, and proclaim to it the message that I tell you." So Jonah set out and went to Nineveh, according to the word of the LORD. Now Nineveh was an exceedingly large city, a three days' walk across. Jonah began to go into the city, going a day's walk. And he cried out, "Forty days more, and Nineveh shall be overthrown!" And the people of Nineveh believed God; they proclaimed a fast, and everyone, great and small, put on sackcloth. When the news reached the king of Nineveh, he rose from his throne, removed his robe, covered himself with sackcloth, and sat in ashes. Then he had a proclamation made in Nineveh: "By the decree of the king and his nobles: No human being or animal, no herd or flock, shall taste anything. They shall not feed, nor shall they drink water. Human beings and animals shall be covered with sackcloth, and they shall cry mightily to God. All shall turn from their evil ways and from the violence that is in their hands. Who knows? God may relent and change his mind; he may turn from his fierce anger, so that we do not perish." When God saw what they did, how they turned from their evil ways, God changed his mind about the calamity that he had said he would bring upon them; and he did not do it. But this was very displeasing to Jonah, and he became angry. He prayed to the LORD and said, "O LORD! Is not this what I said while I was still in my own country? That is why I fled to Tarshish at the beginning; for I knew that you are a gracious God and merciful, slow to anger, and abounding in steadfast love, and ready to relent from punishing. And now, O LORD, please take my life from me, for it is better for me to die than to live." And the LORD said, "Is it right for you to be angry?" Then Jonah went out of the city and sat down east of the city, and made a booth for himself there. He sat under it in the shade, waiting to see what would become of the city. The LORD God appointed a bush, and made it come up over Jonah, to give shade over his head, to save him from his discomfort; so Jonah was very happy about the bush. But when dawn came up the next day, God appointed a worm that attacked the bush, so that it withered. When the sun rose, God prepared a sultry east wind, and the sun beat down on the head of Jonah so that he was faint and asked that he might die. He said, "It is better for me to die than to live." But God said to Jonah, "Is it right for you to be angry about the bush?" And he said, "Yes, angry enough to die." Then the LORD said, "You are concerned about the bush, for which you did not labor and which you did not grow; it came into being in a night and perished in a night. And should I not be concerned about Nineveh, that great city, in which there are more than a hundred and twenty thousand persons who do not know their right hand from their left, and also many animals?"

A Reading (Lesson) from the Letter to the Hebrews [12:1–14]

Therefore, since we are surrounded by so great a cloud of witnesses, let us also lay aside every weight and the sin that clings so closely, and let us run with perseverance the race that is set before us, looking to Jesus the pioneer and perfecter of our faith, who for the sake of the joy that was set before him endured the cross, disregarding its shame, and has taken his seat at the right hand of the throne of God. Consider him who endured such hostility against himself from sinners, so that you may not grow weary or lose heart. In your struggle against sin you have not yet resisted to the point of shedding your blood. And you have forgotten the exhortation that addresses you as children—"My child, do not regard lighty the discipline of the Lord, or lose heart when you are punished by him; for the Lord disciplines those whom he loves, and chastises every child whom he accepts." Endure trials for the sake of discipline. God is treating you as children; for what child is there whom a parent does not discipline? If you do not have that discipline in which all children share, then you are illegitimate and not his children. Moreover, we had human parents to discipline us, and we respected them. Should we not be even more willing to be subject to the Father of spirits and live? For they disciplined us for a short time as seemed best to them, but he disciplines us for our good, in order that we may share his holiness. Now, discipline always seems painful rather than pleasant at the time, but later it yields the peaceful fruit of righteousness to those who have been trained by it. Therefore lift your drooping hands and strengthen your weak knees, and make straight paths for your feet, so that what is lame may not be put out of joint, but rather be healed. Pursue peace with everyone, and the holiness without which no one will see the Lord.

A Reading (Lesson) from the Gospel according to Luke [18:9–14]

Jesus told this parable to some who trusted in themselves that they were righteous and regarded others with contempt: "Two men went up to the temple to pray, one a Pharisee and the other a tax collector. The Pharisee, standing by himself, was praying thus, 'God, I thank you that I am not like other people: thieves, rogues, adulterers, or even like this tax collector. I fast twice a week; I give a tenth of all my income.' But the tax collector, standing far off, would not even look up to heaven, but was beating his breast and saying, 'God, be merciful to me, a sinner!' I tell you, this man went down to his home justified rather than the other; for all who exalt themselves will be humbled, but all who humble themselves will be exalted."

Thursday

A Reading (Lesson) from the Book of Deuteronomy [7:6–11]

Moses convened all Israel, and said to them: You are a people holy to the LORD your God; the LORD your God has chosen you out of all the peoples on earth to be his people, his treasured possession. It was not because you were more numerous than any other people that the LORD set his heart on you and chose you—for you were the fewest of all peoples. It was because the LORD loved you and kept the oath that he swore to your ancestors, that the LORD has brought you out with a mighty hand, and redeemed you from the house of slavery, from the hand of Pharaoh king of Egypt. Know therefore that the LORD your God is God, the faithful God who maintains covenant loyalty with those who love him and keep his commandments, to a thousand generations, and who repays in their own person those who reject him. He does not delay but repays in their own person those who reject him. Therefore, observe diligently the commandment—the statutes, and the ordinances—that I am commanding you today.

A Reading (Lesson) from the Letter of Paul to Titus [1:1–16]

Paul, a servant of God and an apostle of Jesus Christ, for the sake of the faith of God's elect and the knowledge of the truth that is in accordance with godliness, in the hope of eternal life that God, who never lies, promised before the ages began—in due time he revealed his word through the proclamation with which I have been entrusted by the command of God our Savior, to Titus, my loyal child in the faith we share: Grace and peace from God the Father and Christ Jesus our Savior. I left you behind in Crete for this reason, so that you should put in order what remained to be done, and should appoint elders in every town, as I directed you: someone who is blameless, married only once, whose children are believers, not accused of debauchery and not rebellious. For a bishop, as God's steward, must be blameless; he must not be arrogant or quick-tempered or addicted to wine or violent or greedy for gain; but he must be hospitable, a lover of goodness, prudent, upright, devout, and self-controlled. He must have a firm grasp of the word that is trustworthy in accordance with the teaching, so that he may be able both to preach with sound doctrine and to refute those who contradict it. There are also many rebellious people, idle talkers and deceivers, especially those of the circumcision; they must be silenced, since they are upsetting whole families by teaching for sordid gain what it is not right to teach. It was one of them, their very own prophet, who said, "Cretans are always liars, vicious brutes, lazy gluttons." That testimony is true. For this reason rebuke them sharply, so that they may become sound in the faith, not paying attention to Jewish myths or to commandments of those who reject the truth. To the pure all things are pure, but to the corrupt and unbelieving nothing is pure. Their very minds and consciences are corrupted. They profess to know God, but they deny him by their actions. They are detestable, disobedient, unfit for any good work.

A Reading (Lesson) from the Gospel according to John [1:29–34]

The next day John saw Jesus coming toward him and declared, "Here is the Lamb of God who takes away the sin of the world! This is he of whom I said, 'After me comes a man who ranks ahead of me because he was before me.' I myself did not know him; but I came baptizing with water for this reason, that he might be revealed to Israel." And John testified, "I saw the Spirit descending from heaven like a dove, and it remained on him. I myself did not know him, but the one who sent me to baptize with water said to me, 'He on whom you see the Spirit descend and remain is the one who baptizes with the Holy Spirit.' And I myself have seen and have testified that this is the Son of God."

Friday

A Reading (Lesson) from the Book of Deuteronomy [7:12–16]

Moses convened all Israel, and said to them: If you heed these ordinances, by diligently observing them, the LORD your God will maintain with you the covenant loyalty that he swore to your ancestors; he will love you, bless you, and multiply you; he will bless the fruit of your womb and the fruit of your ground, your grain and your wine and your oil, the increase of your cattle and the issue of your flock, in the land that he swore to your ancestors to give you. You shall be the most blessed of peoples, with neither sterility nor barrenness among you or your livestock. The LORD will turn away from you every illness; all the dread diseases of Egypt that you experienced, he will not inflict on you, but he will lay them on all who hate you. You shall devour all the peoples that the LORD your God is giving over to you, showing them no pity; you shall not serve their gods, for that would be a snare to you.

A Reading (Lesson) from the Letter of Paul to Titus [2:1–15]

As for you, teach what is consistent with sound doctrine. Tell the older men to be temperate, serious, prudent, and sound in faith, in love, and in endurance. Likewise, tell the older women to be reverent in behavior, not to be slanderers or slaves to drink; they are to teach what is good, so that they may encourage the young women to love their husbands, to love their children, to be self-controlled, chaste, good managers of the household, kind, being submissive to their husbands, so that the word of God may not be discredited. Likewise, urge the younger men to be self-controlled. Show yourself in all respects a model of good works, and in your teaching show integrity, gravity, and sound speech that cannot be censured, then any opponent will be put to shame, having nothing evil to say of us. Tell slaves to be submissive to their masters and to give satisfaction in every respect; they are not to talk back, not to pilfer, but to show complete and perfect fidelity, so that in everything they may be an ornament to the doctrine of God our Savior. For the grace of God has appeared, bringing salvation to all, training us to renounce impiety and worldly passions, and in the present age to live lives that are self-controlled, upright, and godly, while we wait for the blessed hope and the manifestation of the glory of our great God and Savior, Jesus Christ. He it is who gave himself for us that he might redeem us from all iniquity and purify for himself a people of his own who are zealous for good deeds. Declare these things; exhort and reprove with all authority. Let no one look down on you.

A Reading (Lesson) from the Gospel according to John [1:35–42]

The next day John again was standing with two of his disciples, and as he watched Jesus walk by, he exclaimed, "Look, here is the Lamb of God!" The two disciples heard him say this, and they followed Jesus. When Jesus turned and saw them following, he said to them, "What are you looking for?" They said to him, "Rabbi" (which translated means Teacher), "where are you staying?" He said to them, "Come and see." They came and saw where he was staying, and they remained with him that day. It was about four o'clock in the afternoon. One of the two who heard John speak and followed him was Andrew, Simon Peter's brother. He first found his brother Simon and said to him, "We have found the Messiah" (which is translated Anointed). He brought Simon to Jesus, who looked at him and said, "You are Simon son of John. You are to be called Cephas" (which is translated Peter).

Saturday

A Reading (Lesson) from the Book of Deuteronomy [7:17–26]

Moses convened all Israel, and said to them: If you say to yourself, "These nations are more numerous than I; how can I dispossess them?" do not be afraid of them. Just remember what the LORD your God did to Pharaoh and to all Egypt, the great trials that your eyes saw, the signs and wonders, the mighty hand and the outstretched arm by which the LORD your God brought you out. The LORD your God will do the same to all the peoples of whom you are afraid. Moreover, the LORD your God will send the pestilence against them, until even the survivors and the fugitives are destroyed. Have no dread of them, for the LORD your God, who is present with you, is a great and awesome God. The LORD your God will clear away these nations before you little by little; you will not be able to make a quick end of them, otherwise the wild animals would become too numerous for you. But the LORD your God will give them over to you, and throw them into great panic, until they are destroyed. He will hand their kings over to you and you shall blot out their name from under heaven; no one will be able to stand against you, until you have destroyed them. The images of their gods you shall burn with fire. Do not covet the silver or the gold that is on them and take it for yourself, because you could be ensnared by it; for it is abhorrent to the LORD your God. Do not bring an abhorrent thing into your house, or you will be set apart for destruction like it. You must utterly detest and abhor it, for it is set apart for destruction.

A Reading (Lesson) from the Letter of Paul to Titus [3:1–15]

Remind them to be subject to rulers and authorities, to be obedient, to be ready for every good work, to speak evil of no one, to avoid quarreling, to be gentle, and to show every courtesy to everyone. For we ourselves were once foolish, disobedient, led astray, slaves to various passions and pleasures, passing our days in malice and envy, despicable, hating one another. But when the goodness and loving kindness of God our Savior appeared, he saved us, not because of any works of righteousness that we had done, but according to his mercy, through the water of rebirth and renewal by the Holy Spirit. This Spirit he poured out on us richly through Jesus Christ our Savior, so that, having been justified by his grace, we might become heirs according to the hope of eternal life. The saying is sure. I desire that you insist on these things, so that those who have come to believe in God may be careful to devote themselves to good works; these things are excellent and profitable to everyone. But avoid stupid controversies, genealogies, dissensions, and quarrels about the law, for they are unprofitable and worthless. After a first and second admonition, have nothing more to do with anyone who causes divisions, since you know that such a person is perverted and sinful, being self-condemned. When I send Artemas to you, or Tychicus, do your best to come to me at Nicopolis, for I have decided to spend the winter there. Make every effort to send Zenas the lawyer and Apollos on their way, and see that they lack nothing. And let people learn to devote themselves to good works in order to meet urgent needs, so that they may not be unproductive. All who are with me send greetings to you. Greet those who love us in the faith. Grace be with all of you.

A Reading (Lesson) from the Gospel according to John [1:43–51]

The next day Jesus decided to go to Galilee. He found Philip and said to him, "Follow me." Now Philip was from Bethsaida, the city of Andrew and Peter. Philip found Nathanael and said to him, "We have found him about whom Moses in the law and also the prophets wrote, Jesus son of Joseph from Nazareth." Nathanael said to him, "Can anything good come out of Nazareth?" Philip said to him, "Come and see." When Jesus saw Nathanael coming toward him, he said of him, "Here is truly an Israelite in whom there is no deceit!" Nathanael asked him, "Where did you get to know me?" Jesus answered, "I saw you under the fig tree before Philip called you." Nathanael replied, "Rabbi, you are the Son of God! You are the King of Israel!" Jesus answered, "Do you believe because I told you that I saw you under the fig tree? You will see greater things than these." And he said to him, "Very truly, I tell you, you will see heaven opened and the angels of God ascending and descending upon the Son of Man."

Week of I Lent

Sunday

A Reading (Lesson) from the Book of Deuteronomy [8:1–10]

Moses convened all Israel, and said to them: This entire commandment that I command you today you must diligently observe, so that you may live and increase, and go in and occupy the land that the LORD promised on oath to your ancestors. Remember the long way that the LORD your God has led you these forty years in the wilderness, in order to humble you, testing you to know what was in your heart, whether or not you would keep his commandments. He humbled you by letting you hunger, then by feeding you with manna, with which neither you nor your ancestors were acquainted, in order to make you understand that one does not live by bread alone, but by every word that comes from the mouth of the LORD. The clothes on your back did not wear out and your feet did not swell these forty years. Know then in your heart that as a parent disciplines a child so the LORD your God disciplines you. Therefore keep the commandments of the LORD your God, by walking in his ways and by fearing him. For the LORD your God is bringing you into a good land, a land with flowing streams, with springs and underground waters welling up in valleys and hills, a land of wheat and barley, of vines and fig trees and pomegranates, a land of olive trees and honey, a land where you may eat bread without scarcity, where you will lack nothing, a land whose stones are iron and from whose hills you may mine copper. You shall eat your fill and bless the LORD your God for the good land that he has given you.

A Reading (Lesson) from the First Letter of Paul to the Corinthians [1:17–31]

Christ did not send me to baptize but to proclaim the gospel, and not with eloquent wisdom, so that the cross of Christ might not be emptied of its power. For the message about the cross is foolishness to those who are perishing, but to us who are being saved it is the power of God. For it is written, "I will destroy the wisdom of the wise, and the discernment of the discerning I will thwart." Where is the one who is wise? Where is the scribe? Where is the debater of this age? Has not God made foolish the wisdom of the world? For since, in the wisdom of God, the world did not know God through wisdom, God decided, through the foolishness of our proclamation, to save those who believe. For Jews demand signs and Greeks desire wisdom, but we proclaim Christ crucified, a stumbling block to Jews and foolishness to Gentiles, but to those who are the called, both Jews and Greeks, Christ the power of God and the wisdom of God. For God's foolishness is wiser than human wisdom, and God's weakness is stronger than human strength. Consider your own call, brothers and sisters: not many of you were wise by human standards, not many were powerful, nor many were of noble birth. But God chose what is foolish in the world to shame the wise; God chose what is weak in the world to shame the strong; God chose what is low and despised in the world, things that are not, to reduce to nothing things that are, so that no one might boast in the presence of God. He is the source of your life in Christ Jesus, who became for us wisdom from God, and righteousness and sanctification and redemption, in order that, as it is written, "Let the one who boasts, boast in the Lord."

A Reading (Lesson) from the Gospel according to Mark [2:18–22]

John's disciples and the Pharisees were fasting; and people came and said to Jesus, "Why do John's disciples and the disciples of the Pharisees fast, but your disciples do not fast?" Jesus said to them, "The wedding guests cannot fast while the bridegroom is with them, can they? As long as they have the bridegroom with them, they cannot fast. The days will come when the bridegroom is taken away from them, and then they will fast on that day. No one sews a piece of unshrunk cloth on an old cloak; otherwise, the patch pulls away from it, the new from the old, and a worse tear is made. And no one puts new wine into old wineskins; otherwise, the wine will burst the skins, and the wine is lost, and so are the skins; but one puts new wine into fresh wineskins."

Monday

A Reading (Lesson) from the Book of Deuteronomy [8:11–20]

Moses convened all Israel, and said to them: Take care that you do not forget the LORD your God, by failing to keep his commandments, his ordinances, and his statutes, which I am commanding you today. When you have eaten your fill and have built fine houses and live in them, and when your herds and flocks have multiplied, and your silver and gold is multiplied, and all that you have is multiplied, then do not exalt yourself, forgetting the LORD your God, who brought you out of the land of Egypt, out of the house of slavery, who led you through the great and terrible wilderness, an arid wasteland with poisonous snakes and scorpions. He made water flow for you from flint rock, and fed you in the wilderness with manna that your ancestors did not know, to humble you and to test you, and in the end to do you good. Do not say to yourself, "My power and the might of my own hand have gotten me this wealth." But remember the LORD your God, for it is he who gives you power to get wealth, so that he may confirm his covenant that he swore to your ancestors, as he is doing today. If you do forget the LORD your God and follow other gods to serve and worship them, I solemnly warn you today that you shall surely perish. Like the nations that the LORD is destroying before you, so shall you perish, because you would not obey the voice of the LORD your God.

A Reading (Lesson) from the Letter to the Hebrews [2:11–18]

The one who sanctifies and those who are sanctified all have one Father. For this reason Jesus is not ashamed to call them brothers and sisters, saying, "I will proclaim your name to my brothers and sisters, in the midst of the congregation I will praise you." And again, "I will put my trust in him." And again, "Here am I and the children whom God has given me." Since, therefore, the children share flesh and blood, he himself likewise shared the same things, so that through death he might destroy the one who has the power of death, that is, the devil, and free those who all their lives were held in slavery by the fear of death. For it is clear that he did not come to help angels, but the descendants of Abraham. Therefore he had to become like his brothers and sisters in every respect, so that he might be a merciful and faithful high priest in the service of God, to make a sacrifice of atonement for the sins of the people. Because he himself was tested by what he suffered, he is able to help those who are being tested.

A Reading (Lesson) from the Gospel according to John [2:1–12]

On the third day there was a wedding in Cana of Galilee, and the mother of Jesus was there. Jesus and his disciples had also been invited to the wedding. When the wine gave out, the mother of Jesus said to him, "They have no wine." And Jesus said to her, "Woman, what concern is that to you and to me? My hour has not yet come." His mother said to the servants, "Do whatever he tells you." Now standing there were six stone water jars for the Jewish rites of purification, each holding twenty or thirty gallons. Jesus said to them, "Fill the jars with water." And they filled them up to the brim. He said to them, "Now draw some out, and take it to the chief steward." So they took it. When the steward tasted the water that had become wine, and did not know where it came from (though the servants who had drawn the water knew), the steward called the bridegroom and said to him, "Everyone serves the good wine first, and then the inferior wine after the guests have become drunk. But you have kept the good wine until now." Jesus did this, the first of his signs, in Cana of Galilee, and revealed his glory; and his disciples believed in him. After this he went down to Capernaum with his mother, his brothers, and his disciples; and they remained there a few days.

Tuesday

A Reading (Lesson) from the Book of Deuteronomy [9:4–12]

Moses convened all Israel, and said to them: When the LORD your God thrusts them out before you, do not say to, yourself, "It is because of my righteousness that the LORD has brought me in to occupy this land;" it is rather because of the wickedness of these nations that the LORD is dispossessing them before you. It is not because of your righteousness or the uprightness of your heart that you are going in to occupy their land; but because of the wickedness of these nations the

Lord your God is dispossessing them before you, in order to fulfill the promise that the Lord made on oath to your ancestors, to Abraham, to Isaac, and to Jacob. Know, then, that the Lord your God is not giving you this good land to occupy because of your righteousness; for you are a stubborn people. Remember and do not forget how you provoked the Lord your God to wrath in the wilderness; you have been rebellious against the Lord from the day you came out of the land of Egypt until you came to this place. Even at Horeb you provoked the Lord to wrath, and the Lord was so angry with you that he was ready to destroy you. When I went up the mountain to receive the stone tablets, the tablets of the covenant that the Lord made with you, I remained on the mountain forty days and forty nights; I neither ate bread nor drank water. And the Lord gave me the two stone tablets written with the finger of God; on them were all the words that the Lord had spoken to you at the mountain out of the fire on the day of the assembly. At the end of forty days and forty nights the Lord gave me the two stone tablets, the tablets of the covenant. Then the Lord said to me, "Get up, go down quickly from here, for your people whom you have brought from Egypt have acted corruptly. They have been quick to turn from the way that I commanded them; they have cast an image for themselves."

A Reading (Lesson) from the Letter to the Hebrews [3:1–11]

Therefore, brothers and sisters, holy partners in a heavenly calling, consider that Jesus, the apostle and high priest of our confession, was faithful to the one who appointed him, just as Moses also "was faithful in all God's house." Yet Jesus is worthy of more glory than Moses, just as the builder of a house has more honor than the house itself. (For every house is built by someone, but the builder of all things is God.) Now Moses was faithful in all God's house as a servant, to testify to the things that would be spoken later. Christ, however, was faithful over God's house as a son, and we are his house if we hold firm the confidence and the pride that belong to hope. Therefore, as the Holy Spirit says, "Today, if you hear his voice, do not harden your hearts as in the rebellion, as on the day of testing in the wilderness, where your ancestors put me to the test, though they had seen my works for forty years. Therefore I was angry with that generation, and I said, 'They always go astray in their hearts, and they have not known my ways.' As in my anger I swore, 'They will not enter my rest.'"

A Reading (Lesson) from the Gospel according to John[2:13–22]

The Passover of the Jews was near, and Jesus went up to Jerusalem. In the temple he found people selling cattle, sheep, and doves, and the money changers seated at their tables. Making a whip of cords, he drove all of them out of the temple, both the sheep and the cattle. He also poured out the coins of the money changers and overturned their tables. He told those who were selling the doves, "Take these things out of here! Stop making my Father's house a marketplace!" His disciples remembered that it was written, "Zeal for your house will consume me." The Jews then said to him, "What sign can you show us for doing this?" Jesus answered them, "Destroy this temple, and in three days I will raise it up." The Jews then said, "This temple has been under construction for forty-six years, and will you raise it up in three days?" But he was speaking of the temple of his body. After he was raised from the dead, his disciples remembered that he had said this; and they believed the scripture and the word that Jesus had spoken.

Wednesday

A Reading (Lesson) from the Book of Deuteronomy [9:13–21]

Moses convened all Israel, and said to them: Furthermore the LORD said to me, "I have seen that this people is indeed a stubborn people. Let me alone that I may destroy them and blot out their name from under heaven; and I will make of you a nation mightier and more numerous than they." So I turned and went down from the mountain, while the mountain was ablaze; the two tablets of the covenant were in my two hands. Then I saw that you had indeed sinned against the LORD your God, by casting for yourselves an image of a calf; you had been quick to turn from the way that the LORD had commanded you. So I took hold of the two tablets and flung them from my two hands, smashing them before your eyes. Then I lay prostrate before the LORD as before, forty days and forty nights; I neither ate bread nor drank water, because of all the sin you had committed, provoking the LORD by doing what was evil in his sight. For I was afraid that the anger that the LORD bore against you was so fierce that he would destroy you. But the LORD listened to me that time also. The LORD was so angry with Aaron that he was ready to destroy him, but I interceded also on behalf of Aaron at that same time. Then I took the sinful thing you had made, the calf, and burned it with fire and crushed it, grinding it thoroughly, until it was reduced to dust; and I threw the dust of it into the stream that runs down the mountain.

A Reading (Lesson) from the Letter to the Hebrews [3:12–19]

Take care, brothers and sisters, that none of you may have an evil, unbelieving heart that turns away from the living God. But exhort one another every day, as long as it is called "today," so that none of you may be hardened by the deceitfulness of sin. For we have become partners of Christ, if only we hold our first confidence firm to the end. As it is said, "Today, if you hear his voice, do not harden your hearts as in the rebellion." Now who were they who heard and yet were rebellious? Was it not all those who left Egypt under the leadership of Moses? But with whom was he angry forty years? Was it not those who sinned, whose bodies fell in the wilderness? And to whom did he swear that they would not enter his rest, if not to those who were disobedient? So we see that they were unable to enter because of unbelief.

A Reading (Lesson) from the Gospel according to John [2:23 — 3:15]

When Jesus was in Jerusalem during the Passover festival, many believed in his name because they saw the signs that he was doing. But Jesus on his part would not entrust himself to them, because he knew all people and needed no one to testify about anyone; for he himself knew what was in everyone. Now there was a Pharisee named Nicodemus, a leader of the Jews. He came to Jesus by night and said to him, "Rabbi, we know that you are a teacher who has come from God; for no one can do these signs that you do apart from the presence of God." Jesus answered him, "Very truly, I tell you, no one can see the kingdom of God without being born from above." Nicodemus said to him, "How can anyone be born after having grown old? Can one enter a second time into the mother's womb and be born?" Jesus answered, "Very truly, I tell you, no one can enter the kingdom of God without being born of water and Spirit. What is born of the flesh is flesh, and what is born of the Spirit is spirit. Do not be astonished that I said to you, 'You must be born from above.' The wind blows where it chooses, and you hear the sound of it, but you do not know where it comes from or where it goes. So it is with everyone who is born of the Spirit." Nicodemus said to him, "How can these things be?" Jesus answered him, "Are you a teacher of Israel, and yet you do not understand these things? Very truly, I tell you, we speak of what we know and testify to what we have seen; yet you do not receive our testimony. If I have told you about earthly things and you do not believe, how can you believe if I tell you about heavenly things? No one has ascended into heaven except the one who descended from heaven, the Son of Man. And just as Moses lifted up the serpent in the wilderness, so must the Son of Man be lifted up, that whoever believes in him may have eternal life."

Thursday

A Reading (Lesson) from the Book of Deuteronomy [9:23 – 10:5]

Moses convened all Israel, and said to them: When the LORD sent you from Kadesh-barnea, saying, "Go up and occupy the land that I have given you," you rebelled against the command of the LORD your God, neither trusting him nor obeying him. You have been rebellious against the LORD as long as he has known you. Throughout the forty days and forty nights that I lay prostrate before the LORD when the LORD intended to destroy you, I prayed to the LORD and said, "LORD GOD, do not destroy the people who are your very own possession, whom you redeemed in your greatness, whom you brought out of Egypt with a mighty hand. Remember your servants, Abraham, Isaac, and Jacob; pay no attention to the stubbornness of this people, their wickedness and their sin, otherwise the land from which you have brought us might say, 'Because the LORD was not able to bring them into the land that he promised them, and because he hated them, he has brought them out to let them die in the wilderness.' For they are the people of your very own possession, whom you brought out by your great power and by your outstretched arm." At that time the LORD said to me, "Carve out two tablets of stone like the former ones, and come up to me on the mountain, and make an ark of wood. I will write on the tablets the words that were on the former tablets, which you smashed, and you shall put them in the ark." So I made an ark of acacia wood, cut two tablets of stone like the former ones, and went up the mountain with the two tablets in my hand. Then he wrote on the tablets the same words as before, the ten commandments that the LORD had spoken to you on the mountain out of the fire on the day of the assembly; and the LORD gave them to me. So I turned and came down from the mountain, and put the tablets in the ark that I had made; and there they are, as the LORD commanded me.

A Reading (Lesson) from the Letter to the Hebrews [4:1–10]

While the promise of entering his rest is still open, let us take care that none of you should seem to have failed to reach it. For indeed the good news came to us just as to them; but the message they heard did not benefit them, because they were not united by faith with those who listened. For we who have believed enter that rest, just as God has said, "As in my anger I swore, 'They shall not enter my rest,'" though his works were finished at the foundation of the world. For in one place it speaks about the seventh day as follows, "And God rested on the seventh day from all his works." And again in this place it says, "They shall not enter my rest." Since therefore it remains open for some to enter it, and those who formerly received the good news failed to enter because of disobedience, again he sets a certain day—"today"—saying through David much later, in the words already quoted, "Today, if you hear his voice, do not harden your hearts." For if Joshua had given them rest, God would not speak later about another day. So then, a sabbath rest still remains for the people of God; for those who enter God's rest also cease from their labors as God did from his.

A Reading (Lesson) from the Gospel according to John [3:16–21]

Jesus said to Nicodemus, "God so loved the world that he gave his only Son, so that everyone who believes in him may not perish but may have eternal life. Indeed, God did not send the Son into the world to condemn the world, but in order that the world might be saved through him. Those who believe in him are not condemned; but those who do not believe are condemned already, because they have not believed in the name of the only Son of God. And this is the judgment, that the light has come into the world, and people loved darkness rather than light because their deeds were evil. For all who do evil hate the light and do not come to the light, so that their deeds may not be exposed. But those who do what is true come to the light, so that it may be clearly seen that their deeds have been done in God."

Friday

A Reading (Lesson) from the Book of Deuteronomy [10:12–22]

Moses convened all Israel, and said to them: So now, O Israel, what does the LORD your God require of you? Only to fear the LORD your God, to walk in all his ways, to love him, to serve the LORD your God with all your heart and with all your soul, and to keep the command-ments of the LORD your God and his decrees that I am commanding you today, for your own well-being. Although heaven and the heaven of heavens belong to the LORD your God, the earth with all that is in it, yet the LORD set his heart in love on your ancestors alone and chose you, their descendants after them, out of all the peoples, as it is today. Circumcise, then, the foreskin of your heart, and do not be stubborn any longer. For the LORD your God is God of gods and LORD of lords, the great God, mighty and awesome, who is not partial and takes no bribe, who executes justice for the orphan and the widow, and who loves the strangers, providing them food and clothing. You shall also love the stranger, for you were strangers in the land of Egypt. You shall fear the LORD your God; him alone you shall worship; to him you shall hold fast, and by his name you shall swear. He is your praise; he is your God, who has done for you these great and awesome things that your own eyes have seen. Your ancestors went down to Egypt seventy persons; and now the LORD your God has made you as numerous as the stars in heaven.

A Reading (Lesson) from the Letter to the Hebrews [4:11–16]

Let us make every effort to enter that rest, so that no one may fall through such disobedience as theirs. Indeed, the word of God is living and active, sharper than any two-edged sword, piercing until it divides soul from spirit, joints from marrow; it is able to judge the thoughts and intentions of the heart. And before him no creature is hidden, but all are naked and laid bare to the eyes of the one to whom we must render an account. Since, then, we have a great high priest who has passed through the heavens, Jesus, the Son of God, let us hold fast to our confession. For we do not have a high priest who is unable to sympathize with our weaknesses, but we have one who in every respect has been tested as we are, yet without sin. Let us therefore approach the throne of grace with boldness, so that we may receive mercy and find grace to help in time of need.

A Reading (Lesson) from the Gospel according to John [3:22–36]

Jesus and his disciples went into the Judean countryside, and he spent some time there with them and baptized. John also was baptizing at Aenon near Salim because water was abundant there; and people kept coming and were being baptized—John, of course, had not yet been thrown into prison. Now a discussion about purification arose between John's disciples and a Jew. They came to John and said to him, "Rabbi, the one who was with you across the Jordan, to whom you testified, here he is baptizing, and all are going to him." John answered, "No one can receive anything except what has been given from heaven. You yourselves are my witnesses that I said, 'I am not the Messiah, but I have been sent ahead of him.' He who has the bride is the bridegroom. The friend of the bridegroom, who stands and hears him, rejoices greatly at the bridegroom's voice. For this reason my joy has been fulfilled. He must increase, but I must decrease." The one who comes from above is above all; the one who is of the earth belongs to the earth and speaks about earthly things. The one who comes from heaven is above all. He testifies to what he has seen and heard, yet no one accepts his testimony. Whoever has accepted his testimony has certified this, that God is true. He whom God has sent speaks the words of God, for he gives the Spirit without measure. The Father loves the Son and has placed all things in his hands. Whoever believes in the Son has eternal life; whoever disobeys the Son will not see life, but must endure God's wrath.

Saturday

A Reading (Lesson) from the Book of Deuteronomy [11:18–28]

Moses convened all Israel, and said to them: You shall put these words of mine in your heart and soul, and you shall bind them as a sign on your hand, and fix them as an emblem on your forehead. Teach them to your children, talking about them when you are at home and when you are away, when you lie down and when you rise. Write them on the doorposts of your house and on your gates, so that your days and the days of your children may be multiplied in the land that the LORD swore to your ancestors to give them, as long as the heavens are above the earth. If you will diligently observe this entire commandment that I am commanding you, loving the LORD your God, walking in all his ways, and holding fast to him, then the LORD will drive out all these nations before you, and you will dispossess nations larger and mightier than yourselves. Every place on which you set foot shall be yours; your territory shall extend from the wilderness to the Lebanon and from the River, the river Euphrates, to the Western Sea. No one will be able to stand against you; the LORD your God will put the fear and dread of you on all the land on which you set foot, as he promised you. See, I am setting before you today a blessing and a curse: the blessing, if you obey the commandments of the LORD your God that I am commanding you today; and the curse, if you do not obey the commandments of the LORD your God, but turn from the way that I am commanding you today, to follow other gods that you have not known.

A Reading (Lesson) from the Letter to the Hebrews [5:1–10]

Every high priest chosen from among mortals is put in charge of things pertaining to God on their behalf, to offer gifts and sacrifices for sins. He is able to deal gently with the ignorant and wayward, since he himself is subject to weakness; and because of this he must offer sacrifice for his own sins as well as for those of the people. And one does not presume to take this honor, but takes it only when called by God, just as Aaron was. So also Christ did not glorify himself in becoming a high priest, but was appointed by the one who said to him, "You are my Son, today I have begotten you"; as he says also in another place, "You are a priest forever, according to the order of Melchizedek." In the days of his flesh, Jesus offered up prayers and supplications, with loud cries and tears, to the one who was able to save him from death, and he was heard because of his reverent submission. Although he was a Son, he learned obedience through what he suffered; and having been made perfect, he became the source of eternal salvation for all who obey him, having been designated by God a high priest according to the order of Melchizedek.

A Reading (Lesson) from the Gospel according to John [4:1–26]

Now when Jesus learned that the Pharisees had heard, "Jesus is making and baptizing more disciples than John"—although it was not Jesus himself but his disciples who baptized—he left Judea and started back to Galilee. But he had to go through Samaria. So he came to a Samaritan city called Sychar, near the plot of ground that Jacob had given to his son Joseph. Jacob's well was there, and Jesus, tired out by his journey, was sitting by the well. It was about noon. A Samaritan woman came to draw water, and Jesus said to her, "Give me a drink." (His disciples had gone to the city to buy food.) The Samaritan woman said to him, "How is it that you, a Jew, ask a drink of me, a woman of Samaria?" (Jews do not share things in common with Samaritans.) Jesus answered her, "If you knew the gift of God, and who it is that is saying to you, 'Give me a drink,' you would have asked him, and he would have given you living water." The woman said to him, "Sir, you have no bucket, and the well is deep. Where do you get that living water? Are you greater than our ancestor Jacob, who gave us the well, and with his sons and his flocks drank from it?" Jesus said to her, "Everyone who drinks of this water will be thirsty again, but those who drink of the water that I will give them will never be thirsty. The water that I will give will become in them a spring of water gushing up to eternal life." The woman said to him, "Sir, give me this water, so that I may never be thirsty or have to keep coming here to draw water." Jesus said to her, "Go, call your husband, and come back." The woman answered him, "I have no husband." Jesus said to her, "You are right in saying, 'I have no husband' for you have had five husbands, and the one you have now is not your husband. What you have said is true!" The woman said to him, "Sir, I see that you are a prophet. Our ancestors worshiped on this mountain, but you say that the place where people must worship is in Jerusalem." Jesus said to her, "Woman, believe me, the hour is coming when you will worship the Father neither on this mountain nor in Jerusalem. You worship what you do not know; we worship what we know, for salvation is from the Jews. But the hour is coming, and is now here, when the true worshipers will worship the Father in spirit and truth, for the Father seeks such as these to worship him. God is spirit, and those who worship him must worship in spirit and truth." The woman said to him, "I know that Messiah is coming" (who is called Christ). "When he comes, he will proclaim all things to us." Jesus said to her, "I am he, the one who is speaking to you."

Week of 2 Lent

Sunday

A Reading (Lesson) from the Book of Jeremiah [1:1–10]

The words of Jeremiah son of Hilkiah, of the priests who were in Anathoth in the land of Benjamin, to whom the word of the LORD came in the days of King Josiah son of Amon of Judah, in the thirteenth year of his reign. It came also in the days of King Jehoiakim son of Josiah of Judah, and until the end of the eleventh year of King Zedekiah son of Josiah of Judah, until the captivity of Jerusalem in the fifth month. Now the word of the LORD came to me saying, "Before I formed you in the womb I knew you, and before you were born I consecrated you; I appointed you a prophet to the nations." Then I said, "Ah, LORD GOD! Truly I do not know how to speak, for I am only a boy." But the LORD said to me, "Do not say, 'I am only a boy'; for you shall go to all to whom I send you, and you shall speak whatever I command you. Do not be afraid of them, for I am with you to deliver you, says the LORD." Then the LORD put out his hand and touched my mouth; and the LORD said to me, "Now I have put my words in your mouth. See, today I appoint you over nations and over kingdoms, to pluck up and to pull down, to destroy and to overthrow, to build and to plant."

A Reading (Lesson) from the First Letter of Paul to the Corinthians [3:11–23]

No one can lay any foundation other than the one that has been laid; that foundation is Jesus Christ. Now if anyone builds on the foundation with gold, silver, precious stones, wood, hay, straw—the work of each builder will become visible, for the Day will disclose it, because it will be revealed with fire, and the fire will test what sort of work each has done. If what has been built on the foundation survives, the builder will receive a reward. If the work is burned up, the builder will suffer loss; the builder will be saved, but only as through fire. Do you not know that you are God's temple and that God's Spirit dwells in you? If anyone destroys God's temple, God will destroy that person. For God's temple is holy, and you are that temple. Do not deceive yourselves. If you think that you are wise in this age, you should become fools so that you may become wise. For the wisdom of this world is foolishness with God. For it is written, "He catches the wise in their craftiness," and again, "The Lord knows the thoughts of the wise, that they are futile." So let no one boast about human leaders. For all things are yours, whether Paul or Apollos or Cephas or the world or life or death or the present or the future—all belong to you, and you belong to Christ, and Christ belongs to God.

A Reading (Lesson) from the Gospel according to Mark [3:31—4:9]

Jesus' mother and his brothers came; and standing outside, they sent to him and called him. A crowd was sitting around him; and they said to him, "Your mother and your brothers and sisters are outside, asking for you." And he replied, "Who are my mother and my brothers?" And looking at those who sat around him, he said, "Here are my mother and my brothers! Whoever does the will of God is my brother and sister and mother." Again he began to teach beside the sea. Such a very large crowd gathered around him that he got into a boat on the sea and sat there, while the whole crowd was beside the sea on the land. He began to teach them many things in parables, and in his teaching he said to them: "Listen! A sower went out to sow. And as he sowed, some seed fell on the path, and the birds came and ate it up. Other seed fell on rocky ground, where it did not have much soil, and it sprang up quickly, since it had no depth of soil. And when the sun rose, it was scorched; and since it had no root, it withered away. Other seed fell among thorns, and the thorns grew up and choked it, and it yielded no grain. Other seed fell into good soil and brought forth grain, growing up and increasing and yielding thirty and sixty and a hundred-fold." And he said, "Let anyone with ears to hear listen!"

Monday

A Reading (Lesson) from the Book of Jeremiah [1:11–19]

The word of the LORD came to me, saying, "Jeremiah, what do you see?" And I said, "I see a branch of an almond tree." Then the LORD said to me, "You have seen well, for I am watching over my word to perform it." The word of the LORD came to me a second time, saying, "What do you see?" And I said, "I see a boiling pot, tilted away from the north." Then the LORD said to me: Out of the north disaster shall break out on all the inhabitants of the land. For now I am calling all the tribes of the kingdoms of the north, says the LORD; and they shall come and all of them shall set their thrones at the entrance of the gates of Jerusalem, against all its surrounding walls and against all the cities of Judah. And I will utter my judgments against them, for all their wickedness in forsaking me; they have made offerings to other gods, and worshiped the works of their own hands. But you, gird up your loins; stand up and tell them everything that I command you. Do not break down before them, or I will break you before them. And I for my part have made you today a fortified city, an iron pillar, and a bronze wall, against the whole land—against the kings of Judah, its princes, its priests, and the people of the land. They will fight against you; but they shall not prevail against you, for I am with you, says the LORD, to deliver you.

A Reading (Lesson) from the Letter of Paul to the Romans [1:1–15]

Paul, a servant of Jesus Christ, called to be an apostle, set apart for the gospel of God, which he promised beforehand through his prophets in the holy scriptures, the gospel concerning his Son, who was descended from David according to the flesh and was declared to be Son of God with power according to the spirit of holiness by resurrection from the dead, Jesus Christ our Lord, through whom we have received grace and apostleship to bring about the obedience of faith among all the Gentiles for the sake of his name, including yourselves who are called to belong to Jesus Christ, to all God's beloved in Rome, who are called to be saints: Grace to you and peace from God our Father and the Lord Jesus Christ. First, I thank my God through Jesus Christ for all of you, because your faith is proclaimed throughout the world. For God, whom I serve with my spirit by announcing the gospel of his Son, is my witness that without ceasing I remember you always in my prayers, asking that by God's will I may somehow at last succeed in coming to you. For I am longing to see you so that I may share with you some spiritual gift to strengthen you—or rather so that we may be mutually encouraged by each other's faith, both yours and mine. I want you to know, brothers and sisters, that I have often intended to come to you (but thus far have been prevented), in order that I may reap some harvest among you as I have among the rest of the Gentiles. I am a debtor both to Greeks and to barbarians, both to the wise and to the foolish— hence my eagerness to proclaim the gospel to you also who are in Rome.

A Reading (Lesson) from the Gospel according to John [4:27–42]

Just then the disciples of Jesus came. They were astonished that he was speaking with a woman, but no one said, "What do you want?" or, "Why are you speaking with her?" Then the woman left her water jar and went back to the city. She said to the people, "Come and see a man who told me everything I have ever done! He cannot be the Messiah, can he?" They left the city and were on their way to him. Meanwhile the disciples were urging him, "Rabbi, eat something." But he said to them, "I have food to eat that you do not know about." So the disciples said to one another, "Surely no one has brought him something to eat?" Jesus said to them, "My food is to do the will of him who sent me and to complete his work. Do you not say, 'Four months more, them comes the harvest'? But I tell you, look around you, and see how the fields are ripe for harvesting. The reaper is already receiving wages and is gathering fruit for eternal life, so that sower and reaper may rejoice together. For here the saying holds true, 'One sows and another reaps.' I sent you to reap that for which you did not labor. Others have labored, and you have entered into their labor." Many Samaritans from that city believed in him because of the woman's testimony, "He told me everything I have ever done." So when the Samaritans came to him, they asked him to stay with them; and he stayed there two days. And many more believed because of his word. They said to the woman, "It is no longer because of what you said that we believe, for we have heard for ourselves, and we know that this is truly the Savior of the world."

Tuesday

A Reading (Lesson) from the Book of Jeremiah [2:1–13]

The word of the LORD came to me, saying: Go and proclaim in the hearing of Jerusalem, Thus says the LORD: I remember the devotion of your youth, your love as a bride, how you followed me in the wilderness, in a land not sown. Israel was holy to the LORD, the first fruits of his harvest. All who ate of it were held guilty; disaster came upon them, says the LORD. Hear the word of the LORD, O house of Jacob, and all the families of the house of Israel. Thus says the LORD: What wrong did your ancestors find in me that they went far from me, and went after worthless things, and became worthless themselves? They did not say, "Where is the LORD who brought us up from the land of Egypt, who led us in the wilderness, in a land of deserts and pits, in a land of drought and deep darkness, in a land that no one passes through, where no one lives?" I brought you into a plentiful land to eat its fruits and its good things. But when you entered you denied my land, and made my heritage an abomination. The priests did not say, "Where is the LORD?" Those who handle the law did not know me; the rulers transgressed against me; the prophets prophesied by Baal, and went after things that do not profit. Therefore once more I accuse you, says the LORD, and I accuse your children's children. Cross to the coasts of Cyprus and look, send to Kedar and examine with care; see if there has ever been such a thing. Has a nation changed its gods, even though they are no gods? But my people have changed their glory for something that does not profit. Be appalled, O heavens, at this, be shocked, be utterly desolate, says the LORD, for my people have committed two evils;

they have forsaken me, the fountain of living water, and dug out cisterns for themselves, cracked cisterns that can hold no water.

A Reading (Lesson) from the Letter of Paul to the Romans [1:16–25]

For I am not ashamed of the gospel; it is the power of God for salvation to everyone who has faith, to the Jew first and also to the Greek. For in it the righteousness of God is revealed through faith for faith; as it is written, "The one who is righteous will live by faith." For the wrath of God is revealed from heaven against all ungodliness and wickedness of those who by their wickedness suppress the truth. For what can be known about God is plain to them, because God has shown it to them. Ever since the creation of the world his eternal power and divine nature, invisible though they are, have been understood and seen through the things he has made. So they are without excuse; for though they knew God, they did not honor him as God or give thanks to him, but they became futile in their thinking, and their senseless minds were darkened. Claiming to be wise, they became fools; and they exchanged the glory of the immortal God for images resembling a mortal human being or birds or four-footed animals or reptiles. Therefore God gave them up in the lusts of their hearts to impurity, to the degrading of their bodies among themselves, because they exchanged the truth about God for a lie and worshiped and served the creature rather than the Creator, who is blessed forever! Amen.

A Reading (Lesson) from the Gospel according to John [4:43–54]

After two days in Samaria Jesus went from that place to Galilee (for Jesus himself had testified that a prophet has no honor in the prophet's own country). When he came to Galilee, the Galileans welcomed him, since they had seen all that he had done in Jerusalem at the festival; for they too had gone to the festival. Then he came again to Cana in Galilee where he had changed the water into wine. Now there was a royal official whose son lay ill in Capernaum. When he heard that Jesus had come from Judea to Galilee, he went and begged him to come down and heal his son, for he was at the point of death. Then Jesus said to him, "Unless you see signs and wonders you will not believe." The official said to him, "Sir, come down before my little boy dies." Jesus said to him, "Go; your son will live." The man believed the word that Jesus spoke to him and started on his way. As he was going down, his slaves met him and told him that his child was alive. So he asked them the hour when he began to recover, and they said to him, "Yesterday at one in the afternoon the fever left him." The father realized that this was the hour when Jesus had said to him, "Your son will live." So he himself believed, along with his whole household. Now this was the second sign that Jesus did after coming from Judea to Galilee.

Wednesday

A Reading (Lesson) from the Book of Jeremiah [3:6–18]

The LORD said to me in the days of King Josiah: Have you seen what she did, that faithless one, Israel, how she went up on every high hill and under every green tree, and played the whore there? And I thought, "After she has done all this she will return to me"; but she did not return, and her false sister Judah saw it. She saw that for all the adulteries of that faithless one, Israel, I had sent her away with a decree of divorce; yet her false sister Judah did not fear, but she too went and played the whore. Because she took her whoredom so lightly, she polluted the land, committing adultery with stone and tree. Yet for all this her false sister Judah did not return to me with her whole heart, but only in pretense, says the LORD. Then the LORD said to me: Faithless Israel has shown herself less guilty than false Judah. Go, and proclaim these words toward the north, and say: Return, faithless Israel, says the LORD. I will not look on you in anger, for I am merciful, says the LORD; I will not be angry forever. Only acknowledge your guilt, that you have rebelled against the LORD your God, and scattered your favors among strangers under every green tree, and have not obeyed my voice, says the LORD. Return, O faithless children, says the LORD, for I am your master; I will take you, one from a city and two from a family, and I will bring you to Zion. I will give you shepherds after my own heart, who will feed you with knowledge and understanding. And when you have multiplied and increased in the land, in those days, says the LORD, they shall no longer say, "The ark of the covenant of the LORD." It shall not come to mind, or be remembered, or missed; nor shall another one be made. At that time Jerusalem shall be called the throne of the LORD, and all nations shall gather to it, to the presence of the LORD in Jerusalem, and they shall no longer stubbornly follow their own evil will. In those days the house of Judah shall join the house of Israel, and together they shall come from the land of the north to the land that I gave your ancestors for a heritage.

A Reading (Lesson) from the Letter of Paul to the Romans [1:28 — 2:11]

Since they did not see fit to acknowledge God, God gave them up to a debased mind and to things that should not be done. They were filled with every kind of wickedness, evil, covetousness, malice. Full of envy, murder, strife, deceit, craftiness, they are gossips, slanderers, God-haters, insolent, haughty, boastful, inventors of evil, rebellious toward parents, foolish, faithless, heartless, ruthless. They know God's decree, that those who practice such things deserve to die—yet they not only do them but even applaud others who practice them. Therefore you have no excuse, whoever you are, when you judge others; for in passing judgment on another you condemn yourself, because you, the judge, are doing the very same things. You say, "We know that God's judgment on those who do such things is in accordance with truth." Do you imagine, whoever you are, that when you judge those who do such things and yet do them yourself, you will escape the judgment of God? Or do you despise the riches of his kindness and forbearance and patience? Do you not realize that God's kindness is meant to lead you to repentance? But by your hard and impenitent heart you are storing up wrath for yourself on the day of wrath, when God's righteous judgment will be revealed. For he will repay according to each one's deeds: to those who by patiently doing good seek for glory and honor and immortality, he will give eternal life; while for those who are self-seeking and who obey not the truth but wickedness, there will be wrath and fury. There will be anguish and distress for everyone who does evil, the Jew first and also the Greek, but glory and honor and peace for everyone who does good, the Jew first and also the Greek. For God shows no partiality.

A Reading (Lesson) from the Gospel according to John [5:1–18]

After the second sign in Cana there was a festival of the Jews, and Jesus went up to Jerusalem. Now in Jerusalem by the Sheep Gate there is a pool, called in Hebrew Beth-zatha, which has five porticoes. In these lay many invalids—blind, lame, and paralyzed. One man was there who had been ill for thirty-eight years. When Jesus saw him lying there and knew that he had been there a long time, he said to him, "Do you want to be made well?" The sick man answered him, "Sir, I have no one to put me into the pool when the water is stirred up; and while I am making my way, someone else steps down ahead of me." Jesus said to him, "Stand up, take your mat and walk." At once the man was made well, and he took up his mat and began to walk. Now that day was a sabbath. So the Jews said to the man who had been cured, "It is the sabbath; it is not lawful for you to carry your mat." But he answered them, "The man who made me well said to me, 'Take up your mat and walk.'" They asked him, "Who is the man who said to you, 'Take it up and walk'?" Now the man who had been healed did not know who it was, for Jesus had disappeared in the crowd that was there. Later Jesus found him in the temple and said to him, "See, you have been made well! Do not sin any more, so that nothing worse happens to you." The man went away and told the Jews that it was Jesus who had made him well. Therefore the Jews started persecuting Jesus, because he was doing such things on the sabbath. But Jesus answered them, "My Father is still working, and I also am working." For this reason the Jews were seeking all the more to kill him, because he was not only breaking the sabbath, but was also calling God his own Father, thereby making himself equal to God.

Thursday

A Reading (Lesson) from the Book of Jeremiah [4:9–10, 19–28]

On that day, says the LORD, courage shall fail the king and the officials; the priests shall be appalled and the prophets astounded. Then I said, "Ah, LORD GOD, how utterly you have deceived this people and Jerusalem, saying, 'It shall be well with you,' even while the sword is at the throat!" My anguish, my anguish! I writhe in pain! Oh, the walls of my heart! My heart is beating wildly; I cannot keep silent; for I hear the sound of the trumpet, the alarm of war. Disaster overtakes disaster, the whole land is laid waste. Suddenly my tents are destroyed, my curtains in a moment. How long must I see the standard, and hear the sound of the trumpet? "For my people are foolish, they do not know me; they are stupid children, they have no understanding. They are skilled in doing evil, but do not know how to do good." I looked on the earth, and lo, it was waste and void; and to the heavens, and they had no light. I looked on the mountains, and lo, they were quaking, and all the hills moved to and fro. I looked, and lo, there was no one at all, and all the birds of the air had fled. I looked, and lo, the fruitful land was a desert, and all its cities were laid in ruins before the LORD, before his fierce anger. For thus says the LORD: The whole land shall be a desolation; yet I will not make a full end. Because of this the earth shall mourn, and the heavens above grow black; for I have spoken, I have purposed; I have not relented nor will I turn back.

A Reading (Lesson) from the Letter of Paul to the Romans [2:12–24]

All who have sinned apart from the law will also perish apart from the law, and all who have sinned under the law will be judged by the law. For it is not the hearers of the law who are righteous in God's sight, but the doers of the law who will be justified. When Gentiles, who do not possess the law, do instinctively what the law requires, these, though not having the law, are a law to themselves. They show that what the law requires is written on their hearts, to which their own conscience also bears witness; and their conflicting thoughts will accuse or perhaps excuse them on the day when, according to my gospel, God, through Jesus Christ, will judge the secret thoughts of all. But if you call yourself a Jew and rely on the law and boast of your relation to God and know his will and determine what is best because you are instructed in the law, and if you are sure that you are a guide to the blind, a light to those who are in darkness, a corrector of the foolish, a teacher of children, having in the law the embodiment of knowledge and truth, you, then, that teach others, will you not teach yourself? While you preach against stealing, do you steal? You that forbid adultery, do you commit adultery? You that abhor idols, do you rob temples? You that boast in the law, do you dishonor God by breaking the law? For, as it is written, "The name of God is blasphemed among the Gentiles because of you."

A Reading (Lesson) from the Gospel according to John [5:19–29]

Jesus said to the Jews, "Very truly, I tell you, the Son can do nothing on his own, but only what he sees the Father doing; for whatever the Father does, the Son does likewise. The Father loves the Son and shows him all that he himself is doing; and he will show him greater works than these, so that you will be astonished. Indeed, just as the Father raises the dead and gives them life, so also the Son gives life to whomever he wishes. The Father judges no one but has given all judgment to the Son, so that all may honor the Son just as they honor the Father. Anyone who does not honor the Son does not honor the Father who sent him. Very truly, I tell you, anyone who hears my word and believes him who sent me has eternal life, and does not come under Judgment, but has passed from death to life. Very truly, I tell you, the hour is coming, and is now here, when the dead will hear the voice of the Son of God, and those who hear will live. For just as the Father has life in himself, so he has granted the Son also to have life in himself; and he has given him authority to execute judgment, because he is the Son of Man. Do not be astonished at this; for the hour is coming when all who are in their graves will hear his voice and will come out—those who have done good, to the resurrection of life, and those who have done evil, to the resurrection of condemnation."

Friday

A Reading (Lesson) from the Book of Jeremiah [5:1–9]

Run to and fro through the streets of Jerusalem, look around and take note! Search its squares and see if you can find one person who acts justly and seeks truth—so that I may pardon Jerusalem. Although they say, "As the LORD lives," yet they swear falsely. O LORD, do your eyes not look for truth? You have struck them, but they felt no anguish, you have consumed them, but they refused to take correction. They have made their faces harder than rock; they have refused to turn back. Then I said, "These are only the poor, they have no sense; for they do not know the way of the LORD, the law of their God. Let me go to the rich and speak to them; surely they know the way of the LORD, the law of their God." But they all alike had broken the yoke, they had burst the bonds. Therefore a lion from the forest shall kill them, a wolf from the desert shall destroy them. A leopard is watching against their cities; everyone who goes out of them shall be torn in pieces—because their transgressions are many, their apostasies are great. How can I pardon you? Your children have forsaken me, and have sworn by those who are no gods. When I fed them to the full, they committed adultery and trooped to the houses of prostitutes. They were well-fed lusty stallions, each neighing for his neighbor's wife. Shall I not punish them for these things? says the LORD; and shall I not bring retribution on a nation such as this?

A Reading (Lesson) from the Letter of Paul to the Romans [2:25 — 3:18]

Circumcision indeed is of value if you obey the law; but if you break the law, your circumcision has become uncircumcision. So, if those who are uncircumcised keep the requirements of the law, will not their uncircumcision be regarded as circumcision? Then those who are physically uncircumcised but keep the law will condemn you that have the written code and circumcision but break the law. For a person is not a Jew who is one outwardly, nor is true circumcision something external and physical. Rather, a person is a Jew who is one inwardly, and real circumcision is a matter of the heart—it is spiritual and not literal. Such a person receives praise not from others but from God. Then what advantage has the Jew? Or what is the value of circumcision? Much, in every way. For in the first place the Jews were entrusted with the oracles of God. What if some were unfaithful? Will their faithlessness nullify the faithfulness of God? By no means! Although everyone is a liar, let God be proved true, as it is written, "So that you may be justified in your words, and prevail in your judging." But if our injustice serves to confirm the justice of God, what should we say? That God is unjust to inflict wrath on us? (I speak in a human way.) By no means! For then how could God judge the world? But if through my falsehood God's truthfulness abounds to his glory, why am I still being condemned as a sinner? And why not say (as some people slander us by saying that we say), "Let us do evil so that good may come"? Their condemnation is deserved! What then? Are we any better off? No, not at all; for we have already charged that all, both Jews and Greeks, are under the power of sin, as it is written: "There is no one who is righteous, not even one; there is no one who has understanding, there is no one who seeks God. All have turned aside, together they have become worthless; there is no one who shows kindness, there is not even one." "Their throats are opened graves; they use their tongues to deceive." "The venom of vipers is under their lips." "Their mouths are full of cursing and bitterness." "Their feet are swift to shed blood; ruin and misery are in their paths, and the way of peace they have not known." "There is no fear of God before their eyes."

A Reading (Lesson) from the Gospel according to John [5:30–47]

Jesus said to the Jews, "I can do nothing on my own. As I hear, I judge; and my judgement is just, because I seek to do not my own will but the will of him who sent me. If I testify about myself, my testimony is not true. There is another who testifies on my behalf, and I know that his testimony to me is true. You sent messengers to John, and he testified to the truth. Not that I accept such human testimony, but I say these things so that you may be saved. He was a burning and shining lamp, and you were willing to rejoice for a while in his light. But I have a testimony greater than John's. The works that the Father has given me to complete, the very works that I am doing, testify on my behalf that the Father has sent me. And the Father who sent me has himself testified on my behalf. You have never heard his voice or seen his form, and you do not have his word abiding in you, because you do not believe him whom he has sent. You search the scriptures because you think that in them you have eternal life; and it is they that testify on my behalf. Yet you refuse to come to me to have life. I do not accept glory from human beings. But I know that you do not have the love of God in you. I have come in my Father's name, and you do not accept me; if another comes in his own name, you will accept him. How can you believe when you accept glory from one another and do not seek the glory that comes from the one who alone is God? Do not think that I will accuse you before the Father; your accuser is Moses, on whom you have set your hope. If you believed Moses, you should believe me, for he wrote about me. But if you do not believe what he wrote, how will you believe what I say?"

Saturday

A Reading (Lesson) from the Book of Jeremiah [5:20–31]

Declare this in the house of Jacob, proclaim it in Judah: Hear this, O foolish and senseless people, who have eyes, but do not see, who have ears, but do not hear. Do you not fear me? says the LORD; Do you not tremble before me? I placed the sand as a boundary for the sea, a perpetual barrier that it cannot pass; though the waves toss, they cannot prevail, though they roar, they cannot pass over it. But this people has a stubborn and rebellious heart; they have turned aside and gone away. They do not say in their hearts, "Let us fear the LORD our God, who gives the rain in its season, the autumn rain and the spring rain, and keeps for us the weeks appointed for the harvest." Your iniquities have turned these away, and your sins have deprived you of good. For scoundrels are found among my people; they take over the goods of others. Like fowlers they set a trap; they catch human beings. Like a cage full of birds, their houses are full of treachery; therefore they have become great and rich, they have grown fat and sleek. They know no limits in deeds of wickedness; they do not judge with justice the cause of the orphan, to make it prosper, and they do not defend the rights of the needy. Shall I not punish them for these things? says the LORD, and shall I not bring retribution on a nation such as this? An appalling and horrible thing has happened in the land: the prophets prophesy falsely, and the priests rule as the prophets direct; my people love to have it so, but what will you do when the end comes?

A Reading (Lesson) from the Letter of Paul to the Romans [3:19–31]

We know that whatever the law says, it speaks to those who are under the law, so that every mouth may be silenced, and the whole world may be held accountable to God. For "no human being will be justified in his sight" by deeds prescribed by the law, for through the law comes the knowledge of sin. But now, apart from law, the righteousness of God has been disclosed, and is attested by the law and the prophets, the righteousness of God through faith in Jesus Christ for all who believe. For there is no distinction, since all have sinned and fall short of the glory of God; they are now justified by his grace as a gift, through the redemption that is in Christ Jesus, whom God put forward as a sacrifice of atonement by his blood, effective through faith. He did this to show his righteousness, because in his divine forbearance he had passed over the sins previously committed; it was to prove at the present time that he himself is righteous and that he justifies the one who has faith in Jesus. Then what becomes of boasting? It is excluded. By what law? By that of works? No, but by the law of faith. For we hold that a person is justified by faith apart from works prescribed by the law. Or is God the God of Jews only? Is he not the God of Gentiles also? Yes, of Gentiles also, since God is one; and he will justify the circumcised on the ground of faith and the uncircumcised through that same faith. Do we then overthrow the law by this faith? By no means! On the contrary, we uphold the law.

A Reading (Lesson) from the Gospel according to John [7:1–13]

Jesus went about in Galilee. He did not wish to go about in Judea because the Jews were looking for an opportunity to kill him. Now the Jewish festival of Booths was near. So his brothers said to him, "Leave here and go to Judea so that your disciples also may see the works you are doing; for no one who wants to be widely known acts in secret. If you do these things, show yourself to the world." (For not even his brothers believed in him.) Jesus said to them, "My time has not yet come, but your time is always here. The world cannot hate you, but it hates me because I testify against it that its works are evil. Go to the festival yourselves. I am not going to this festival, for my time has not yet fully come." After saying this, he remained in Galilee. But after his brothers had gone to the festival, then he also went, not publicly but as it were in secret. The Jews were looking for him at the festival and saying, "Where is he?" And there was considerable complaining about him among the crowds. While some were saying, "He is a good man," others were saying, "No, he is deceiving the crowd." Yet no one would speak openly about him for fear of the Jews.

Week of 3 Lent

Sunday

A Reading (Lesson) from the Book of Jeremiah [6:9–15]

Thus says the LORD of hosts: Glean thoroughly as a vine the remnant of Israel; like a grape-gatherer, pass your hand again over its branches. To whom shall I speak and give warning, that they may hear? See, their ears are closed, they cannot listen. The word of the LORD is to them an object of scorn; they take no pleasure in it. But I am full of the wrath of the LORD; I am weary of holding it in. Pour it out on the children in the street, and on the gatherings of young men as well; both husband and wife shall be taken, the old folk and the very aged. Their houses shall be turned over to others, their fields and wives together; for I will stretch out my hand against the inhabitants of the land, says the LORD. For from the least to the greatest of them, everyone is greedy for unjust gain; and from prophet to priest, everyone deals falsely. They have treated the wound of my people carelessly, saying, "Peace, peace," when there is no peace. They acted shamefully, they committed abomination; yet they were not ashamed, they did not know how to blush. Therefore they shall fall among those who fall; at the time that I punish them, they shall be overthrown, says the LORD.

A Reading (Lesson) from the First Letter of Paul to the Corinthians [6:12–20]

"All things are lawful for me," but not all things are beneficial. "All things are lawful for me," but I will not be dominated by anything. "Food is meant for the stomach and the stomach for food," and God will destroy both one and the other. The body is meant not for fornication but for the Lord, and the Lord for the body. And God raised the Lord and will also raise us by his power. Do you not know that your bodies are members of Christ? Should I therefore take the members of Christ and make them members of a prostitute? Never! Do you not know that whoever is united to a prostitute becomes one body with her? For it is said, "The two shall be one flesh." But anyone united to the Lord becomes one spirit with him. Shun fornication! Every sin that a person commits is outside the body; but the fornicator sins against the body itself. Or do you not know that your body is a temple of the Holy Spirit within you, which you have from God, and that you are not your own? For you were bought with a price; therefore glorify God in your body.

A Reading (Lesson) from the Gospel according to Mark [5:1–20]

Jesus and his disciples came to the other side of the sea, to the country of the Gerasenes. And when he had stepped out of the boat, immediately a man out of the tombs with an unclean spirit met him. He lived among the tombs; and no one could restrain him any more, even with a chain; for he had often been restrained with shackles and chains, but the chains he wrenched apart, and the shackles he broke in pieces; and no one had the strength to subdue him. Night and day among the tombs and on the mountains he was always howling and bruising himself with stones. When he saw Jesus from a distance, he ran and bowed down before him; and he shouted at the top of his voice, "What have you to do with me, Jesus, Son of the Most High God? I adjure you by God, do not torment me." For he had said to him, "Come out of the man, you unclean spirit!" Then Jesus asked him, "What is your name?" He replied, "My name is Legion; for we are many." He begged him earnestly not to send them out of the country. Now there on the hillside a great herd of swine was feeding; and the unclean spirits begged him, "Send us into the swine; let us enter them." So he gave them permission. And the unclean spirits came out and entered the swine; and the herd, numbering about two thousand, rushed down the steep bank into the sea, and were drowned in the sea. The swineherds ran off and told it in the city and in the country. Then people came to see what it was that had happened. They came to Jesus and saw the demoniac sitting there, clothed and in his right mind, the very man who had had the legion; and they were afraid. Those who had seen what had happened to the demoniac and to the swine reported it. Then they began to beg Jesus to leave their neighborhood. As he was getting into the boat, the man who had been possessed by demons begged him that he might be with him. But Jesus refused, and said to him, "Go home to your friends, and tell them how much the Lord has done for you, and what mercy he has shown you." And he went away and began to proclaim in the Decapolis how much Jesus had done for him; and everyone was amazed.

Monday

A Reading (Lesson) from the Book of Jeremiah [7:1–15]

The word that came to Jeremiah from the LORD: Stand in the gate of the LORD's house, and proclaim there this word, and say, Hear the word of the LORD, all you people of Judah, you that enter these gates to worship the LORD. Thus says the LORD of hosts, the God of Israel: Amend your ways and your doings, and let me dwell with you in this place. Do not trust in these deceptive words: "This is the temple of the LORD, the temple of the LORD, the temple of the LORD." For if you truly amend your ways and your doings, if you truly act justly one with another, if you do not oppress the alien, the orphan, and the widow, or shed innocent blood in this place, and if you do not go after other gods to your own hurt, then I will dwell with you in this place, in the land that I gave of old to your ancestors forever and ever. Here you are, trusting in deceptive words to no avail. Will you steal, murder, commit adultery, swear falsely, make offerings to Baal, and go after other gods that you have not known, and then come and stand before me in this house, which is called by my name, and say, "We are safe!"—only to go on doing all these abominations? Has this house, which is called by my name, become a den of robbers in your sight? You know, I too am watching, says the LORD. Go now to my place that was in Shiloh, where I made my name dwell at first, and see what I did to it for the wickedness of my people Israel. And now, because you have done all these things, says the LORD, and when I spoke to you persistently, you did not listen, and when I called you, you did not answer, therefore I will do to the house that is called by my name, in which you trust, and to the place that I gave to you and to your ancestors, just what I did to Shiloh. And I will cast you out of my sight, just as I cast out all your kinsfolk, all the offspring of Ephraim.

A Reading (Lesson) from the Letter of Paul to the Romans [4:1–12]

What then are we to say was gained by Abraham, our ancestor according to the flesh? For if Abraham was justified by works, he has something to boast about, but not before God. For what does the scripture say? "Abraham believed God, and it was reckoned to him as righteousness." Now to one who works, wages are not reckoned as a gift but as something due. But to one who without works trusts him who justifies the ungodly, such faith is reckoned as righteousness. So also David speaks of the blessedness of those to whom God reckons righteousness apart from works: "Blessed are those whose iniquities are forgiven and whose sins are covered; blessed is the one against whom the Lord will not reckon sin." Is this blessedness, then, pronounced only on the circumcised, or also on the uncircumcised? We say, "Faith was reckoned to Abraham as righteousness." How then was it reckoned to him? Was it before or after he had been circumcised? It was not after, but before he was circumcised. He received the sign of circumcision as a seal of the righteousness that he had by faith while he was still uncircumcised. The purpose was to make him the ancestor of all who believe without being circumcised and who thus have righteousness reckoned to them, and likewise the ancestor of the circumcised who are not only circumcised but who also follow the example of the faith that our ancestor Abraham had before he was circumcised.

A Reading (Lesson) from the Gospel according to John [7:14–36]

About the middle of the festival Jesus went up into the temple and began to teach. The Jews were astonished at it, saying, "How does this man have such learning, when he has never been taught?" Then Jesus answered them, "My teaching is not mine but his who sent me. Anyone who resolves to do the will of God will know whether the teaching is from God or whether I am speaking on my own. Those who speak on their own seek their own glory; but the one who seeks the glory of him who sent him is true, and there is nothing false in him. Did not Moses give you the law? Yet none of you keeps the law. Why are you looking for an opportunity to kill me?" The crowd answered, "You have a demon! Who is trying to kill you?" Jesus answered them, "I performed one work, and all of you are astonished. Moses gave you circumcision (it is, of course, not from Moses, but from the patriarchs), and you circumcise a man on the sabbath. If a man receives circumcision on the sabbath in order that the law of Moses may not be broken, are you angry with me because I healed a man's whole body on the sabbath? Do not judge by appearances, but judge with right judgment." Now some of the people of Jerusalem were saying, "Is not this the man whom they are trying to kill? And here he is, speaking openly, but they say nothing to him! Can it be that the authorities really know that this is the Messiah? Yet we know where this man is from; but when the Messiah comes, no one will know where he is from." Then Jesus cried out as he was teaching in the temple, "You know me, and you know where I am from. I have not come on my own. But the one who sent me is true, and you do not know him. I know him, because I am from him, and he sent me." Then they tried to arrest him, but no one laid hands on him, because his hour had not yet come. Yet many in the crowd believed in him and were saying, "When the Messiah comes, will he do more signs than this man has done?" The Pharisees heard the crowd muttering such things about him, and the chief priests and Pharisees sent temple police to arrest him. Jesus then said, "I will be with you a little while longer, and then I am going to him who sent me. You will search for me, but you will not find me; and where I am, you cannot come." The Jews said to one another, "Where does this man intend to go that we will not find him? Does he intend to go to the Dispersion among the Greeks and teach the Greeks? What does he mean by saying, 'You will search for me and you will not find me' and 'Where I am, you cannot come'?"

Tuesday

A Reading (Lesson) from the Book of Jeremiah [7:21–34]

Thus says the LORD of hosts, the God of Israel: Add your burnt offerings to your sacrifices, and eat the flesh. For in the day that I brought your ancestors out of the land of Egypt, I did not speak to them or command them concerning burnt offerings and sacrifices. But this command I gave them, "Obey my voice, and I will be your God, and you shall be my people; and walk only in the way that I command you, so that it may be well with you." Yet they did not obey or incline their ear, but, in the stubbornness of their evil will, they walked in their own counsels, and looked backward rather than forward. From the day that your ancestors came out of the land of Egypt until this day, I have persistently sent all my servants the prophets to them, day after day; yet they did not listen to me, or pay attention, but they stiffened their necks. They did worse than their ancestors did. So you shall speak all these words to them, but they will not listen to you. You shall call to them, but they will not answer you. You shall say to them: This is the nation that did not obey the voice of the LORD their God, and did not accept discipline; truth has perished; it is cut off from their lips. Cut off your hair and throw it away; raise a lamentation on the bare heights, for the LORD has rejected and forsaken the generation that provoked his wrath. For the people of Judah have done evil in my sight, says the LORD; they have set their abominations in the house that is called by my name, defiling it. And they go on building the high place of Topheth, which is in the valley of the son of Hinnom, to burn their sons and their daughters in the fire—which I did not command, nor did it come into my mind. Therefore, the days are surely coming, says the LORD, when it will no more be called Topheth, or the valley of the son of Hinnom, but the valley of Slaughter: for they will bury in Topheth until there is no more room. The corpses of this people will be food for the birds of the air, and for the animals of the earth; and no one will frighten them away. And I will bring to an end the sound of mirth and gladness, the voice of the bride and bridegroom in the cities of Judah and in the streets of Jerusalem; for the land shall become a waste.

A Reading (Lesson) from the Letter of Paul to the Romans [4:13–25]

The promise that he would inherit the world did not come to Abraham or to his descendants through the law but through the righteousness of faith. If it is the adherents of the law who are to be the heirs, faith is null and the promise is void. For the law brings wrath; but where there is no law, neither is there violation. For this reason it depends on faith, in order that the promise may rest on grace and be guaranteed to all his descendants, not only to the adherents of the law but also to those who share the faith of Abraham (for he is the father of all of us, as it is written, "I have made you the father of many nations")—in the presence of the God in whom he believed, who gives life to the dead and calls into existence the things that do not exist. Hoping against hope, he believed that he would become "the father of many nations," according to what was said, "So numerous shall your descendants be." He did not weaken in faith when he considered his own body, which was already as good as dead (for he was about a hundred years old), or when he considered the barrenness of Sarah's womb. No distrust made him waver concerning the promise of God, but he grew strong in his faith as he gave glory to God, being fully convinced that God was able to do what he had promised. Therefore his faith "was reckoned to him as righteousness." Now the words, "it was reckoned to him," were written not for his sake alone, but for ours also. It will be reckoned to us who believe in him who raised Jesus our Lord from the dead, who was handed over to death for our trespasses and was raised for our justification.

A Reading (Lesson) from the Gospel according to John [7:37–52]

On the last day of the festival, the great day, while Jesus was standing there, he cried out, "Let anyone who is thirsty come to me, and let the one who believes in me drink. As the scripture has said, 'Out of the believer's heart shall flow rivers of living water.'" Now he said this about the Spirit, which believers in him were to receive; for as yet there was no Spirit, because Jesus was not yet glorified. When they heard these words, some in the crowd said, "This is really the prophet." Others said, "This is the Messiah." But some asked, "Surely the Messiah does not come from Galilee, does he? Has not the scripture said that the Messiah is descended from David and comes from Bethlehem, the village where David lived?" So there was a division in the crowd because of him. Some of them wanted to arrest him, but no one laid hands on him. Then the temple police went back to the chief priests and Pharisees, who asked them, "Why did you not arrest him?" The police answered, "Never has anyone spoken like this!" Then the Pharisees replied, "Surely you have not been deceived too, have you? Has any one of the authorities or of the Pharisees believed in him? But this crowd, which does not know the law—they are accursed." Nicodemus, who had gone to Jesus before, and who was one of them, asked, "Our Law does not judge people without first giving them a hearing to find out what they are doing, does it?" They replied, "Surely you are not also from Galilee, are you? Search and you will see that no prophet is to arise from Galilee."

Wednesday

A Reading (Lesson) from the Book of Jeremiah [8:18—9:6]

My joy is gone, grief is upon me, my heart is sick. Hark, the cry of my poor people from far and wide in the land: "Is the LORD not in Zion? Is her King not in her?" ("Why have they provoked me to anger with their images, with their foreign idols?") "The harvest is past, the summer is ended, and we are not saved." For the hurt of my poor people I am hurt, I mourn, and dismay has taken hold of me. Is there no balm in Gilead? Is there no physician there? Why then has the health of my poor people not been restored? O that my head were a spring of water, and my eyes a fountain of tears, so that I might weep day and night for the slain of my poor people! O that I had in the desert a traveler's lodging place, that I might leave my people and go away from them! For they are all adulterers, a band of traitors. They bend their tongues like bows; they have grown strong in the land for falsehood, and not for truth; for they proceed from evil to evil, and they do not know me, says the LORD. Beware of your neighbors, and put no trust in any of your kin; for all your kin are supplanters, and every neighbor goes around like a slanderer. They all deceive their neighbors, and no one speaks the truth; they have taught their tongues to speak lies; they commit iniquity and are too weary to repent. Oppression upon oppression, deceit upon deceit! They refuse to know me, says the LORD.

A Reading (Lesson) from the Letter of Paul to the Romans [5:1–11]

Since we are justified by faith, we have peace with God through our Lord Jesus Christ, through whom we have obtained access to this grace in which we stand; and we boast in our hope of sharing the glory of God. And not only that, but we also boast in our sufferings, knowing that suffering produces endurance, and endurance produces character, and character produces hope, and hope does not disappoint us, because God's love has been poured into our hearts through the Holy Spirit that has been given to us. For while we were still weak, at the right time Christ died for the ungodly. Indeed, rarely will anyone die for a righteous person—though perhaps for a good person someone might actually dare to die. But God proves his love for us in that while we still were sinners Christ died for us. Much more surely then, now that we have been justified by his blood, will we be saved through him from the wrath of God. For if while we were enemies, we were reconciled to God through the death of his Son, much more surely, having been reconciled, will we be saved by his life. But more than that, we even boast in God through our Lord Jesus Christ, through whom we have now received reconciliation.

A Reading (Lesson) from the Gospel according to John [8:12–20]

Again Jesus spoke to the crowd, saying, "I am the light of the world. Whoever follows me will never walk in darkness but will have the light of life." Then the Pharisees said to him, "You are testifying on your own behalf; your testimony is not valid." Jesus answered, "Even if I testify on my own behalf, my testimony is valid because I know where I have come from and where I am going, but you do not know where I come from or where I am going. You judge by human standards; I judge no one. Yet even if I do judge, my judgment is valid; for it is not I alone who judge, but I and the Father who sent me. In your law it is written that the testimony of two witnesses is valid. I testify on my own behalf, and the Father who sent me testifies on my behalf." Then they said to him, "Where is your Father?" Jesus answered, "You know neither me nor my Father. If you knew me, you would know my Father also." He spoke these words while he was teaching in the treasury of the temple, but no one arrested him, because his hour had not yet come.

Thursday

A Reading (Lesson) from the Book of Jeremiah [10:11–24]

Thus shall you say to them: The gods who did not make the heavens and the earth shall perish from the earth and from under the heavens. It is the LORD who made the earth by his power, who established the world by his wisdom, and by his understanding stretched out the heavens. When he utters his voice, there is a tumult of waters in the heavens, and he makes the mist rise from the ends of the earth. He makes lightnings for the rain, and he brings out the wind from his storehouses. Everyone is stupid and without knowledge; goldsmiths are all put to shame by their idols; for their images are false, and there is no breath in them. They are worthless, a work of delusion; at the time of their punishment they shall perish. Not like these is the LORD, the portion of Jacob, for he is the one who formed all things, and Israel is the tribe of his inheritance; the LORD of hosts is his name. Gather up your bundle from the ground, O you who live under siege! For thus says the LORD: I am going to sling out the inhabitants of the land at this time, and I will bring distress on them, so that they shall feel it. Woe is me because of my hurt! My wound is severe. But I said, "Truly this is my punishment, and I must bear it." My tent is destroyed, and all my cords are broken; my children have gone from me, and they are no more; there is no one to spread my tent again, and to set up my curtains. For the shepherds are stupid, and do not inquire of the LORD; therefore they have not prospered, and all their flock is scattered. Hear, a noise! Listen, it is coming—a great commotion from the land of the north to make the cities of Judah a desolation, a lair of jackals. I know, O LORD, that the way of human beings is not in their control, that mortals as they walk cannot direct their steps. Correct me, O LORD, but in just measure; not in your anger, or you will bring me to nothing.

A Reading (Lesson) from the Letter of Paul to the Romans [5:12–21]

Just as sin came into the world through one man, and death came through sin, and so death spread to all because all have sinned—sin was indeed in the world before the law, but sin is not reckoned when there is no law. Yet death exercised dominion from Adam to Moses, even over those whose sins were not like the transgression of Adam, who is a type of the one who was to come. But the free gift is not like the trespass. For if the many died through the one man's trespass, much more surely have the grace of God and the free gift in the grace of the one man, Jesus Christ, abounded for the many. And the free gift is not like the effect of the one man's sin. For the judgment following one trespass brought condemnation, but the free gift following many trespasses brings justification. If, because of the one man's trespass, death exercised dominion through that one, much more surely will those who receive the abundance of grace and the free gift of righteousness exercise dominion in life through the one man, Jesus Christ. Therefore just as one man's trespass led to condemnation for all, so one man's act of righteousness leads to justification and life for all. For just as by the one man's disobedience the many were made sinners, so by the one man's obedience the many will be made righteous. But law came in, with the result that the trespass multiplied; but where sin increased, grace abounded all the more, so that, just as sin exercised dominion in death, so grace might also exercise dominion through justification leading to eternal life through Jesus Christ our Lord.

A Reading (Lesson) from the Gospel according to John [8:21–32]

Again Jesus said to the crowd, "I am going away, and you will search for me, but you will die in your sin. Where I am going, you cannot come." Then the Jews said, "Is he going to kill himself? Is that what he means by saying, 'Where I am going, you cannot come'?" He said to them, "You are from below, I am from above; you are of this world, I am not of this world. I told you that you would die in your sins, for you will die in your sins unless you believe that I am he." They said to him, "Who are you?" Jesus said to them, "Why do I speak to you at all? I have much to say about you and much to condemn; but the one who sent me is true, and I declare to the world what I have heard from him." They did not understand that he was speaking to them about the Father. So Jesus said, "When you have lifted up the Son of Man, then you will realize that I am he, and that I do nothing on my own, but I speak these things as the Father instructed me. And the one who sent me is with me; he has not left me alone, for I always do what is pleasing to him." As he was saying these things, many believed in him. Then Jesus said to the Jews who had believed in him, "If you continue in my word, you are truly my disciples; and you will know the truth, and the truth will make you free."

Friday

A Reading (Lesson) from the Book of Jeremiah [11:1–8, 14–20]

The word that came to Jeremiah from the LORD: Hear the words of this covenant, and speak to the people of Judah and the inhabitants of

Jerusalem. You shall say to them, Thus says the LORD, the God of Israel: Cursed be anyone who does not heed the words of this covenant, which I commanded your ancestors when I brought them out of the land of Egypt, from the iron-smelter, saying, Listen to my voice, and do all that I command you. So shall you be my people, and I will be your God, that I may perform the oath that I swore to your ancestors, to give them a land flowing with milk and honey, as at this day. Then I answered, "So be it, LORD." And the LORD said to me: Proclaim all these words in the cities of Judah, and in the streets of Jerusalem: Hear the words of this covenant and do them. For I solemnly warned your ancestors when I brought them up out of the land of Egypt, warning them persistently, even to this day, saying, Obey my voice. Yet they did not obey or incline their ear, but everyone walked in the stubbornness of an evil will. So I brought upon them all the words of this covenant, which I commanded them to do, but they did not. As for you, do not pray for this people, or lift up a cry or prayer on their behalf, for I will not listen when they call to me in the time of their trouble. What right has my beloved in my house, when she has done vile deeds? Can vows and sacrificial flesh avert your doom? Can you then exult? The LORD once called you, "A green olive tree, fair with goodly fruit"; but with the roar of a great tempest he will set fire to it, and its branches will be consumed. The LORD of hosts, who planted you, has pronounced evil against you, because of the evil that the house of Israel and the house of Judah have done, provoking me to anger by making offerings to Baal. It was the LORD who made it known to me, and I knew; then you showed me their evil deeds. But I was like a gentle lamb led to the slaughter. And I did not know it was against me that they devised schemes, saying, "Let us destroy the tree with its fruit, let us cut him off from the land of the living, so that his name will no longer be remembered!" But you, O LORD of hosts, who judge righteously, who try the heart and the mind, let me see your retribution upon them, for to you I have committed my cause.

A Reading (Lesson) from the Letter of Paul to the Romans [6:1–11]

What then are we to say? Should we continue in sin in order that grace may abound? By no means! How can we who died to sin go on living in it? Do you not know that all of us who have been baptized into Christ Jesus were baptized into his death? Therefore we have been buried with him by baptism into death, so that, just as Christ was raised from the dead by the glory of the Father, so we too might walk in newness of life. For if we have been united with him in a death like his, we will certainly be united with him in a resurrection like his. We know that our old self was crucified with him so that the body of sin might be destroyed, and we might no longer be enslaved to sin. For whoever has died is freed from sin. But if we have died with Christ, we believe that we will also live with him. We know that Christ, being raised from the dead, will never die again; death no longer has dominion over him. The death he died, he died to sin, once for all; but the life he lives, he lives to God. So you also must consider yourselves dead to sin and alive to God in Christ Jesus.

A Reading (Lesson) from the Gospel according to John [8:33–47]

The Jews answered Jesus, "We are descendants of Abraham and have never been slaves to anyone. What do you mean by saying, 'You will be made free'?" Jesus answered them, "Very truly, I tell you, everyone who commits sin is a slave to sin. The slave does not have a permanent place in the household; the son has a place there forever. So if the Son makes you free, you will be free indeed. I know that you are descendants of Abraham; yet you look for an opportunity to kill me, because there is no place in you for my word. I declare what I have seen in the Father's presence; as for you, you should do what you have heard from the Father." They answered him, "Abraham is our father." Jesus said to them, "If you were Abraham's children, you would be doing what Abraham did, but now you are trying to kill me, a man who has told you the truth that I heard from God. This is not what Abraham did. You are indeed doing what your father does." They said to him, "We are not illegitimate children; we have one father, God himself." Jesus said to them, "If God were your Father, you would love me, for I came from God and now I am here. I did not come on my own, but he sent me. Why do you not understand what I say? It is because you cannot accept my word. You are from your father the devil, and you choose to do your father's desires. He was a murderer from the beginning and does not stand in the truth, because there is no truth in him. When he lies, he speaks according to his own nature, for he is a liar and the father of lies. But because I tell the truth, you do not believe me. Which of you convicts me of sin? If I tell the truth, why do you not believe me? Whoever is from God hears the words of God. The reason you do not hear them is that you are not from God."

Saturday

A Reading (Lesson) from the Book of Jeremiah [13:1–11]

Thus said the LORD to me, "Go and buy yourself a linen loincloth, and put it on your loins, but do not dip it in water." So I bought a loincloth according to the word of the LORD, and put it on my loins. And the word of the LORD came to me a second time, saying, "Take the loincloth that you bought and are wearing, and go now to the Euphrates, and hide it there in a cleft of the rock." So I went, and hid it by the Euphrates, as the LORD commanded me. And after many days the LORD said to me, "Go now to the Euphrates, and take from there the loincloth that I commanded you to hide there." Then I went to the Euphrates, and dug, and I took the loincloth from the place where I had hidden it. But now the loincloth was ruined; it was good for nothing. Then the word of the LORD came to me: Thus says the LORD: Just so I will ruin the pride of Judah and the great pride of Jerusalem. This evil people, who refuse to hear my words, who stubbornly follow their own will and have gone after other gods to serve them and worship them, shall be like this loincloth, which is good for nothing. For as the loincloth clings to one's loins, so I made the whole house of Israel and the whole house of Judah cling to me, says the LORD, in order that they might be for me a people, a name, a praise, and a glory. But they would not listen.

A Reading (Lesson) from the Letter of Paul to the Romans [6:12–23]

Do not let sin exercise dominion in your mortal bodies, to make you obey their passions. No longer present your members to sin as instruments of wickedness, but present yourselves to God as those who have been brought from death to life, and present your members to God as instruments of righteousness. For sin will have no dominion over you, since you are not under law but under grace. What then? Should we sin because we are not under law but under grace? By no means! Do you not know that if you present yourselves to anyone as obedient slaves, you are slaves of the one whom you obey, either of sin, which leads to death, or of obedience, which leads to righteousness? But thanks be to God that you, having once been slaves of sin, have become obedient from the heart to the form of teaching to which you were entrusted, and that you, having been set free from sin, have become slaves of righteousness. I am speaking in human terms because of your natural limitations. For just as you once presented your members as slaves to impurity and to greater and greater iniquity, so now present your members as slaves to righteousness for sanctification. When you were slaves of sin, you were free in regard to righteousness. So what advantage did you then get from the things of which you now are ashamed? The end of those things is death. But now that you have been freed from sin and enslaved to God, the advantage you get is sanctification. The end is eternal life. For the wages of sin is death, but the free gift of God is eternal life in Christ Jesus our Lord.

A Reading (Lesson) from the Gospel according to John [8:47–59]

Jesus said to the Jews, "Whoever is from God hears the words of God. The reason you do not hear them is that you are not from God." The Jews answered him, "Are we not right in saying that you are a Samaritan and have a demon?" Jesus answered, "I do not have a demon; but I honor my Father, and you dishonor me. Yet I do not seek my own glory; there is one who seeks it and he is the judge. Very truly, I tell you, whoever keeps my word will never see death." The Jews said to him, "Now we know that you have a demon. Abraham died, and so did the prophets; yet you say,'Whoever keeps my word will never taste death.' Are you greater than our father Abraham, who died? The prophets also died. Who do you claim to be?" Jesus answered, "If I glorify myself, my glory is nothing. It is my Father who glorifies me, he of whom you say, 'He is our God,' though you do not know him. But I know him; if I would say that I do not know him, I would be a liar like you. But I do know him and I keep his word. Your ancestor Abraham rejoiced that he would see my day; he saw it and was glad." Then the Jews said to him, "You are not yet fifty years old, and have you seen Abraham?" Jesus said to them, "Very truly, I tell you, before Abraham was, I am." So they picked up stones to throw at him, but Jesus hid himself and went out of the temple.

Week of 4 Lent

Sunday

A Reading (Lesson) from the Book of Jeremiah [14:1–9,17–22]

The word of the LORD that came to Jeremiah concerning the drought: Judah mourns and her gates languish; they lie in gloom on the ground, and the cry of Jerusalem goes up. Her nobles send their servants for water; they come to the cisterns, they find no water, they return with their vessels empty. They are ashamed and dismayed and cover their heads, because the ground is cracked. Because there has been no rain on the land the farmers are dismayed; they cover their heads. Even the doe in the field forsakes her newborn fawn because there is no grass. The wild asses stand on the bare heights, they pant for air like jackals; their eyes fail because there is no herbage. Although our iniquities testify against us, act, O LORD, for your name's sake; our apostasies indeed are many, and we have sinned against you. O hope of Israel, its savior in time of trouble, why should you be like a stranger in the land, like a traveler turning aside for the night? Why should you be like someone confused, like a mighty warrior who cannot give help? Yet you, O LORD, are in the midst of us, and we are called by your name; do not forsake us! You shall say to them this word: Let my eyes run down with tears night and day, and let them not cease, for the virgin daughter—my people—is struck down with a crushing blow, with a very grievous wound. If I go out into the field, look—those killed by the sword! And if I enter the city, look—those sick with famine! For both prophet and priest ply their trade throughout the land, and have no knowledge. Have you completely rejected Judah? Does your heart loathe Zion? Why have you struck us down so that there is no healing for us? We look for peace, but find no good; for a time of healing, but there is terror instead. We acknowledge our wickedness, O LORD, the iniquity of our ancestors, for we have sinned against you. Do not spurn us, for your name's sake; do not dishonor your glorious throne; remember and do not break your covenant with us. Can any idols of the nations bring rain? Or can the heavens give showers? Is it not you, O LORD our God? We set our hope on you, for it is you who do all this.

A Reading (Lesson) from the Letter of Paul to the Galatians [4:21–5:1]

Tell me, you who desire to be subject to the law, will you not listen to the law? For it is written that Abraham had two sons, one by a slave woman and the other by a free woman. One, the child of the slave, was born according to the flesh; the other, the child of the free woman, was born through the promise. Now this is an allegory: these women are two covenants. One woman, in fact, is Hagar, from Mount Sinai, bearing children for slavery. Now Hagar is Mount Sinai in Arabia and corresponds to the present Jerusalem, for she is in slavery with her children. But the other woman corresponds to the Jerusalem above; she is free, and she is our mother. For it is written, "Rejoice, you childless one, you who bear no children, burst into song and shout, you who endure no birth pangs; for the children of the desolate woman are more numerous than the children of the one who is married." Now you, my friends, are children of the promise, like Isaac. But just as at that time the child who was born according to the flesh persecuted the child who was born according to the Spirit, so it is now also. But what does the scripture say? "Drive out the slave and her child; for the child of the slave will not share the inheritance with the child of the free woman." So then, friends, we are children, not of the slave but of the free woman. For freedom Christ has set us free. Stand firm, therefore, and do not submit again to a yoke of slavery.

The Pharisees came and began to argue with Jesus, asking him for a sign from heaven, to test him. And he sighed deeply in his spirit and said, "Why does this generation ask for a sign? Truly I tell you, no sign will be given to this generation." And he left them, and getting into the boat again, he went across to the other side. Now the disciples had forgotten to bring any bread; and they had only one loaf with them in the boat. And he cautioned them, saying, "Watch out—beware of the yeast of the Pharisees and the yeast of Herod." They said to one another, "It is because we have no bread." And becoming aware of it, Jesus said to them, "Why are you talking about having no bread? Do you still not perceive or understand? Are your hearts hardened? Do you have eyes, and fail to see? Do you have ears, and fail to hear? And do you not remember? When I broke the five loaves for the five thousand, how many baskets full of broken pieces did you collect?" They said to him, "Twelve." "And the seven for the four thousand, how many baskets full of broken pieces did you collect?" And they said to him, "Seven." Then he said to them, "Do you not yet understand?"

Monday

A Reading (Lesson) from the Book of Jeremiah [16:10–21]

The word of the LORD came to me: When you tell this people all these words, and they say to you, "Why has the LORD pronounced all this great evil against us? What is our iniquity? What is the sin that we have committed against the LORD our God?" then you shall say to them: It is because your ancestors have forsaken me, says the LORD, and have gone after other gods and have served and worshiped them, and have forsaken me and have not kept my law; and because you have behaved worse than your ancestors, for here you are, every one of you, following your stubborn evil will, refusing to listen to me. Therefore I will hurl you out of this land into a land that neither you nor your ancestors have known, and there you shall serve other gods day and night, for I will show you no favor. Therefore, the days are surely coming, says the LORD, when it shall no longer be said, "As the LORD lives who brought the people of Israel up out of the land of Egypt," but "As the LORD lives who brought the people of Israel up out of the land of the north and out of all the lands where he had driven them." For I will bring them back to their own land that I gave to their ancestors. I am now sending for many fishermen, says the LORD, and they shall catch them; and afterward I will send for many hunters, and they shall hunt them from every mountain and every hill, and out of the clefts of the rocks. For my eyes are on all their ways; they are not hidden from my presence, nor is their iniquity concealed from my sight. And I will doubly repay their iniquity and their sin, because they have polluted my land with the carcasses of their detestable idols, and have filled my inheritance with their abominations. O LORD, my strength and my stronghold, my refuge in the day of trouble, to you shall the nations come from the ends of the earth and say: Our ancestors have inherited nothing but lies, worthless things in which there is no profit. Can mortals make for themselves gods? Such are no gods! "Therefore I am surely going to teach them, this time I am going to teach them my power and my might, and they shall know that my name is the LORD."

A Reading (Lesson) from the Letter of Paul to the Romans [7:1–12]

Do you not know, brothers and sisters—for I am speaking to those who know the law—that the law is binding on a person only during that person's lifetime? Thus a married woman is bound by the law to her husband as long as he lives; but if her husband dies, she is discharged from the law concerning the husband. Accordingly, she will be called an adulteress if she lives with another man while her husband is alive. But if her husband dies, she is free from that law, and if she marries another man, she is not an adulteress. In the same way, my friends, you have died to the law through the body of Christ, so that you may belong to another, to him who has been raised from the dead in order that we may bear fruit for God. While we were living in the flesh, our sinful passions, aroused by the law, were at work in our members to bear fruit for death. But now we are discharged from the law, dead to that which held us captive, so that we are slaves not under the old written code but in the new life of the Spirit. What then should we say? That the law is sin? By no means! Yet, if it had not been for the law, I would not have known sin. I would not have known what it is to covet if the law had not said, "You shall not covet," But sin, seizing an opportunity in the commandment, produced in me all kinds of covetousness. Apart from the law sin lies dead. I was once alive apart from the law, but when the commandment came, sin revived and I died, and the very commandment that promised life proved to be death to me. For sin, seizing an opportunity in the commandment, deceived me and through it killed me. So the law is holy, and the commandment is holy and just and good.

A Reading (Lesson) from the Gospel according to John [6:1–15]

After this Jesus went to the other side of the Sea of Galilee, also called the Sea of Tiberias. A large crowd kept following him, because they saw the signs that he was doing for the sick. Jesus went up the mountain and sat down there with his disciples. Now the Passover, the festival of the

Jews, was near. When he looked up and saw a large crowd coming toward him, Jesus said to Philip, "Where are we to buy bread for these people to eat?" He said this to test him, for he himself knew what he was going to do. Philip answered him, "Six months' wages would not buy enough bread for each of them to get a little." One of his disciples, Andrew, Simon Peter's brother, said to him, "There is a boy here who has five barley loaves and two fish. But what are they among so many people?" Jesus said, "Make the people sit down." Now there was a great deal of grass in the place; so they sat down, about five thousand in all. Then Jesus took the loaves, and when he had given thanks, he distributed them to those who were seated; so also the fish, as much as they wanted. When they were satisfied, he told his disciples, "Gather up the fragments left over, so that nothing may be lost." So they gathered them up, and from the fragments of the five barley loaves, left by those who had eaten, they filled twelve baskets. When the people saw the sign that he had done, they began to say, "This is indeed the prophet who is to come into the world." When Jesus realized that they were about to come and take him by force to make him king, he withdrew again to the mountain by himself.

Tuesday

A Reading (Lesson) from the Book of Jeremiah [17:19–27]

Thus said the LORD to me: Go and stand in the People's Gate, by which the kings of Judah enter and by which they go out, and in all the gates of Jerusalem, and say to them: Hear the word of the LORD, you kings of Judah, and all Judah, and all the inhabitants of Jerusalem, who enter by these gates. Thus says the LORD: For the sake of your lives, take care that you do not bear a burden on the sabbath day or bring it in by the gates of Jerusalem. And do not carry a burden out of your houses on the sabbath or do any work, but keep the sabbath day holy, as I commanded your ancestors. Yet they did not listen or incline their ear; they stiffened their necks and would not hear or receive instruction. But if you listen to me, says the LORD, and bring in no burden by the gates of this city on the sabbath day, but keep the sabbath day holy and do not work on it, then there shall enter by the gates of this city kings who sit on the throne of David, riding in chariots and on horses, they and their officials, the people of Judah and the inhabitants of Jerusalem; and this city shall be inhabited forever. And people shall come from the towns of Judah and the places around Jerusalem, from the land of Benjamin, from the Shephelah, from the hill country, and from the Negeb, bringing burnt offerings and sacrifices, grain offerings and frankincense, and bringing thank offerings to the house of the LORD. But if you do not listen to me, to keep the sabbath day holy, and to carry in no burden through the gates of Jerusalem on the sabbath day, then I will kindle a fire in its gates; it shall devour the palaces of Jerusalem and shall not be quenched.

A Reading (Lesson) from the Letter of Paul to the Romans [7:13–25]

Did what is good, then, bring death to me? By no means! It was sin, working death in me through what is good, in order that sin might be shown to be sin, and through the commandment might become sinful beyond measure. For we know that the law is spiritual; but I am of the flesh, sold into slavery under sin. I do not understand my own actions. For I do not do what I want, but I do the very thing I hate. Now if I do what I do not want, I agree that the law is good. But in fact it is no longer I that do it, but sin that dwells within me. For I know that nothing good dwells within me, that is, in my flesh. I can will what is right, but I cannot do it. For I do not do the good I want, but the evil I do not want is what I do. Now if I do what I do not want, it is no longer I that do it, but sin that dwells within me. So I find it to be a law that when I want to do what is good, evil lies close at hand. For I delight in the law of God in my inmost self, but I see in my members another law at war with the law of my mind, making me captive to the law of sin that dwells in my members. Wretched man that I am! Who will rescue me from this body of death? Thanks be to God through Jesus Christ our Lord! So then, with my mind I am a slave to the law of God, but with my flesh I am a slave to the law of sin.

A Reading (Lesson) from the Gospel according to John [6:15–27]

When Jesus realized that they were about to come and take him by force to make him king, he withdrew again to the mountain by himself. When evening came, his disciples went down to the sea, got into a boat, and started across the sea to Capernaum. It was now dark, and Jesus had not yet come to them. The sea became rough because a strong wind was blowing. When they had rowed about three or four miles, they saw Jesus walking on the sea and drawing near to the boat, and they were terrified. But he said to them, "It is I; do not be afraid." Then they wanted to take him into the boat, and immediately the boat reached the land toward which they were going. The next day the crowd that had stayed on the other side of the sea saw that there had been only one boat there. They also saw that Jesus had not got into the boat with his disciples, but that his disciples had gone away alone. Then some boats from Tiberias came near the place where they had eaten the bread after the Lord had given thanks. So when the crowd saw that neither Jesus nor his disciples were there, they themselves got into the boats, and went to Capernaum looking for Jesus. When they found him on the other side of the sea, they said to him, "Rabbi, when did you come here?" Jesus answered them, "Very truly, I tell you, you are looking for me, not because you saw signs, but because you ate your fill of the loaves. Do not work for the food that perishes, but for the food that endures for eternal life, which the Son of Man will give you. For it is on him that God the Father has set his seal."

Wednesday

A Reading (Lesson) from the Book of Jeremiah [18:1–11]

The word that came to Jeremiah from the LORD: "Come, go down to the potter's house, and there I will let you hear my words." So I went down to the potter's house, and there he was working at his wheel. The vessel he was making of clay was spoiled in the potter's hand, and he reworked it into another vessel, as seemed good to him. Then the word of the LORD came to me: Can I not do with you, O house of Israel, just as this potter has done? says the LORD. Just like the clay in the potter's hand, so are you in my hand, O house of Israel. At one moment I may declare concerning a nation or a kingdom, that I will pluck up and break down and destroy it, but if that nation, concerning which I have spoken, turns from its evil, I will change my mind about the disaster that I intended to bring on it. And at another moment I may declare concerning a nation or a kingdom that I will build and plant it, but if it does evil in my sight, not listening to my voice, then I will change my mind about the good that I had intended to do to it. Now, therefore, say to the people of Judah and the inhabitants of Jerusalem: Thus says the LORD: Look, I am a potter shaping evil against you and devising a plan against you. Turn now, all of you from your evil way, and amend your ways and your doings.

A Reading (Lesson) from the Letter of Paul to the Romans [8:1–11]

There is therefore now no condemnation for those who are in Christ Jesus. For the law of the Spirit of life in Christ Jesus has set you free from the law of sin and of death. For God has done what the law, weakened by the flesh, could not do: by sending his own Son in the likeness of sinful flesh, and to deal with sin, he condemned sin in the flesh, so that the just requirement of the law might be fulfilled in us, who walk not according to the flesh but according to the Spirit. For those who live according to the flesh set their minds on the things of the flesh, but those who live according to the Spirit set their minds on the things of the Spirit. To set the mind on the flesh is death, but to set the mind on the Spirit is life and peace. For this reason the mind that is set on the flesh is hostile to God; it does not submit to God's law—indeed it cannot, and those who are in the flesh cannot please God. But you are not in the flesh; you are in the Spirit, since the Spirit of God dwells in you. Anyone who does not have the Spirit of Christ does not belong to him. But if Christ is in you, though the body is dead because of sin, the Spirit is life because of righteousness. If the Spirit of him who raised Jesus from the dead dwells in you, he who raised Christ from the dead will give life to your mortal bodies also through his Spirit that dwells in you.

A Reading (Lesson) from the Gospel according to John [6:27–40]

Jesus said to the people, "Do not work for the food that perishes, but for the food that endures for eternal life, which the Son of Man will give you. For it is on him that God the Father has set his seal." Then they said to him, "What must we do to perform the works of God?" Jesus answered them, "This is the work of God, that you believe in him whom he has sent." So they said to him, "What sign are you going to give us then, so that we may see it and believe you? What work are you performing? Our ancestors ate the manna in the wilderness; as it is written, 'He gave them bread from heaven to eat.'" Then Jesus said to them, "Very truly, I tell you, it was not Moses who gave you the bread from heaven, but it is my Father who gives you the true bread from heaven. For the bread of God is that which comes down from heaven and gives life to the world." They said to him, "Sir, give us this bread always." Jesus said to them, "I am the bread of life. Whoever comes to me will never be hungry, and whoever believes in me will never be thirsty. But I said to you that you have seen me and yet do not believe. Everything that the Father gives me will come to me, and anyone who comes to me I will never drive away; for I have come down from heaven, not to do my own will, but the will of him who sent me. And this is the will of him who sent me, that I should lose nothing of all that he has given me, but raise it up on the last day. This is indeed the will of my Father, that all who see the Son and believe in him may have eternal life; and I will raise them up on the last day."

Thursday

A Reading (Lesson) from the Book of Jeremiah [22:13–23]

Woe to him who builds his house by unrighteousness, and his upper rooms by injustice; who makes his neighbors work for nothing, and does not give them their wages; who says, "I will build myself a spacious house with large upper rooms," and who cuts out windows for it, paneling it with cedar, and painting it with vermilion. Are you a king because you compete in cedar? Did not your father eat and drink and do justice and righteousness? Then it was well with him. He judged the cause of the poor and needy; then it was well. Is not this to know me? says the LORD. But your eyes and heart are only on your dishonest gain, for shedding innocent blood, and for practicing oppression and violence. Therefore thus says the LORD concerning King Jehoiakim son of Josiah of Judah: They shall not lament for him, saying, "Alas, my brother!" or "Alas, sister!" They shall not lament for him, saying, "Alas, lord!" or "Alas, his majesty!" With the burial of a donkey he shall be buried—dragged off and thrown out beyond the gates of Jerusalem. Go up to Lebanon, and cry out, and lift up your voice in Bashan; cry out from Abarim, for all your lovers are crushed. I spoke to you in your prosperity, but you said, "I will not listen." This has been your way from your youth, for you have not obeyed my voice. The wind shall shepherd all your shepherds, and your lovers shall go into captivity; then you will be ashamed and dismayed because of all your wickedness. O inhabitant of Lebanon, nested among the cedars, how you will groan when pangs come upon you, pain as of a woman in labor!

A Reading (Lesson) from the Letter of Paul to the Romans [8:12–27]

Brothers and sisters, we are debtors, not to the flesh, to live according to the flesh—for if you live according to the flesh, you will die; but if by the Spirit you put to death the deeds of the body, you will live. For all who are led by the Spirit of God are children of God. For you did not receive a spirit of slavery to fall back into fear, but you have received a spirit of adoption. When we cry, "Abba! Father!" it is that very Spirit bearing witness with our spirit that we are children of God, and if children, then heirs, heirs of God and joint heirs with Christ—if, in fact, we suffer with him so that we may also be glorified with him. I consider that the sufferings of this present time are not worth comparing with the glory about to be revealed to us. For the creation waits with eager longing for the revealing of the children of God; for the creation was subjected to futility, not of its own will but by the will of the one who subjected it, in hope that the creation itself will be set free from its bondage to decay and will obtain the freedom of the glory of the children of God. We know that the whole creation has been groaning in labor pains until now; and not only the creation, but we ourselves, who have the first fruits of the Spirit, groan inwardly while we wait for adoption, the redemption of our bodies. For in hope we were saved. Now hope that is seen is not hope. For who hopes for what is seen? But if we hope for what we do not see, we wait for it with patience. Likewise the Spirit helps us in our weakness; for we do not know how to pray as we ought, but that very Spirit intercedes with sighs too deep for words. And God, who searches the heart, knows what is the mind of the Spirit, because the Spirit intercedes for the saints according to the will of God.

A Reading (Lesson) from the Gospel according to John [6:41–51]

The Jews began to complain about Jesus because he said, "I am the bread that came down from heaven." They were saying, "Is not this Jesus, the son of Joseph, whose father and mother we know? How can he now say, 'I have come down from heaven'?" Jesus answered them, "Do not complain among yourselves. No one can come to me unless drawn by the Father who sent me; and I will raise that person up on the last day. It is written in the prophets, 'And they shall all be taught by God.' Everyone who has heard and learned from the Father comes to me. Not that anyone has seen the Father except the one who is from God; he has seen the Father. Very truly, I tell you, whoever believes has eternal life. I am the bread of life. Your ancestors ate the manna in the wilderness, and they died. This is the bread that comes down from heaven, so that one may eat of it and not die. I am the living bread that came down from heaven. Whoever eats of this bread will live forever; and the bread that I will give for the life of the world is my flesh."

Friday

A Reading (Lesson) from the Book of Jeremiah [23:1–8]

Woe to the shepherds who destroy and scatter the sheep of my pasture! says the LORD. Therefore thus says the LORD, the God of Israel, concerning the shepherds who shepherd my people: It is you who have scattered my flock, and have driven them away, and you have not attended to them. So I will attend to you for your evil doings, says the LORD. Then I myself will gather the remnant of my flock out of all the lands where I have driven them, and I will bring them back to their fold, and they shall be fruitful and multiply. I will raise up shepherds over them who will shepherd them, and they shall not fear any longer, or be dismayed, nor shall any be missing, says the LORD. The days are surely coming, says the LORD, when I will raise up for David a righteous Branch, and he shall reign as king and deal wisely, and shall execute justice and righteousness in the land. In his days Judah will be saved and Israel will live in safety. And this is the name by which he will be called: "The LORD is our righteousness." Therefore, the days are surely coming, says the LORD, when it shall no longer be said, "As the LORD lives who brought the people of Israel up out of the land of Egypt," but "As the LORD lives who brought out and led the offspring of the house of Israel out of the land of the north and out of all the lands where he had driven them." Then they shall live in their own land.

A Reading (Lesson) from the Letter of Paul to the Romans [8:28–39]

We know that all things work together for good for those who love God, who are called according to his purpose. For those whom he foreknew he also predestined to be conformed to the image of his Son, in order that he might be the firstborn within a large family. And those whom he predestined he also called; and those whom he called he also justified; and those whom he justified he also glorified. What then are we to say about these things? If God is for us, who is against us? He who did not withhold his own Son, but gave him up for all of us, will he not with him also give us everything else? Who will bring any charge against God's elect? It is God who justifies. Who is to condemn? It is Christ Jesus, who died, yes, who was raised, who is at the right hand of God, who indeed intercedes for us. Who will separate us from the love of Christ? Will hardship, or distress, or persecution, or famine, or nakedness, or peril, or sword? As it is written, "For your sake we are being killed all day long; we are accounted as sheep to be slaughtered." No, in all these things we are more than conquerors through him who loved us. For I am convinced that neither death, nor life, nor angels, nor rulers, nor things present, nor things to come, nor powers, nor height, nor depth, nor anything else in all creation, will be able to separate us from the love of God in Christ Jesus our Lord.

A Reading (Lesson) from the Gospel according to John [6:52–59]

The Jews disputed among themselves, saying, "How can this man give us his flesh to eat?" So Jesus said to them, "Very truly, I tell you, unless you eat the flesh of the Son of Man and drink his blood, you have no life in you. Those who eat my flesh and drink my blood have eternal life, and I will raise them up on the last day; for my flesh is true food and my blood is true drink. Those who eat my flesh and drink my blood abide in me, and I in them. Just as the living Father sent me, and I live because of the Father, so whoever eats me will live because of me. This is the bread that came down from heaven, not like that which your ancestors ate, and they died. But the one who eats this bread will live forever." He said these things while he was teaching in the synagogue at Capernaum.

Saturday

A Reading (Lesson) from the Book of Jeremiah [23:9–15]

Concerning the prophets: My heart is crushed within me, all my bones shake; I have become like a drunkard, like one overcome by wine, because of the LORD and because of his holy words. For the land is full of adulterers; because of the curse the land mourns, and the pastures of the wilderness are dried up. Their course has been evil, and their might is not right. Both prophet and priest are ungodly; even in my house I have found their wickedness, says the LORD. Therefore their way shall be to them like slippery paths in the darkness, into which they shall be driven and fall; for I will bring disaster upon them in the year of their punishment, says the LORD. In the prophets of Samaria I saw a disgusting thing: they prophesied by Baal and led my people Israel astray. But in the prophets of Jerusalem I have seen a more shocking thing: they commit adultery and walk in lies; they strengthen the hands of evildoers, so that no one turns from wickedness; all of them have become like Sodom to me, and its inhabitants like Gomorrah. Therefore thus says the LORD of hosts concerning the prophets: "I am going to make them eat wormwood, and give them poisoned water to drink; for from the prophets of Jerusalem ungodliness has spread throughout the land."

A Reading (Lesson) from the Letter of Paul to the Romans [9:1–18]

I am speaking the truth in Christ—I am not lying; my conscience confirms it by the Holy Spirit—I have great sorrow and unceasing anguish in my heart. For I could wish that I myself were accursed and cut off from Christ for the sake of my own people, my kindred according to the flesh. They are Israelites, and to them belong the adoption, the glory, the covenants, the giving of the law, the worship, and the promises; to them belong the patriarchs, and from them, according to the flesh, comes the Messiah, who is over all, God blessed forever. Amen. It is not as though the word of God had failed. For not all Israelites truly belong to Israel, and not all of Abraham's children are his true descendants; but "It is through Isaac that descendants shall be named for you." This means that it is not the children of the flesh who are the children of God, but the children of the promise are counted as descendants. For this is what the promise said, "About this time I will return and Sarah shall have a son." Nor is that all; something similar happened to Rebecca when she had conceived children by one husband, our ancestor Isaac. Even before they had been born or had done anything good or bad (so that God's purpose of election might continue, not by works but by his call) she was told, "The elder shall serve the younger." As it is written, "I have loved Jacob, but I have hated Esau." What then are we to say? Is there injustice on God's part? By no means! For he says to Moses, "I will have mercy on whom I have mercy, and I will have compassion on whom I have compassion." So it depends not on human will or exertion, but on God who shows mercy. For the scripture says to Pharaoh, "I have raised you up for the very purpose of showing my power in you, so that my name may be proclaimed in all the earth." So then he has mercy on whomever he chooses, and he hardens the heart of whomever he chooses.

A Reading (Lesson) from the Gospel according to John [6:60–71]

When many of Jesus' disciples heard him say, "Whoever eats of this bread will live forever," they said, "This teaching is difficult; who can accept it?" But Jesus, being aware that his disciples were complaining about it, said to them, "Does this offend you? Then what if you were to see the Son of Man ascending to where he was before? It is the spirit that gives life; the flesh is useless. The words that I have spoken to you are spirit and life. But among you there are some who do not believe." For Jesus knew from the first who were the ones that did not believe, and who was the one that would betray him. And he said, "For this reason I have told you that no one can come to me unless it is granted by the Father." Because of this many of his disciples turned back and no longer went about with him. So Jesus asked the twelve, "Do you also wish to go away?" Simon Peter answered him, "Lord, to whom can we go? You have the words of eternal life. We have come to believe and know that you are the Holy One of God." Jesus answered them, "Did I not choose you, the twelve? Yet one of you is a devil." He was speaking of Judas son of Simon Iscariot, for he, though one of the twelve, was going to betray him.

Week of 5 Lent

Sunday

A Reading (Lesson) from the Book of Jeremiah [23:16–32]

Thus says the LORD of hosts: Do not listen to the words of the prophets who prophesy to you; they are deluding you. They speak visions of their own minds, not from the mouth of the LORD. They keep saying to those who despise the word of the LORD, "It shall be well with you"; and to all who stubbornly follow their own stubborn hearts, they say, "No calamity shall come upon you." For who has stood in the council of the LORD so as to see and to hear his word? Who has given heed to his word so as to proclaim it? Look, the storm of the LORD! Wrath has gone forth, a whirling tempest; it will burst upon the head of the wicked. The anger of the LORD will not turn back until he has executed and accomplished the intents of his mind. In the latter days you will understand it clearly. I did not send the prophets, yet they ran; I did not speak to them, yet they prophesied. But if they had stood in my council, then they would have proclaimed my words to my people, and they would have turned them from their evil way, and from the evil of their doings. Am I a God near by, says the LORD, and not a God far off? Who can hide in secret places so that I cannot see them? says the LORD. Do I not fill heaven and earth? says the LORD. I have heard what the prophets have said who prophesy lies in my name, saying, "I have dreamed, I have dreamed!" How long? Will the hearts of the prophets ever turn back—those who prophesy lies, and who prophesy the deceit of their own heart? They plan to make my people forget my name by their dreams that they tell one another, just as their ancestors forgot my name for Baal. Let the prophet who has a dream tell the dream, but let the one who has my word speak my word faithfully. What has straw in common with wheat? says the LORD. Is not my word like fire, says the LORD, and like a hammer that breaks a rock in pieces? See, therefore, I am against the prophets, says the LORD, who steal my words from one another. See, I am against the prophets, says the LORD, who use their own tongues and say, "Says the LORD." See, I am against those who prophesy lying dreams, says the LORD, and who tell them, and who lead my people astray by their lies and their recklessness, when I did not send them or appoint them; so they do not profit this people at all, says the LORD.

A Reading (Lesson) from the First Letter of Paul to the Corinthians [9:19—27]

Though I am free with respect to all, I have made myself a slave to all, so that I might win more of them. To the Jews I became as a Jew, in order to win Jews. To those under the law I became as one under the law (though I myself am not under the law) so that I might win those under the law. To those outside the law I became as one outside the law (though I am not free from God's law but am under Christ's law) so that I might win those outside the law. To the weak I became weak, so that I might win the weak. I have become all things to all people, that I might by all means save some. I do it all for the sake of the gospel, so that I may share in its blessings. Do you not know that in a race the runners all compete, but only one receives the prize? Run in such a way that you may win it. Athletes exercise self-control in all things; they do it to receive a perishable wreath, but we an imperishable one. So I do not run aimlessly, nor do I box as though beating the air; but I punish my body and enslave it, so that after proclaiming to others I myself should not be disqualified.

A Reading (Lesson) from the Gospel according to Mark [8:31—9:1]

Jesus began to teach his disciples that the Son of Man must undergo great suffering, and be rejected by the elders, the chief priests, and the scribes, and be killed, and after three days rise again. He said all this quite openly. And Peter took him aside and began to rebuke him. But turning and looking at his disciples, he rebuked Peter and said, "Get behind me, Satan! For you are setting your mind not on divine things but on human things." He called the crowd with his disciples, and said to them, "If any want to become my followers, let them deny themselves and take up their cross and follow me. For those who want to save their life will lose it, and those who lose their life for my sake, and for the sake of the gospel, will save it. For what will it profit them to gain the whole world and forfeit their life? Indeed, what can they give in return for their life? Those who are ashamed of me and of my words in this adulterous and sinful generation, of them the Son of Man will also be ashamed when he comes in the glory of his Father with the holy angels." And he said to them, "Truly I tell you, there are some standing here who will not taste death until they see that the kingdom of God has come with power."

Monday

A Reading (Lesson) from the Book of Jeremiah [24:1–10]

The LORD showed me two baskets of figs placed before the temple of the LORD. This was after King Nebuchadrezzar of Babylon had taken into exile from Jerusalem King Jeconiah son of Jehoiakim of Judah, together with the officials of Judah, the artisans, and the smiths, and had brought them to Babylon. One basket had very good figs, like first-ripe figs, but the other basket had very bad figs, so bad that they could not be eaten. And the LORD said to me, "What do you see, Jeremiah?" I said, "Figs, the good figs very good, and the bad figs very bad, so bad that they cannot be eaten." Then the word of the LORD came to me: Thus says the LORD, the God of Israel: Like these good figs, so I will regard as good the exiles from Judah, whom I have sent away from this place to the land of the Chaldeans. I will set my eyes upon them for good, and I will bring them back to this land. I will build them up, and not tear them down; I will plant them, and not pluck them up. I will give them a heart to know that I am the LORD; and they shall be my people and I will be their God, for they shall return to me with their whole heart. But thus says the LORD: Like the bad figs that are so bad they cannot be eaten, so will I treat King Zedekiah of Judah, his officials, the remnant of Jerusalem who remain in this land, and those who live in the land of Egypt. I will make them a horror, an evil thing, to all the kingdoms of the earth—a disgrace, a byword, a taunt, and a curse in all the places where I shall drive them. And I will send sword, famine, and pestilence upon them, until they are utterly destroyed from the land that I gave to them and their ancestors.

A Reading (Lesson) from the Letter of Paul to the Romans [9:19–33]

You will say to me then, "Why then does he still find fault? For who can resist his will?" But who indeed are you, a human being, to argue with God? Will what is molded say to the one who molds it, "Why have you made me like this?" Has the potter no right over the clay, to make out of the same lump one object for special use and another for ordinary use? What if God, desiring to show his wrath and to make known his power, has endured with much patience the objects of wrath that are made for destruction; and what if he has done so in order to make known the riches of his glory for the objects of mercy, which he has prepared beforehand for glory—including us whom he has called, not from the Jews only but also from the Gentiles? As indeed he says in Hosea, "Those who were not my people I will call 'my people,' and her who was not beloved I will call 'beloved.'" "And in the very place where it was said to them, 'You are not my people,' there they shall be called children of the living God." And Isaiah cries out concerning Israel, "Though the number of the children of Israel were like the sand of the sea, only a remnant of them will be saved; for the Lord will execute his sentence on the earth quickly and decisively." And as Isaiah predicted, "If the Lord of hosts had not left survivors to us, we would have fared like Sodom and been made like Gomorrah." What then are we to say? Gentiles, who did not strive for righteousness, have attained it, that is, righteousness through faith; but Israel, who did strive for the righteousness that is based on the law, did not succeed in fulfilling that law. Why not? Because they did not strive for it on the basis of faith, but as if it were based on works. They have stumbled over the stumbling stone, as it is written, "See, I am laying in Zion a stone that will make people stumble, a rock that will make them fall, and whoever believes in him will not be put to shame."

A Reading (Lesson) from the Gospel according to John [9:1–17]

As he walked along, Jesus saw a man blind from birth. His disciples asked him, "Rabbi, who sinned, this man or his parents, that he was born blind?" Jesus answered, "Neither this man nor his parents sinned; he was born blind so that God's works might be revealed in him. We must work the works of him who sent me while it is day; night is coming when no one can work. As long as I am in the world, I am the light of the world." When he had said this, he spat on the ground and made mud with the saliva and spread the mud on the man's eyes, saying to him, "Go, wash in the pool of Siloam" (which means Sent). Then he went and washed and came back able to see. The neighbors and those who had seen him before as a beggar began to ask, "Is this not the man who used to sit and beg?" Some were saying, "It is he." Others were saying, "No, but it is someone like him." He kept saying, "I am the man." But they kept asking him, "Then how were your eyes opened?" He answered, "The man called Jesus made mud, spread it on my eyes, and said to me, 'Go to Siloam and wash.' Then I went and washed and received my sight." They said to him, "Where is he?" He said, "I do not know." They brought to the Pharisees the man who had formerly been blind. Now it was a sabbath day when Jesus made the mud and opened his eyes. Then the Pharisees also began to ask him how he had received his sight. He said to them, "He put mud on my eyes. Then I washed, and now I see." Some of the Pharisees said, "This man is not from God, for he does not observe the sabbath." But others said, "How can a man who is a sinner perform such signs?" And they were divided. So they said again to the blind man, "What do you say about him? It was your eyes he opened." He said, "He is a prophet."

Tuesday

A Reading (Lesson) from the Book of Jeremiah [25:8–17]

Thus says the Lord of hosts: Because you have not obeyed my words, I am going to send for all the tribes of the north, says the Lord, even for King Nebuchadrezzar of Babylon, my servant, and I will bring them against this land and its inhabitants, and against all these nations around; I will utterly destroy them, and make them an object of horror and of hissing, and an everlasting disgrace. And I will banish from them the sound of mirth and the sound of gladness, the voice of the bridegroom and the voice of the bride, the sound of the millstones and the light of the lamp. This whole land shall become a ruin and a waste, and these nations shall serve the king of Babylon seventy years. Then after seventy years are completed, I will punish the king of Babylon and that nation, the land of the Chaldeans, for their iniquity, says the Lord, making the land an everlasting waste. I will bring upon that land all the words that I have uttered against it, everything written in this book, which Jeremiah prophesied against all the nations. For many nations and great kings shall make slaves of them also; and I will repay them according to their deeds and the work of their hands. For thus the Lord, the God of Israel, said to me: Take from my hand this cup of the wine of wrath, and make all the nations to whom I send you drink it. They shall drink and stagger and go out of their minds because of the sword that I am sending among them. So I took the cup from the

LORD's hand, and made all the nations to whom the LORD sent me drink it.

A Reading (Lesson) from the Letter of Paul to the Romans [10:1–13]

Brothers and sisters, my heart's desire and prayer to God for them is that they may be saved. I can testify that they have a zeal for God, but it is not enlightened. For, being ignorant of the righteousness that comes from God, and seeking to establish their own, they have not submitted to God's righteousness. For Christ is the end of the law so that there may be righteousness for everyone who believes. Moses writes concerning the righteousness that comes from the law, that "the person who does these things will live by them." But the righteousness that comes from faith says, "Do not say in your heart, 'Who will ascend into heaven?'" (that is, to bring Christ down) "or 'Who will descend into the abyss?'" (that is, to bring Christ up from the dead). But what does it say? "The word is near you, on your lips and in your heart" (that is, the word of faith that we proclaim); because if you confess with your lips that Jesus is Lord and believe in your heart that God raised him from the dead, you will be saved. For one believes with the heart and so is justified, and one confesses with the mouth and so is saved. The scripture says, "No one who believes in him will be put to shame." For there is no distinction between Jew and Greek; the same Lord is Lord of all and is generous to all who call on him. For, "Everyone who calls on the name of the Lord shall be saved."

A Reading (Lesson) from the Gospel according to John [9:18–41]

The Jews did not believe that the man had been blind and had received his sight until they called the parents of the man who had received his sight and asked them, "Is this your son, who you say was born blind? How then does he now see?" His parents answered, "We know that this is our son, and that he was born blind; but we do not know how it is that now he sees, nor do we know who opened his eyes. Ask him; he is of age. He will speak for himself." His parents said this because they were afraid of the Jews; for the Jews had already agreed that anyone who confessed Jesus to be the Messiah would be put out of the synagogue. Therefore his parents said, "He is of age; ask him." So for the second time they called the man who had been blind, and they said to him, "Give glory to God! We know that this man is a sinner." He answered, "I do not know whether he is a sinner. One thing I do know, that though I was blind, now I see." They said to him, "What did he do to you? How did he open your eyes?" He answered them, "I have told you already, and you would not listen. Why do you want to hear it again? Do you also want to become his disciples?" Then they reviled him, saying, "You are his disciple, but we are disciples of Moses. We know that God has spoken to Moses, but as for this man, we do not know where he comes from." The man answered, "Here is an astonishing thing! You do not know where he comes from, and yet he opened my eyes. We know that God does not listen to sinners, but he does listen to one who worships him and obeys his will. Never since the world began has it been heard that anyone opened the eyes of a person born blind. If this man were not from God, he could do nothing." They answered him, "You were born entirely in sins, and are you trying to teach us?" And they drove him out. Jesus heard that they had driven him out, and when he found him, he said, "Do you believe in the Son of Man?" He answered, "And who is he, sir? Tell me, so that I may believe in him." Jesus said to him, "You have seen him, and the one speaking with you is he." He said, "Lord, I believe." And he worshiped him. Jesus said, "I came into this world for judgment so that those who do not see may see, and those who do see, may become blind." Some of the Pharisees near him heard this and said to him, "Surely we are not blind, are we?" Jesus said to them, "If you were blind, you would not have sin. But now that you say, 'We see,' your sin remains."

Wednesday

A Reading (Lesson) from the Book of Jeremiah [25:30–38]

You, therefore, shall prophesy against them all these words, and say to them: The LORD will roar from on high, and from his holy habitation utter his voice; he will roar mightily against his fold, and shout, like those who tread grapes, against all the inhabitants of the earth. The clamor will resound to the ends of the earth, for the LORD has an indictment against the nations; he is entering into judgment with all flesh, and the guilty he will put to the sword, says the LORD. Thus says the LORD of hosts: See, disaster is spreading from nation to nation, and a great tempest is stirring from the farthest parts of the earth! Those slain by the LORD on that day shall extend from one end of the earth to the other. They shall not be lamented, or gathered, or buried; they shall become dung on the surface of the ground. Wail, you shepherds, and cry out; roll in ashes, you lords of the flock, for the days of your slaughter have come—and your dispersions, and you shall fall like a choice vessel. Flight shall fail the shepherds, and there shall be no escape for the lords of the flock. Hark! the cry of the shepherds, and the wail of the lords of the flock! For the LORD is despoiling their pasture, and the peaceful folds are devastated, because of the fierce anger of the LORD. Like a lion he has left his covert; for their land has become a waste because of the cruel sword, and because of his fierce anger.

A Reading (Lesson) from the Letter of Paul to the Romans [10:14–21]

How are they to call on one in whom they have not believed? And how are they to believe in one of whom they have never heard? And how are they to hear without someone to proclaim him? And how are they to proclaim him unless they are sent? As it is written, "How beautiful are the feet of those who bring good news!" But not all have obeyed the good news; for Isaiah says, "LORD, who has believed our message?" So faith comes from what is heard, and what is heard comes through the word of Christ. But I ask, have they not heard? Indeed they have; for "Their voice has gone out to all the earth, and their words to the ends of the world." Again I ask, did Israel not understand? First Moses says, "I will make you jealous of those who are not a nation; with a foolish nation I will make you angry." Then Isaiah is so bold as to say, "I have been found by those who did not seek me; I have shown myself to those who did not ask for me." But of Israel he says, "All day long I have held out my hands to a disobedient and contrary people."

A Reading (Lesson) from the Gospel according to John [10:1–18]

Jesus said to the crowd, "Very truly, I tell you, anyone who does not enter the sheepfold by the gate but climbs in by another way is a thief and a bandit. The one who enters by the gate is the shepherd of the sheep. The gatekeeper opens the gate for him, and the sheep hear his voice. He calls his own sheep by name and leads them out. When he has brought out all his own, he goes ahead of them, and the sheep follow him because they know his voice. They will not follow a stranger, but they will run from him because they do not know the voice of strangers." Jesus used this figure of speech with them, but they did not understand what he was saying to them. So again Jesus said to them, "Very truly, I tell you, I am the gate for the sheep. All who came before me are thieves and bandits; but the sheep did not listen to them. I am the gate. Whoever enters by me will be saved, and will come in and go out and find pasture. The thief comes only to steal and kill and destroy. I came that they may have life, and have it abundantly. I am the good shepherd. The good shepherd lays down his life for the sheep. The hired hand, who is not the shepherd and does not own the sheep, sees the wolf coming and leaves the sheep and runs away—and the wolf snatches them and scatters them. The hired hand runs away because a hired hand does not care for the sheep. I am the good shepherd. I know my own and my own know me, just as the Father knows me and I know the Father. And I lay down my life for the sheep. I have other sheep that do not belong to this fold. I must bring them also, and they will listen to my voice. So there will be one flock, one shepherd. For this reason the Father loves me, because I lay down my life in order to take it up again. No one takes it from me, but I lay it down of my own accord. I have power to lay it down, and I have power to take it up again. I have received this command from my Father."

Thursday

A Reading (Lesson) from the Book of Jeremiah [26:1–16]

At the beginning of the reign of King Jehoiakim son of Josiah of Judah, this word came from the LORD: Thus says the LORD: Stand in the court of the LORD's house, and speak to all the cities of Judah that come to worship in the house of the LORD; speak to them all the words that I command you; do not hold back a word. It may be that they will listen, all of them, and will turn from their evil way, that I may change my mind about the disaster that I intend to bring on them because of their evil doings. You shall say to them: Thus says the LORD: If you will not listen to me, to walk in my law that I have set before you, and to heed the words of my servants the prophets whom I send to you urgently—though you have not heeded—then I will make this house like Shiloh, and I will make this city a curse for all the nations of the earth. The priests and the prophets and all the people heard Jeremiah speaking these words in the house of the LORD. And when Jeremiah had finished speaking all that the LORD had commanded him to speak to all the people, then the priests and the prophets and all the people laid hold of him, saying, "You shall die! Why have you prophesied in the name of the LORD, saying, 'This house shall be like Shiloh, and this city shall be desolate, without inhabitant'?" And all the people gathered around Jeremiah in the house of the LORD. When the officials of Judah heard these things, they came up from the king's house to the house of the LORD and took their seat in the entry of the New Gate of the house of the LORD. Then the priests and the prophets said to the officials and to all the people, "This man deserves the sentence of death because he has prophesied against this city, as you have heard with your own ears." Then Jeremiah spoke to all the officials and all the people, saying, "It is the LORD who sent me to prophesy against this house and this city all the words you have heard. Now therefore amend your ways and your doings, and obey the voice of the LORD your God, and the LORD will change his mind about the disaster that he has pronounced against you. But as for me, here I am in your hands. Do with me as seems good and right to you. Only know for certain that if you put me to death, you will be bringing innocent blood upon yourselves and upon this city and its inhabitants, for in truth the LORD sent me to you to speak all these words in your ears." Then the officials and all the people said to the priests and the prophets, "This man does not deserve the sentence of death, for he has spoken to us in the name of the LORD our God."

A Reading (Lesson) from the Letter of Paul to the Romans [11:1–12]

I ask, then, has God rejected his people? By no means! I myself am an Israelite, a descendant of Abraham, a member of the tribe of Benjamin. God has not rejected his people whom he foreknew. Do you not know what the scripture says of Elijah, how he pleads with God against Israel? "Lord, they have killed your prophets, they have demolished your altars; I alone am left, and they are seeking my life." But what is the divine reply to him? "I have kept for myself seven thousand who have not bowed the knee to Baal." So too at the present time there is a remnant, chosen by grace. But if it is by grace, it is no longer on the basis of works, otherwise grace would no longer be grace. What then? Israel failed to obtain what it was seeking. The elect obtained it, but the rest were hardened, as it is written, "God gave them a sluggish spirit, eyes that would not see and ears that would not hear, down to this very day." And David says, "Let their table become a snare and a trap, a stumbling block and a retribution for them; let their eyes be darkened so that they cannot see, and keep their backs forever bent." So I ask, have they stumbled so as to fall? By no means! But through their stumbling salvation has come to the Gentiles, so as to make Israel jealous. Now if their stumbling means riches for the world, and if their defeat means riches for Gentiles, how much more will their full inclusion mean!

A Reading (Lesson) from the Gospel according to John [10:19–42]

Again the Jews were divided because of Jesus' words. Many of them were saying, "He has a demon and is out of his mind. Why listen to him?" Others were saying, "These are not the words of one who has a demon. Can a demon open the eyes of the blind?" At that time the festival of the Dedication took place in Jerusalem. It was winter, and Jesus was walking in the temple, in the portico of Solomon. So the Jews gathered around him and said to him, "How long will you keep us in suspense? If you are the Messiah, tell us plainly." Jesus answered, "I have told you, and you do not believe. The works that I do in my Father's name testify to me; but you do not believe, because you do not belong to my sheep. My sheep hear my voice. I know them, and they follow me. I give them eternal life, and they will never perish. No one will snatch them out of my hand. What my Father has given me is greater than all else, and no one can snatch it out of the Father's hand. The Father and I are one." The Jews took up stones again to stone him. Jesus replied, "I have shown you many good works from the Father. For which of these are you going to stone me?" The Jews answered, "It is not for a good work that we are going to stone you, but for blasphemy, because you, though only a human being, are making yourself God." Jesus answered, "Is it not written in your law, 'I said, you are gods'? If those to whom the word of God came were called 'gods'—and the scripture cannot be annulled—can you say that the one whom the Father has sanctified and sent into the world is blaspheming because I said, 'I am God's Son'? If I am not doing the works of my Father, then do not believe me. But if I do them, even though you do not believe me, believe the works, so that you may know and understand that the Father is in me and I am in the Father." Then they tried to arrest him again, but he escaped from their hands. He went away again across the Jordan to the place where John had been baptizing earlier, and he remained there. Many came to him, and they were saying, "John performed no sign, but everything that John said about this man was true." And many believed in him there.

Friday

A Reading (Lesson) from the Book of Jeremiah [29:1,4–13]

These are the words of the letter that the prophet Jeremiah sent from Jerusalem to the remaining elders among the exiles, and to the priests, the prophets, and all the people, whom Nebuchadnezzar had taken into exile from Jerusalem to Babylon. Thus says the LORD of hosts, the God of Israel, to all the exiles whom I have sent into exile from Jerusalem to Babylon: Build houses and live in them; plant gardens and eat what they produce. Take wives and have sons and daughters; take wives for your sons, and give your daughters in marriage, that they may bear sons and daughters; multiply there, and do not decrease. But seek the welfare of the city where I have sent you into exile, and pray to the LORD on its behalf, for in its welfare you will find your welfare. For thus says the LORD of hosts, the God of Israel: Do not let the prophets and the diviners who are among you deceive you, and do not listen to the dreams that they dream, for it is a lie that they are prophesying to you in my name; I did not send them, says the LORD. For thus says the LORD: Only when Babylon's seventy years are completed will I visit you, and I will fulfill to you my promise and bring you back to this place. For surely I know the plans I have for you, says the LORD, plans for your welfare and not for harm, to give you a future with hope. Then when you call upon me and come and pray to me, I will hear you. When you search for me, you will find me; if you seek me with all your heart.

A Reading (Lesson) from the Letter of Paul to the Romans [11:13–24]

Now I am speaking to you Gentiles. Inasmuch then as I am an apostle to the Gentiles, I glorify my ministry in order to make my own people jealous, and thus save some of them. For if their rejection is the reconciliation of the world, what will their acceptance be but life from the dead! If the part of the dough offered as first fruits is holy, then the whole batch is holy; and if the root is holy, then the branches also are holy. But if some of the branches were broken off, and you, a wild olive shoot, were grafted in their place to share the rich root of the olive tree, do not boast over the branches. If you do boast, remember that it is not you that support the root, but the root that supports you. You will say, "Branches were broken off so that I might be grafted in." That is true. They were broken off because of their unbelief, but you stand only through faith. So do not become proud, but stand in awe. For if God did not spare the natural branches, perhaps he will not spare you. Note then the kindness and the severity of God: severity toward those who have fallen, but God's kindness toward you, provided you continue in his kindness; otherwise you also will be cut off. And even those of Israel, if they do not persist in unbelief, will be grafted in, for God has the power to graft them in again. For if you have been cut from what is by nature a wild olive tree and grafted, contrary to nature, into a cultivated olive tree, how much more will these natural branches be grafted back into their own olive tree.

A Reading (Lesson) from the Gospel according to John [11:1–27]

Now a certain man was ill, Lazarus of Bethany, the village of Mary and her sister Martha. Mary was the one who anointed the Lord with perfume and wiped his feet with her hair; her brother Lazarus was ill. So the sisters sent a message to Jesus, "Lord, he whom you love is ill." But when Jesus heard it, he said, "This illness does not lead to death; rather it is for God's glory, so that the Son of God may be glorified through it." Accordingly, though Jesus loved Martha and her sister and Lazarus, after having heard that Lazarus was ill, he stayed two days longer in the place where he was. Then after this he said to the disciples, "Let us go to Judea again." The disciples said to him, "Rabbi, the Jews were just now trying to stone you, and are you going there again?" Jesus answered, "Are there not twelve hours of daylight? Those who walk during the day do not stumble, because they see the light of this world. But those who walk at night stumble, because the light is not in them." After saying this, he told them, "Our friend Lazarus has fallen asleep, but I am going there to awaken him." The disciples said to him, "Lord, if he has fallen asleep, he will be all right." Jesus, however, had been speaking about his death, but they thought that he was referring merely to sleep. Then Jesus told them plainly, "Lazarus is dead. For your sake I am glad I was not there, so that you may believe. But let us go to him." Thomas, who was called the Twin, said to his fellow disciples, "Let us also go, that we may die with him." When Jesus arrived, he found that Lazarus had already been in the tomb four days. Now Bethany was near Jerusalem, some two miles away, and many of the Jews had come to Martha and Mary to console them about their brother. When Martha heard that Jesus was coming, she went and met him, while Mary stayed at home. Martha said to Jesus, "Lord, if you had been here, my brother would not have died. But even now I know that God will give you whatever you ask of him." Jesus said to her, "Your brother will rise again." Martha said to him, "I know that he will rise again in the resurrection on the last day." Jesus said to her, "I am the resurrection and the life. Those who believe in me, even though they die, will live, and everyone who lives and believes in me will never die. Do you believe this?" She said to him, "Yes, Lord, I believe that you are the Messiah, the Son of God, the one coming into the world."

or this

A Reading (Lesson) from the Gospel according to John [12:1–10]

Six days before the Passover Jesus came to Bethany, the home of Lazarus, whom he had raised from the dead. There they gave a dinner for him. Martha served, and Lazarus was one of those at the table with him. Mary took a pound of costly perfume made of pure nard, anointed Jesus' feet, and wiped them with her hair. The house was filled with the fragrance of the perfume. But Judas Iscariot, one of his disciples (the one who was about to betray him), said, "Why was this perfume not sold for three hundred denarii and the money given to the poor?" (He said this not because he cared about the poor, but because he was a thief; he kept the common purse and used to steal what was put into it.) Jesus said, "Leave her alone. She bought it so that she might keep it for the day of my burial. You always have the poor with you, but you do not always have me." When the great crowd of the Jews learned that he was there, they came not only because of Jesus but also to see Lazarus, whom he had raised from the dead. So the chief priests planned to put Lazarus to death as well.

Saturday

A Reading (Lesson) from the Book of Jeremiah [31:27–34]

The days are surely coming, says the LORD, when I will sow the house of Israel and the house of Judah with the seed of humans and the seed of animals. And just as I have watched over them to pluck up and break down, to overthrow, destroy, and bring evil, so I will watch over them to build and to plant, says the LORD. In those days they shall no longer say: "The parents have eaten sour grapes, and the children's teeth are set on edge." But all shall die for their own sins; the teeth of everyone who eats sour grapes shall be set on edge. The days are surely coming, says the LORD, when I will make a new covenant with the house of Israel and the house of Judah. It will not be like the covenant that I made with their ancestors when I took them by the hand to bring them out of the land of Egypt—a covenant that they broke, though I was their husband, says the LORD. But this is the covenant that I will make with the house of Israel after those days, says the LORD: I will put my law within them, and I will write it on their hearts; and I will be their God, and they shall be my people. No longer shall they teach one another, or say to each other, "Know the LORD," for they shall all know me, from the least of them to the greatest, says the LORD; for I will forgive their iniquity, and remember their sin no more.

A Reading (Lesson) from the Letter of Paul to the Romans [11:25–36]

So that you may not claim to be wiser than you are, brothers and sisters, I want you to understand this mystery: a hardening has come upon part of Israel, until the full number of the Gentiles has come in. And so all Israel will be saved; as it is written, "Out of Zion will come the Deliverer; he will banish ungodliness from Jacob." "And this is my covenant with them, when I take away their sins." As regards the gospel they are enemies of God for your sake; but as regards election they are beloved, for the sake of their ancestors; for the gifts and the calling of God are irrevocable. Just as you were once disobedient to God but have now received mercy because of their disobedience, so they have now been disobedient in order that, by the mercy shown to you, they too may now receive mercy. For God has imprisoned all in disobedience so that he may be merciful to all. O the depth of the riches and wisdom and knowledge of God! How unsearchable are his judgments and how inscrutable his ways! "For who has known the mind of the Lord? Or who has been his counselor?" "Or who has given a gift to him, to receive a gift in return?" For from him and through him and to him are all things. To him be the glory forever. Amen.

A Reading (Lesson) from the Gospel according to John [11:28–44]

When Martha had said this, she went back and called her sister Mary, and told her privately, "The Teacher is here and is calling for you." And when she heard it, she got up quickly and went to him. Now Jesus had not yet come to the village, but was still at the place where Martha had met him. The Jews who were with her in the house, consoling her, saw Mary get up quickly and go out. They followed her because they thought that she was going to the tomb to weep there. When Mary came where Jesus was and saw him, she knelt at his feet and said to him, "Lord, if you had been here, my brother would not have died." When Jesus saw her weeping, and the Jews who came with her also weeping, he was greatly disturbed in spirit and deeply moved. He said, "Where have you laid him?" They said to him, "Lord, come and see." Jesus began to weep. So the Jews said, "See how he loved him!" But some of them said, "Could not he who opened the eyes of the blind man have kept this man from dying?" Then Jesus, again greatly disturbed, came to the tomb. It was a cave, and a stone was lying against it. Jesus said, "Take away the stone." Martha, the sister of the dead man, said to him, "Lord, already there is a stench because he has been dead four days." Jesus said to her, "Did I not tell you that if you believed, you would see the glory of God?" So they took away the stone. And Jesus looked upward and said, "Father, I thank you for having heard me. I knew that you always hear me, but I have said this for the sake of the crowd standing here, so that they may believe that you sent me." When he had said this, he cried with a loud voice, "Lazarus, come out!" The dead man came out, his hands and feet bound with strips of cloth, and his face wrapped in a cloth. Jesus said to them, "Unbind him, and let him go."

or this

A Reading (Lesson) from the Gospel according to John [12:37–50]

Although Jesus had performed so many signs in their presence, they did not believe in him. This was to fulfill the word spoken by the prophet Isaiah: "Lord, who has believed our message, and to whom has the arm of the Lord been revealed?" And so they could not believe, because Isaiah also said, "He has blinded their eyes and hardened their heart, so that they might not look with their eyes, and understand with their heart and turn—and I would heal them." Isaiah said this because he saw his glory and spoke about him. Nevertheless many, even of the authorities, believed in him. But because of the Pharisees they did not confess it, for fear that they would be put out of the synagogue; for they loved human glory more than the glory that comes from God.

Then Jesus cried aloud: "Whoever believes in me believes not in me but in him who sent me. And whoever sees me sees him who sent me. I have come as light into the world, so that everyone who believes in me should not remain in the darkness. I do not judge anyone who hears my words and does not keep them, for I came not to judge the world, but to save the world. The one who rejects me and does not receive my word has a judge; on the last day the word that I have spoken will serve as judge, for I have not spoken on my own, but the Father who sent me has himself given me a commandment about what to say and what to speak. And I know that his commandment is eternal life. What I speak, therefore, I speak just as the Father has told me."

Holy Week

Palm Sunday

A Reading (Lesson) from the Book of Zechariah [9:9–12]

Intended for use in the morning

Rejoice greatly, O daughter Zion! Shout aloud, O daughter Jerusalem! Lo, your king comes to you; triumphant and victorious is he, humble and riding on a donkey, on a colt, the foal of a donkey. He will cut off the chariot from Ephraim and the war horse from Jerusalem; and the battle bow shall be cut off, and he shall command peace to the nations; his dominion shall be from sea to sea, and from the River to the ends of the earth. As for you also, because of the blood of my covenant with you, I will set your prisoners free from the waterless pit. Return to your stronghold, O prisoners of hope; today I declare that I will restore to you double.

A Reading (Lesson) from the First Letter of Paul to Timothy [6:12–16]

Intended for use in the morning

Fight the good fight of the faith; take hold of the eternal life, to which you were called and for which you made the good confession in the presence of many witnesses. In the presence of God, who gives life to all things, and of Christ Jesus, who in his testimony before Pontius Pilate made the good confession, I charge you to keep the command-ment without spot or blame until the manifestation of our Lord Jesus Christ, which he will bring about at the right time—he who is the blessed and only Sovereign, the King of kings and Lord of lords. It is he alone who has immortality and dwells in unapproachable light, whom no one has ever seen or can see; to him be honor and eternal dominion. Amen.

A Reading (Lesson) from the Book of Zechariah [12:9–11;13:1, 7–9]

Intended for use in the evening

Thus says the LORD: On that day I will seek to destroy all the nations that come against Jerusalem. And I will pour out a spirit of compassion and supplication on the house of David and the inhabitants of Jerusalem, so that, when they look on the one whom they have pierced, they shall mourn for him as one mourns for an only child, and weep bitterly over him, as one weeps over a firstborn. On that day the mourning in Jerusalem will be as great as the mourning for Hadad-rimmon in the plain of Megiddo. On that day a fountain shall be opened for the house of David and the inhabitants of Jerusalem, to cleanse them from sin and impurity. "Awake, O sword, against my shepherd, against the man who is my associate," says the LORD of hosts. Strike the shepherd, that the sheep may be scattered; I will turn my hand against the little ones. In the whole land, says the LORD, two-thirds shall be cut off and perish, and one-third shall be left alive. And I will put this third into the fire, refine them as one refines silver, and test them as gold is tested. They will call on my name, and I will answer them. I will say, "They are my people"; and they will say, "The LORD is our God."

A Reading (Lesson) from the Gospel according to Matthew [21:12–17]

Intended for use in the evening

Jesus entered the temple and drove out all who were selling and buying in the temple, and he overturned the tables of the money changers and the seats of those who sold doves. He said to them, "It is written, 'My house shall be called a house of prayer'; but you are making it a den of robbers." The blind and the lame came to him in the temple, and he cured them. But when the chief priests and the scribes saw the amazing things that he did, and heard the children crying out in the temple, "Hosanna to the Son of David," they became angry and said to him, "Do you hear what these are saying?" Jesus said to them, "Yes; have you never read, 'Out of the mouths of infants and nursing babies you have prepared praise for yourself'?" He left them, went out of the city to Bethany, and spent the night there.

Monday

A Reading (Lesson) from the Book of Jeremiah [12:1–16]

You will be in the right, O LORD, when I lay charges against you; but
let me put my case to you. Why does the way of the guilty prosper?
Why do all who are treacherous thrive? You plant them, and they take
root; they grow and bring forth fruit; you are near in their mouths yet
far from their hearts. But you, O LORD, know me; You see me and test
me—my heart is with you. Pull them out like sheep for the slaughter,
and set them apart for the day of slaughter. How long will the land
mourn, and the grass of every field wither? For the wickedness of those
who live in it the animals and the birds are swept away, and because
people said, "He is blind to our ways." If you have raced with foot-
runners and they have wearied you, how will you compete with horses?
And if in a safe land you fall down, how will you fare in the thickets of
the Jordan? For even your kinsfolk and your own family, even they
have dealt treacherously with you; they are in full cry after you; do not
believe them, though they speak friendly words to you. I have forsaken
my house, I have abandoned my heritage; I have given the beloved of
my heart into the hands of her enemies. My heritage has become to me
like a lion in the forest; she has lifted up her voice against me—therefore I hate her. Is the hyena greedy for my heritage at my command?
Are the birds of prey all around her? Go, assemble all the wild animals;
bring them to devour her. Many shepherds have destroyed my vineyard, they have trampled down my portion, they have made my pleasant portion a desolate wilderness. They have made it a desolation;
desolate, it mourns to me. The whole land is made desolate, but no one
lays it to heart. Upon all the bare heights in the desert spoilers have
come; for the sword of the LORD devours from one end of the land to
the other; no one shall be safe. They have sown wheat and have
reaped thorns, they have tired themselves out but profit nothing. They
shall be ashamed of their harvests because of the fierce anger of the
LORD. Thus says the LORD concerning all my evil neighbors who touch
the heritage that I have given my people Israel to inherit: I am about
to pluck them up from their land, and I will pluck up the house of
Judah from among them. And after I have plucked them up, I will
again have compassion on them, and I will bring them again to their
heritage and to their land, every one of them. And then, if they will
diligently learn the ways of my people, to swear by my name, "As the
LORD lives," as they taught my people to swear by Baal, then they
shall be built up in the midst of my people.

A Reading (Lesson) from the Letter of Paul to the Philippians [3:1–14]

Finally, my brothers and sisters, rejoice in the Lord. To write the same things to you is not troublesome to me, and for you it is a safeguard. Beware of the dogs, beware of the evil workers, beware of those who mutilate the flesh! For it is we who are the circumcision, who worship in the Spirit of God and boast in Christ Jesus and have no confidence in the flesh—even though I, too, have reason for confidence in the flesh. If anyone else has reason to be confident in the flesh, I have more: circumcised on the eighth day, a member of the people of Israel, of the tribe of Benjamin, a Hebrew born of Hebrews; as to the law, a Pharisee; as to zeal, a persecutor of the church; as to righteousness under the law, blameless. Yet whatever gains I had, these I have come to regard as loss because of Christ. More than that, I regard everything as loss because of the surpassing value of knowing Christ Jesus my Lord. For his sake I have suffered the loss of all things, and I regard them as rubbish, in order that I may gain Christ and be found in him, not having a righteousness of my own that comes from the law, but one that comes through faith in Christ, the righteousness from God based on faith. I want to know Christ and the power of his resurrection and the sharing of his sufferings by becoming like him in his death, if somehow I may attain the resurrection from the dead. Not that I have already obtained this or have already reached the goal, but I press on to make it my own, because Christ Jesus has made me his own. Beloved, I do not consider that I have made it my own, but this one thing I do: forgetting what lies behind and straining forward to what lies ahead, I press on toward the goal for the prize of the heavenly call of God in Christ Jesus.

A Reading (Lesson) from the Gospel according to John [12:9–19]

When the great crowd of the Jews learned that he was there, they came not only because of Jesus but also to see Lazarus, whom he had raised from the dead. So the chief priests planned to put Lazarus to death as well, since it was on account of him that many of the Jews were deserting and were believing in Jesus. The next day the great crowd that had come to the festival heard that Jesus was coming to Jerusalem. So they took branches of palm trees and went out to meet him, shouting, "Hosanna! Blessed is the one who comes in the name of the Lord—the King of Israel!" Jesus found a young donkey and sat on it; as it is written: "Do not be afraid, daughter of Zion. Look, your king is coming, sitting on a donkey's colt!" His disciples did not understand these things at first; but when Jesus was glorified, then they remembered that these things had been written of him and had been done to him. So the crowd that had been with him when he called Lazarus out of the tomb and raised him from the dead continued to testify. It was also because they heard that he had performed this sign that the crowd went to meet him. The Pharisees then said to one another, "You see, you can do nothing. Look, the world has gone after him!"

Tuesday

A Reading (Lesson) from the Book of Jeremiah [15:10–21]

Woe is me, my mother, that you ever bore me, a man of strife and contention to the whole land! I have not lent, nor have I borrowed, yet all of them curse me. The LORD said: Surely I have intervened in your life for good, surely I have imposed enemies on you in a time of trouble and in a time of distress. Can iron and bronze break iron from the north? Your wealth and your treasures I will give as plunder, without price, for all your sins, throughout all your territory, I will make you serve your enemies in a land that you do not know, for in my anger a fire is kindled that shall burn forever. O LORD, you know; remember me and visit me, and bring down retribution for me on my persecutors. In your forbearance do not take me away; know that on your account I suffer insult. Your words were found, and I ate them, and your words became to me a joy and the delight of my heart; for I am called by your name, O LORD, God of hosts. I did not sit in the company of merrymakers, nor did I rejoice; under the weight of your hand I sat alone, for you had filled me with indignation. Why is my pain unceasing, my wound incurable, refusing to be healed? Truly, you are to me like a deceitful brook, like waters that fail. Therefore thus says the LORD: If you turn back, I will take you back, and you shall stand before me. If you utter what is precious, and not what is worthless, you shall serve as my mouth. It is they who will turn to you, not you who will turn to them. And I will make you to this people a fortified wall of bronze; they will fight against you, but they shall not prevail over you, for I am with you to save you and deliver you, says the LORD. I will deliver you out of the hand of the wicked, and redeem you from the grasp of the ruthless.

A Reading (Lesson) from the Letter of Paul to the Philippians [3:15–21]

Let those of us then who are mature be of the same mind; and if you think differently about anything, this too God will reveal to you. Only let us hold fast to what we have attained. Brothers and sisters, join in imitating me, and observe those who live according to the example you have in us. For many live as enemies of the cross of Christ; I have often told you of them, and now I tell you even with tears. Their end is destruction; their god is the belly; and their glory is in their shame; their minds are set on earthly things. But our citizenship is in heaven, and it is from there that we are expecting a Savior, the Lord Jesus Christ. He will transform the body of our humiliation that it may be conformed to the body of his glory, by the power that also enables him to make all things subject to himself.

A Reading (Lesson) from the Gospel according to John [12:20–26]

Among those who went up to worship at the festival were some Greeks. They came to Philip, who was from Bethsaida in Galilee, and said to him, "Sir, we wish to see Jesus." Philip went and told Andrew; then Andrew and Philip went and told Jesus. Jesus answered them, "The hour has come for the Son of Man to be glorified. Very truly, I tell you, unless a grain of wheat falls into the earth and dies, it remains just a single grain; but if it dies, it bears much fruit. Those who love their life lose it, and those who hate their life in this world will keep it for eternal life. Whoever serves me must follow me, and where I am, there will my servant be also. Whoever serves me, the Father will honor."

Wednesday

A Reading (Lesson) from the Book of Jeremiah [17:5–10,14–17]

Thus says the LORD: Cursed are those who trust in mere mortals and make mere flesh their strength, whose hearts turn away from the LORD. They shall be like a shrub in the desert, and shall not see when relief comes. They shall live in the parched places of the wilderness, in an uninhabited salt land. Blessed are those who trust in the LORD, whose trust is the LORD. They shall be like a tree planted by water, sending out its roots by the stream. It shall not fear when heat comes, and its leaves shall stay green; in the year of drought it is not anxious, and it does not cease to bear fruit. The heart is devious above all else; it is perverse—who can understand it? I the LORD test the mind and search the heart, to give to all according to their ways, according to the fruit of their doings. Heal me, O LORD, and I shall be healed; save me, and I shall be saved; for you are my praise. See how they say to me, "Where is the word of the LORD? Let it come!" But I have not run away from being a shepherd in your service, nor have I desired the fatal day. You know what came from my lips; it was before your face. Do not become a terror to me; you are my refuge in the day of disaster.

A Reading (Lesson) from the Letter of Paul to the Philippians [4:1–13]

My brothers and sisters, whom I love and long for, my joy and crown, stand firm in the Lord in this way, my beloved. I urge Euodia and I urge Syntyche to be of the same mind in the Lord. Yes, and I ask you also, my loyal companion, help these women, for they have struggled beside me in the work of the gospel, together with Clement and the rest of my co-workers, whose names are in the book of life. Rejoice in the Lord always; again I will say, Rejoice. Let your gentleness be known to everyone. The Lord is near. Do not worry about anything, but in everything by prayer and supplication with thanksgiving let your requests be made known to God. And the peace of God, which surpasses all understanding, will guard your hearts and your minds in Christ Jesus. Finally, beloved, whatever is true, whatever is honorable, whatever is just, whatever is pure, whatever is pleasing, whatever is commendable, if there is any excellence and if there is anything worthy of praise, think about these things. Keep on doing the things that you have learned and received and heard and seen in me, and the God of peace will be with you. I rejoice in the Lord greatly that now at last you have revived your concern for me; indeed, you were concerned for me, but had no opportunity to show it. Not that I am referring to being in need; for I have learned to be content with whatever I have. I know what it is to have little, and I know what it is to have plenty. In any and all circumstances I have learned the secret of being well-fed and of going hungry, of having plenty and of being in need. I can do all things through him who strengthens me.

A Reading (Lesson) from the Gospel according to John [12:27–36]

Jesus said, "Now my soul is troubled. And what should I say—'Father, save me from this hour'? No, it is for this reason that I have come to this hour. Father, glorify your name." Then a voice came from heaven, "I have glorified it, and I will glorify it again." The crowd standing there heard it and said that it was thunder. Others said. "An angel has spoken to him." Jesus answered, "This voice has come for your sake, not for mine. Now is the judgment of this world; now the ruler of this world will be driven out. And I, when I am lifted up from the earth, will draw all people to myself." He said this to indicate the kind of death he was to die. The crowd answered him, "We have heard from the law that the Messiah remains forever. How can you say that the Son of Man must be lifted up? Who is this Son of Man?" Jesus said to them, "The light is with you for a little longer. Walk while you have the light, so that the darkness may not overtake you. If you walk in the darkness, you do not know where you are going. While you have the light, believe in the light, so that you may become children of light." After Jesus had said this, he departed and hid from them.

Maundy Thursday

A Reading (Lesson) from the Book of Jeremiah [20:7–11]

O LORD you have enticed me, and I was enticed; you have overpowered me, and you have prevailed. I have become a laughingstock all day long; everyone mocks me. For whenever I speak, I must cry out, I must shout, "Violence and destruction!" For the word of the LORD has become for me a reproach and derision all day long. If I say, "I will not mention him, or speak any more in his name," then within me there is something like a burning fire shut up in my bones; I am weary with holding it in, and I cannot. For I hear many whispering: "Terror is all around! Denounce him! Let us denounce him!" All my close friends are watching for me to stumble. "Perhaps he can be enticed, and we can prevail against him, and take our revenge on him." But the LORD is with me like a dread warrior; therefore my persecutors will stumble, and they will not prevail. They will be greatly shamed, for they will not succeed. Their eternal dishonor will never be forgotten.

A Reading (Lesson) from the First Letter of Paul to the Corinthians [10:14–17,11:27–32]

My dear friends, flee from the worship of idols. I speak as to sensible people; judge for yourselves what I say. The cup of blessing that we bless, is it not a sharing in the blood of Christ? The bread that we break, is it not a sharing in the body of Christ? Because there is one bread, we who are many are one body, for we all partake of the one bread. Whoever, therefore, eats the bread or drinks the cup of the Lord in an unworthy manner will be answerable for the body and blood of the Lord. Examine yourselves, and only then eat of the bread and drink of the cup. For all who eat and drink without discerning the body, eat and drink judgment against themselves. For this reason many of you are weak and ill, and some have died. But if we judged ourselves, we would not be judged. But when we are judged by the Lord, we are disciplined so that we may not be condemned along with the world.

A Reading (Lesson) from the Gospel according to John [17:1–11(12–26)]

After Jesus had spoken, he looked up to heaven and said, "Father, the hour has come; glorify your Son so that the Son may glorify you, since you have given him authority over all people, to give eternal life to all whom you have given him. And this is eternal life, that they may know you, the only true God, and Jesus Christ whom you have sent. I glorified you on earth by finishing the work that you gave me to do. So now, Father, glorify me in your own presence with the glory that I had in your presence before the world existed. I have made your name known to those whom you gave me from the world. They were yours, and you gave them to me, and they have kept your word. Now they know that everything you have given me is from you; for the words that you gave to me I have given to them, and they have received them and know in truth that I came from you; and they have believed that you sent me. I am asking on their behalf; I am not asking on behalf of the world, but on behalf of those whom you gave me, because they are yours. All mine are yours, and yours are mine; and I have been glorified in them. And now I am no longer in the world, but they are in the world, and I am coming to you. Holy Father, protect them in your name that you have given me, so that they may be one, as we are one."

"While I was with them, I protected them in your name that you have given me. I guarded them, and not one of them was lost except the one destined to be lost, so that the scripture might be fulfilled. But now I am coming to you, and I speak these things in the world so that they may have my joy made complete in themselves. I have given them your word, and the world has hated them because they do not belong to the world, just as I do not belong to the world. I am not asking you to take them out of the world, but I ask you to protect them from the evil one. They do not belong to the world, just as I do not belong to the world. Sanctify them in the truth; your word is truth. As you have sent me into the world, so I have sent them into the world. And for their sakes I sanctify myself, so that they also may be sanctified in truth. I ask not only on behalf of these, but also on behalf of those who will believe in me through their word, that they may all be one. As you, Father, are in me and I am in you, may they also be in us, so that the world may believe that you have sent me. The glory that you have given me I have given them, so that they may be one, as we are one, I in them and you in me, that they may become completely one, so that the world may know that you have sent me and have loved them even as you have loved me. Father, I desire that those also, whom you have given me, may be with me where I am, to see my glory, which you have given me because you loved me before the foundation of the world. Righteous Father, the world does not know you, but I know you; and these know that you have sent me. I made your name known to them, and I will make it known, so that the love with which you have loved me may be in them, and I in them."

Good Friday

A Reading (Lesson) from the Book of Wisdom [1:16—2:1,12–22]

The ungodly by their words and deeds summoned death; considering him a friend, they pined away and made a covenant with him, because they are fit to belong to his company. For they reasoned unsoundly, saying to themselves, "Short and sorrowful is our life, and there is no remedy when a life comes to its end, and no one has been known to return from Hades. Let us lie in wait for the righteous man, because he is inconvenient to us and opposes our actions; he reproaches us for sins against the law, and accuses us of sins against our training. He professes to have knowledge of God, and calls himself a child of the LORD. He became to us a reproof of our thoughts; the very sight of him is a burden to us, because his manner of life is unlike that of others, and his ways are strange. We are considered by him as something base, and he avoids our ways as unclean; he calls the last end of the righteous happy, and boasts that God is his father. Let us see if his words are true, and let us test what will happen at the end of his life; for if the righteous man is God's child, he will help him, and will deliver him from the hand of his adversaries. Let us test him with insult and torture, so that we may find out how gentle he is, and make trial of his forbearance. Let us condemn him to a shameful death, for, according to what he says, he will be protected." Thus they reasoned, but they were led astray, for their wickedness blinded them, and they did not know the secret purposes of God, nor hoped for the wages of holiness, nor discerned the prize for blameless souls.

or this

A Reading (Lesson) from the Book of Genesis [22:1–14]

God tested Abraham. He said to him, "Abraham!" And he said, "Here I am." He said, "Take your son, your only son Isaac, whom you love, and go to the land of Moriah, and offer him there as a burnt offering on one of the mountains that I shall show you." So Abraham rose early in the morning, saddled his donkey, and took two of his young men with him, and his son Isaac; he cut the wood for the burnt offering, and set out and went to the place in the distance that God had shown him. On the third day Abraham looked up and saw the place far away. Then Abraham said to his young men, "Stay here with the donkey; the boy and I will go over there; we will worship, and then we will come back to you." Abraham took the wood of the burnt offering and laid it on his son Isaac, and he himself carried the fire and the knife. So the two of them walked on together. Isaac said to his father Abraham, "Father!" And he said, "Here I am, my son." He said, "The fire and the wood are here, but where is the lamb for a burnt offering?" Abraham said, "God himself will provide the lamb for a burnt offering, my son." So the two of them walked on together. When they came to the place that God had shown him, Abraham built an altar there and laid the wood in order. He bound his son Isaac, and laid him on the altar, on top of the wood. Then Abraham reached out his hand and took the knife to kill his son. But the angel of the Lord called to him from heaven, and said, "Abraham, Abraham!" And he said, "Here I am." He said, "Do not lay your hand on the boy or do anything to him; for now I know that you fear God, since you have not withheld your son, your only son, from me." And Abraham looked up and saw a ram, caught in a thicket by its horns. Abraham went and took the ram and offered it up as a burnt offering instead of his son. So Abraham called that place "The Lord will provide"; as it is said to this day, "On the mount of the Lord it shall be provided."

A Reading (Lesson) from the First Letter of Peter [1:10–20]

Concerning salvation, the prophets who prophesied of the grace that was to be yours made careful search and inquiry, inquiring about the person or time that the Spirit of Christ within them indicated when it testified in advance to the sufferings destined for Christ and the subsequent glory. It was revealed to them that they were serving not themselves but you, in regard to the things that have now been announced to you through those who brought you good news by the Holy Spirit sent from heaven—things into which angels long to look! Therefore prepare your minds for action; discipline yourselves; set all your hope on the grace that Jesus Christ will bring you when he is revealed. Like obedient children, do not be conformed to the desires that you formerly had in ignorance. Instead, as he who called you is holy, be holy yourselves in all your conduct; for it is written, "You shall be holy, for I am holy." If you invoke as Father the one who judges all people impartially according to their deeds, live in reverent fear during the time of your exile. You know that you were ransomed from the futile ways inherited from your ancestors, not with perishable things like silver or gold, but with the precious blood of Christ, like that of a lamb without defect or blemish. He was destined before the foundation of the world, but was revealed at the end of the ages for your sake.

A Reading (Lesson) from the Gospel according to John [13:36–38]

Intended for use in the morning

Simon Peter said to Jesus, "Lord, where are you going?" Jesus answered, "Where I am going, you cannot follow me now; but you will follow afterward." Peter said to him, "Lord, why can I not follow you now? I will lay down my life for you." Jesus answered, "Will you lay down your life for me? Very truly, I tell you, before the cock crows, you will have denied me three times."

A Reading (Lesson) from the Gospel according to John [19:38–42]

Intended for use in the evening

Joseph of Arimathea, who was a disciple of Jesus, though a secret one because of his fear of the Jews, asked Pilate to let him take away the body of Jesus. Pilate gave him permission; so he came and removed his body. Nicodemus, who had at first come to Jesus by night, also came, bringing a mixture of myrrh and aloes, weighing about a hundred pounds. They took the body of Jesus and wrapped it with the spices in linen cloths, according to the burial custom of the Jews. Now there was a garden in the place where he was crucified, and in the garden there was a new tomb in which no one had ever been laid. And so, because it was the Jewish day of Preparation, and the tomb was nearby, they laid Jesus there.

Holy Saturday

A Reading (Lesson) from the Book of Job [19:21–27a]

Job answered Bildad the Shuhite: "Have pity on me, have pity on me, O you my friends, for the hand of God has touched me! Why do you, like God, pursue me, never satisfied with my flesh? O that my words were written down! O that they were inscribed in a book! O that with an iron pen and with lead they were engraved on a rock forever! For I know that my Redeemer lives, and that at the last he will stand upon the earth; and after my skin has been thus destroyed, then in my flesh I shall see God, whom I shall see on my side, and my eyes shall behold, and not another."

A Reading (Lesson) from the Letter to the Hebrews [4:1–16]

Intended for use in the morning

While the promise of entering his rest is still open, let us take care that none of you should seem to have failed to reach it. For indeed the good news came to us just as to them; but the message they heard did not benefit them, because they were not united by faith with those who listened. For we who have believed enter that rest, just as God has said, "As in my anger I swore, 'They shall not enter my rest,'" though his works were finished at the foundation of the world. For in one place it speaks about the seventh day as follows, "And God rested on the seventh day from all his works." And again in this place it says, "They shall not enter my rest." Since therefore it remains open for some to enter it, and those who formerly received the good news failed to enter because of disobedience, again he sets a certain day—"today"—saying through David much later, in the words already quoted, "Today, if you hear his voice, do not harden your hearts." For if Joshua had given them rest, God would not speak later about another day. So then, a sabbath rest still remains for the people of God; for those who enter God's rest also cease from their labors as God did from his. Let us therefore make every effort to enter that rest, so that no one may fall through such disobedience as theirs. Indeed, the word of God is living and active, sharper than any two-edged sword, piercing until it divides soul from spirit, joints from marrow; it is able to judge the thoughts and intentions of the heart. And before him no creature is hidden, but all are naked and laid bare to the eyes of the one to whom we must render an account. Since, then, we have a great high priest who has passed through the heavens, Jesus, the Son of God, let us hold fast to our confession. For we do not have a high priest who is unable to sympathize with our weaknesses, but we have one who in every respect has been tested as we are, yet without sin. Let us therefore approach the throne of grace with boldness, so that we may receive mercy and find grace to help in time of need.

A Reading (Lesson) from the Letter of Paul to the Romans [8:1–11]

Intended for use in the evening

There is therefore now no condemnation for those who are in Christ Jesus. For the law of the Spirit of life in Christ Jesus has set you free from the law of sin and of death. For God has done what the law, weakened by the flesh, could not do: by sending his own Son in the likeness of sinful flesh, and to deal with sin, he condemned sin in the flesh, so that the just requirement of the law might be fulfilled in us, who walk not according to the flesh but according to the Spirit. For those who live according to the flesh set their minds on the things of the flesh, but those who live according to the Spirit, set their minds on the things of the Spirit. To set the mind on the flesh is death, but to set the mind on the Spirit is life and peace. For this reason the mind that is set on the flesh is hostile to God; it does not submit to God's law—indeed it cannot, and those who are in the flesh cannot please God. But you are not in the flesh; you are in the Spirit, since the Spirit of God dwells in you. Anyone who does not have the Spirit of Christ does not belong to him. But if Christ is in you, though the body is dead because of sin, the Spirit is life because of righteousness. If the Spirit of him who raised Jesus from the dead dwells in you, he who raised Christ from the dead will give life to your mortal bodies also through his Spirit that dwells in you.

Year Two

Ash Wednesday

A Reading (Lesson) from the Book of Amos [5:6–15]

Seek the LORD and live, or he will break out against the house of Joseph like fire, and it will devour Bethel, with no one to quench it. Ah, you that turn justice to wormwood, and bring righteousness to the ground! The one who made the Pleiades and Orion, and turns deep darkness into the morning, and darkens the day into night, who calls for the waters of the sea, and pours them out on the surface of the earth, the LORD is his name, who makes destruction flash out against the strong, so that destruction comes upon the fortress. They hate the one who reproves in the gate, and they abhor the one who speaks the truth. Therefore because you trample on the poor and take from them levies of grain, you have built houses of hewn stone, but you shall not live in them; you have planted pleasant vineyards, but you shall not drink their wine. For I know how many are your transgressions, and how great are your sins—you who afflict the righteous, who take a bribe, and push aside the needy in the gate. Therefore the prudent will keep silent in such a time; for it is an evil time. Seek good and not evil, that you may live; and so the LORD, the God of hosts, will be with you, just as you have said. Hate evil and love good, and establish justice in the gate; it may be that the LORD, the God of hosts, will be gracious to the remnant of Joseph.

A Reading (Lesson) from the Letter to the Hebrews [12:1–14]

Since we are surrounded by so great a cloud of witnesses, let us also lay aside every weight and the sin that clings so closely, and let us run with perseverance the race that is set before us, looking to Jesus the pioneer and perfecter of our faith, who for the sake of the joy that was set before him endured the cross, disregarding its shame, and has taken his seat at the right hand of the throne of God. Consider him who endured such hostility against himself from sinners, so that you may not grow weary or lose heart. In your struggle against sin you have not yet resisted to the point of shedding your blood. And you have forgotten the exhortation that addresses you as children—"My child, do not regard lightly the discipline of the Lord, or lose heart when you are punished by him; for the Lord disciplines those whom he loves, and chastises every child whom he accepts." Endure trials for the sake of discipline. God is treating you as children; for what child is there whom a parent does not discipline? If you do not have that discipline in which all children share, then you are illegitimate and not his children. Moreover, we had human parents to discipline us, and we respected them. Should we not be even more willing to be subject to the Father of spirits and live? For they disciplined us for a short time as seemed best to them, but he disciplines us for our good, in order that we may share his holiness. Now, discipline always seems painful rather than pleasant at the time, but later it yields the peaceful fruit of righteousness to those who have been trained by it. Therefore, lift your drooping hands and strengthen your weak knees, and make straight paths for your feet, so that what is lame may not be put out of joint, but rather be healed. Pursue peace with everyone, and the holiness without which no one will see the Lord.

A Reading (Lesson) from the Gospel according to Luke [18:9–14]

Jesus also told this parable to some who trusted in themselves that they were righteous and regarded others with contempt: "Two men went up to the temple to pray, one a Pharisee and the other a tax collector. The Pharisee, standing by himself, was praying thus, 'God, I thank you that I am not like other people: thieves, rogues, adulterers, or even like this tax collector. I fast twice a week; I give a tenth of all my income.' But the tax collector, standing far off, would not even look up to heaven, but was beating his breast and saying, 'God, be merciful to me, a sinner!' I tell you, this man went down to his home justified rather than the other; for all who exalt themselves will be humbled, but all who humble themselves will be exalted."

Thursday

A Reading (Lesson) from the Book of Habakkuk
[3:1–10(11–15)16–18]

A prayer of the prophet Habakkuk according to Shigionoth. O LORD, I have heard of your renown, and I stand in awe, O LORD, of your work. In our own time revive it; in our own time make it known; in wrath may you remember mercy. God came from Teman, the Holy One from Mount Paran. His glory covered the heavens, and the earth was full of his praise. The brightness was like the sun; rays came forth from his hand, where his power lay hidden. Before him went pestilence, and plague followed close behind. He stopped and shook the earth; he looked and made the nations tremble. The eternal mountains were shattered; along his ancient pathways the everlasting hills sank low. I saw the tents of Cushan under affliction; the tent-curtains of the land of Midian trembled. Was your wrath against the rivers, O LORD? Or your anger against the rivers, or your rage against the sea, when you drove your horses, your chariots to victory? You brandished your naked bow, sated were the arrows at your command. You split the earth with rivers. The mountains saw you, and writhed; a torrent of water swept by; the deep gave forth its voice. The sun raised high its hands;

the moon stood still in its exalted place, at the light of your arrows speeding by, at the gleam of your flashing spear. In fury you trod the earth, in anger you trampled nations. You came forth to save your people, to save your anointed. You crushed the head of the wicked house, laying it bare from foundation to roof. You pierced with his own arrows the head of his warriors, who came like a whirlwind to scatter us, gloating as if ready to devour the poor who were in hiding. You trampled the sea with your horses, churning the mighty waters.

I hear, and I tremble within; my lips quiver at the sound. Rottenness enters into my bones, and my steps tremble beneath me. I wait quietly for the day of calamity to come upon the people who attack us. Though the fig tree does not blossom, and no fruit is on the vines; though the produce of the olive fails and the fields yield no food; though the flock is cut off from the fold and there is no herd in the stalls, yet I will rejoice in the LORD; I will exult in the God of my salvation.

A Reading (Lesson) from the Letter of Paul to the Philippians [3:12–21]

Not that I have already obtained the resurrection from the dead or have already reached the goal; but I press on to make it my own, because Christ Jesus has made me his own. Beloved, I do not consider that I have made it my own; but this one thing I do: forgetting what lies behind and straining forward to what lies ahead, I press on toward the goal for the prize of the heavenly call of God in Christ Jesus. Let those of us then who are mature be of the same mind; and if you think differently about anything, this too God will reveal to you. Only let us hold fast to what we have attained. Brothers and sisters, join in imitating me, and observe those who live according to the example you have in us. For many live as enemies of the cross of Christ; I have often told you of them, and now I tell you even with tears. Their end is destruction; their god is the belly; and their glory is in their shame; their minds are set on earthly things. But our citizenship is in heaven, and it is from there that we are expecting a Savior, the Lord Jesus Christ. He will transform the body of our humiliation that it may be conformed to the body of his glory, by the power that also enables him to make all things subject to himself.

A Reading (Lesson) from the Gospel according to John [17:1–8]

After Jesus had spoken, he looked up to heaven and said, "Father, the hour has come; glorify your Son so that the Son may glorify you, since you have given him authority over all people, to give eternal life to all whom you have given him. And this is eternal life, that they may know you, the only true God, and Jesus Christ whom you have sent. I glorified you on earth by finishing the work that you gave me to do. So now, Father, glorify me in your own presence with the glory that I had in your presence before the world existed. I have made your name known to those whom you gave me from the world. They were yours, and you gave them to me, and they have kept your word. Now they know that everything you have given me is from you; for the words that you gave to me I have given to them, and they have received them and know in truth that I came from you; and they have believed that you sent me."

Friday

A Reading (Lesson) from the Book of Ezekiel [18:1–4,25–32]

The word of the LORD came to me: What do you mean by repeating this proverb concerning the land of Israel, "The parents have eaten sour grapes, and the children's teeth are set on edge"? As I live, says the LORD God, this proverb shall no more be used by you in Israel. Know that all lives are mine; the life of the parent as well as the life of the child is mine: it is only the person who sins that shall die. Yet you say, "The way of the LORD is unfair." Hear now, O house of Israel: Is my way unfair? Is it not your ways that are unfair? When the righteous turn away from their righteousness and commit iniquity, they shall die for it; for the iniquity that they have committed they shall die. Again, when the wicked turn away from the wickedness they have committed and do what is lawful and right, they shall save their life. Because they considered and turned away from all the transgressions that they had committed, they shall surely live; they shall not die. Yet the house of Israel says, "The way of the LORD is unfair." O house of Israel, are my ways unfair? Is it not your ways that are unfair? Therefore I will judge you, O house of Israel, all of you according to your ways, says the LORD GOD. Repent and turn from all your transgressions; otherwise iniquity will be your ruin. Cast away from you all the transgressions that you have committed against me, and get yourselves a new heart and a new spirit! Why will you die, O house of Israel? For I have no pleasure in the death of anyone, says the LORD GOD. Turn, then, and live.

A Reading (Lesson) from the Letter of Paul to the Philippians [4:1–9]

Therefore, my brothers and sisters, whom I love and long for, my joy and crown, stand firm in the Lord in this way, my beloved. I urge

Euodia and I urge Syntyche to be of the same mind in the Lord. Yes, and I ask you also, my loyal companion, help these women, for they have struggled beside me in the work of the gospel, together with Clement and the rest of my co-workers, whose names are in the book of life. Rejoice in the Lord always; again I will say, Rejoice. Let your gentleness be known to everyone. The Lord is near. Do not worry about anything, but in everything by prayer and supplication with thanksgiving let your requests be made known to God. And the peace of God, which surpasses all understanding, will guard your hearts and your minds in Christ Jesus. Finally, beloved, whatever is true, whatever is honorable, whatever is just, whatever is pure, whatever is pleasing, whatever is commendable, if there is any excellence and if there is any-thing worthy of praise, think about these things. Keep on doing the things that you have learned and received and heard and seen in me, and the God of peace will be with you.

A Reading (Lesson) from the Gospel according to John [17:9–19]

Jesus lifted up his eyes to heaven and said, "I am asking on their behalf; I am not asking on behalf of the world, but on behalf of those whom you gave me, because they are yours. All mine are yours, and yours are mine; and I have been glorified in them. And now I am no longer in the world, but they are in the world, and I am coming to you. Holy Father, protect them in your name that you have given me, so that they may be one, as we are one. While I was with them, I pro-tected them in your name that you have given me. I guarded them, and not one of them was lost except the one destined to be lost, so that the scripture might be fulfilled. But now I am coming to you, and I speak these things in the world so that they may have my joy made complete in themselves. I have given them your word, and the world has hated them because they do not belong to the world, just as I do not belong to the world. I am not asking you to take them out of the world, but I ask you to protect them from the evil one. They do not belong to the world, just as I do not belong to the world. Sanctify them in the truth; your word is truth. As you have sent me into the world, so I have sent them into the world. And for their sakes I sanctify myself, so that they also may be sanctified in truth."

Saturday

A Reading (Lesson) from the Book of Ezekiel [39:21–29]

The word of the Lord came to me: I will display my glory among the nations; and all the nations shall see my judgment that I have executed, and my hand that I have laid on them. The house of Israel shall know that I am the Lord their God, from that day forward. And the nations shall know that the house of Israel went into captivity for their iniquity, because they dealt treacherously with me. So I hid my face from them and gave them into the hand of their adversaries, and they all fell by the sword. I dealt with them according to their uncleanness and their transgressions, and hid my face from them. Therefore thus says the Lord God: Now I will restore the fortunes of Jacob, and have mercy on the whole house of Israel; and I will be jealous for my holy name. They shall forget their shame, and all the treachery they have practiced against me, when they live securely in their land with no one to make them afraid, when I have brought them back from the peoples and gathered them from their enemies' lands, and through them have displayed my holiness in the sight of many nations. Then they shall know that I am the Lord their God because I sent them into exile among the nations, and then gathered them into their own land. I will leave none of them behind; and I will never again hide my face from them, when I pour out my spirit upon the house of Israel, says the Lord God.

A Reading (Lesson) from the Letter of Paul to the Philippians [4:10–20]

I rejoice in the Lord greatly that now at last you have revived your concern for me; indeed, you were concerned for me, but had no opportunity to show it. Not that I am referring to being in need; for I have learned to be content with whatever I have. I know what it is to have little, and I know what it is to have plenty. In any and all circumstances I have learned the secret of being well-fed and of going hungry, of having plenty and of being in need. I can do all things through him who strengthens me. In any case, it was kind of you to share my distress. You Philippians indeed know that in the early days of the gospel, when I left Macedonia, no church shared with me in the matter of giving and receiving, except you alone. For even when I was in Thessalonica, you sent me help for my needs more than once. Not that I seek the gift, but I seek the profit that accumulates to your account. I have been paid in full and have more than enough; I am fully satisfied, now that I have received from Epaphroditus the gifts you sent, a fragrant offering, a sacrifice acceptable and pleasing to God. And my God will fully satisfy every need of yours according to his riches in glory in Christ Jesus. To our God and Father be glory forever and ever. Amen.

A Reading (Lesson) from the Gospel according to John [17:20–26]

Jesus lifted up his eyes to heaven and said, "I ask not only on behalf of these, but also on behalf of those who will believe in me through their word, that they may all be one. As you, Father, are in me and I am in you, may they also be in us, so that the world may believe that you have sent me. The glory that you have given me I have given them, so that they may be one, as we are one, I in them and you in me, that they may become completely one, so that the world may know that you have sent me and have loved them even as you have loved me. Father, I desire that those also, whom you have given me, may be with me where I am, to see my glory, which you have given me because you loved me before the foundation of the world. Righteous Father, the world does not know you, but I know you; and these know that you have sent me. I made your name known to them, and I will make it known, so that the love with which you have loved me may be in them, and I in them."

Week of I Lent

Sunday

A Reading (Lesson) from the Book of Daniel [9:3–10]

Then I turned to the LORD GOD, to seek an answer by prayer and supplication with fasting and sackcloth and ashes. I prayed to the LORD my God and made confession, saying, "Ah, LORD, great and awesome GOD, keeping covenant and steadfast love with those who love you and keep your commandments, we have sinned and done wrong, acted wickedly and rebelled, turning aside from your commandments and ordinances. We have not listened to your servants the prophets, who spoke in your name to our kings, our princes, and our ancestors, and to all the people of the land. Righteousness is on your side, O LORD, but open shame, as at this day, falls on us, the people of Judah, the inhabitants of Jerusalem, and all Israel, those who are near and those who are far away, in all the lands to which you have driven them, because of the treachery that they have committed against you. Open shame, O LORD, falls on us, our kings, our officials, and our ancestors, because we have sinned against you. To the LORD our GOD belong mercy and forgiveness, for we have rebelled against him, and have not obeyed the voice of the LORD our God by following his laws, which he set before us by his servants the prophets."

A Reading (Lesson) from the Letter to the Hebrews [2:10–18]

It was fitting that God, for whom and through whom all things exist, in bringing many children to glory, should make the pioneer of their salvation perfect through sufferings. For the one who sanctifies and those who are sanctified all have one Father. For this reason Jesus is not ashamed to call them brothers and sisters, saying, "I will proclaim your name to my brothers and sisters, in the midst of the congregation I will praise you." And again, "I will put my trust in him." And again, "Here am I and the children whom God has given me." Since, therefore, the children share flesh and blood, he himself likewise shared the same things, so that through death he might destroy the one who has the power of death, that is, the devil, and free those who all their lives were held in slavery by the fear of death. For it is clear that he did not come to help angels, but the descendants of Abraham. Therefore he had to become like his brothers and sisters in every respect, so that he might be a merciful and faithful high priest in the service of God, to make a sacrifice of atonement for the sins of the people. Because he himself was tested by what he suffered, he is able to help those who are being tested.

A Reading (Lesson) from the Gospel according to John [12:44–50]

Jesus cried aloud: "Whoever believes in me believes not in me but in him who sent me. And whoever sees me sees him who sent me. I have come as light into the world, so that everyone who believes in me should not remain in the darkness. I do not judge anyone who hears my words and does not keep them, for I came not to judge the world, but to save the world. The one who rejects me and does not receive my word has a judge; on the last day the word that I have spoken will serve as judge, for I have not spoken on my own, but the Father who sent me has himself given me a commandment about what to say and what to speak. And I know that his commandment is eternal life. What I speak, therefore, I speak just as the Father has told me."

Monday

A Reading (Lesson) from the Book of Genesis [37:1-11]

Jacob settled in the land where his father had lived as an alien, the land of Canaan. This is the story of the family of Jacob. Joseph, being seventeen years old, was shepherding the flock with his brothers; he was a helper to the sons of Bilhah and Zilpah, his father's wives; and Joseph brought a bad report of them to their father. Now Israel loved Joseph more than any other of his children, because he was the son of his old age; and he had made him a long robe with sleeves. But when his brothers saw that their father loved him more than all his brothers, they hated him, and could not speak peaceably to him. Once Joseph had a dream, and when he told it to his brothers, they hated him even more. He said to them, "Listen to this dream that I dreamed. There we were, binding sheaves in the field. Suddenly my sheaf rose and stood upright; then your sheaves gathered around it, and bowed down to my sheaf." His brothers said to him, "Are you indeed to reign over us? Are you indeed to have dominion over us?" So they hated him even more because of his dreams and his words. He had another dream, and told it to his brothers, saying, "Look, I have had another dream: the sun, the moon, and eleven stars were bowing down to me." But when he told it to his father and to his brothers, his father rebuked him, and said to him, "What kind of dream is this that you have had? Shall we indeed come, I and your mother and your brothers, and bow to the ground before you?" So his brothers were jealous of him, but his father kept the matter in mind.

A Reading (Lesson) from the First Letter of Paul to the Corinthians [1:1–19]

Paul, called to be an apostle of Christ Jesus by the will of God, and our brother Sosthenes, to the church of God that is in Corinth, to those who are sanctified in Christ Jesus, called to be saints, together with all those who in every place call on the name of our Lord Jesus Christ, both their Lord and ours: Grace to you and peace from God our Father and the Lord Jesus Christ. I give thanks to my God always for you because of the grace of God that has been given you in Christ Jesus, for in every way you have been enriched in him, in speech and knowledge of every kind—just as the testimony of Christ has been strengthened among you—so that you are not lacking in any spiritual gift as you wait for the revealing of our Lord Jesus Christ. He will also strengthen you to the end, so that you may be blameless on the day of our Lord Jesus Christ. God is faithful; by him you were called into the fellowship of his Son, Jesus Christ our Lord. Now I appeal to you, brothers and sisters, by the name of our Lord Jesus Christ, that all of you be in agreement and that there be no divisions among you, but that you be united in the same mind and the same purpose. For it has been reported to me by Chloe's people that there are quarrels among you, my brothers and sisters. What I mean is that each of you says, "I belong to Paul," or "I belong to Apollos," or "I belong to Cephas," or "I belong to Christ." Has Christ been divided? Was Paul crucified for you? Or were you baptized in the name of Paul? I thank God that I baptized none of you except Crispus and Gaius, so that no one can say that you were baptized in my name. (I did baptize also the household of Stephanas; beyond that, I do not know whether I baptized anyone else.) For Christ did not send me to baptize but to proclaim the gospel, and not with eloquent wisdom, so that the cross of Christ might not be emptied of its power. For the message about the cross is foolishness to those who are perishing, but to us who are being saved it is the power of God. For it is written, "I will destroy the wisdom of the wise, and the discernment of the discerning I will thwart."

A Reading (Lesson) from the Gospel according to Mark [1:1–13]

The beginning of the good news of Jesus Christ, the Son of God. As it is written in the prophet Isaiah, "See, I am sending my messenger ahead of you, who will prepare your way; the voice of one crying out in the wilderness: 'Prepare the way of the Lord, make his paths straight,'" John the baptizer appeared in the wilderness, proclaiming a baptism of repentance for the forgiveness of sins. And people from the whole Judean countryside and all the people of Jerusalem were going out to him, and were baptized by him in the river Jordan, confessing their sins. Now John was clothed with camel's hair, with a leather belt around his waist, and he ate locusts and wild honey. He proclaimed, "The one who is more powerful than I is coming after me; I am not worthy to stoop down and untie the thong of his sandals. I have baptized you with water; but he will baptize you with the Holy Spirit." In those days Jesus came from Nazareth of Galilee and was baptized by John in the Jordan. And just as he was coming up out of the water, he saw the heavens torn apart and the Spirit descending like a dove on him. And a voice came from heaven, "You are my Son, the Beloved; with you I am well pleased." And the Spirit immediately drove him out into the wilderness. He was in the wilderness forty days, tempted by Satan; and he was with the wild beasts; and the angels waited on him.

Tuesday

A Reading (Lesson) from the Book of Genesis [37:12–24]

Joseph's brothers went to pasture their father's flock near Shechem. And Israel said to Joseph, "Are not your brothers pasturing the flock at Shechem? Come, I will send you to them." He answered, "Here I am." So he said to him, "Go now, see if it is well with your brothers and with the flock; and bring word back to me." So he sent him from the valley of Hebron. He came to Shechem, and a man found him wandering in the fields; the man asked him, "What are you seeking?" "I am seeking my brothers," he said; "tell me, please, where they are pasturing the flock." The man said, "They have gone away, for I heard them say, 'Let us go to Dothan.'" So Joseph went after his brothers, and found them at Dothan. They saw him from a distance, and before he came near to them, they conspired to kill him. They said to one another, "Here comes this dreamer. Come now, let us kill him and throw him into one of the pits; then we shall say that a wild animal has devoured him, and we shall see what will become of his dreams." But when Reuben heard it, he delivered him out of their hands, saying, "Let us not take his life." Reuben said to them, "Shed no blood; throw him into this pit here in the wilderness, but lay no hand on him"—that he might rescue him out of their hand and restore him to his father. So when Joseph came to his brothers, they stripped him of his robe, the long robe with sleeves that he wore; and they took him and threw him into a pit. The pit was empty; there was no water in it.

A Reading (Lesson) from the First Letter of Paul to the Corinthians [1:20–31]

Where is the one who is wise? Where is the scribe? Where is the debater of this age? Has not God made foolish the wisdom of the world? For since, in the wisdom of God, the world did not know God through wisdom, God decided, through the foolishness of our proclamation, to save those who believe. For Jews demand signs and Greeks desire wisdom, but we proclaim Christ crucified, a stumbling block to Jews and foolishness to Gentiles, but to those who are the called, both Jews and Greeks, Christ the power of God and the wisdom of God. For God's foolishness is wiser than human wisdom, and God's weakness is stronger than human strength. Consider your own call, brothers and sisters: not many of you were wise by human standards, not many were powerful, not many were of noble birth. But God chose what is foolish in the world to shame the wise; God chose what is weak in the world to shame the strong; God chose what is low and despised in the world, things that are not, to reduce to nothing things that are, so that no one might boast in the presence of God. He is the source of your life in Christ Jesus, who became for us wisdom from God, and righteousness and sanctification and redemption, in order that, as it is written, "Let the one who boasts, boast in the Lord."

A Reading (Lesson) from the Gospel according to Mark [1:14–28]

After John was arrested, Jesus came to Galilee, proclaiming the good news of God, and saying, "The time is fulfilled, and the kingdom of God has come near; repent, and believe in the good news." As Jesus passed along the Sea of Galilee, he saw Simon and his brother Andrew casting a net into the sea—for they were fishermen. And Jesus said to them, "Follow me and I will make you fish for people." And immediately they left their nets and followed him. As he went a little farther, he saw James son of Zebedee and his brother John, who were in their boat mending the nets. Immediately he called them; and they left their father Zebedee in the boat with the hired men, and followed him. They went to Capernaum; and when the sabbath came, he entered the synagogue and taught. They were astounded at his teaching, for he taught them as one having authority, and not as the scribes. Just then there was in their synagogue a man with an unclean spirit, and he cried out, "What have you to do with us, Jesus of Nazareth? Have you come to destroy us? I know who you are, the Holy One of God." But Jesus rebuked him, saying, "Be silent, and come out of him!" And the unclean spirit, convulsing him and crying with a loud voice, came out of him. They were all amazed, and they kept on asking one another, "What is this? A new teaching—with authority! He commands even the unclean spirits, and they obey him." At once his fame began to spread throughout the surrounding region of Galilee.

Wednesday

A Reading (Lesson) from the Book of Genesis [37:25–36]

The brothers of Joseph sat down to eat; and looking up they saw a caravan of Ishmaelites coming from Gilead, with their camels carrying gum, balm, and resin, on their way to carry it down to Egypt. Then Judah said to his brothers, "What profit is it if we kill our brother and conceal his blood? Come, let us sell him to the Ishmaelites, and not lay our hands on him, for he is our brother, our own flesh." And his brothers agreed. When some Midianite traders passed by, they drew Joseph up, lifting him out of the pit, and sold him to the Ishmaelites for twenty pieces of silver. And they took Joseph to Egypt. When Reuben returned to the pit and saw that Joseph was not in the pit, he tore his clothes. He returned to his brothers, and said, "The boy is gone; and I, where can I turn?" Then they took Joseph's robe, slaughtered a goat, and dipped the robe in the blood. They had the long robe with sleeves taken to their father, and they said, "This we have found; see now whether it is your son's robe or not." He recognized it, and said, "It is my son's robe! A wild animal has devoured him; Joseph is without doubt torn to pieces." Then Jacob tore his garments, and put sackcloth on his loins, and mourned for his son many days. All his sons and all his daughters sought to comfort him; but he refused to be comforted, and said, "No, I shall go down to Sheol to my son, mourning." Thus his father bewailed him. Meanwhile the Midianites had sold him in Egypt to Potiphar, one of Pharaoh's officials, the captain of the guard.

A Reading (Lesson) from the First Letter of Paul to the Corinthians [2:1–13]

When I came to you, brothers and sisters, I did not come proclaiming the mystery of God to you in lofty words or wisdom. For I decided to know nothing among you except Jesus Christ, and him crucified. And I came to you in weakness and in fear and in much trembling. My speech and my proclamation were not with plausible words of wisdom, but with a demonstration of the Spirit and of power, so that your faith might rest not on human wisdom but on the power of God. Yet among the mature we do speak wisdom, though it is not a wisdom of this age or of the rulers of this age, who are doomed to perish. But we speak God's wisdom, secret and hidden, which God decreed before the ages for our glory. None of the rulers of this age understood this; for if they had, they would not have crucified the Lord of glory. But, as it is written, "What no eye has seen, nor ear heard, nor the human heart conceived, what God has prepared for those who love him"—these things God has revealed to us through the Spirit; for the Spirit searches everything, even the depths of God. For what human being knows what is truly human except the human spirit that is within? So also no one comprehends what is truly God's except the Spirit of God. Now we have received not the spirit of the world, but the Spirit that is from God, so that we may understand the gifts bestowed on us by God. And we speak of these things in words not taught by human wisdom but taught by the Spirit, interpreting spiritual things to those who are spiritual.

A Reading (Lesson) from the Gospel according to Mark [1:29–45]

As soon as Jesus left the synagogue, they entered the house of Simon and Andrew, with James and John. Now Simon's mother-in-law was in bed with a fever, and they told him about her at once. He came and took her by the hand and lifted her up. Then the fever left her, and she began to serve them. That evening, at sundown, they brought to him all who were sick or possessed with demons. And the whole city was gathered around the door. And he cured many who were sick with various diseases, and cast out many demons; and he would not permit the demons to speak, because they knew him. In the morning, while it was still very dark, he got up and went out to a deserted place, and there he prayed. And Simon and his companions hunted for him. When they found him, they said to him, "Everyone is searching for you." He answered, "Let us go on to the neighboring towns, so that I may proclaim the message there also; for that is what I came out to do." And he went throughout Galilee, proclaiming the message in their synagogues and casting out demons. A leper came to him begging him, and kneeling he said to him, "If you choose, you can make me clean." Moved with pity, Jesus stretched out his hand and touched him, and said to him, "I do choose. Be made clean!" Immediately the leprosy left him, and he was made clean. After sternly warning him he sent him away at once, saying to him, "See that you say nothing to anyone; but go, show yourself to the priest, and offer for your cleansing what Moses commanded, as a testimony to them." But he went out and began to proclaim it freely, and to spread the word, so that Jesus could no longer go into a town openly, but stayed out in the country; and people came to him from every quarter.

Thursday

A Reading (Lesson) from the Book of Genesis [39:1–23]

Joseph was taken down to Egypt, and Potiphar, an officer of Pharaoh, the captain of the guard, an Egyptian, bought him from the Ishmaelites who had brought him down there. The LORD was with Joseph, and he became a successful man; he was in the house of his Egyptian master. His master saw that the LORD was with him, and that the LORD caused all that he did to prosper in his hands. So Joseph found favor in his sight and attended him; he made him overseer of his house and put him in charge of all that he had. From the time that he made him overseer in his house and over all that he had, the LORD blessed the Egyptian's house for Joseph's sake; the blessing of the LORD was on all that he had, in house and field. So he left all that he had in Joseph's charge; and, with him there, he had no concern for anything but the food that he ate. Now Joseph was handsome and good-looking. And after a time his master's wife cast her eyes on Joseph and said, "Lie with me." But he refused and said to his master's wife, "Look, with me here, my master has no concern about anything in the house, and he has put everything that he has in my hand. He is not greater in this house than I am, nor has he kept back anything from me except yourself, because you are his wife. How then could I do this great wickedness, and sin against God?" And although she spoke to Joseph day after day, he would not consent to lie beside her or to be with her. One day, however, when he went into the house to do his work, and while no one else was in the house, she caught hold of his garment, saying, "Lie with me!" But he left his garment in her hand, and fled and ran outside. When she saw that he had left his garment in her hand and had fled outside, she called out to the members of her household and said to them, "See, my husband has brought among us a Hebrew to insult us! He came in to me to lie with me, and I cried out with a loud voice; and when he heard me raise my voice and cry out, he left his garment beside me, and fled outside." Then she kept his garment by her until his master came home, and she told him the same story, saying, "The Hebrew servant, whom you have brought among us, came in to me to insult me; but as soon as I raised my voice and cried out, he left his garment beside me and fled outside." When his master heard the words that his wife spoke to him, saying, "This is the way your servant treated me," he became enraged. And Joseph's master took him and put him into the prison, the place where the king's prisoners were confined; he remained there in prison. But the LORD was with Joseph and showed him steadfast love; he gave him favor in the sight of the chief jailer. The chief jailer committed to Joseph's care all the prisoners who were in the prison, and whatever was done there, he was the one who did it. The chief jailer paid no heed to anything that was in Joseph's care, because the LORD was with him; and whatever he did, the LORD made it prosper.

A Reading (Lesson) from the First Letter of Paul to the Corinthians [2:14—3:15]

Those who are unspiritual do not receive the gifts of God's Spirit, for they are foolishness to them, and they are unable to understand them because they are spiritually discerned. Those who are spiritual discern all things, and they are themselves subject to no one else's scrutiny. "For who has known the mind of the Lord so as to instruct him?" But we have the mind of Christ. And so, brothers and sisters, I could not speak to you as spiritual people, but rather as people of the flesh, as infants in Christ. I fed you with milk, not solid food, for you were not ready for solid food. Even now you are still not ready, for you are still of the flesh. For as long as there is jealousy and quarreling among you, are you not of the flesh, and behaving according to human inclinations? For when one says, "I belong to Paul," and another, "I belong to Apollos," are you not merely human? What then is Apollos? What is Paul? Servants through whom you came to believe, as the Lord assigned to each. I planted, Apollos watered, but God gave the growth. So neither the one who plants nor the one who waters is anything, but only God who gives the growth. The one who plants and the one who waters have a common purpose, and each will receive wages according to the labor of each. For we are God's servants, working together; you are God's field, God's bpuilding. According to the grace of God given to me, like a skilled master builder I laid a foundation, and someone else is building on it. Each builder must choose with care how to build on it. For no one can lay any foundation other than the one that has been laid; that foundation is Jesus Christ. Now if anyone builds on the foundation with gold, silver, precious stones, wood, hay, straw—the work of each builder will become visible, for the Day will disclose it, because it will be revealed with fire, and the fire will test what sort of work each has done. If what has been built on the foundation survives, the builder will receive a reward. If the work is burned up, the builder will suffer loss; the builder will be saved, but only as through fire.

A Reading (Lesson) from the Gospel according to Mark [2:1–12]

When Jesus returned to Capernaum after some days, it was reported that he was at home. So many gathered around that there was no longer room for them, not even in front of the door; and he was speaking the word to them. Then some people came, bringing to him a paralyzed man, carried by four of them. And when they could not bring him to Jesus because of the crowd, they removed the roof above him; and after having dug through it, they let down the mat on which the paralytic lay. When Jesus saw their faith, he said to the paralytic. "Son, your sins are forgiven." Now some of the scribes were sitting there, questioning in their hearts, "Why does this fellow speak in this way? It is blasphemy! Who can forgive sins but God alone?" At once Jesus perceived in his spirit that they were discussing these questions among themselves; and he said to them, "Why do you raise such questions in your hearts? Which is easier, to say to the paralytic, 'Your sins are forgiven,' or to say, 'stand up and take your mat and walk'? But so that you may know that the Son of Man has authority on earth to forgive sins"—he said to the paralytic—"I say to you, stand up, take your mat and go to your home." And he stood up, and immediately took the mat and went out before all of them; so that they were all amazed and glorified God, saying, "We have never seen anything like this!"

Friday

A Reading (Lesson) from the Book of Genesis [40:1–23]

Some time after Joseph's master had put him into the prison, the cupbearer of the king of Egypt and his baker offended their lord the king of Egypt. Pharaoh was angry with his two officers, the chief cupbearer and the chief baker, and he put them in custody in the house of the captain of the guard, in the prison where Joseph was confined. The captain of the guard charged Joseph with them, and he waited on them; and they continued for some time in custody. One night they both dreamed—the cupbearer and the baker of the king of Egypt, who were confined in the prison—each his own dream, and each dream with its own meaning. When Joseph came to them in the morning, he saw that they were troubled. So he asked Pharaoh's officers, who were with him in custody in his master's house, "Why are your faces downcast today?" They said to him, "We have had dreams, and there is no one to interpret them." And Joseph said to them, "Do not interpretations belong to God? Please tell them to me." So the chief cupbearer told his dream to Joseph, and said to him, "In my dream there was a vine before me, and on the vine there were three branches. As soon as it budded, its blossoms came out and the clusters ripened into grapes.

Pharaoh's cup was in my hand; and I took the grapes and pressed them into Pharaoh's cup, and placed the cup in Pharaoh's hand." Then Joseph said to him, "This is its interpretation: the three branches are three days; within three days Pharaoh will lift up your head and restore you to your office; and you shall place Pharaoh's cup in his hand, just as you used to do when you were his cupbearer. But remember me when it is well with you; please do me the kindness to make mention of me to Pharaoh, and so get me out of this place. For in fact I was stolen out of the land of the Hebrews; and here also I have done nothing that they should have put me into the dungeon." When the chief baker saw that the interpretation was favorable, he said to Joseph, "I also had a dream: there were three cake baskets on my head, and in the uppermost basket there were all sorts of baked food for Pharaoh, but the birds were eating it out of the basket on my head." And Joseph answered, "This is its interpretation: the three baskets are three days; within three days Pharaoh will lift up your head—from you!—and hang you on a pole; and the birds will eat the flesh from you." On the third day, which was Pharaoh's birthday, he made a feast for all his servants, and lifted up the head of the chief cupbearer and the head of the chief baker among his servants. He restored the chief cupbearer to his cupbearing, and he placed the cup in Pharaoh's hand; but the chief baker he hanged, just as Joseph had interpreted to them. Yet the chief cupbearer did not remember Joseph, but forgot him.

A Reading (Lesson) from the First Letter of Paul to the Corinthians [3:16–23]

Do you not know that you are God's temple and that God's Spirit dwells in you? If anyone destroys God's temple, God will destroy that person. For God's temple is holy, and you are that temple. Do not deceive yourselves. If you think that you are wise in this age, you should become fools so that you may become wise. For the wisdom of this world is foolishness with God. For it is written, "He catches the wise in their craftiness," and again, "The Lord knows the thoughts of the wise, that they are futile." So let no one boast about human leaders. For all things are yours, whether Paul or Apollos or Cephas or the world or life or death or the present or the future—all belong to you, and you belong to Christ, and Christ belongs to God.

A Reading (Lesson) from the Gospel according to Mark [2:13–22]

Jesus went out again beside the sea; the whole crowd gathered around him, and he taught them. As he was walking along, he saw Levi son of Alphaeus sitting at the tax booth, and he said to him, "Follow me." And he got up and followed him. And as he sat at dinner in Levi's house, many tax collectors and sinners were also sitting with Jesus and his disciples—for there were many who followed him. When the scribes of the Pharisees saw that he was eating with sinners and tax collectors, they said to his disciples, "Why does he eat with tax collectors and sinners?" When Jesus heard this, he said to them, "Those who are well have no need of a physician, but those who are sick; I have come to call not the righteous but sinners." Now John's disciples and the Pharisees were fasting; and people came and said to him, "Why do John's disciples and the disciples of the Pharisees fast, but your disciples do not fast?" Jesus said to them, "The wedding guests cannot fast while the bridegroom is with them, can they? As long as they have the bridegroom with them, they cannot fast. The days will come when the bridegroom is taken away from them, and then they will fast on that day. No one sews a piece of unshrunk cloth on an old cloak; otherwise, the patch pulls away from it, the new from the old, and a worse tear is made. And no one puts new wine into old wineskins; otherwise, the wine will burst the skins, and the wine is lost, and so are the skins; but one puts new wine into fresh wineskins."

Saturday

A Reading (Lesson) from the Book of Genesis [41:1–13]

After two whole years, Pharaoh dreamed that he was standing by the Nile, and there came up out of the Nile seven sleek and fat cows, and they grazed in the reed grass. Then seven other cows, ugly and thin, came up out of the Nile after them, and stood by the other cows on the bank of the Nile. The ugly and thin cows ate up the seven sleek and fat cows. And Pharaoh awoke. Then he fell asleep and dreamed a second time; seven ears of grain, plump and good, were growing on one stalk. Then seven ears, thin and blighted by the east wind, sprouted after them. The thin ears swallowed up the seven plump and full ears. Pharaoh awoke, and it was a dream. In the morning his spirit was troubled; so he sent and called for all the magicians of Egypt and all its wise men. Pharaoh told them his dreams, but there was no one who could interpret them to Pharaoh. Then the chief cupbearer said to Pharaoh, "I remember my faults today. Once Pharaoh was angry with his servants, and put me and the chief baker in custody in the house of the captain of the guard. We dreamed on the same night, he and I, each having a dream with its own meaning. A young Hebrew was there with us, a servant of the captain of the guard. When we told him, he interpreted our dreams to us, giving an interpretation to each according to his dream. As he interpreted to us, so it turned out; I was restored to my office, and the baker was hanged."

A Reading (Lesson) from the First Letter of Paul to the Corinthians [4:1–7]

Think of us in this way, as servants of Christ and stewards of God's mysteries. Moreover, it is required of stewards that they be found trustworthy. But with me it is a very small thing that I should be judged by you or by any human court. I do not even judge myself. I am not aware of anything against myself, but I am not thereby acquitted. It is the Lord who judges me. Therefore do not pronounce judgment before the time, before the Lord comes, who will bring to light the things now hidden in darkness and will disclose the purposes of the heart. Then each one will receive commendation from God. I have applied all this to Apollos and myself for your benefit, brothers and sisters, so that you may learn through us the meaning of the saying, "Nothing beyond what is written," so that none of you will be puffed up in favor of one against another. For who sees anything different in you? What do you have that you did not receive? And if you received it, why do you boast as if it were not a gift?

A Reading (Lesson) from the Gospel according to Mark [2:23 – 3:6]

One sabbath Jesus was going through the grainfields; and as they made their way his disciples began to pluck heads of grain. The Pharisees said to him, "Look, why are they doing what is not lawful on the sabbath?" And he said to them, "Have you never read what David did when he and his companions were hungry and in need of food? He entered the house of God, when Abiathar was high priest, and ate the bread of the Presence, which it is not lawful for any but the priests to eat, and he gave some to his companions." Then he said to them, "The sabbath was made for humankind, and not humankind for the sabbath; so the Son of Man is lord even of the sabbath." Again he entered the synagogue, and a man was there who had a withered hand. They watched him to see whether he would cure him on the sabbath, so that they might accuse him. And he said to the man who had the withered hand, "Come forward." Then he said to them, "Is it lawful to do good or to do harm on the sabbath, to save life or to kill?" But they were silent. He looked around at them with anger; he was grieved at their hardness of heart and said to the man, "Stretch out your hand." He stretched it out, and his hand was restored. The Pharisees went out and immediately conspired with the Herodians against him, how to destroy him.

Week of 2 Lent

Sunday

A Reading (Lesson) from the Book of Genesis [41:14–45]

Pharaoh sent for Joseph, and he was hurriedly brought out of the dungeon. When he had shaved himself and changed his clothes, he came in before Pharaoh. And Pharaoh said to Joseph, "I have had a dream, and there is no one who can interpret it. I have heard it said of you that when you hear a dream you can interpret it." Joseph answered Pharaoh, "It is not I; God will give Pharaoh a favorable answer." Then Pharaoh said to Joseph, "In my dream I was standing on the banks of the Nile; and seven cows, fat and sleek, came up out of the Nile and fed in the reed grass. Then seven other cows came up after them, poor, very ugly, and thin. Never had I seen such ugly ones in all the land of Egypt. The thin and ugly cows ate up the first seven fat cows, but when they had eaten them no one would have known that they had done so, for they were still as ugly as before. Then I awoke. I fell asleep a second time and I saw in my dream seven ears of grain, full and good, growing on one stalk, and seven ears, withered, thin, and blighted by the east wind, sprouting after them; and the thin ears swallowed up the seven good ears. But when I told it to the magicians, there was no one who could explain it to me." Then Joseph said to Pharaoh, "Pharaoh's dreams are one and the same; God has revealed to Pharaoh what he is about to do. The seven good cows are seven years, and the seven good ears are seven years; the dreams are one. The seven lean and ugly cows that came up after them are seven years, as are the seven empty ears blighted by the east wind. They are seven years of famine. It is as I told Pharaoh; God has shown to Pharaoh what he is about to do. There will come seven years of great plenty throughout all the land of Egypt. After them there will arise seven years of famine, and all the plenty will be forgotten in the land of Egypt; the famine will consume the land. The plenty will no longer be known in the land because of the famine that will follow, for it will be very grievous. And the doubling of Pharaoh's dream means that the thing is fixed by God, and God will shortly bring it about. Now therefore let Pharaoh select a man who is discerning and wise, and set him over the land of Egypt. Let Pharaoh proceed to appoint overseers over the land, and take one-fifth of the produce of the land of Egypt during the seven plenteous years. Let them gather all the food of these good years that are coming, and lay up grain under the authority of Pharaoh for food in the cities, and let them keep it. That food shall be a reserve for the land against the seven years of famine that are to befall the land of Egypt, so that the land may not perish through the famine." The proposal pleased Pharaoh and all his servants. Pharaoh said to his servants, "Can we find anyone else like this—one in whom is the spirit of God?" So Pharaoh said to Joseph, "Since God has shown you all this, there is no one so discerning and wise as you. You shall be over my house, and all my people shall order themselves as you command; only with regard to the throne will I be greater than you." And Pharaoh said to Joseph, "See, I have set you over all the land of Egypt." Removing his signet ring from his hand, Pharaoh put it on Joseph's hand; he arrayed him in garments of fine linen, and put a gold chain around his neck. He had him ride in the chariot of his second-in-command; and they cried out in front of him, "Bow the knee!" Thus he set him over all the land of Egypt. Moreover Pharaoh said to Joseph, "I am Pharaoh, and without your consent no one shall lift up hand or foot in all the land of Egypt." Pharaoh gave Joseph the name Zaphenath-paneah; and he gave him Asenath daughter of Potiphera, priest of On, as his wife. Thus Joseph gained authority over the land of Egypt.

A Reading (Lesson) from the Letter of Paul to the Romans [6:3–14]

Do you not know that all of us who have been baptized into Christ Jesus were baptized into his death? Therefore we have been buried with him by baptism into death, so that, just as Christ was raised from the dead by the glory of the Father, so we too might walk in newness of life. For if we have been united with him in a death like his, we will certainly be united with him in a resurrection like his. We know that our old self was crucified with him so that the body of sin might be destroyed, and we might no longer be enslaved to sin. For whoever has died is freed from sin. But if we have died with Christ, we believe that we will also live with him. We know that Christ, being raised from the dead, will never die again; death no longer has dominion over him. The death he died, he died to sin, once for all; but the life he lives, he lives to God. So you also must consider yourselves dead to sin and alive to God in Christ Jesus. Therefore, do not let sin exercise dominion in your mortal bodies, to make you obey their passions. No longer present your members to sin as instruments of wickedness, but present yourselves to God as those who have been brought from death to life, and present your members to God as instruments of righteousness. For sin will have no dominion over you, since you are not under law but under grace.

A Reading (Lesson) from the Gospel according to John [5:19–24]

Jesus said to the Jews, "Very truly, I tell you, the Son can do nothing on his own, but only what he sees the Father doing; for whatever the Father does, the Son does likewise. The Father loves the Son and shows him all that he himself is doing; and he will show him greater works than these, so that you will be astonished. Indeed, just as the Father raises the dead and gives them life, so also the Son gives life to whomever he wishes. The Father judges no one but has given all judgment to the Son, so that all may honor the Son just as they honor the Father. Anyone who does not honor the Son does not honor the Father who sent him. Very truly, I tell you, anyone who hears my word and believes him who sent me has eternal life, and does not come under judgment, but has passed from death to life."

Monday

A Reading (Lesson) from the Book of Genesis [41:46–57]

Joseph was thirty years old when he entered the service of Pharaoh king of Egypt. And Joseph went out from the presence of Pharaoh, and went through all the land of Egypt. During the seven plenteous years the earth produced abundantly. He gathered up all the food of the seven years when there was plenty in the land of Egypt, and stored up food in the cities; he stored up in every city the food from the fields around it. So Joseph stored up grain in such abundance—like the sand of the sea—that he stopped measuring it; it was beyond measure. Before the years of famine came, Joseph had two sons, whom Asenath daughter of Potiphera, priest of On, bore to him. Joseph named the firstborn Manasseh, "For," he said, "God has made me forget all my hardship and all my father's house." The second he named Ephraim, "For God has made me fruitful in the land of my misfortunes." The seven years of plenty that prevailed in the land of Egypt came to an end; and the seven years of famine began to come, just as Joseph had said. There was famine in every country, but throughout the land of Egypt there was bread. When all the land of Egypt was famished, the people cried to Pharaoh for bread. Pharaoh said to all the Egyptians, "Go to Joseph; what he says to you, do." And since the famine had spread over all the land, Joseph opened all the storehouses, and sold to the Egyptians, for the famine was severe in the land of Egypt. Moreover, all the world came to Joseph in Egypt to buy grain, because the famine became severe throughout the world.

A Reading (Lesson) from the First Letter of Paul to the Corinthians [4:8–20(21)]

Already you have all you want! Already you have become rich! Quite apart from us you have become kings! Indeed, I wish that you had become kings, so that we might be kings with you! For I think that God has exhibited us apostles as last of all, as though sentenced to death, because we have become a spectacle to the world, to angels and to mortals. We are fools for the sake of Christ, but you are wise in Christ. We are weak, but you are strong. You are held in honor, but we in disrepute. To the present hour we are hungry and thirsty, we are poorly clothed and beaten and homeless, and we grow weary from the work of our own hands. When reviled, we bless; when persecuted, we endure; when slandered, we speak kindly. We have become like the rubbish of the world, the dregs of all things, to this very day. I am not writing this to make you ashamed, but to admonish you as my beloved children. For though you might have ten thousand guardians in Christ, you do not have many fathers. Indeed, in Christ Jesus I became your father through the gospel. I appeal to you, then, be imitators of me. For this reason I sent you Timothy, who is my beloved and faithful child in the Lord, to remind you of my ways in Christ Jesus, as I teach them everywhere in every church. But some of you, thinking that I am not coming to you, have become arrogant. But I will come to you soon, if the Lord wills, and I will find out not the talk of these arrogant people but their power. For the kingdom of God depends not on talk but on power.

What would you prefer? Am I to come to you with a stick, or with love in a spirit of gentleness?

A Reading (Lesson) from the Gospel according to Mark [3:7–19a]

Jesus departed with his disciples to the sea, and a great multitude from Galilee followed him; hearing all that he was doing, they came to him in great numbers from Judea, Jerusalem, Idumea, beyond the Jordan, and the region around Tyre and Sidon. He told his disciples to have a boat ready for him because of the crowd, so that they would not crush him; for he had cured many, so that all who had diseases pressed upon him to touch him. Whenever the unclean spirits saw him, they fell down before him and shouted, "You are the Son of God!" But he sternly ordered them not to make him known. He went up the mountain and called to him those whom he wanted, and they came to him. And he appointed twelve, whom he also named apostles, to be with him, and to be sent out to proclaim the message, and to have authority to cast out demons. So he appointed the twelve: Simon (to whom he gave the name Peter); James son of Zebedee and John the brother of James (to whom he gave the name Boanerges, that is, Sons of Thunder); and Andrew, and Philip, and Bartholomew, and Matthew, and Thomas, and James son of Alphaeus, and Thaddaeus, and Simon the Cananaean, and Judas Iscariot, who betrayed him.

Tuesday

A Reading (Lesson) from the Book of Genesis [42:1–17]

When Jacob learned that there was grain in Egypt, he said to his sons, "Why do you keep looking at one another? I have heard," he said, "that there is grain in Egypt; go down and buy grain for us there, that we may live and not die." So ten of Joseph's brothers went down to buy grain in Egypt. But Jacob did not send Joseph's brother Benjamin with his brothers, for he feared that harm might come to him. Thus the sons of Israel were among the other people who came to buy grain, for the famine had reached the land of Canaan. Now Joseph was governor over the land; it was he who sold to all the people of the land. And Joseph's brothers came and bowed themselves before him with their faces to the ground. When Joseph saw his brothers, he recognized them, but he treated them like strangers and spoke harshly to them. "Where do you come from?" he said. They said, "From the land of Canaan, to buy food." Although Joseph had recognized his brothers, they did not recognize him. Joseph also remembered the dreams that he had dreamed about them. He said to them, "You are spies; you have come to see the nakedness of the land!" They said to him, "No, my lord; your servants have come to buy food. We are all sons of one man; we are honest men; your servants have never been spies." But he said to them, "No, you have come to see the nakedness of the land!" They said, "We, your servants, are twelve brothers, the sons of a certain man in the land of Canaan; the youngest, however, is now with our father, and one is no more." But Joseph said to them, "It is just as I have said to you: you are spies! Here is how you shall be tested: as Pharaoh lives, you shall not leave this place unless your youngest brother comes here! Let one of you go and bring your brother, while the rest of you remain in prison, in order that your words may be tested, whether there is truth in you; or else, as Pharaoh lives, surely you are spies." And he put them all together in prison for three days.

A Reading (Lesson) from the First Letter of Paul to the Corinthians [5:1–8]

It is actually reported that there is sexual immorality among you, and of a kind that is not found even among pagans; for a man is living with his father's wife. And you are arrogant! Should you not rather have mourned, so that he who has done this would have been removed from among you? For though absent in body, I am present in spirit; and as if present I have already pronounced judgment in the name of the Lord Jesus on the man who has done such a thing. When you are assembled, and my spirit is present with the power of our Lord Jesus, you are to hand this man over to Satan for the destruction of the flesh, so that his spirit may be saved in the day of the Lord. Your boasting is not a good thing. Do you not know that a little yeast leavens the whole batch of dough? Clean out the old yeast so that you may be a new batch, as you really are unleavened. For our paschal lamb, Christ, has been sacrificed. Therefore, let us celebrate the festival, not with the old yeast, the yeast of malice and evil, but with the unleavened bread of sincerity and truth.

A Reading (Lesson) from the Gospel according to Mark [3:19b–35]

Jesus went home; and the crowd came together again, so that they could not even eat. When his family heard it, they went out to restrain him, for people were saying, "He has gone out of his mind." And the scribes who came down from Jerusalem said, "He has Beelzebul, and by the ruler of the demons he casts out demons." And he called them to him, and spoke to them in parables, "How can Satan cast out Satan? If a kingdom is divided against itself, that kingdom cannot stand. And if a house is divided against itself, that house will not be able to stand. And if Satan has risen up against himself and is divided, he cannot stand, but his end has come. But no one can enter a strong man's house and plunder his property without first tying up the strong man; then indeed the house can be plundered. Truly I tell you, people will be forgiven for their sins and whatever blasphemies they utter; but whoever blasphemes against the Holy Spirit can never have forgiveness, but is guilty of an eternal sin"—for they had said, "He has an unclean spirit." Then his mother and his brothers came; and standing outside, they sent to him and called him. A crowd was sitting around him; and they said to him, "Your mother and your brothers and sisters are outside, asking for you." And he replied, "Who are my mother and my brothers?" And looking at those who sat around him, he said, "Here are my mother and my brothers! Whoever does the will of God is my brother and sister and mother."

Wednesday

A Reading (Lesson) from the Book of Genesis [42:18–28]

On the third day Joseph said to his brothers, "Do this and you will live, for I fear God: if you are honest men, let one of your brothers stay here where you are imprisoned. The rest of you shall go and carry grain for the famine of your households, and bring your youngest brother to me. Thus your words will be verified, and you shall not die." And they agreed to do so. They said to one another, "Alas, we are paying the penalty for what we did to our brother; we saw his anguish when he pleaded with us, but we would not listen. That is why this anguish has come upon us." Then Reuben answered them, "Did I not tell you not to wrong the boy? But you would not listen. So now there comes a reckoning for his blood." They did not know that Joseph understood them, since he spoke with them through an interpreter. He turned away from them and wept; then he returned and spoke to them. And he picked out Simeon and had him bound before their eyes. Joseph then gave orders to fill their bags with grain, to return every man's money to his sack, and to give them provisions for their journey. This was done for them. They loaded their donkeys with their grain, and departed. When one of them opened his sack to give his donkey fodder at the lodging place, he saw his money at the top of the sack. He said to his brothers, "My money has been put back; here it is in my sack!" At this they lost heart and turned trembling to one another, saying, "What is this that God has done to us?"

A Reading (Lesson) from the First Letter of Paul to the Corinthians [5:9—6:8]

I wrote to you in my letter not to associate with sexually immoral persons—not at all meaning the immoral of this world, or the greedy and robbers, or idolaters, since you would then need to go out of the world. But now I am writing to you not to associate with anyone who bears the name of brother or sister who is sexually immoral or greedy, or is an idolater, reviler, drunkard, or robber. Do not even eat with such a one. For what have I to do with judging those outside? Is it not those who are inside that you are to judge? God will judge those outside. "Drive out the wicked person from among you." When any of you has a grievance against another, do you dare to take it to court before the unrighteous, instead of taking it before the saints? Do you not know that the saints will judge the world? And if the world is to be judged by you, are you incompetent to try trivial cases? Do you not know that we are to judge angels—to say nothing of ordinary matters? If you have ordinary cases, then, do you appoint as judges those who have no standing in the church? I say this to your shame. Can it be that there is no one among you wise enough to decide between one believer and another, but a believer goes to court against a believer—and before unbelievers at that? In fact, to have lawsuits at all with one another is already a defeat for you. Why not rather be wronged? Why not rather be defrauded? But you yourselves wrong and defraud—and believers at that.

A Reading (Lesson) from the Gospel according to Mark [4:1–20]

Again Jesus began to teach beside the sea. Such a very large crowd gathered around him that he got into a boat on the sea and sat there, while the whole crowd was beside the sea on the land. He began to teach them many things in parables, and in his teaching he said to them: "Listen! A sower went out to sow. And as he sowed, some seed fell on the path, and the birds came and ate it up. Other seed fell on rocky ground, where it did not have much soil, and it sprang up quickly, since it had no depth of soil. And when the sun rose, it was scorched; and since it had no root, it withered away. Other seed fell among thorns, and the thorns grew up and choked it, and it yielded no grain. Other seed fell into good soil and brought forth grain, growing up and increasing and yielding thirty and sixty and a hundredfold." And he said, "Let anyone with ears to hear listen!" When he was alone, those who were around him along with the twelve asked him about the parables. And he said to them, "To you has been given the secret of the kingdom of God, but for those outside, everything comes in parables; in order that 'they may indeed look, but not perceive, and may indeed listen, but not understand; so that they may not turn again and be forgiven.'" And he said to them, "Do you not understand this parable? Then how will you understand all the parables? The sower sows the word. These are the ones on the path where the word is sown: when they hear, Satan immediately comes and takes away the word that is sown in them. And these are the ones sown on rocky ground: when they hear the word, they immediately receive it with joy. But they have no root, and endure only for a while; then, when trouble or persecution arises on account of the word, immediately they fall away. And others are those sown among the thorns: these are the ones who hear the word, but the cares of the world, and the lure of wealth, and the desire for other things come in and choke the word, and it yields nothing. And these are the ones sown on the good soil: they hear the word and accept it and bear fruit, thirty and sixty and a hundredfold."

Thursday

A Reading (Lesson) from the Book of Genesis [42:29–38]

When the brothers of Joseph came to their father Jacob in the land of Canaan, they told him all that had happened to them, saying, "The man, the lord of the land, spoke harshly to us, and charged us with spying on the land. But we said to him, 'We are honest men, we are not spies. We are twelve brothers, sons of our father; one is no more, and the youngest is now with our father in the land of Canaan.' Then the man, the lord of the land, said to us, 'By this I shall know that you are honest men: leave one of your brothers with me, take grain for the famine of your households, and go your way. Bring your youngest brother to me, and I shall know that you are not spies but honest men. Then I will release your brother to you, and you may trade in the land.'"

As they were emptying their sacks, there in each one's sack was his bag of money. When they and their father saw their bundles of money, they were dismayed. And their father Jacob said to them, "I am the one you have bereaved of children: Joseph is no more, and Simeon is no more, and now you would take Benjamin. All this has happened to me!" Then Reuben said to his father, "You may kill my two sons if I do not bring him back to you. Put him in my hands, and I will bring him back to you." But he said, "My son shall not go down with you, for his brother is dead, and he alone is left. If harm should come to him on the journey that you are to make, you would bring down my gray hairs with sorrow to Sheol."

A Reading (Lesson) from the First Letter of Paul to the Corinthians [6:12–20]

"All things are lawful for me," but not all things are beneficial. "All things are lawful for me," but I will not be dominated by anything. "Food is meant for the stomach and the stomach for food," and God will destroy both one and the other. The body is meant not for fornication but for the Lord, and the Lord for the body. And God raised the Lord and will also raise us by his power. Do you not know that your bodies are members of Christ? Should I therefore take the members of Christ and make them members of a prostitute? Never! Do you not know that whoever is united to a prostitute becomes one body with her? For it is said, "The two shall be one flesh." But anyone united to the Lord becomes one spirit with him. Shun fornication! Every sin that a person commits is outside the body; but the fornicator sins against the body itself. Or do you not know that your body is a temple of the Holy Spirit within you, which you have from God, and that you are not your own? For you were bought with a price; therefore glorify God in your body.

A Reading (Lesson) from the Gospel according to Mark [4:21–34]

Jesus said to the disciples, "Is a lamp brought in to be put under the bushel basket, or under the bed, and not on the lampstand? For there is nothing hidden, except to be disclosed; nor is anything secret, except to come to light. Let anyone with ears to hear listen!" And he said to them, "Pay attention to what you hear; the measure you give will be the measure you get, and still more will be given you. For to those who have, more will be given; and from those who have nothing, even what they have will be taken away." He also said, "The kingdom of God is as if someone would scatter seed on the ground, and would sleep and rise night and day, and the seed would sprout and grow, he does not know how. The earth produces of itself, first the stalk, then the head, then the full grain in the head. But when the grain is ripe, at once he goes in with his sickle, because the harvest has come." He also said, "With what can we compare the kingdom of God, or what parable will we use for it? It is like a mustard seed, which, when sown upon the ground, is the smallest of all the seeds on earth; yet when it is sown it grows up and becomes the greatest of all shrubs, and puts forth large branches, so that the birds of the air can make nests in its shade." With many such parables he spoke the word to them, as they were able to hear it; he did not speak to them except in parables, but he explained everything in private to his disciples.

Friday

A Reading (Lesson) from the Book of Genesis [43:1–15]

Now the famine was severe in the land. And when they had eaten up the grain that they had brought from Egypt, their father said to them, "Go again, buy us a little more food." But Judah said to him, "The man solemnly warned us, saying, 'You shall not see my face unless your brother is with you.' If you will send our brother with us, we will go down and buy you food; but if you will not send him, we will not go down, for the man said to us, 'You shall not see my face, unless your brother is with you.'" Israel said, "Why did you treat me so badly as to tell the man that you had another brother?" They replied, "The man questioned us carefully about ourselves and our kindred, saying, 'Is your father still alive? Have you another brother?' What we told him was in answer to these questions. Could we in any way know that he would say, 'Bring your brother down'?" Then Judah said to his father Israel, "Send the boy with me, and let us be on our way, so that we may live and not die—you and we and also our little ones. I myself will be surety for him; you can hold me accountable for him. If I do not bring him back to you and set him before you, then let me bear the blame forever. If we had not delayed, we would now have returned twice." Then their father Israel said to them, "If it must be so, then do this: take some of the choice fruits of the land in your bags, and carry them down as a present to the man—a little balm and a little honey, gum, resin, pistachio nuts, and almonds. Take double the money with you. Carry back with you the money that was returned in the top of your sacks; perhaps it was an oversight. Take your brother also, and be on your way again to the man; may God Almighty grant you mercy before the man, so that he may send back your other brother and Benjamin. As for me, if I am bereaved of my children, I am bereaved." So the men took the present, and they took double the money with them, as well as Benjamin. Then they went on their way down to Egypt, and stood before Joseph.

A Reading (Lesson) from the First Letter of Paul to the Corinthians [7:1–9]

Now concerning the matters about which you wrote: "It is well for a man not to touch a woman." But because of cases of sexual immorality, each man should have his own wife and each woman her own husband. The husband should give to his wife her conjugal rights, and likewise the wife to her husband. For the wife does not have authority over her own body, but the husband does; likewise the husband does not have authority over his own body, but the wife does. Do not deprive one another except perhaps by agreement for a set time, to devote yourselves to prayer, and then come together again, so that Satan may not tempt you because of your lack of self-control. This I say by way of concession, not of command. I wish that all were as I myself am. But each has a particular gift from God, one having one kind and another a different kind. To the unmarried and the widows I say that it is well for them to remain unmarried as I am. But if they are not practicing self-control, they should marry. For it is better to marry than to be aflame with passion.

A Reading (Lesson) from the Gospel according to Mark [4:35–41]

On that day, when evening had come, Jesus said to them, "Let us go across to the other side." And leaving the crowd behind, they took him with them in the boat, just as he was. Other boats were with him. A great windstorm arose, and the waves beat into the boat, so that the boat was already being swamped. But he was in the stern, asleep on the cushion; and they woke him up and said to him, "Teacher, do you not care that we are perishing?" He woke up and rebuked the wind, and said to the sea, "Peace! Be still!" Then the wind ceased, and there was a dead calm. He said to them, "Why are you afraid? Have you still no faith?" And they were filled with great awe and said to one another, "Who then is this, that even the wind and the sea obey him?"

Saturday

A Reading (Lesson) from the Book of Genesis [43:16–34]

When Joseph saw Benjamin with them, he said to the steward of his house, "Bring the men into the house, and slaughter an animal and make ready, for the men are to dine with me at noon." The man did as Joseph said, and brought the men to Joseph's house. Now the men were afraid because they were brought to Joseph's house, and they said, "It is because of the money, replaced in our sacks the first time, that we have been brought in, so that he may have an opportunity to fall upon us, to make slaves of us and take our donkeys." So they went up to the steward of Joseph's house and spoke with him at the entrance to the house. They said, "Oh, my lord, we came down the first time to buy food; and when we came to the lodging place we opened our sacks, and there was each one's money in the top of his sack, our money in full weight. So we have brought it back with us. Moreover we have brought down with us additional money to buy food. We do not know who put our money in our sacks." He replied, "Rest assured, do not be afraid; your God and the God of your father must have put treasure in your sacks for you; I received your money." Then he brought Simeon out to them. When the steward had brought the men into Joseph's house, and given them water, and they had washed their feet, and when he had given their donkeys fodder, they made the present ready for Joseph's coming at noon, for they had heard that they would dine there. When Joseph came home, they brought him the present that they had carried into the house, and bowed to the ground before him. He inquired about their welfare, and said, "Is your father well, the old man of whom you spoke? Is he still alive?" They said, "Your servant our father is well; he is still alive." And they bowed their heads and did obeisance. Then he looked up and saw his brother Benjamin, his mother's son, and said, "Is this your youngest brother, of whom you spoke to me? God be gracious to you, my son!" With that, Joseph hurried out, because he was overcome with affection for his brother, and he was about to weep. So he went into a private room and wept there. Then he washed his face and came out; and controlling himself he said, "Serve the meal." They served him by himself, and them by themselves, and the Egyptians who ate with him by themselves, because the Egyptians could not eat with the Hebrews, for that is an abomination to the Egyptians. When they were seated before him, the firstborn according to his birthright and the youngest according to his youth, the men looked at one another in amazement. Portions were taken to them from Joseph's table, but Benjamin's portion was five times as much as any of theirs. So they drank and were merry with him.

A Reading (Lesson) from the First Letter of Paul to the Corinthians [7:10–24]

To the married I give this command—not I but the Lord—that the wife should not separate from her husband (but if she does separate, let her remain unmarried or else be reconciled to her husband), and that the husband should not divorce his wife. To the rest I say—I and not the Lord—that if any believer has a wife who is an unbeliever, and she consents to live with him, he should not divorce her. And if any woman has a husband who is an unbeliever, and he consents to live with her, she should not divorce him. For the unbelieving husband is made holy through his wife, and the unbelieving wife is made holy through her husband. Otherwise, your children would be unclean, but as it is, they are holy. But if the unbelieving partner separates, let it be so; in such a case the brother or sister is not bound. It is to peace that God has called you. Wife, for all you know, you might save your husband. Husband, for all you know, you might save your wife. However that may be, let each of you lead the life that the Lord has assigned, to which God called you. This is my rule in all the churches. Was anyone at the time of his call already circumcised? Let him not seek to remove the marks of circumcision. Was anyone at the time of his call uncircumcised? Let him not seek circumcision. Circumcision is nothing, and uncircumcision is nothing; but obeying the commandments of God is everything. Let each of you remain in the condition in which you were called. Were you a slave when called? Do not be concerned about it. Even if you can gain your freedom, make use of your present condition now more than ever. For whoever was called in the Lord as a slave is a freed person belonging to the Lord, just as whoever was free when called is a slave of Christ. You were bought with a price; do not become slaves of human masters. In whatever condition you were called, brothers and sisters, there remain with God.

A Reading (Lesson) from the Gospel according to Mark [5:1–20]

Jesus and his disciples came to the other side of the sea, to the country of the Gerasenes. And when he had stepped out of the boat, immediately a man out of the tombs with an unclean spirit met him. He lived among the tombs; and no one could restrain him any more, even with a chain; for he had often been restrained with shackles and chains, but the chains he wrenched apart, and the shackles he broke in pieces; and no one had the strength to subdue him. Night and day among the tombs and on the mountains he was always howling and bruising himself with stones. When he saw Jesus from a distance, he ran and bowed down before him; and he shouted at the top of his voice, "What have you to do with me, Jesus, Son of the Most High God? I adjure you by God, do not torment me." For he had said to him, "Come out of the man, you unclean spirit!" Then Jesus asked him, "What is your name?" He replied, "My name is Legion; for we are many." He begged him earnestly not to send them out of the country. Now there on the hillside a great herd of swine was feeding; and the unclean spirits begged him, "Send us into the swine; let us enter them." So he gave them permission. And the unclean spirits came out and entered the swine; and the herd, numbering about two thousand, rushed down the steep bank into the sea, and were drowned in the sea. The swineherds ran off and told it in the city and in the country. Then people came to see what it was that had happened. They came to Jesus and saw the demoniac sitting there, clothed and in his right mind, the very man who had had the legion; and they were afraid. Those who had seen what had happened to the demoniac and to the swine reported it. Then they began to beg Jesus to leave their neighborhood. As he was getting into the boat, the man who had been possessed by demons begged him that he might be with him. But Jesus refused, and said to him, "Go home to your friends, and tell them how much the Lord has done for you, and what mercy he has shown you." And he went away and began to proclaim in the Decapolis how much Jesus had done for him; and everyone was amazed.

Week of 3 Lent

Sunday

A Reading (Lesson) from the Book of Genesis [44:1–17]

Joseph commanded the steward of his house, "Fill the men's sacks with food, as much as they can carry, and put each man's money in the top of his sack. Put my cup, the silver cup, in the top of the sack of the youngest, with his money for the grain." And he did as Joseph told him. As soon as the morning was light, the men were sent away with their donkeys. When they had gone only a short distance from the city, Joseph said to his steward, "Go, follow after the men; and when you overtake them, say to them, 'Why have you returned evil for good? Why have you stolen my silver cup? Is it not from this that my lord drinks? Does he not indeed use it for divination? You have done wrong in doing this.'" When he overtook them, he repeated these words to them. They said to him, "Why does my lord speak such words as these? Far be it from your servants that they should do such a thing! Look, the money that we found at the top of our sacks, we brought back to you from the land of Canaan; why then would we steal silver or gold from your lord's house? Should it be found with any one of your servants, let him die; moreover the rest of us will become my lord's slaves." He said, "Even so; in accordance with your words, let it be: he with whom it is found shall become my slave, but the rest of you shall go free." Then each one quickly lowered his sack to the ground, and each opened his sack. He searched, beginning with the eldest and ending with the youngest; and the cup was found in Benjamin's sack.

At this they tore their clothes. Then each one loaded his donkey, and they returned to the city. Judah and his brothers came to Joseph's house while he was still there; and they fell to the ground before him. Joseph said to them, "What deed is this that you have done? Do you not know that one such as I can practice divination?" And Judah said, "What can we say to my lord? What can we speak? How can we clear ourselves? God has found out the guilt of your servants; here we are then, my lord's slaves, both we and also the one in whose possession the cup has been found." But he said, "Far be it from me that I should do so! Only the one in whose possession the cup was found shall be my slave; but as for you, go up in peace to your father."

A Reading (Lesson) from the Letter of Paul to the Romans [8:1–10]

There is therefore now no condemnation for those who are in Christ Jesus. For the law of the Spirit of life in Christ Jesus has set you free from the law of sin and of death. For God has done what the law, weakened by the flesh, could not do: by sending his own Son in the likeness of sinful flesh, and to deal with sin, he condemned sin in the flesh, so that the just requirement of the law might be fulfilled in us, who walk not according to the flesh but according to the Spirit. For those who live according to the flesh set their minds on the things of the flesh, but those who live according to the Spirit set their minds on the things of the Spirit. To set the mind on the flesh is death, but to set the mind on the Spirit is life and peace. For this reason the mind that is set on the flesh is hostile to God; it does not submit to God's law— indeed it cannot, and those who are in the flesh cannot please God. But you are not in the flesh; you are in the Spirit, since the Spirit of God dwells in you. Anyone who does not have the Spirit of Christ does not belong to him. But if Christ is in you, though the body is dead because of sin, the Spirit is life because of righteousness.

A Reading (Lesson) from the Gospel according to John [5:25–29]

Jesus said to the Jews, "Very truly, I tell you, the hour is coming, and is now here, when the dead will hear the voice of the Son of God, and those who hear will live. For just as the Father has life in himself, so he has granted the Son also to have life in himself; and he has given him authority to execute judgment, because he is the Son of Man. Do not be astonished at this; for the hour is coming when all who are in their graves will hear his voice and will come out—those who have done good, to the resurrection of life, and those who have done evil, to the resurrection of condemnation."

Monday

A Reading (Lesson) from the Book of Genesis [44:18–34]

Then Judah stepped up to Joseph and said, "O my lord, let your servant please speak a word in my lord's ears, and do not be angry with your servant; for you are like Pharaoh himself. My lord asked his servants, saying, 'Have you a father or a brother?' And we said to my lord, 'We have a father, an old man, and a young brother, the child of his old age. His brother is dead; he alone is left of his mother's children, and his father loves him.' Then you said to your servants, 'Bring him down to me, so that I may set my eyes on him.' We said to my lord, 'The boy cannot leave his father, for if he should leave his father, his father would die.' Then you said to your servants, 'Unless your youngest brother comes down with you, you shall see my face no more.' When we went back to your servant my father we told him the words of my lord. And when our father said, 'Go again, buy us a little food,' we said, 'We cannot go down. Only if our youngest brother goes with us, will we go down; for we cannot see the man's face unless our youngest brother is with us.' Then your servant my father said to us, 'You know that my wife bore me two sons; one left me, and I said, Surely he has been torn to pieces; and I have never seen him since. If you take this one also from me, and harm comes to him, you will bring down my gray hairs in sorrow to Sheol.' Now therefore, when I come to your servant my father and the boy is not with us, then, as his life is bound up in the boy's life, when he sees that the boy is not with us, he will die; and your servants will bring down the gray hairs of your servant our father with sorrow to Sheol. For your servant became surety for the boy to my father, saying, 'If I do not bring him back to you, then I will bear the blame in the sight of my father all my life.' Now therefore, please let your servant remain as a slave to my lord in place of the boy; and let the boy go back with his brothers. For how can I go back to my father if the boy is not with me? I fear to see the suffering that would come upon my father."

A Reading (Lesson) from the First Letter of Paul to the Corinthians [7:25–31]

Now concerning virgins, I have no command of the Lord, but I give my opinion as one who by the Lord's mercy is trustworthy. I think that, in view of the impending crisis, it is well for you to remain as you are. Are you bound to a wife? Do not seek to be free. Are you free from a wife? Do not seek a wife. But if you marry, you do not sin, and if a virgin marries, she does not sin. Yet those who marry will experience distress in this life, and I would spare you that. I mean, brothers and sisters, the appointed time has grown short; from now on, let even those who have wives be as though they had none, and those who mourn as though they were not mourning, and those who rejoice as though they were not rejoicing, and those who buy as though they had no possessions, and those who deal with the world as though they had no dealings with it. For the present form of this world is passing away.

A Reading (Lesson) from the Gospel according to Mark [5:21–43]

When Jesus had crossed again in the boat to the other side, a great crowd gathered around him; and he was by the sea. Then one of the leaders of the synagogue named Jairus came and, when he saw him, fell at his feet and begged him repeatedly, "My little daughter is at the point of death. Come and lay your hands on her, so that she may be made well, and live." So he went with him. And a large crowd followed him and pressed in on him. Now there was a woman who had been suffering from hemorrhages for twelve years. She had endured much under many physicians, and had spent all that she had; and she was no better, but rather grew worse. She had heard about Jesus, and came up behind him in the crowd and touched his cloak, for she said, "If I but touch his clothes, I will be made well." Immediately her hemorrhage stopped; and she felt in her body that she was healed of her disease. Immediately aware that power had gone forth from him, Jesus turned about in the crowd and said, "Who touched my clothes?" And his disciples said to him, "You see the crowd pressing in on you; how can you say, 'Who touched me?'" He looked all around to see who had done it. But the woman, knowing what had happened to her, came in fear and trembling, fell down before him, and told him the whole truth. He said to her, "Daughter, your faith has made you well; go in peace, and be healed of your disease." While he was still speaking, some people came from the leader's house to say, "Your daughter is dead. Why trouble the teacher any further?" But overhearing what they said, Jesus said to the leader of the synagogue, "Do not fear, only believe." He allowed no one to follow him except Peter, James, and John, the brother of James. When they came to the house of the leader of the synagogue, he saw a commotion, people weeping and wailing loudly. When he had entered, he said to them, "Why do you make a commotion and weep? The child is not dead but sleeping." And they laughed at him. Then he put them all outside, and took the child's father and mother and those who were with him, and went in where the child was. He took her by the hand and said to her, "Talitha cum," which means, "Little girl, get up!" And immediately the girl got up and began to walk about (she was twelve years of age). At this they were overcome with amazement. He strictly ordered them that no one should know this, and told them to give her something to eat.

Tuesday

A Reading (Lesson) from the Book of Genesis [45:1–15]

Joseph could no longer control himself before all those who stood by him, and he cried out, "Send everyone away from me." So no one stayed with him when Joseph made himself known to his brothers. And he wept so loudly that the Egyptians heard it, and the household of Pharaoh heard it. Joseph said to his brothers, "I am Joseph. Is my father still alive?" But his brothers could not answer him, so dismayed were they at his presence. Then Joseph said to his brothers, "Come closer to me." And they came closer. He said, "I am your brother, Joseph, whom you sold into Egypt. And now do not be distressed, or angry with yourselves, because you sold me here; for God sent me before you to preserve life. For the famine has been in the land these two years; and there are five more years in which there will be neither plowing nor harvest. God sent me before you to preserve for you a remnant on earth, and to keep alive for you many survivors. So it was not you who sent me here, but God; he has made me a father to Pharaoh, and lord of all his house and ruler over all the land of Egypt. Hurry and go up to my father and say to him, 'Thus says your son Joseph, God has made me lord of all Egypt; come down to me, do not delay. You shall settle in the land of Goshen, and you shall be near me, you and your children and your children's children, as well as your flocks, your herds, and all that you have. I will provide for you there— since there are five more years of famine to come—so that you and your household, and all that you have, will not come to poverty.' And now your eyes and the eyes of my brother Benjamin see that it is my own mouth that speaks to you. You must tell my father how greatly I am honored in Egypt, and all that you have seen. Hurry and bring my father down here." Then he fell upon his brother Benjamin's neck and wept, while Benjamin wept upon his neck. And he kissed all his brothers and wept upon them; and after that his brothers talked with him.

A Reading (Lesson) from the First Letter of Paul to the Corinthians [7:32–40]

I want you to be free from anxieties. The unmarried man is anxious about the affairs of the Lord, how to please the Lord; but the married man is anxious about the affairs of the world, how to please his wife, and his interests are divided. And the unmarried woman and the virgin are anxious about the affairs of the Lord, so that they may be holy in body and spirit; but the married woman is anxious about the affairs of the world, how to please her husband. I say this for your own benefit, not to put any restraint upon you, but to promote good order and unhindered devotion to the Lord. If anyone thinks that he is not behaving properly toward his fiancée, if his passions are strong, and so it has to be, let him marry as he wishes; it is no sin. Let them marry. But if someone stands firm in his resolve, being under no necessity but having his own desire under control, and has determined in his own mind to keep her as his fiancé;e, he will do well. So then, he who marries his fiancée does well; and he who refrains from marriage will do better. A wife is bound as long as her husband lives. But if the husband dies, she is free to marry anyone she wishes, only in the Lord. But in my judgment she is more blessed if she remains as she is. And I think that I too have the Spirit of God.

A Reading (Lesson) from the Gospel according to Mark [6:1–13]

Jesus left that place and came to his hometown, and his disciples followed him. On the sabbath he began to teach in the synagogue, and many who heard him were astounded. They said, "Where did this man get all this? What is this wisdom that has been given to him? What deeds of power are being done by his hands! Is not this the carpenter, the son of Mary and brother of James and Joses and Judas and Simon, and are not his sisters here with us?" And they took offense at him. Then Jesus said to them, "Prophets are not without honor, except in their hometown, and among their own kin, and in their own house." And he could do no deed of power there, except that he laid his hands on a few sick people and cured them. And he was amazed at their unbelief. Then he went about among the villages teaching. He called the twelve and began to send them out two by two, and gave them authority over the unclean spirits. He ordered them to take nothing for their journey except a staff; no bread, no bag, no money in their belts; but to wear sandals and not to put on two tunics. He said to them, "Wherever you enter a house, stay there until you leave the place. If any place will not welcome you and they refuse to hear you, as you leave, shake off the dust that is on your feet as a testimony against them." So they went out and proclaimed that all should repent. They cast out many demons, and anointed with oil many who were sick and cured them.

Wednesday

A Reading (Lesson) from the Book of Genesis [45:16–28]

When the report was heard in Pharaoh's house, "Joseph's brothers have come," Pharaoh and his servants were pleased. Pharaoh said to Joseph, "Say to your brothers, 'Do this: load your animals and go back to the land of Canaan. Take your father and your households and come to me, so that I may give you the best of the land of Egypt, and you may enjoy the fat of the land.' You are further charged to say, 'Do this: take wagons from the land of Egypt for your little ones and for your wives, and bring your father, and come. Give no thought to your possessions, for the best of all the land of Egypt is yours.'" The sons of Israel did so. Joseph gave them wagons according to the instruction of Pharaoh, and he gave them provisions for the journey. To each one of them he gave a set of garments; but to Benjamin he gave three hundred pieces of silver and five sets of garments. To his father he sent the following: ten donkeys loaded with the good things of Egypt, and ten female donkeys loaded with grain, bread, and provision for his father on the journey. Then he sent his brothers on their way, and as they were leaving he said to them, "Do not quarrel along the way." So they went up out of Egypt and came to their father Jacob in the land of Canaan. And they told him, "Joseph is still alive! He is even ruler over all the land of Egypt." He was stunned; he could not believe them. But when they told him all the words of Joseph that he had said to them, and when he saw the wagons that Joseph had sent to carry him, the spirit of their father Jacob revived. Israel said, "Enough! My son Joseph is still alive. I must go and see him before I die."

A Reading (Lesson) from the First Letter of Paul to the Corinthians [8:1–13]

Now concerning food sacrificed to idols: we know that "all of us possess knowledge." Knowledge puffs up, but love builds up. Anyone who claims to know something does not yet have the necessary knowledge; but anyone who loves God is known by him. Hence, as to the eating of food offered to idols, we know that "no idol in the world really exists," and that "there is no God but one." Indeed, even though there may be so-called gods in heaven or on earth—as in fact there are many gods and many lords—yet for us there is one God, the Father, from whom are all things and for whom we exist, and one Lord, Jesus Christ, through whom are all things and through whom we exist. It is not everyone, however, who has this knowledge. Since some have become so accustomed to idols until now, they still think of the food they eat as food offered to an idol; and their conscience, being weak, is defiled. "Food will not bring us close to God." We are no worse off if we do not eat, and no better off if we do. But take care that this liberty of yours does not somehow become a stumbling block to the weak. For if others see you, who possess knowledge, eating in the temple of an idol, might they not, since their conscience is weak, be encouraged to the point of eating food sacrificed to idols? So by your knowledge those weak believers for whom Christ died are destroyed. But when you thus sin against members of your family, and wound their conscience when it is weak, you sin against Christ. Therefore, if food is a cause of their falling, I will never eat meat, so that I may not cause one of them to fall.

A Reading (Lesson) from the Gospel according to Mark [6:13–29]

The twelve cast out many demons, and anointed with oil many that were sick and healed them. King Herod heard of it, for Jesus' name had become known. Some were saying, "John the baptizer has been raised from the dead; and for this reason these powers are at work in him." But others said, "It is Elijah." And others said, "It is a prophet, like one of the prophets of old." But when Herod heard of it, he said, "John, whom I beheaded, has been raised." For Herod himself had sent men who arrested John, bound him, and put him in prison on account of Herodias, his brother Philip's wife, because Herod had married her. For John had been telling Herod, "It is not lawful for you to have your brother's wife." And Herodias had a grudge against him, and wanted to kill him. But she could not, for Herod feared John, knowing that he was a righteous and holy man, and he protected him. When he heard him, he was greatly perplexed; and yet he liked to listen to him. But an opportunity came when Herod on his birthday gave a banquet for his courtiers and officers and for the leaders of Galilee. When his daughter Herodias came in and danced, she pleased Herod and his guests; and the king said to the girl, "Ask me for whatever you wish, and I will give it." And he solemnly swore to her, "Whatever you ask me, I will give you, even half of my kingdom." She went out and said to her mother, "What should I ask for?" She replied, "The head of John the baptizer." Immediately she rushed back to the king and requested, "I want you to give me at once the head of John the Baptist on a platter." The king was deeply grieved; yet out of regard for his oaths and for the guests, he did not want to refuse her. Immediately the king sent a soldier of the guard with orders to bring John's head. He went and beheaded him in the prison, brought his head on a platter, and gave it to the girl. Then the girl gave it to her mother. When his disciples heard about it, they came and took his body, and laid it in a tomb.

Thursday

A Reading (Lesson) from the Book of Genesis [46:1–7,28–34]

When Israel set out on his journey with all that he had and came to Beer–sheba, he offered sacrifices to the God of his father Isaac. God spoke to Israel in visions of the night, and said, "Jacob, Jacob." And he said, "Here I am." Then he said, "I am God, the God of your father;

do not be afraid to go down to Egypt, for I will make of you a great nation there. I myself will go down with you to Egypt, and I will also bring you up again; and Joseph's own hand shall close your eyes." Then Jacob set out from Beer–sheba; and the sons of Israel carried their father Jacob, their little ones, and their wives, in the wagons that Pharaoh had sent to carry him. They also took their livestock and the goods that they had acquired in the land of Canaan, and they came into Egypt, Jacob and all his offspring with him, his sons, and his sons' sons with him, his daughters, and his sons' daughters; all his offspring he brought with him into Egypt. Israel sent Judah ahead to Joseph to lead the way before him into Goshen. When they came to the land of Goshen, Joseph made ready his chariot and went up to meet his father Israel in Goshen. He presented himself to him, fell on his neck, and wept on his neck a good while. Israel said to Joseph, "I can die now, having seen for myself that you are still alive." Joseph said to his brothers and to his father's household, "I will go up and tell Pharaoh, and will say to him, 'My brothers and my father's household, who were in the land of Canaan, have come to me. The men are shepherds, for they have been keepers of livestock; and they have brought their flocks, and their herds, and all that they have.' When Pharaoh calls you, and says, 'What is your occupation?' you shall say, 'Your servants have been keepers of livestock from our youth even until now, both we and our ancestors'—in order that you may settle in the land of Goshen, because all shepherds are abhorrent to the Egyptians."

A Reading (Lesson) from the First Letter of Paul to the Corinthians [9:1–15]

Am I not free? Am I not an apostle? Have I not seen Jesus our Lord? Are you not my work in the Lord? If I am not an apostle to others, at least I am to you; for you are the seal of my apostleship in the Lord. This is my defense to those who would examine me. Do we not have the right to our food and drink? Do we not have the right to be accompanied by a believing wife, as do the other apostles and the brothers of the Lord and Cephas? Or is it only Barnabas and I who have no right to refrain from working for a living? Who at any time pays the expenses for doing military service? Who plants a vineyard and does not eat any of its fruit? Or who tends a flock and does not get any of its milk? Do I say this on human authority? Does not the law also say the same? For it is written in the law of Moses, "You shall not muzzle an ox while it is treading out the grain." Is it for oxen that God is concerned? Or does he not speak entirely for our sake? It was indeed written for our sake, for whoever plows should plow in hope and whoever threshes should thresh in hope of a share in the crop. If we have sown spiritual good among you, is it too much if we reap your material benefits? If others share this rightful claim on you, do not we still more? Nevertheless, we have not made use of this right, but we endure anything rather than put an obstacle in the way of the gospel of Christ. Do you not know that those who are employed in the temple service get their food from the temple, and those who serve at the altar share in what is sacrificed on the altar? In the same way, the Lord commanded that those who proclaim the gospel should get their living by the gospel. But I have made no use of any of these rights, nor am I writing this so that they may be applied in my case. Indeed, I would rather die than that no one will deprive me of my ground for boasting!

A Reading (Lesson) from the Gospel according to Mark [6:30–46]

The apostles gathered around Jesus, and told him all that they had done and taught. He said to them, "Come away to a deserted place all by yourselves and rest a while." For many were coming and going, and they had no leisure even to eat. And they went away in the boat to a deserted place by themselves. Now many saw them going and recognized them, and they hurried there on foot from all the towns and arrived ahead of them. As he went ashore, he saw a great crowd; and he had compassion for them, because they were like sheep without a shepherd; and he began to teach them many things. When it grew late, his disciples came to him and said, "This is a deserted place, and the hour is now very late; send them away so that they may go into the surrounding country and villages and buy something for themselves to eat." But he answered them, "You give them something to eat." They said to him, "Are we to go and buy two hundred denarii worth of bread, and give it to them to eat?" And he said to them, "How many loaves have you? Go and see." When they had found out, they said, "Five, and two fish." Then he ordered them to get all the people to sit down in groups on the green grass. So they sat down in groups of hundreds and of fifties. Taking the five loaves and the two fish, he looked up to heaven, and blessed and broke the loaves, and gave them to his disciples to set before the people; and he divided the two fish among them all. And all ate and were filled; and they took up twelve baskets full of broken pieces and of the fish. Those who had eaten the loaves numbered five thousand men. Immediately he made his disciples get into the boat and go on ahead to the other side, to Bethsaida, while he dismissed the crowd. After saying farewell to them, he went up on the mountain to pray.

Friday

A Reading (Lesson) from the Book of Genesis [47:1–26]

So Joseph went and told Pharaoh, "My father and my brothers, with their flocks and herds and all that they possess, have come from the land of Canaan; they are now in the land of Goshen." From among his brothers he took five men and presented them to Pharaoh. Pharaoh said to his brothers, "What is your occupation?" And they said to Pharaoh, "Your servants are shepherds, as our ancestors were." They said to Pharaoh, "We have come to reside as aliens in the land; for there is no pasture for your servants' flocks because the famine is severe in the land of Canaan. Now, we ask you, let your servants settle in the land of Goshen." Then Pharaoh said to Joseph, "Your father and your brothers have come to you. The land of Egypt is before you; settle your father and your brothers in the best part of the land; let them live in the land of Goshen; and if you know that there are capable men among them, put them in charge of my livestock." Then Joseph brought in his father Jacob, and presented him before Pharaoh, and Jacob blessed Pharaoh. Pharaoh said to Jacob, "How many are the years of your life?" Jacob said to Pharaoh, "The years of my earthly sojourn are one hundred thirty; few and hard have been the years of my life. They do not compare with the years of the life of my ancestors during their long sojourn." Then Jacob blessed Pharaoh, and went out from the presence of Pharaoh. Joseph settled his father and his brothers, and granted them a holding in the land of Egypt, in the best part of the land, in the land of Rameses, as Pharaoh had instructed. And Joseph provided his father, his brothers, and all his father's household with food, according to the number of their dependents. Now there was no food in all the land, for the famine was very severe. The land of Egypt and the land of Canaan languished because of the famine. Joseph collected all the money to be found in the land of Egypt and in the land of Canaan, in exchange for the grain that they bought; and Joseph brought the money into Pharaoh's house. When the money from the land of Egypt and from the land of Canaan was spent, all the Egyptians came to Joseph, and said, "Give us food! Why should we die before your eyes? For our money is gone." And Joseph answered, "Give me your livestock, and I will give you food in exchange for your livestock, if your money is gone." So they brought their livestock to Joseph; and Joseph gave them food in exchange for the horses, the flocks, the herds, and the donkeys. That year he supplied them with food in exchange for all their livestock. When that year was ended, they came to him the following year, and said to him, "We can not hide from my lord that our money is all spent; and the herds of cattle are my lord's. There is nothing left in the sight of my lord but our bodies and our lands. Shall we die before your eyes, both we and our land? Buy us and our land in exchange for food. We with our land will become slaves to Pharaoh; just give us seed, so that we may live and not die, and that the land may not become desolate." So Joseph bought all the land of Egypt for Pharaoh. All the Egyptians sold their fields, because the famine was severe upon them; and the land became

Pharaoh's. As for the people, he made slaves of them from one end of Egypt to the other. Only the land of the priests he did not buy; for the priests had a fixed allowance from Pharaoh, and lived on the allowance that Pharaoh gave them; therefore they did not sell their land. Then Joseph said to the people, "Now that I have this day bought you and your land for Pharaoh, here is seed for you; sow the land. And at the harvests you shall give one–fifth to Pharaoh, and four–fifths shall be your own, as seed for the field and as food for yourselves and your households, and as food for your little ones." They said, "You have saved our lives; may it please my lord, we will be slaves to Pharaoh." So Joseph made it a statute concerning the land of Egypt, and it stands to this day, that Pharaoh should have the fifth. The land of the priests alone did not become Pharaoh's.

A Reading (Lesson) from the First Letter of Paul to the Corinthians [9:16–27]

If I proclaim the gospel, this gives me no ground for boasting, for an obligation is laid on me, and woe to me if I do not proclaim the gospel! For if I do this of my own will, I have a reward; but if not of my own will, I am entrusted with a commission. What then is my reward? Just this: that in my proclamation I may make the gospel free of charge, so as not to make full use of my rights in the gospel. For though I am free with respect to all, I have made myself a slave to all, so that I might win more of them. To the Jews I became as a Jew, in order to win Jews. To those under the law I became as one under the law (though I myself am not under the law) so that I might win those under the law. To those outside the law I became as one outside the law (though I am not free from God's law but am under Christ's law) so that I might win those outside the law. To the weak I became weak, so that I might win the weak. I have become all things to all people, that I might by all means save some. I do it all for the sake of the gospel, so that I may share in its blessings. Do you not know that in a race the runners all compete, but only one receives the prize? Run in such a way that you may win it. Athletes exercise self-control in all things; they do it to receive a perishable wreath, but we an imperishable one. So I do not run aimlessly, nor do I box as though beating the air; but I punish my body and enslave it, so that after proclaiming to others I myself should not be disqualified.

A Reading (Lesson) from the Gospel according to Mark [6:47–56]

When evening came, the boat was out on the sea, and Jesus was alone on the land. When he saw that they were straining at the oars against an adverse wind, he came towards them early in the morning, walking on the sea. He intended to pass them by. But when they saw him walking on the sea, they thought it was a ghost and cried out; for they all saw him and were terrified. But immediately he spoke to them and said, "Take heart, it is I; do not be afraid." Then he got into the boat with them and the wind ceased. And they were utterly astounded, for they did not understand about the loaves, but their hearts were hardened. When they had crossed over, they came to land at Gennesaret and moored the boat. When they got out of the boat, people at once recognized him, and rushed about that whole region and began to bring the sick on mats to wherever they heard he was. And wherever he went, into villages or cities or farms, they laid the sick in the marketplaces, and begged him that they might touch even the fringe of his cloak; and all who touched it were healed.

Saturday

A Reading (Lesson) from the Book of Genesis [47:27–48:7]

Thus Israel settled in the land of Egypt, in the region of Goshen; and they gained possessions in it, and were fruitful and multiplied exceedingly. Jacob lived in the land of Egypt seventeen years; so the days of Jacob, the years of his life, were one hundred forty–seven years. When the time of Israel's death drew near, he called his son Joseph and said to him, "If I have found favor with you, put your hand under my thigh and promise to deal loyally and truly with me. Do not bury me in Egypt. When I lie down with my ancestors, carry me out of Egypt and bury me in their burial place." He answered, "I will do as you have said." And he said, "Swear to me"; and he swore to him. Then Israel bowed himself on the head of his bed. After this Joseph was told, "Your father is ill." So he took with him his two sons, Manasseh and Ephraim. When Jacob was told, "Your son Joseph has come to you," he summoned his strength and sat up in bed. And Jacob said to Joseph, "God Almighty appeared to me at Luz in the land of Canaan, and he blessed me, and said to me, 'I am going to make you fruitful and increase your numbers; I will make of you a company of peoples, and will give this land to your offspring after you for a perpetual holding.' Therefore your two sons, who were born to you in the land of Egypt before I came to you in Egypt, are now mine; Ephraim and Manasseh shall be mine, just as Reuben and Simeon are. As for the offspring born to you after them, they shall be yours. They shall be recorded under the names of their brothers with regard to their inheritance. For when I came from Paddan, Rachel, alas, died in the land of Canaan on the way, while there was still some distance to go to Ephrath; and I buried her there on the way to Ephrath" (that is, Bethlehem).

A Reading (Lesson) from the First Letter of Paul to the Corinthians [10:1–13]

I do not want you to be unaware, brothers and sisters, that our ancestors were all under the cloud, and all passed through the sea, and all were baptized into Moses in the cloud and in the sea, and all ate the same spiritual food, and all drank the same spiritual drink. For they drank from the spiritual rock that followed them, and the rock was Christ. Nevertheless, God was not pleased with most of them, and they were struck down in the wilderness. Now these things occurred as examples for us, so that we might not desire evil as they did. Do not become idolaters as some of them did; as it is written, "The people sat down to eat and drink, and they rose up to play." We must not indulge in sexual immorality as some of them did, and twenty–three thousand fell in a single day. We must not put Christ to the test, as some of them did, and were destroyed by serpents. And do not complain as some of them did, and were destroyed by the destroyer. These things happened to them to serve as an example, and they were written down to instruct us, on whom the ends of the ages have come. So if you think you are standing, watch out that you do not fall. No testing has overtaken you that is not common to everyone. God is faithful, and he will not let you be tested beyond your strength, but with the testing he will also provide the way out so that you may be able to endure it.

A Reading (Lesson) from the Gospel according to Mark [7:1–23]

Now when the Pharisees and some of the scribes who had come from Jerusalem gathered around Jesus, they noticed that some of his disciples were eating with defiled hands, that is, without washing them. (For the Pharisees, and all the Jews, do not eat unless they thoroughly wash their hands, thus observing the tradition of the elders; and they do not eat anything from the market unless they wash it; and there are also many other traditions that they observe, the washing of cups, pots, and bronze kettles.) So the Pharisees and the scribes asked him, "Why do your disciples not live according to the tradition of the elders, but eat with defiled hands?" He said to them, "Isaiah prophesied rightly about you hypocrites, as it is written, 'This people honors me with their lips, but their hearts are far from me; in vain do they worship me, teaching human precepts as doctrines.' You abandon the commandment of God and hold to human tradition." Then he said to them, "You have a fine way of rejecting the commandment of God in order to keep your tradition! For Moses said, 'Honor your father and mother'; and, 'Whoever speaks evil of father or mother must surely die.' But you say that if anyone tells father or mother, 'Whatever support you might have had from me is Corban' (that is, an offering to God)—then you no longer permit doing anything for a father or mother, thus making void the word of God through your tradition that you have handed on. And you do many things like this." Then he called the crowd again and said to them, "Listen to me, all of you, and understand: there is nothing outside a person that by going in can defile, but the things that come out are what defile." When he had left the crowd and entered the house, his disciples asked him about the parable. He said to them, "Then do you also fail to understand? Do you not see that whatever goes into a person from outside cannot defile, since it enters, not the heart but the stomach, and goes out into the sewer?" (Thus he declared all foods clean.) And he said, "It is what comes out of a person that defiles. For it is from within, from the human heart, that evil intentions come: fornication, theft, murder, adultery, avarice, wickedness, deceit, licentiousness, envy, slander, pride, folly. All these evil things come from within, and they defile a person."

Week of 4 Lent

Sunday

A Reading (Lesson) from the Book of Genesis [48:8–22]

When Israel saw Joseph's sons, he said, "Who are these?" Joseph said to his father, "They are my sons, whom God has given me here." And he said, "Bring them to me, please, that I may bless them." Now the eyes of Israel were dim with age, and he could not see well. So Joseph brought them near him; and he kissed them and embraced them. Israel said to Joseph, "I did not expect to see your face; and here God has let me see your children also." Then Joseph removed them from his father's knees, and he bowed himself with his face to the earth. Joseph took them both, Ephraim in his right hand toward Israel's left, and Manasseh in his left hand toward Israel's right, and brought them near him. But Israel stretched out his right hand and laid it on the head of Ephraim, who was the younger, and his left hand on the head of Manasseh, crossing his hands, for Manasseh was the firstborn. He blessed Joseph, and said, "The God before whom my ancestors Abraham and Isaac walked, the God who has been my shepherd all my life to this day, the angel who has redeemed me from all harm, bless the boys; and in them let my name be perpetuated, and the name of my ancestors Abraham and Isaac; and let them grow into a multitude on the earth." When Joseph saw that his father laid his right hand on the head of Ephraim, it displeased him; so he took his father's hand, to remove it from Ephraim's head to Manasseh's head. Joseph said to his father, "Not so, my father! Since this one is the firstborn, put your right hand on his head." But his father refused, and said, "I know, my son, I know; he also shall become a people, and he also shall be great. Nevertheless his younger brother shall be greater than he, and his offspring shall become a multitude of nations." So he blessed them that day, saying, "By you Israel will invoke blessings, saying, 'God make you like Ephraim and like Manasseh.'" So he put Ephraim ahead of Manasseh. Then Israel said to Joseph, "I am about to die, but God will be with you and will bring you again to the land of your ancestors. I now give to you one portion more than to your brothers, the portion that I took from the hand of the Amorites with my sword and with my bow."

A Reading (Lesson) from the Letter of Paul to the Romans [8:11–25]

If the Spirit of him who raised Jesus from the dead dwells in you, he who raised Christ from the dead will give life to your mortal bodies also through his Spirit that dwells in you. So then, brothers and sisters, we are debtors, not to the flesh, to live according to the flesh—for if you live according to the flesh, you will die; but if by the Spirit you put to death the deeds of the body, you will live. For all who are led by the Spirit of God are children of God. For you did not receive a spirit of slavery to fall back into fear, but you have received a spirit of adoption. When we cry, "Abba! Father!" it is that very Spirit bearing witness with our spirit that we are children of God, and if children, then heirs, heirs of God and joint heirs with Christ—if, in fact, we suffer with him so that we may also be glorified with him. I consider that the sufferings of this present time are not worth comparing with the glory about to be revealed to us. For the creation waits with eager longing for the revealing of the children of God; for the creation was subjected to futility, not of its own will but by the will of the one who subjected it, in hope that the creation itself will be set free from its bondage to decay and will obtain the freedom of the glory of the children of God. We know that the whole creation has been groaning in labor pains until now; and not only the creation, but we ourselves, who have the first fruits of the Spirit, groan inwardly while we wait for adoption, the redemption of our bodies. For in hope we were saved. Now hope that is seen is not hope. For who hopes for what is seen? But if we hope for what we do not see, we wait for it with patience.

A Reading (Lesson) from the Gospel according to John [6:27–40]

Jesus said to the people, "Do not work for the food that perishes, but for the food that endures for eternal life, which the Son of Man will give you. For it is on him that God the Father has set his seal." Then they said to him, "What must we do to perform the works of God?" Jesus answered them, "This is the work of God, that you believe in him whom he has sent." So they said to him, "What sign are you going to give us then, so that we may see it and believe you? What work are you performing? Our ancestors ate the manna in the wilderness; as it is written, 'He gave them bread from heaven to eat.'" Then Jesus said to them, "Very truly, I tell you, it was not Moses who gave you the bread from heaven, but it is my Father who gives you the true bread from heaven. For the bread of God is that which comes down from heaven and gives life to the world." They said to him, "Sir, give us this bread always." Jesus said to them, "I am the bread of life. Whoever comes to me will never be hungry, and whoever believes in me will never be thirsty. But I said to you that you have seen me and yet do not believe. Everything that the Father gives me will come to me, and anyone who comes to me I will never drive away; for I have come down from heaven, not to do my own will, but the will of him who sent me. And this is the will of him who sent me, that I should lose nothing of all that he has given me, but raise it up on the last day. This is indeed the will of my Father, that all who see the Son and believe in him may have eternal life; and I will raise them up on the last day."

Monday

A Reading (Lesson) from the Book of Genesis [49:1–28]

Then Jacob called his sons, and said: "Gather around, that I may tell you what will happen to you in days to come. Assemble and hear, O sons of Jacob; listen to Israel your father. Reuben, you are my first-born, my might and the first fruits of my vigor, excelling in rank and excelling in power. Unstable as water, you shall no longer excel because you went up onto your father's bed; then you defiled it—you went up onto my couch! Simeon and Levi are brothers; weapons of violence are their swords. May I never come into their council; may I not be joined to their company— for in their anger they killed men, and at their whim they hamstrung oxen. Cursed be their anger, for it is fierce, and their wrath, for it is cruel! I will divide them in Jacob, and scatter them in Israel. Judah, your brothers shall praise you; your hand shall be on the neck of your enemies; your father's sons shall bow down before you. Judah is a lion's whelp; from the prey, my son, you have gone up. He crouches down, he stretches out like a lion, like a lioness—who dares rouse him up? The scepter shall not depart from Judah, nor the ruler's staff from between his feet, until tribute comes to him; and the obedience of the peoples is his. Binding his foal to the vine and his donkey's colt to the choice vine, he washes his garments in wine and his robe in the blood of grapes; his eyes are darker than wine, and his teeth whiter than milk. Zebulun shall settle at the shore of the sea; he shall be a haven for ships, and his border shall be at Sidon. Issachar is a strong donkey, lying down between the sheepfolds; he saw that a resting place was good, and that the land was pleasant; so he bowed his shoulder to the burden, and became a slave at forced labor. Dan shall judge his people as one of the tribes of Israel. Dan shall be a snake by the roadside, a viper along the path, that bites the horse's heels so that its rider falls backward. I wait for your salvation, O LORD. Gad shall be raided by raiders, but he shall raid at their heels. Asher's food shall be rich, and he shall provide royal delicacies. Naphtali is a doe let loose that bears lovely fawns. Joseph is a fruitful bough, a fruitful bough by a spring; his branches run over the wall. The archers fiercely attacked him; they shot at him and pressed him hard. Yet his bow remained taut, and his arms were made agile by the hands of the Mighty One of Jacob, by the name of the Shepherd, the Rock of Israel, by the God of your father, who will help you, by the Almighty who will bless you with blessings of heaven above, blessings of the deep that lies beneath, blessings of the breasts and of the womb. The blessings of your father are stronger than the blessings of the eternal mountains, the bounties of the everlasting hills; may they be on the head of Joseph, on the brow of him who was set apart from his brothers. Benjamin is a ravenous wolf, in the morning devouring the prey, and at evening dividing the spoil." All these are the twelve tribes of Israel, and this is what their father said to them when he blessed them, blessing each one of them with a suitable blessing.

A Reading (Lesson) from the First Letter of Paul to the Corinthians [10:14 — 11:1]

Therefore, my dear friends, flee from the worship of idols. I speak as to sensible people; judge for yourselves what I say. The cup of blessing that we bless, is it not a sharing in the blood of Christ? The bread that we break, is it not a sharing in the body of Christ? Because there is one bread, we who are many are one body, for we all partake of the one bread. Consider the people of Israel; are not those who eat the sacrifices partners in the altar? What do I imply then? That food sacrificed to idols is anything, or that an idol is anything? No, I imply that what pagans sacrifice, they sacrifice to demons and not to God. I do not want you to be partners with demons. You cannot drink the cup of the Lord and the cup of demons. You cannot partake of the table of the Lord and the table of demons. Or are we provoking the Lord to jealousy? Are we stronger than he? "All things are lawful," but not all things are beneficial. "All things are lawful," but not all things build up. Do not seek your own advantage, but that of the other. Eat whatever is sold in the meat market without raising any question on the ground of conscience, for "the earth and its fullness are the Lord's." If an unbeliever invites you to a meal and you are disposed to go, eat whatever is set before you without raising any question on the ground of conscience. But if someone says to you, "This has been offered in sacrifice," then do not eat it, out of consideration for the one who informed you, and for the sake of conscience—I mean the other's conscience, not your own. For why should my liberty be subject to the judgment of someone else's conscience? If I partake with thankfulness, why should I be denounced because of that for which I give thanks? So, whether you eat or drink, or whatever you do, do everything for the glory of God. Give no offense to Jews or to Greeks or to the church of God, just as I try to please everyone in everything I do, not seeking my own advantage, but that of many, so that they may be saved. Be imitators of me, as I am of Christ.

A Reading (Lesson) from the Gospel according to Mark [7:24–37]

From Gennesaret Jesus set out and went away to the region of Tyre. He entered a house and did not want anyone to know he was there. Yet he could not escape notice, but a woman whose little daughter had an unclean spirit immediately heard about him, and she came and bowed down at his feet. Now the woman was a Gentile, of Syrophoenician origin. She begged him to cast the demon out of her daughter. He said to her, "Let the children be fed first, for it is not fair to take the children's food and throw it to the dogs." But she answered him, "Sir, even the dogs under the table eat the children's crumbs." Then he said to her, "For saying that, you may go—the demon has left your daughter." So she went home, found the child lying on the bed, and the demon gone. Then he returned from the region of Tyre, and went by way of Sidon towards the Sea of Galilee, in the region of the Decapolis. They brought to him a deaf man who had an impediment in his speech; and they begged him to lay his hand on him. He took him aside in private, away from the crowd, and put his fingers into his ears, and he spat and touched his tongue. Then looking up to heaven, he sighed and said to him, "Ephphatha," that is, "Be opened." And immediately his ears were opened, his tongue was released, and he spoke plainly. Then Jesus ordered them to tell no one; but the more he ordered them, the more zealously they proclaimed it. They were astounded beyond measure, saying, "He has done everything well; he even makes the deaf to hear and the mute to speak."

Tuesday

A Reading (Lesson) from the Book of Genesis [49:29 — 50:14]

Then Israel charged his sons, saying to them, "I am about to be gathered to my people. Bury me with my ancestors—in the cave in the field of Ephron the Hittite, in the cave in the field at Machpelah, near Mamre, in the land of Canaan, in the field that Abraham bought from Ephron the Hittite as a burial site. There Abraham and his wife Sarah were buried; there Isaac and his wife Rebekah were buried; and there I buried Leah—the field and the cave that is in it were purchased from the Hittites." When Jacob ended his charge to his sons, he drew up his feet into the bed, breathed his last, and was gathered to his people. Then Joseph threw himself on his father's face and wept over him and kissed him. Joseph commanded the physicians in his service to embalm his father. So the physicians embalmed Israel; they spent forty days in doing this, for that is the time required for embalming. And the Egyptians wept for him seventy days. When the days of weeping for him were past, Joseph addressed the household of Pharaoh, "If now I have found favor with you, please speak to Pharaoh as follows: My father made me swear an oath; he said, 'I am about to die. In the tomb that I hewed out for myself in the land of Canaan, there you shall bury me.' Now therefore let me go up, so that I may bury my father; then I will return." Pharaoh answered, "Go up, and bury your father, as he made you swear to do." So Joseph went up to bury his father. With him went up all the servants of Pharaoh, the elders of his household, and all the elders of the land of Egypt, as well as all the household of Joseph, his brothers, and his father's household. Only their children, their flocks, and their herds were left in the land of Goshen. Both chariots and charioteers went up with him. It was a very great company. When they came to the threshing floor of Atad, which is beyond the Jordan, they held there a very great and sorrowful lamentation; and he observed a time of mourning for his father seven days. When the Canaanite inhabitants of the land saw the mourning on the threshing floor of Atad, they said, "This is a grievous mourning on the part of the Egyptians." Therefore the place was named Abel-mizraim; it is beyond the Jordan. Thus his sons did for him as he had instructed them. They carried him to the land of Canaan and buried him in the cave of the field at Machpelah, the field near Mamre, which Abraham bought as a burial site from Ephron the Hittite. After he had buried his father, Joseph returned to Egypt with his brothers and all who had gone up with him to bury his father.

A Reading (Lesson) from the First Letter of Paul to the Corinthians [11:17–34]

Now in the following instructions I do not commend you, because when you come together it is not for the better but for the worse. For, to begin with, when you come together as a church, I hear that there are divisions among you; and to some extent I believe it. Indeed, there have to be factions among you, for only so will it become clear who among you are genuine. When you come together, it is not really to eat the Lord's supper. For when the time comes to eat, each of you goes ahead with your own supper, and one goes hungry and another becomes drunk. What! Do you not have homes to eat and drink in? Or do you show contempt for the church of God and humiliate those who have nothing? What should I say to you? Should I commend you? In this matter I do not commend you! For I received from the Lord what I also handed on to you, that the Lord Jesus on the night when he was betrayed took a loaf of bread, and when he had given thanks, he broke it and said, "This is my body that is for you. Do this in remembrance of me." In the same way he took the cup also, after supper, saying, "This cup is the new covenant in my blood. Do this, as often as you drink it, in remembrance of me." For as often as you eat this bread and drink the cup, you proclaim the Lord's death until he comes. Whoever, therefore, eats the bread or drinks the cup of the Lord in an unworthy manner will be answerable for the body and blood of the Lord. Examine yourselves, and only then eat of the bread and drink of the cup. For all who eat and drink without discerning the body, eat and drink judgment against themselves. For this reason many of you are weak and ill, and some have died. But if we judged ourselves, we would not be judged. But when we are judged by the Lord, we are disciplined so that we may not be condemned along with the world. So then, my brothers and sisters, when you come together to eat, wait for one another. If you are hungry, eat at home, so that when you come together, it will not be for your condemnation. About the other things I will give instructions when I come.

A Reading (Lesson) from the Gospel according to Mark [8:1–10]

In those days when there was again a great crowd without anything to eat, he called his disciples and said to them, "I have compassion for the crowd, because they have been with me now for three days and have nothing to eat. If I send them away hungry to their homes, they will faint on the way—and some of them have come from a great distance."

His disciples replied, "How can one feed these people with bread here in the desert?" He asked them, "How many loaves do you have?" They said, "Seven." Then he ordered the crowd to sit down on the ground; and he took the seven loaves, and after giving thanks he broke them and gave them to his disciples to distribute; and they distributed them to the crowd. They had also a few small fish; and after blessing them, he ordered that these too should be distributed. They ate and were filled; and they took up the broken pieces left over, seven baskets full. Now there were about four thousand people. And he sent them away. And immediately he got into the boat with his disciples and went to the district of Dalmanutha.

Wednesday

A Reading (Lesson) from the Book of Genesis [50:15–26]

Realizing that their father was dead, Joseph's brothers said, "What if Joseph still bears a grudge against us and pays us back in full for all the wrong that we did to him?" So they approached Joseph, saying, "Your father gave this instruction before he died, 'Say to Joseph: I beg you, forgive the crime of your brothers and the wrong they did in harming you.' Now therefore please forgive the crime of the servants of the God of your father." Joseph wept when they spoke to him. Then his brothers also wept, fell down before him, and said, "We are here as your slaves." But Joseph said to them, "Do not be afraid! Am I in the place of God? Even though you intended to do harm to me, God intended it for good, in order to preserve a numerous people, as he is doing today. So have no fear; I myself will provide for you and your little ones." In this way he reassured them, speaking kindly to them. So Joseph remained in Egypt, he and his father's household; and Joseph lived one hundred ten years. Joseph saw Ephraim's children of the third generation; the children of Machir son of Manasseh were also born on Joseph's knees. Then Joseph said to his brothers, "I am about to die; but God will surely come to you, and bring you up out of this land to the land that he swore to Abraham, to Isaac, and to Jacob." So Joseph made the Israelites swear, saying, "When God comes to you, you shall carry up my bones from here." And Joseph died, being one hundred ten years old; he was embalmed and placed in a coffin in Egypt.

A Reading (Lesson) from the First Letter of Paul to the Corinthians [12:1–11]

Now concerning spiritual gifts, brothers and sisters, I do not want you to be uninformed. You know that when you were pagans, you were enticed and led astray to idols that could not speak. Therefore I want you to understand that no one speaking by the Spirit of God ever says "Let Jesus be cursed!" and no one can say "Jesus is Lord" except by the Holy Spirit. Now there are varieties of gifts, but the same Spirit; and there are varieties of services, but the same Lord; and there are varieties of activities, but it is the same God who activates all of them in everyone. To each is given the manifestation of the Spirit for the common good. To one is given through the Spirit the utterance of wisdom, and to another the utterance of knowledge according to the same Spirit, to another faith by the same Spirit, to another gifts of healing by the one Spirit, to another the working of miracles, to another prophecy, to another the discernment of spirits, to another various kinds of tongues, to another the interpretation of tongues. All these are activated by one and the same Spirit, who allots to each one individually just as the Spirit chooses.

A Reading (Lesson) from the Gospel according to Mark [8:11–26]

The Pharisees came and began to argue with Jesus, asking him for a sign from heaven, to test him. And he sighed deeply in his spirit and said, "Why does this generation ask for a sign? Truly I tell you, no sign will be given to this generation." And he left them, and getting into the boat again, he went across to the other side. Now the disciples had forgotten to bring any bread; and they had only one loaf with them in the boat. And he cautioned them, saying, "Watch out—beware of the yeast of the Pharisees and the yeast of Herod." They said to one another, "It is because we have no bread." And becoming aware of it, Jesus said to them, "Why are you talking about having no bread? Do you still not perceive or understand? Are your hearts hardened? Do you have eyes, and fail to see? Do you have ears, and fail to hear? And do you not remember? When I broke the five loaves for the five thousand, how many baskets full of broken pieces did you collect?" They said to him, "Twelve." "And the seven for the four thousand, how many baskets full of broken pieces did you collect?" And they said to him, "Seven." Then he said to them, "Do you not yet understand?" They came to Bethsaida. Some people brought a blind man to him and begged him to touch him. He took the blind man by the hand and led him out of the village; and when he had put saliva on his eyes and laid his hands on him, he asked him, "Can you see anything?" And the man looked up and said, "I can see people, but they look like trees, walking." Then Jesus laid his hands on his eyes again; and he looked intently and his sight was restored, and he saw everything clearly. Then he sent him away to his home, saying, "Do not even go into the village."

Thursday

A Reading (Lesson) from the Book of Exodus [1:6–22]

Joseph died, and all his brothers, and that whole generation. But the Israelites were fruitful and prolific; they multiplied and grew exceedingly strong, so that the land was filled with them. Now a new king arose over Egypt, who did not know Joseph. He said to his people, "Look, the Israelite people are more numerous and more powerful than we. Come, let us deal shrewdly with them, or they will increase and, in the event of war, join our enemies and fight against us and escape from the land." Therefore they set taskmasters over them to oppress them with forced labor. They built supply cities, Pithom and Rameses, for Pharaoh. But the more they were oppressed, the more they multiplied and spread, so that the Egyptians came to dread the Israelites. The Egyptians became ruthless in imposing tasks on the Israelites, and made their lives bitter with hard service in mortar and brick and in every kind of field labor. They were ruthless in all the tasks that they imposed on them. The king of Egypt said to the Hebrew midwives, one of whom was named Shiphrah and the other Puah, "When you act as midwives to the Hebrew women, and see them on the birthstool, if it is a boy, kill him; but if it is a girl, she shall live." But the midwives feared God; they did not do as the king of Egypt commanded them, but they let the boys live. So the king of Egypt summoned the midwives and said to them, "Why have you done this, and allowed the boys to live?" The midwives said to Pharaoh, "Because the Hebrew women are not like the Egyptian women; for they are vigorous and give birth before the midwife comes to them." So God dealt well with the midwives; and the people multiplied and became very strong. And because the midwives feared God, he gave them families. Then Pharaoh commanded all his people, "Every boy that is born to the Hebrews you shall throw into the Nile, but you shall let every girl live."

A Reading (Lesson) from the First Letter of Paul to the Corinthians [12:12–26]

Just as the body is one and has many members, and all the members of the body, though many, are one body, so it is with Christ. For in the one Spirit we were all baptized into one body—Jews or Greeks, slaves or free—and we were all made to drink of one Spirit. Indeed, the body does not consist of one member but of many. If the foot would say, "Because I am not a hand, I do not belong to the body," that would not make it any less a part of the body. And if the ear would say, "Because I am not an eye, I do not belong to the body," that would not make it any less a part of the body. If the whole body were an eye, where would the hearing be? If the whole body were hearing, where would the sense of smell be? But as it is, God arranged the members in the body, each one of them, as he chose. If all were a single member, where would the body be? As it is, there are many members, yet one body. The eye cannot say to the hand, "I have no need of you," nor again the head to the feet, "I have no need of you." On the contrary, the members of the body that seem to be weaker are indispensable, and those members of the body that we think less honorable we clothe with greater honor, and our less respectable members are treated with greater respect; whereas our more respectable members do not need this. But God has so arranged the body, giving the greater honor to the inferior member, that there may be no dissension within the body, but the members may have the same care for one another. If one member suffers, all suffer together with it; if one member is honored, all rejoice together with it.

A Reading (Lesson) from the Gospel according to Mark [8:27—9:1]

Jesus went on with his disciples to the villages of Caesarea Philippi; and on the way he asked his disciples, "Who do people say that I am?" And they answered him, "John the Baptist; and others, Elijah; and still others, one of the prophets." He asked them, "But who do you say that I am?" Peter answered him, "You are the Messiah." And he sternly ordered them not to tell anyone about him. Then he began to teach them that the Son of Man must undergo great suffering, and be rejected by the elders, the chief priests, and the scribes, and be killed, and after three days rise again. He said all this quite openly. And Peter took him aside and began to rebuke him. But turning and looking at his disciples, he rebuked Peter and said, "Get behind me, Satan! For you are setting your mind not on divine things but on human things." He called the crowd with his disciples, and said to them, "If any want to become my followers, let them deny themselves and take up their cross and follow me. For those who want to save their life will lose it, and those who lose their life for my sake, and for the sake of the gospel, will save it. For what will it profit them to gain the whole world and forfeit their life? Indeed, what can they give in return for their life? Those who are ashamed of me and of my words in this adulterous and sinful generation, of them the Son of Man will also be ashamed when he comes in the glory of his Father with the holy angels." And he said to them, "Truly I tell you, there are some standing here who will not taste death until they see that the kingdom of God has come with power."

Friday

A Reading (Lesson) from the Book of Exodus [2:1–22]

A man from the house of Levi went and married a Levite woman. The woman conceived and bore a son; and when she saw that he was a fine baby, she hid him three months. When she could hide him no longer she got a papyrus basket for him, and plastered it witĚ bitumen and pitch; she put the child in it and placed it among the reeds on the bank of the river. His sister stood at a distance, to see what would happen to him. The daughter of Pharaoh came down to bathe at the river, while her attendants walked beside the river. She saw the basket among the reeds and sent her maid to bring it. When she opened it, she saw the child. He was crying, and she took pity on him, "This must be one of the Hebrews' children," she said. Then his sister said to Pharaoh's daughter, "Shall I go and get you a nurse from the Hebrew women to nurse the child for you?" Pharaoh's daughter said to her, "Yes." So the girl went and called the child's mother. Pharaoh's daughter said to her, "Take this child and nurse it for me, and I will give you your wages." So the woman took the child and nursed it. When the child grew up, she brought him to Pharaoh's daughter, and she took him as her son. She named him Moses, "because," she said, "I drew him out of the water." One day, after Moses had grown up, he went out to his people and saw their forced labor. He saw an Egyptian beating a Hebrew, one of his kinsfolk. He looked this way and that, and seeing no one he killed the Egyptian and hid him in the sand. When he went out the next day, he saw two Hebrews fighting; and he said to the one who was in the wrong, "Why do you strike your fellow Hebrew?" He answered, "Who made you a ruler and judge over us? Do you mean to kill me as you killed the Egyptian?" Then Moses was afraid and thought, "Surely the thing is known." When Pharaoh heard of it, he sought to kill Moses. But Moses fled from Pharaoh. He settled in the land of Midian, and sat down by a well. The priest of Midian had seven daughters. They came to draw water, and filled the troughs to water their father's flock. But some shepherds came and drove them away. Moses got up and came to their defense and watered their flock. When they returned to their father Reuel, he said, "How is it that you have come back so soon today?" They said, "An Egyptian helped us against the shepherds; he even drew water for us and watered the flock." He said to his daughters, "Where is he? Why did you leave the man? Invite him to break bread." Moses agreed to stay with the man, and he gave Moses his daughter Zipporah in marriage. She bore a son, and he named him Gershom; for he said, "I have been an alien residing in a foreign land."

A Reading (Lesson) from the First Letter of Paul to the Corinthians [12:27 – 13:3]

Now you are the body of Christ and individually members of it. And God has appointed in the church first apostles, second prophets, third teachers; then deeds of power, then gifts of healing, forms of assistance, forms of leadership, various kinds of tongues. Are all apostles? Are all prophets? Are all teachers? Do all work miracles? Do all possess gifts of healing? Do all speak in tongues? Do all interpret? But strive for the greater gifts. And I will show you a still more excellent way. If I speak in the tongues of mortals and of angels, but do not have love, I am a noisy gong or a clanging cymbal. And if I have prophetic powers, and understand all mysteries and all knowledge, and if I have all faith, so as to remove mountains, but do not have love, I am nothing. If I give away all my possessions, and if I hand over my body so that I may boast, but do not have love, I gain nothing.

A Reading (Lesson) from the Gospel according to Mark [9:2–13]

Six days later, Jesus took with him Peter and James and John, and led them up a high mountain apart, by themselves. And he was transfigured before them, and his clothes became dazzling white, such as no one on earth could bleach them. And there appeared to them Elijah with Moses, who were talking with Jesus. Then Peter said to Jesus, "Rabbi, it is good for us to be here; let us make three dwellings, one for you, one for Moses, and one for Elijah." He did not know what to say, for they were terrified. Then a cloud overshadowed them, and from the cloud there came a voice, "This is my Son, the Beloved; listen to him!" Suddenly when they looked around, they saw no one with them any more, but only Jesus. As they were coming down the mountain, he ordered them to tell no one about what they had seen, until after the Son of Man had risen from the dead. So they kept the matter to themselves, questioning what this rising from the dead could mean. Then they asked him, "Why do the scribes say that Elijah must come first?" He said to them, "Elijah is indeed coming first to restore all things. How then is it written about the Son of Man, that he is to go through many sufferings and be treated with contempt? But I tell you that Elijah has come, and they did to him whatever they pleased, as it is written about him."

Saturday

A Reading (Lesson) from the Book of Exodus [2:23 – 3:15]

After a long time the king of Egypt died. The Israelites groaned under their slavery, and cried out. Out of the slavery their cry for help rose up to God. God heard their groaning, and God remembered his covenant with Abraham, Isaac, and Jacob. God looked upon the Israelites, and God took notice of them. Moses was keeping the flock of his father–in–law Jethro, the priest of Midian; he led his flock beyond the wilderness, and came to Horeb, the mountain of God. There the angel of the LORD appeared to him in a flame of fire out of a bush; he looked, and the bush was blazing, yet it was not consumed. Then Moses said, "I must turn aside and look at this great sight, and see why the bush is not burned up." When the LORD saw that he had turned aside to see, God called to him out of the bush, "Moses, Moses!" And he said, "Here I am." Then he said, "Come no closer! Remove the sandals from your feet, for the place on which you are standing is holy ground." He said further, "I am the God of your father, the God of Abraham, the God of Isaac, and the God of Jacob." And Moses hid his face, for he was afraid to look at God. Then the LORD said, "I have observed the misery of my people who are in Egypt; I have heard their cry on account of their taskmasters. Indeed, I know their sufferings, and I have come down to deliver them from the Egyptians, and to bring them up out of that land to a good and broad land, a land flowing with milk and honey, to the country of the Canaanites, the Hittites, the Amorites, the Perizzites, the Hivites, and the Jebusites. The cry of the Israelites has now come to me; I have also seen how the Egyptians oppress them. So come, I will send you to Pharaoh to bring my people, the Israelites, out of Egypt." But Moses said to God, "Who am I that I should go to Pharaoh, and bring the Israelites out of Egypt?" He said, "I will be with you; and this shall be the sign for you that it is I who sent you: when you have brought the people out of Egypt, you shall worship God on this mountain." But Moses said to God, "If I come to the Israelites and say to them, 'The God of your ancestors has sent me to you,' and they ask me, 'What is his name?' what shall I say to them?" God said to Moses, "I AM WHO I AM." He said further, "Thus you shall say to the Israelites, 'I AM has sent me to you.'" God also said to Moses, "Thus you shall say to the Israelites, 'The LORD, the God of your ancestors, the God of Abraham, the God of Isaac, and the God of Jacob, has sent me to you': This is my name forever, and this my title for all generations."

A Reading (Lesson) from the First Letter of Paul to the Corinthians [13:1–13]

If I speak in the tongues of mortals and of angels, but do not have love, I am a noisy gong or a clanging cymbal. And if I have prophetic powers, and understand all mysteries and all knowledge, and if I have all faith, so as to remove mountains, but do not have love, I am nothing. If I give away all my possessions, and if I hand over my body so that I may boast, but do not have love, I gain nothing. Love is patient; love is kind; love is not envious or boastful or arrogant or rude. It does not insist on its own way; it is not irritable or resentful; it does not rejoice in wrongdoing, but rejoices in the truth. It bears all things, believes all things, hopes all things, endures all things. Love never ends. But as for prophecies, they will come to an end; as for tongues, they will cease; as for knowledge, it will come to an end. For we know only in part, and we prophesy only in part; but when the complete comes, the partial will come to an end. When I was a child, I spoke like a child, I thought like a child, I reasoned like a child; when I became an adult, I put an end to childish ways. For now we see in a mirror, dimly, but then we will see face to face. Now I know only in part; then I will know fully, even as I have been fully known. And now faith, hope, and love abide, these three; and the greatest of these is love.

A Reading (Lesson) from the Gospel according to Mark [9:14–29]

When Jesus, Peter, James and John came to the disciples, they saw a great crowd around them, and some scribes arguing with them. When the whole crowd saw him, they were immediately overcome with awe, and they ran forward to greet him. He asked them, "What are you arguing about with them?" Someone from the crowd answered him, "Teacher, I brought you my son; he has a spirit that makes him unable to speak; and whenever it seizes him, it dashes him down; and he foams and grinds his teeth and becomes rigid; and I asked your disciples to cast it out, but they could not do so." He answered them, "You faithless generation, how much longer must I be among you? How much longer must I put up with you? Bring him to me." And they brought the boy to him. When the spirit saw him, immediately it convulsed the boy, and he fell on the ground and rolled about, foaming at the mouth. Jesus asked the father, "How long has this been happening to him?" And he said, "From childhood. It has often cast him into the fire and into the water, to destroy him; but if you are able to do anything, have pity on us and help us." Jesus said to him, "If you are able!—All things can be done for the one who believes." Immediately the father of the child cried out, "I believe; help my unbelief!" When Jesus saw that a crowd came running together, he rebuked the unclean spirit, saying to it, "You spirit that keeps this boy from speaking and hearing, I command you, come out of him, and never enter him again!" After crying out and convulsing him terribly, it came out, and the boy was like a corpse, so that most of them said, "He is dead." But Jesus took him by the hand and lifted him up, and he was able to stand. When he had entered the house, his disciples asked him privately, "Why could we not cast it out?" He said to them, "This kind can come out only through prayer."

Week of 5 Lent

Sunday

A Reading (Lesson) from the Book of Exodus [3:16 — 4:12]

God said to Moses, "Go and assemble the elders of Israel, and say to them, 'The LORD, the God of your ancestors, the God of Abraham, of Isaac, and of Jacob, has appeared to me, saying: I have given heed to you and to what has been done to you in Egypt. I declare that I will bring you up out of the misery of Egypt, to the land of the Canaanites, the Hittites, the Amorites, the Perizzites, the Hivites, and the Jebusites, a land flowing with milk and honey.' They will listen to your voice; and you and the elders of Israel shall go to the king of Egypt and say to him, 'The LORD, the God of the Hebrews, has met with us; let us now go a three days' journey into the wilderness, so that we may sacrifice to the LORD our God.' I know, however, that the king of Egypt will not let you go unless compelled by a mighty hand. So I will stretch out my hand and strike Egypt with all my wonders that I will perform in it; after that he will let you go. I will bring this people into such favor with the Egyptians that, when you go, you will not go empty-handed; each woman shall ask her neighbor and any woman living in the neighbor's house for jewelry of silver and of gold, and clothing, and you shall put them on your sons and on your daughters; and so you shall plunder the Egyptians." Then Moses answered, "But suppose they do not believe me or listen to me, but say, 'The LORD did not appear to you.'" The LORD said to him, "What is that in your hand?" He said, "A staff." And he said, "Throw it on the ground." So he threw the staff on the ground, and it became a snake; and Moses drew back from it. Then the LORD said to Moses, "Reach out your hand, and seize it by the tail"—so he reached out his hand and grasped it, and it became a staff in his hand—"so that they may believe that the LORD, the God of their ancestors, the God of Abraham, the God of Isaac, and the God of Jacob, has appeared to you." Again, the LORD said to him, "Put your hand inside your cloak." He put his hand into his cloak; and when he took it out, his hand was leprous, as white as snow. Then God said, "Put your hand back into your cloak"—so he put his hand back into his cloak, and when he took it out, it was restored like the rest of his body—"If they will not believe you or heed the first sign, they may believe the second sign. If they will not believe even these two signs or heed you, you shall take some water from the Nile and pour it on the dry ground; and the water that you shall take from the Nile will become blood on the dry ground." But Moses said to the LORD, "O my

LORD, I have never been eloquent, neither in the past nor even now that you have spoken to your servant; but I am slow of speech and slow of tongue." Then the LORD said to him, "Who gives speech to mortals? Who makes them mute or deaf, seeing or blind? Is it not I, the LORD? Now go, and I will be with your mouth and teach you what you are to speak."

A Reading (Lesson) from the Letter of Paul to the Romans[12:1–21]

I appeal to you therefore, brothers and sisters, by the mercies of God, to present your bodies as a living sacrifice, holy and acceptable to God, which is your spiritual worship. Do not be conformed to this world, but be transformed by the renewing of your minds, so that you may discern what is the will of God—what is good and acceptable and perfect. For by the grace given to me I say to everyone among you not to think of yourself more highly than you ought to think, but to think with sober judgment, each according to the measure of faith that God has assigned. For as in one body we have many members, and not all the members have the same function, so we, who are many, are one body in Christ, and individually we are members one of another. We have gifts that differ according to the grace given to us: prophecy, in proportion to faith; ministry, in ministering; the teacher, in teaching; the exhorter, in exhortation; the giver, in generosity; the leader, in diligence; the compassionate, in cheerfulness. Let love be genuine; hate what is evil, hold fast to what is good; love one another with mutual affection; outdo one another in showing honor. Do not lag in zeal, be ardent in spirit, serve the Lord. Rejoice in hope, be patient in suffering, persevere in prayer. Contribute to the needs of the saints; extend hospitality to strangers. Bless those who persecute you; bless and do not curse them. Rejoice with those who rejoice, weep with those who weep. Live in harmony with one another; do not be haughty, but associate with the lowly; do not claim to be wiser than you are. Do not repay anyone evil for evil, but take thought for what is noble in the sight of all. If it is possible, so far as it depends on you, live peaceably with all. Beloved, never avenge yourselves, but leave room for the wrath of God; foÚ it is written, "Vengeance is mine, I will repay, says the Lord." No, "if your enemies are hungry, feed them; if they are thirsty, give them something to drink; for by doing this you will heap burning coals on their heads." Do not be overcome by evil, but overcome evil with good.

A Reading (Lesson) from the Gospel according to John [8:46–59]

Jesus said to the crowd, "Which of you convicts me of sin? If I tell the truth, why do you not believe me? Whoever is from God hears the words of God. The reason you do not hear them is that you are not from God." The Jews answered him, "Are we not right in saying that you are a Samaritan and have a demon?" Jesus answered, "I do not have a demon; but I honor my Father, and you dishonor me. Yet I do not seek my own glory; there is one who seeks it and he is the judge. Very truly, I tell you, whoever keeps my word will never see death." The Jews said to him, "Now we know that you have a demon. Abraham died, and so did the prophets; yet you say, 'Whoever keeps my word will never taste death.' Are you greater than our father Abraham, who died? The prophets also died. Who do you claim to be?" Jesus answered, "If I glorify myself, my glory is nothing. It is my Father who glorifies me, he of whom you say, 'He is our God,' though you do not know him. But I know him; if I would say that I do not know him, I would be a liar like you. But I do know him and I keep his word. Your ancestor Abraham rejoiced that he would see my day; he saw it and was glad." Then the Jews said to him, "You are not yet fifty years old, and have you seen Abraham?" Jesus said to them, "Very truly, I tell you, before Abraham was, I am." So they picked up stones to throw at him, but Jesus hid himself and went out of the temple.

Monday

A Reading (Lesson) from the Book of Exodus [4:10–20(21–26)27–31]

Moses said to the LORD, "O my LORD, I have never been eloquent, neither in the past nor even now that you have spoken to your servant; but I am slow of speech and slow of tongue." Then the LORD said to him, "Who gives speech to mortals? Who makes them mute or deaf, seeing or blind? Is it not I, the LORD? Now go, and I will be with your mouth and teach you what you are to speak." But he said, "O my LORD, please send someone else." Then the anger of the LORD was kindled against Moses and he said, "What of your brother Aaron, the Levite? I know that he can speak fluently; even now he is coming out to meet you, and when he sees you his heart will be glad. You shall speak to him and put the words in his mouth; and I will be with your mouth and with his mouth, and will teach you what you shall do. He indeed shall speak for you to the people; he shall serve as a mouth for you, and you shall serve as God for him. Take in your hand this staff, with which you shall perform the signs." Moses went back to his father–in–law Jethro and said to him, "Please let me go back to my kindred in Egypt and see whether they are still living." And Jethro said to Moses, "Go in peace." The LORD said to Moses in Midian, "Go back to Egypt; for all those who were seeking your life are dead." So

Moses took his wife and his sons, put them on a donkey and went back to the land of Egypt; and Moses carried the staff of God in his hand.

And the LORD said to Moses, "When you go back to Egypt, see that you perform before Pharaoh all the wonders that I have put in your power; but I will harden his heart, so that he will not let the people go. Then you shall say to Pharaoh, 'Thus says the LORD: Israel is my firstborn son. I said to you, "Let my son go that he may worship me." But you refused to let him go; now I will kill your firstborn son.'" On the way, at a place where they spent the night, the LORD met him and tried to kill him. But Zipporah took a flint and cut off her son's foreskin, and touched Moses' feet with it, and said, "Truly you are a bridegroom of blood to me!" So he let him alone. It was then she said, "A bridegroom of blood by circumcision."

The LORD said to Aaron, "Go into the wilderness to meet Moses." So he went; and he met him at the mountain of God and kissed him. Moses told Aaron all the words of the LORD with which he had sent him, and all the signs with which he had charged him. Then Moses and Aaron went and assembled all the elders of the Israelites. Aaron spoke all the words that the LORD had spoken to Moses, and performed the signs in the sight of the people. The people believed; and when they heard that the LORD had given heed to the Israelites and that he had seen their misery, they bowed down and worshiped.

A Reading (Lesson) from the First Letter of Paul to the Corinthians[14:1-19]

Pursue love and strive for the spiritual gifts, and especially that you may prophesy. For those who speak in a tongue do not speak to other people but to God; for nobody understands them, since they are speaking mysteries in the Spirit. On the other hand, those who prophesy speak to other people for their upbuilding and encouragement and consolation. Those who speak in a tongue build up themselves, but those who prophesy build up the church. Now I would like all of you to speak in tongues, but even more to prophesy. One who prophesies is greater than one who speaks in tongues, unless someone interprets, so that the church may be built up. Now, brothers and sisters, if I come to you speaking in tongues, how will I benefit you unless I speak to you in some revelation or knowledge or prophecy or teaching? It is the same way with lifeless instruments that produce sound, such as the flute or the harp. If they do not give distinct notes, how will anyone know what is being played? And if the bugle gives an indistinct sound, who will get ready for battle? So with yourselves; if in a tongue you utter speech that is not intelligible, how will anyone know what is being said? For you will be speaking into the air. There are doubtless many different kinds of sounds in the world, and nothing is without sound. If then I do not know the meaning of a sound, I will be a foreigner to the speaker and the speaker a foreigner to me. So with yourselves; since you are eager for spiritual gifts, strive to excel in them for building up the church. Therefore, one who speaks in a tongue should pray for the power to interpret. For if I pray in a tongue, my spirit prays but my mind is unproductive. What should I do then? I will pray with the spirit, but I will pray with the mind also; I will sing praise with the spirit, but I will sing praise with the mind also. Otherwise, if you say a blessing with the spirit, how can anyone in the position of an outsider say the "Amen" to your thanksgiving, since the outsider does not know what you are saying? For you may give thanks well enough, but the other person is not built up. I thank God that I speak in tongues more than all of you; nevertheless, in church I would rather speak five words with my mind, in order to instruct others also, than ten thousand words in a tongue.

A Reading (Lesson) from the Gospel according to Mark [9:30–41]

Jesus and the disciples went on from there and passed through Galilee. He did not want anyone to know it; for he was teaching his disciples, saying to them, "The Son of Man is to be betrayed into human hands, and they will kill him, and three days after being killed, he will rise again." But they did not understand what he was saying and were afraid to ask him. Then they came to Capernaum; and when he was in the house he asked them, "What were you arguing about on the way?" But they were silent, for on the way they had argued with one another who was the greatest. He sat down, called the twelve, and said to them, "Whoever wants to be first must be last of all and servant of all." Then he took a little child and put it among them; and taking it in his arms, he said to them, "Whoever welcomes one such child in my name welcomes me, and whoever welcomes me welcomes not me but the one who sent me." John said to him, "Teacher, we saw someone casting out demons in your name, and we tried to stop him, because he was not following us." But Jesus said, "Do not stop him; for no one who does a deed of power in my name will be able soon afterward to speak evil of me. Whoever is not against us is for us. For truly I tell you, whoever gives you a cup of water to drink because you bear the name of Christ will by no means lose the reward."

Tuesday

A Reading (Lesson) from the Book of Exodus [5:1—6:1]

Moses and Aaron went to Pharaoh and said, "Thus says the LORD, the God of Israel, 'Let my people go, so that they may celebrate a festival to me in the wilderness.'" But Pharaoh said, "Who is the LORD, that I should heed him and let Israel go? I do not know the LORD, and I will not let Israel go." Then they said, "The God of the Hebrews has revealed himself to us; let us go a three days' journey into the wilderness to sacrifice to the LORD our God, or he will fall upon us with pestilence or sword." But the king of Egypt said to them, "Moses and Aaron, why are you taking the people away from their work? Get to your labors!" Pharaoh continued, "Now they are more numerous than the people of the land and yet you want them to stop working!" That same day Pharaoh commanded the taskmasters of the people, as well as their supervisors, "You shall no longer give the people straw to make bricks, as before; let them go and gather straw for themselves. But you shall require of them the same quantity of bricks as they have made previously; do not diminish it, for they are lazy; that is why they cry, 'Let us go and offer sacrifice to our God.' Let heavier work be laid on them; then they will labor at it and pay no attention to deceptive words." So the taskmasters and the supervisors of the people went out and said to the people, "Thus says Pharaoh, 'I will not give you straw. Go and get straw yourselves, wherever you can find it; but your work will not be lessened in the least.'" So the people scattered throughout the land of Egypt, to gather stubble for straw. The taskmasters were urgent, saying, "Complete your work, the same daily assignment as when you were given straw." And the supervisors of the Israelites, whom Pharaoh's taskmasters had set over them, were beaten, and were asked, "Why did you not finish the required quantity of bricks yesterday and today, as you did before?" Then the Israelite supervisors came to Pharaoh and cried, "Why do you treat your servants like this? No straw is given to your servants, yet they say to us, 'Make bricks!' Look how your servants are beaten! You are unjust to your own people." He said, "You are lazy, lazy; that is why you say, 'Let us go and sacrifice to the LORD.' Go now, and work; for no straw shall be given you, but you shall still deliver the same number of bricks." The Israelite supervisors saw that they were in trouble when they were told, "You shall not lessen your daily number of bricks." As they left Pharaoh, they came upon Moses and Aaron who were waiting to meet them. They said to them, "The LORD look upon you and judge! You have brought us into bad odor with Pharaoh and his officials, and have put a sword in their hand to kill us." Then Moses turned again to the LORD and said, "O LORD, why have you mistreated this people? Why did you ever send me? Since I first came to Pharaoh to speak in your name, he has mistreated this people, and you have done nothing at all to deliver your people." Then the LORD said to Moses, "Now you shall see what I will do to Pharaoh: Indeed, by a mighty hand he will let them go; by a mighty hand he will drive them out of his land."

A Reading (Lesson) from the First Letter of Paul to the Corinthians [14:20–33a,39–40]

Brothers and sisters, do not be children in your thinking; rather, be infants in evil, but in thinking be adults. In the law it is written, "By people of strange tongues and by the lips of foreigners I will speak to this people; yet even then they will not listen to me," says the Lord. Tongues, then, are a sign not for believers but for unbelievers, while prophecy is not for unbelievers but for believers. If, therefore, the whole church comes together and all speak in tongues, and outsiders or unbelievers enter, will they not say that you are out of your mind? But if all prophesy, an unbeliever or outsider who enters is reproved by all and called to account by all. After the secrets of the unbeliever's heart are disclosed, that person will bow down before God and worship him, declaring, "God is really among you." What should be done then, my friends? When you come together, each one has a hymn, a lesson, a revelation, a tongue, or an interpretation. Let all things be done for building up. If anyone speaks in a tongue, let there be only two or at most three, and each in turn; and let one interpret. But if there is no one to interpret, let them be silent in church and speak to themselves and to God. Let two or three prophets speak, and let the others weigh what is said. If a revelation is made to someone else sitting nearby, let the first person be silent. For you can all prophesy one by one, so that all may learn and all be encouraged. And the spirits of prophets are subject to the prophets, for God is a God not of disorder but of peace. So, my friends, be eager to prophesy, and do not forbid speaking in tongues; but all things should be done decently and in order.

A Reading (Lesson) from the Gospel according to Mark (9:42–50)

Jesus said, "If any of you put a stumbling block before one of these little ones who believe in me, it would be better for you if a great millstone were hung around your neck and you were thrown into the sea. If your hand causes you to stumble, cut it off; it is better for you to enter life maimed than to have two hands and to go to hell, to the unquenchable fire. And if your foot causes you to stumble, cut it off; it is better for you to enter life lame than to have two feet and to be thrown into hell. And if your eye causes you to stumble, tear it out; it is better for you to enter the kingdom of God with one eye than to have two eyes and to be thrown into hell, where their worm never dies, and the fire is never quenched. For everyone will be salted with fire. Salt is good; but if salt has lost its saltiness, how can you season it? Have salt in yourselves, and be at peace with one another."

Wednesday

A Reading (Lesson) from the Book of Exodus [7:8–24]

The LORD said to Moses and Aaron, "When Pharaoh says to you, 'Perform a wonder,' then you shall say to Aaron, 'Take your staff and throw it down before Pharaoh, and it will become a snake.'" So Moses and Aaron went to Pharaoh and did as the LORD had commanded: Aaron threw down his staff before Pharaoh and his officials, and it became a snake. Then Pharaoh summoned the wise men and the sorcerers; and they also, the magicians of Egypt, did the same by their secret arts. Each one threw down his staff, and they became snakes; but Aaron's staff swallowed up theirs. Still Pharaoh's heart was hardened, and he would not listen to them, as the LORD had said. Then the LORD said to Moses, "Pharaoh's heart is hardened; he refuses to let the people go. Go to Pharaoh in the morning, as he is going out to the water; stand by at the river bank to meet him, and take in your hand the staff that was turned into a snake. Say to him, 'The LORD, the God of the Hebrews, sent me to you to say, "Let my people go, so that they may worship me in the wilderness." But until now you have not listened.' Thus says the LORD, "By this you shall know that I am the LORD." See, with the staff that is in my hand I will strike the water that is in the Nile, and it shall be turned to blood. The fish in the river shall die, the river itself shall stink, and the Egyptians shall be unable to drink water from the Nile.'" The LORD said to Moses, "Say to Aaron, 'Take your staff and stretch out your hand over the waters of Egypt—over its rivers, its canals, and its ponds, and all its pools of water—so that they may become blood; and there shall be blood throughout the whole land of Egypt, even in vessels of wood and in vessels of stone.'" Moses and Aaron did just as the LORD commanded. In the sight of Pharaoh and of his officials he lifted up the staff and struck the water in the river, and all the water in the river was turned into blood, and the fish in the river died. The river stank so that the Egyptians could not drink its water, and there was blood throughout the whole land of Egypt. But the magicians of Egypt did the same by their secret arts; so Pharaoh's heart remained hardened, and he would not listen to them; as the LORD had said. Pharaoh turned and went into his house, and he did not take even this to heart. And all the Egyptians had to dig along the Nile for water to drink, for they could not drink the water of the river.

A Reading (Lesson) from the Second Letter of Paul to the Corinthians [2:14—3:6]

Thanks be to God, who in Christ always leads us in triumphal procession, and through us spreads in every place the fragrance that comes from knowing him. For we are the aroma of Christ to God among those who are being saved and among those who are perishing; to the one a fragrance from death to death, to the other a fragrance from life to life. Who is sufficient for these things? For we are not peddlers of God's word like so many; but in Christ we speak as persons of sincerity, as persons sent from God and standing in his presence. Are we beginning to commend ourselves again? Surely we do not need, as some do, letters of recommendation to you or from you, do we? You yourselves are our letter, written on our hearts, to be known and read by all; and you show that you are a letter of Christ, prepared by us, written not with ink but with the Spirit of the living God, not on tablets of stone but on tablets of human hearts. Such is the confidence that we have through Christ toward God. Not that we are competent of ourselves to claim anything as coming from us; our competence is from God, who has made us competent to be ministers of a new covenant, not of letter but of spirit; for the letter kills, but the Spirit gives life.

A Reading (Lesson) from the Gospel according to Mark [10:1–16]

Jesus left Capernaum and went to the region of Judea and beyond the Jordan. And crowds again gathered around him; and, as was his custom, he again taught them. Some Pharisees came, and to test him they asked, "Is it lawful for a man to divorce his wife?" He answered them, "What did Moses command you?" They said, "Moses allowed a man to write a certificate of dismissal and to divorce her." But Jesus said to them, "Because of your hardness of heart he wrote this commandment for you. But from the beginning of creation, 'God made them male and female.' 'For this reason a man shall leave his father and mother and be joined to his wife, and the two shall become one flesh.' So they are no longer two, but one flesh. Therefore what God has joined together, let no one separate." Then in the house the disciples asked him again about this matter. He said to them, "Whoever divorces his wife and marries another commits adultery against her; and if she divorces her husband and marries another, she commits adultery." People were bringing little children to him in order that he might touch them; and the disciples spoke sternly to them. But when Jesus saw this, he was indignant and said to them, "Let the little children come to me; do not stop them; for it is to such as these that the kingdom of God belongs.

Truly I tell you, whoever does not receive the kingdom of God as a little child will never enter it." And he took them up in his arms, laid his hands on them, and blessed them.

Thursday

A Reading (Lesson) from the Book of Exodus [7:25 — 8:19]

Seven days passed after the LORD had struck the Nile. Then the LORD said to Moses, "Go to Pharaoh and say to him, 'Thus says the LORD: Let my people go, so that they may worship me. If you refuse to let them go, I will plague your whole country with frogs. The river shall swarm with frogs; they shall come up into your palace, into your bedchamber and your bed, and into the houses of your officials and of your people, and into your ovens and your kneading bowls. The frogs shall come up on you and on your people and on all your officials.'" And the LORD said to Moses, "Say to Aaron, 'Stretch out your hand with your staff over the rivers, the canals, and the pools, and make frogs come up on the land of Egypt.'" So Aaron stretched out his hand over the waters of Egypt; and the frogs came up and covered the land of Egypt. But the magicians did the same by their secret arts, and brought frogs up on the land of Egypt. Then Pharaoh called Moses and Aaron, and said, "Pray to the LORD to take away the frogs from me and my people, and I will let the people go to sacrifice to the LORD." Moses said to Pharaoh, "Kindly tell me when I am to pray for you and for your officials and for your people, that the frogs may be removed from you and your houses and be left only in the Nile." And he said, "Tomorrow." Moses said, "As you say! So that you may know that there is no one like the LORD our God, the frogs shall leave you and your houses and your officials and your people; they shall be left only in the Nile." Then Moses and Aaron went out from Pharaoh; and Moses cried out to the LORD concerning the frogs that he had brought upon Pharaoh. And the LORD did as Moses requested: the frogs died in the houses, the courtyards, and the fields. And they gathered them together in heaps, and the land stank. But when Pharaoh saw that there was a respite, he hardened his heart, and would not listen to them, just as the LORD had said. Then the LORD said to Moses, "Say to Aaron, 'Stretch out your staff and strike the dust of the earth, so that it may become gnats throughout the whole land of Egypt.'" And they did so; Aaron stretched out his hand with his staff and struck the dust of the earth, and gnats came on humans and animals alike; all the dust of the earth turned into gnats throughout the whole land of Egypt. The magicians tried to produce gnats by their secret arts, but they could not.

There were gnats on both humans and animals. And the magicians said to Pharaoh, "This is the finger of God!" But Pharaoh's heart was hardened, and he would not listen to them, just as the LORD had said.

A Reading (Lesson) from the Second Letter of Paul to the Corinthians [3:7–18]

Now if the ministry of death, chiselled in letters on stone tablets, came in glory so that the people of Israel could not gaze at Moses' face because of the glory of his face, a glory now set aside, how much more will the ministry of the Spirit come in glory? For if there was glory in the ministry of condemnation, much more does the ministry of justification abound in glory! Indeed, what once had glory has lost its glory because of the greater glory; for if what was set aside came through glory, much more has the permanent come in glory! Since, then, we have such a hope, we act with great boldness, not like Moses, who put a veil over his face to keep the people of Israel from gazing at the end of the glory that was being set aside. But their minds were hardened. Indeed, to this very day, when they hear the reading of the old covenant, that same veil is still there, since only in Christ is it set aside. Indeed, to this very day whenever Moses is read, a veil lies over their minds; but when one turns to the Lord, the veil is removed. Now the Lord is the Spirit, and where the Spirit of the Lord is, there is freedom. And all of us, with unveiled faces, seeing the glory of the Lord as though reflected in a mirror, are being transformed into the same image from one degree of glory to another; for this comes from the Lord, the Spirit.

A Reading (Lesson) from the Gospel according to Mark [10:17–31]

As Jesus was setting out on a journey, a man ran up and knelt before him, and asked him, "Good Teacher, what must I do to inherit eternal life?" Jesus said to him, "Why do you call me good? No one is good but God alone. You know the commandments: 'You shall not murder; You shall not commit adultery; You shall not steal; You shall not bear false witness; You shall not defraud; Honor your father and mother.'" He said to him, "Teacher, I have kept all these since my youth." Jesus, looking at him, loved him and said, "You lack one thing; go, sell what you own, and give the money to the poor, and you will have treasure in heaven; then come, follow me." When he heard this, he was shocked and went away grieving, for he had many possessions. Then Jesus looked around and said to his disciples, "How hard it will be for those who have wealth to enter the kingdom of God!" And the disciples were perplexed at these words. But Jesus said to them again, "Children, how hard it is to enter the kingdom of God! It is easier for a camel to go through the eye of a needle than for someone who is rich to enter the kingdom of God." They were greatly astounded and said to one another, "Then who can be saved?" Jesus looked at them and said, "For mortals it is impossible, but not for God; for God all things are possible." Peter began to say to him, "Look, we have left everything and followed you." Jesus said, "Truly I tell you, there is no one who has left house or brothers or sisters or mother or father or children or fields, for my sake and for the sake of the good news, who will not receive a hundredfold now in this age—houses, brothers and sisters, mothers and children, and fields, with persecutions—and in the age to come eternal life. But many who are first will be last, and the last will be first."

Friday

A Reading (Lesson) from the Book of Exodus [9:13–35]

The LORD said to Moses, "Rise early in the morning and present yourself before Pharaoh, and say to him, 'Thus says the LORD, the God of the Hebrews: Let my people go, so that they may worship me. For this time I will send all my plagues upon you yourself, and upon your officials, and upon your people, so that you may know that there is no one like me in all the earth. For by now I could have stretched out my hand and struck you and your people with pestilence, and you would have been cut off from the earth. But this is why I have let you live: to show you my power, and to make my name resound through all the earth. You are still exalting yourself against my people, and will not let them go. Tomorrow at this time I will cause the heaviest hail to fall that has ever fallen in Egypt from the day it was founded until now. Send, therefore, and have your livestock and everything that you have in the open field brought to a secure place; every human or animal that is in the open field and is not brought under shelter will die when the hail comes down upon them.'" Those officials of Pharaoh who feared the word of the LORD hurried their slaves and livestock off to a secure place. Those who did not regard the word of the LORD left their slaves and livestock in the open field. The LORD said to Moses, "Stretch out your hand toward heaven so that hail may fall on the whole land of Egypt, on humans and animals and all the plants of the field in the land of Egypt." Then Moses stretched out his staff toward heaven, and the LORD sent thunder and hail, and fire came down on the earth. And the LORD rained hail on the land of Egypt; there was hail with fire flashing continually in the midst of it, such heavy hail as had never fallen in all the land of Egypt since it became a nation. The hail struck down everything that was in the open field throughout all the land of

Egypt, both human and animal; the hail also struck down all the plants of the field, and shattered every tree in the field. Only in the land of Goshen, where the Israelites were, there was no hail. Then Pharaoh summoned Moses and Aaron, and said to them, "This time I have sinned; the LORD is in the right, and I and my people are in the wrong. Pray to the LORD! Enough of God's thunder and hail! I will let you go; you need stay no longer." Moses said to him, "As soon as I have gone out of the city, I will stretch out my hands to the LORD; the thunder will cease, and there will be no more hail, so that you may know that the earth is the LORD's. But as for you and your officials, I know that you do not yet fear the LORD GOD." (Now the flax and the barley were ruined, for the barley was in the ear and the flax was in bud. But the wheat and the spelt were not ruined, for they are late in coming up.) So Moses left Pharaoh, went out of the city, and stretched out his hands to the LORD; then the thunder and the hail ceased, and the rain no longer poured down on the earth. But when Pharaoh saw that the rain and the hail and the thunder had ceased, he sinned once more and hardened his heart, he and his officials. So the heart of Pharaoh was hardened, and he would not let the Israelites go, just as the LORD had spoken through Moses.

A Reading (Lesson) from the Second Letter of Paul to the Corinthians [4:1–12]

Therefore, since it is by God's mercy that we are engaged in this ministry, we do not lose heart. We have renounced the shameful things that one hides; we refuse to practice cunning or to falsify God's word; but by the open statement of the truth we commend ourselves to the conscience of everyone in the sight of God. And even if our gospel is veiled, it is veiled to those who are perishing. In their case the god of this world has blinded the minds of the unbelievers, to keep them from seeing the light of the gospel of the glory of Christ, who is the image of God. For we do not proclaim ourselves; we proclaim Jesus Christ as Lord and ourselves as your slaves for Jesus' sake. For it is the God who said, "Let light shine out of darkness," who has shone in our hearts to give the light of the knowledge of the glory of God in the face of Jesus Christ. But we have this treasure in clay jars, so that it may be made clear that this extraordinary power belongs to God and does not come from us. We are afflicted in every way, but not crushed; perplexed, but not driven to despair; persecuted, but not forsaken; struck down, but not destroyed; always carrying in the body the death of Jesus, so that the life of Jesus may also be made visible in our bodies. For while we live, we are always being given up to death for Jesus' sake, so that the life of Jesus may be made visible in our mortal flesh. So death is at work in us, but life in you.

A Reading (Lesson) from the Gospel according to Mark [10:32–45]

The disciples were on the road, going up to Jerusalem, and Jesus was walking ahead of them; they were amazed, and those who followed were afraid. He took the twelve aside again and began to tell them what was to happen to him, saying, "See, we are going up to Jerusalem, and the Son of Man will be handed over to the chief priests and the scribes, and they will condemn him to death; then they will hand him over to the Gentiles; they will mock him, and spit upon him, and flog him, and kill him; and after three days he will rise again." James and John, the sons of Zebedee, came forward to him and said to him, "Teacher, we want you to do for us whatever we ask of you." And he said to them, "What is it you want me to do for you?" And they said to him, "Grant us to sit, one at your right hand and one at your left, in your glory." But Jesus said to them, "You do not know what you are asking. Are you able to drink the cup that I drink, or be baptized with the baptism that I am baptized with?" They replied, "We are able." Then Jesus said to them, "The cup that I drink you will drink; and with the baptism with which I am baptized, you will be baptized; but to sit at my right hand or at my left is not mine to grant, but it is for those for whom it has been prepared." When the ten heard this, they began to be angry with James and John. So Jesus called them and said to them, "You know that among the Gentiles those whom they recognize as their rulers lord it over them, and their great ones are tyrants over them. But it is not so among you; but whoever wishes to become great among you must be your servant, and whoever wishes to be first among you must be slave of all. For the Son of Man came not to be served but to serve, and to give his life a ransom for many."

Saturday

A Reading (Lesson) from the Book of Exodus [10:21–11:8]

The LORD said to Moses, "Stretch out your hand toward heaven so that there may be darkness over the land of Egypt, a darkness that can be felt." So Moses stretched out his hand toward heaven, and there was dense darkness in all the land of Egypt for three days. People could not see one another, and for three days they could not move from where they were; but all the Israelites had light where they lived. Then Pharaoh summoned Moses, and said, "Go, worship the LORD. Only your flocks and your herds shall remain behind. Even your children may go with you." But Moses said, "You must also let us have sacrifices and burnt offerings to sacrifice to the LORD our God. Our livestock also must go with us; not a hoof shall be left behind, for we must choose some of them for the worship of the LORD our God, and we will not know what to use to worship the LORD until we arrive there." But the LORD hardened Pharaoh's heart, and he was unwilling to let them go. Then Pharaoh said to him, "Get away from me! Take care that you do not see my face again, for on the day you see my face you shall die." Moses said, "Just as you say! I will never see your face again." The LORD said to Moses, "I will bring one more plague upon Pharaoh and upon Egypt; afterwards he will let you go from here; indeed, when he lets you go, he will drive you away. Tell the people that every man is to ask his neighbor and every woman is to ask her neighbor for objects of silver and gold." The LORD gave the people favor in the sight of the Egyptians. Moreover, Moses himself was a man of great importance in the land of Egypt, in the sight of Pharaoh's officials and in the sight of the people. Moses said, "Thus says the LORD: About midnight I will go out through Egypt. Every firstborn in the land of Egypt shall die, from the firstborn of Pharaoh who sits on his throne to the firstborn of the female slave who is behind the handmill, and all the firstborn of the livestock. Then there will be a loud cry throughout the whole land of Egypt, such as has never been or will ever be again. But not a dog shall growl at any of the Israelites—not at people, not at animals—so that you may know that the LORD makes a distinction between Egypt and Israel. Then all these officials of yours shall come down to me, and bow low to me, saying, 'Leave us, you and all the people who follow you.' After that I will leave." And in hot anger he left Pharaoh.

A Reading (Lesson) from the Second Letter of Paul to the Corinthians [4:13–18]

Just as we have the same spirit of faith that is in accordance with scripture—"I believed, and so I spoke"—we also believe, and so we speak, because we know that the one who raised the Lord Jesus will raise us also with Jesus, and will bring us with you into his presence. Yes, everything is for your sake, so that grace, as it extends to more and more people, may increase thanksgiving, to the glory of God. So we do not lose heart. Even though our outer nature is wasting away, our inner nature is being renewed day by day. For this slight momentary affliction is preparing us for an eternal weight of glory beyond all measure, because we look not at what can be seen but at what cannot be seen; for what can be seen is temporary, but what cannot be seen is eternal.

A Reading (Lesson) from the Gospel according to Mark [10:46–52]

They came to Jericho; and as Jesus and his disciples and a large crowd were leaving Jericho, Bartimaeus son of Timaeus, a blind beggar, was sitting by the roadside. When he heard that it was Jesus of Nazareth, he began to shout out and say, "Jesus, Son of David, have mercy on me!" Many sternly ordered him to be quiet, but he cried out even more loudly, "Son of David, have mercy on me!" Jesus stood still and said, "Call him here." And they called the blind man, saying to him, "Take heart; get up, he is calling you." So throwing off his cloak, he sprang up and came to Jesus. Then Jesus said to him, "What do you want me to do for you?" The blind man said to him, "My teacher, let me see again." Jesus said to him, "Go; your faith has made you well." Immediately he regained his sight and followed him on the way.

Holy Week

Palm Sunday

A Reading (Lesson) from the Book of Zechariah [9:9–12]

Intended for use in the morning

Rejoice greatly, O daughter Zion! Shout aloud, O daughter Jerusalem! Lo, your king comes to you; triumphant and victorious is he, humble and riding on a donkey, on a colt, the foal of a donkey. He will cut off the chariot from Ephraim and the war-horse from Jerusalem; and the battle bow shall be cut off, and he shall command peace to the nations; his dominion shall be from sea to sea, and from the River to the ends of the earth. As for you also, because of the blood of my covenant with you, I will set your prisoners free from the waterless pit. Return to your stronghold, O prisoners of hope; today I declare that I will restore to you double.

A Reading (Lesson) from the First Letter of Paul to Timothy [6:12–16]

Intended for use in the morning

Fight the good fight of the faith; take hold of the eternal life, to which you were called and for which you made the good confession in the presence of many witnesses. In the presence of God, who gives life to all things, and of Christ Jesus, who in his testimony before Pontius Pilate made the good confession, I charge you to keep the command-ment without spot or blame until the manifestation of our Lord Jesus Christ, which he will bring about at the right time—he who is the blessed and only Sovereign, the King of kings and Lord of lords. It is he alone who has immortality and dwells in unapproachable light, whom no one has ever seen or can see; to him be honor and eternal dominion. Amen.

A Reading (Lesson) from the Book of Zechariah [12:9–11;13:1,7–9]

Intended for use in the evening

Thus says the LORD: And on that day I will seek to destroy all the nations that come against Jerusalem. And I will pour out a spirit of compassion and supplication on the house of David and the inhabitants of Jerusalem, so that, when they look on the one whom they have pierced, they shall mourn for him, as one mourns for an only child, and weep bitterly over him, as one weeps over a firstborn. On that day the mourning in Jerusalem will be as great as the mourning for Hadad-rimmon in the plain of Megiddo. On that day a fountain shall be opened for the house of David and the inhabitants of Jerusalem, to cleanse them from sin and impurity. "Awake, O sword, against my shepherd, against the man who is my associate," says the LORD of hosts. Strike the shepherd, that the sheep may be scattered; I will turn my hand against the little ones. In the whole land, says the LORD, two-thirds shall be cut off and perish, and one-third shall be left alive. And I will put this third into the fire, refine them as one refines silver, and test them as gold is tested. They will call on my name, and I will answer them. I will say, "They are my people"; and they will say, "The LORD is our God."

A Reading (Lesson) from the Gospel according to Luke [19:41–48]

Intended for the use in the evening

As Jesus came near and saw the city, he wept over it, saying, "If you, even you, had only recognized on this day the things that make for peace! But now they are hidden from your eyes. Indeed, the days will come upon you, when your enemies will set up ramparts around you and surround you, and hem you in on every side. They will crush you to the ground, you and your children within you, and they will not leave within you one stone upon another; because you did not recognize the time of your visitation from God." Then he entered the temple and began to drive out those who were selling things there; and he said, "It is written, 'My house shall be a house of prayer'; but you have made it a den of robbers." Every day he was teaching in the temple. The chief priests, the scribes, and the leaders of the people kept looking for a way to kill him; but they did not find anything they could do, for all the people were spellbound by what they heard.

Monday

A Reading (Lesson) from the Book of Lamentations [1:1–2,6–12]

How lonely sits the city that once was full of people! How like a widow she has become, she that was great among the nations! She that was a princess among the provinces has become a vassal. She weeps bitterly in the night, with tears on her cheeks; among all her lovers she has no one to comfort her; all her friends have dealt treacherously with her, they have become her enemies. From daughter Zion has departed all her majesty. Her princes have become like stags that find no pasture; they fled without strength before the pursuer. Jerusalem remembers, in the days of her affliction and wandering, all the precious things that were hers in days of old. When her people fell into the hand of the foe, and there was no one to help her, the foe looked on mocking over her downfall. Jerusalem sinned grievously, so she has become a mockery; all who honored her despise her, for they have seen her nakedness; she herself groans, and turns her face away. Her uncleanness was in her skirts; she took no thought of her future; her downfall was appalling, with none to comfort her. "O Lord, look at my affliction, for the enemy has triumphed!" Enemies have stretched out their hands over all her precious things; she has even seen the nations invade her sanctuary, those whom you forbade to enter your congregation. All her people groan as they search for bread; they trade their treasures for food to revive their strength. Look, O Lord, and see how worthless I have become. Is it nothing to you, all you who pass by? Look and see if there is any sorrow like my sorrow, which was brought upon me, which the Lord inflicted on the day of his fierce anger.

A Reading (Lesson) from the Second Letter of Paul to the Corinthians [1:1–7]

Paul, an apostle of Christ Jesus by the will of God, and Timothy our brother, to the church of God that is in Corinth, including all the saints throughout Achaia: Grace to you and peace from God our Father and the Lord Jesus Christ. Blessed be the God and Father of our Lord Jesus Christ, the Father of mercies and the God of all consolation, who consoles us in all our affliction, so that we may be able to console those who are in any affliction with the consolation with which we ourselves are consoled by God. For just as the sufferings of Christ are abundant for us, so also our consolation is abundant through Christ. If we are being afflicted, it is for your consolation and salvation; if we are being consoled, it is for your consolation, which you experience when you patiently endure the same sufferings that we are also suffering. Our hope for you is unshaken; for we know that as you share in our sufferings, so also you share in our consolation.

A Reading (Lesson) from the Gospel according to Mark [11:12–25]

On the following day, when Jesus and the disciples came from Bethany, he was hungry. Seeing in the distance a fig tree in leaf, he went to see whether perhaps he would find anything on it. When he came to it, he found nothing but leaves, for it was not the season for figs. He said to it, "May no one ever eat fruit from you again." And his disciples heard it. Then they came to Jerusalem. And he entered the temple and began to drive out those who were selling and those who were buying in the temple, and he overturned the tables of the money changers and the seats of those who sold doves; and he would not allow anyone to carry anything through the temple. He was teaching and saying, "Is it not written, 'My house shall be called a house of prayer for all the nations'? But you have made it a den of robbers." And when the chief priests and the scribes heard it, they kept looking for a way to kill him; for they were afraid of him, because the whole crowd was spellbound by his teaching. And when evening came, Jesus and his disciples went out of the city. In the morning as they passed by, they saw the fig tree withered away to its roots. Then Peter remembered and said to him, "Rabbi, look! The fig tree that you cursed has withered." Jesus answered them, "Have faith in God. Truly I tell you, if you say to this mountain, 'Be taken up and thrown into the sea,' and if you do not doubt in your heart, but believe that what you say will come to pass, it will be done for you. So I tell you, whatever you ask for in prayer, believe that you have received it, and it will be yours. Whenever you stand praying, forgive, if you have anything against anyone; so that your Father in heaven may also forgive you your trespasses."

Tuesday

A Reading (Lesson) from the Book of Lamentations [1:17–22]

Zion stretches out her hands, but there is no one to comfort her; the LORD has commanded against Jacob that his neighbors should become his foes; Jerusalem has become a filthy thing among them. The LORD is in the right, for I have rebelled against his word; but hear, all you peoples, and behold my suffering; my young women and young men have gone into captivity. I called to my lovers but they deceived me; my priests and elders perished in the city while seeking food to revive their strength. See, O LORD, how distressed I am; my stomach churns, my heart is wrung within me, because I have been very rebellious. In the street the sword bereaves; in the house it is like death. They heard how I was groaning, with no one to comfort me. All my enemies heard of my trouble; they are glad that you have done it. Bring on the day you have announced, and let them be as I am. Let all their evildoing come before you; and deal with them as you have dealt with me because of all my transgressions; for my groans are many and my heart is faint.

A Reading (Lesson) from the Second Letter of Paul to the Corinthians [1:8–22]

We do not want you to be unaware, brothers and sisters, of the affliction we experienced in Asia; for we were so utterly, unbearably crushed that we despaired of life itself. Indeed, we felt that we had received the sentence of death so that we would rely not on ourselves but on God who raises the dead. He who rescued us from so deadly a peril will continue to rescue us; on him we have set our hope that he will rescue us again, as you also join in helping us by your prayers, so that many will give thanks on our behalf for the blessing granted us through the prayers of many. Indeed, this is our boast, the testimony of our conscience: we have behaved in the world with frankness and godly sincerity, not by earthly wisdom but by the grace of God—and all the more toward you. For we write you nothing other than what you can read and also understand; I hope you will understand until the end—as you have already understood us in part—that on the day of the Lord Jesus we are your boast even as you are our boast. Since I was sure of this, I wanted to come to you first, so that you might have a double favor; I wanted to visit you on my way to Macedonia, and to come back to you from Macedonia and have you send me on to Judea. Was I vacillating when I wanted to do this? Do I make my plans according to ordinary human standards, ready to say "Yes, yes" and "No, no" at the same time? As surely as God is faithful, our word to you has not been "Yes and No." For the Son of God, Jesus Christ, whom we proclaimed among you, Silvanus and Timothy and I, was not "Yes and No"; but in him it is always "Yes." For in him every one of God's promises is a "Yes." For this reason it is through him that we say the "Amen," to the glory of God. But it is God who establishes us with you in Christ and has anointed us, by putting his seal on us and giving us his Spirit in our hearts as a first installment.

A Reading (Lesson) from the Gospel according to Mark [11:27–33]

Again Jesus and the disciples came to Jerusalem. As he was walking in the temple, the chief priests, the scribes, and the elders came to him and said, "By what authority are you doing these things? Who gave you this authority to do them?" Jesus said to them, "I will ask you one question; answer me, and I will tell you by what authority I do these things. Did the baptism of John come from heaven, or was it of human origin? Answer me." They argued with one another, "If we say, 'From heaven,' he will say, 'Why then did you not believe him?' But shall we say, 'Of human origin'?"—they were afraid of the crowd, for all regarded John as truly a prophet. So they answered Jesus, "We do not know." And Jesus said to them, "Neither will I tell you by what authority I am doing these things."

Wednesday

A Reading (Lesson) from the Book of Lamentations [2:1–9]

How the LORD in his anger has humiliated daughter Zion! He has thrown down from heaven to earth the splendor of Israel; he has not remembered his footstool in the day of his anger. The LORD has destroyed without mercy all the dwellings of Jacob; in his wrath he has broken down the strongholds of daughter Judah; he has brought down to the ground in dishonor the kingdom and its rulers. He has cut down in fierce anger all the might of Israel; he has withdrawn his right hand from them in the face of the enemy; he has burned like a flaming fire in Jacob, consuming all around. He has bent his bow like an enemy, with his right hand set like a foe; he has killed all in whom we took pride in the tent of daughter Zion; he has poured out his fury like fire. The LORD has become like an enemy; he has destroyed Israel. He has destroyed all its palaces, laid in ruins its strongholds, and multiplied in daughter Judah mourning and lamentation. He has broken down his booth like a garden, he has destroyed his tabernacle; the LORD has abolished in Zion festival and sabbath, and in his fierce indignation has spurned king and priest. The LORD has scorned his altar, disowned his sanctuary; he has delivered into the hand of the enemy the walls of her palaces; a clamor was raised in the house of the LORD as on a day of festival. The LORD determined to lay in ruins the wall of daughter Zion; he stretched the line; he did not withhold his hand from destroying; he caused rampart and wall to lament; they languish together. Her gates have sunk into the ground; he has ruined and broken her bars; her king and princes are among the nations; guidance is no more, and her prophets obtain no vision from the LORD.

A Reading (Lesson) from the Second Letter of Paul to the Corinthians [1:23–2:11]

I call on God as witness against me: it was to spare you that I did not come again to Corinth. I do not mean to imply that we lord it over your faith; rather, we are workers with you for your joy, because you stand firm in the faith. So I made up my mind not to make you another painful visit. For if I cause you pain, who is there to make me glad but the one whom I have pained? And I wrote as I did, so that when I came, I might not suffer pain from those who should have made me rejoice; for I am confident about all of you, that my joy would be the joy of all of you. For I wrote you out of much distress and anguish of heart and with many tears, not to cause you pain, but to let you know the abundant love that I have for you. But if anyone has caused pain, he has caused it not to me, but to some extent—not to exaggerate it—to all of you. This punishment by the majority is enough for such a person; so now instead you should forgive and console him, so that he may not be overwhelmed by excessive sorrow. So I urge you to reaffirm your love for him. I wrote for this reason: to test you and to know whether you are obedient in everything. Anyone whom you forgive, I also forgive. What I have forgiven, if I have forgiven anything, has been for your sake in the presence of Christ. And we do this so that we may not be outwitted by Satan; for we are not ignorant of his designs.

A Reading (Lesson) from the Gospel according to Mark [12:1–11]

Jesus began to speak to them in parables. "A man planted a vineyard, put a fence around it, dug a pit for the wine press, and built a watchtower; then he leased it to tenants and went to another country. When the season came, he sent a slave to the tenants to collect from them his share of the produce of the vineyard. But they seized him, and beat him, and sent him away empty-handed. And again he sent another slave to them; this one they beat over the head and insulted. Then he sent another, and that one they killed. And so it was with many others; some they beat, and others they killed. He had still one other, a beloved son. Finally he sent him to them, saying, 'They will respect my son.' But those tenants said to one another, 'This is the heir; come, let us kill him, and the inheritance will be ours.' So they seized him, killed him, and threw him out of the vineyard. What then will the owner of the vineyard do? He will come and destroy the tenants and give the vineyard to others. Have you not read this scripture: 'The stone that the builders rejected has become the cornerstone; this was the Lord's doing, and it is amazing in our eyes'?"

Maundy Thursday

A Reading (Lesson) from the Book of Lamentations [2:10–18]

The elders of daughter Zion sit on the ground in silence; they have thrown dust on their heads and put on sackcloth; the young girls of Jerusalem have bowed their heads to the ground. My eyes are spent with weeping; my stomach churns; my bile is poured out on the ground because of the destruction of my people, because infants and babes faint in the streets of the city. They cry to their mothers, "Where is bread and wine?" as they faint like the wounded in the streets of the city, as their life is poured out on their mothers' bosom. What can I say for you, to what compare you, O daughter Jerusalem? To what can I liken you, that I may comfort you, O virgin daughter Zion? For vast as the sea is your ruin; who can heal you? Your prophets have seen for you false and deceptive visions; they have not exposed your iniquity to restore your fortunes, but have seen oracles for you that are false and misleading. All who pass along the way clap their hands at you; they hiss and wag their heads at daughter Jerusalem; "Is this the city that was called the perfection of beauty, the joy of all the earth?" All your enemies open their mouths against you; they hiss, they gnash their teeth, they cry: "We have devoured her! Ah, this is the day we longed for; at last we have seen it!" The LORD has done what he purposed, he has carried out his threat; as he ordained long ago, he has demolished without pity; he has made the enemy rejoice over you, and exalted the might of your foes. Cry aloud to the LORD! O wall of daughter Zion! Let tears stream down like a torrent day and night! Give yourself no rest, your eyes no respite!

A Reading (Lesson) from the First Letter of Paul to the Corinthians [10:14–17;11:27–32]

My dear friends, flee from the worship of idols. I speak as to sensible people; judge for yourselves what I say. The cup of blessing that we bless, is it not a sharing in the blood of Christ? The bread that we break, is it not a sharing in the body of Christ? Because there is one bread, we who are many are one body, for we all partake of the one bread. Whoever, therefore, eats the bread or drinks the cup of the Lord in an unworthy manner will be answerable for the body and blood of the Lord. Examine yourselves, and only then eat of the bread and drink of the cup. For all who eat and drink without discerning the body, eat and drink judgment against themselves. For this reason many of you are weak and ill, and some have died. But if we judged ourselves, we would not be judged. But when we are judged by the Lord, we are disciplined so that we may not be condemned along with the world.

A Reading (Lesson) from the Gospel according to Mark [14:12–25]

On the first day of Unleavened Bread, when the Passover lamb is sacrificed, his disciples said to Jesus, "Where do you want us to go and make the preparations for you to eat the Passover?" So he sent two of his disciples, saying to them, "Go into the city, and a man carrying a jar of water will meet you; follow him, and wherever he enters, say to the owner of the house, 'The Teacher asks, Where is my guest room where I may eat the Passover with my disciples?' He will show you a large room upstairs, furnished and ready. Make preparations for us there." So the disciples set out and went to the city, and found everything as he had told them; and they prepared the Passover meal. When it was evening, he came with the twelve. And when they had taken their places and were eating, Jesus said, "Truly I tell you, one of you will betray me, one who is eating with me." They began to be distressed and to say to him one after another, "Surely, not I?" He said to them, "It is one of the twelve, one who is dipping bread into the bowl with me. For the Son of Man goes as it is written of him, but woe to that one by whom the Son of Man is betrayed! It would have been better for that one not to have been born." While they were eating, he took a loaf of bread, and after blessing it he broke it, gave it to them, and said, "Take; this is my body." Then he took a cup, and after giving thanks he gave it to them, and all of them drank from it. He said to them, "This is my blood of the covenant, which is poured out for many. Truly I tell you, I will never again drink of the fruit of the vine until that day when I drink it new in the kingdom of God."

Good Friday

A Reading (Lesson) from the Book of Lamentations [3:1–9, 19–33]

I am one who has seen affliction under the rod of God's wrath; he has driven and brought me into darkness without any light; against me alone he turns his hand, again and again, all day long. He has made my flesh and my skin waste away, and broken my bones; he has besieged and enveloped me with bitterness and tribulation; he has made me sit in darkness like the dead of long ago. He has walled me about so that I cannot escape; he has put heavy chains on me; though I call and cry for help, he shuts out my prayer; he has blocked my ways with hewn stones, he has made my paths crooked. The thought of my affliction and my homelessness is wormwood and gall! My soul continually thinks of it and is bowed down within me. But this I call to mind, and therefore I have hope: The steadfast love of the LORD never ceases, his mercies never come to an end; they are new every morning; great is your faithfulness. "The LORD is my portion," says my soul, "therefore I will hope in him." The LORD is good to those who wait for him, to the soul that seeks him. It is good that one should wait quietly for the salvation of the LORD. It is good for one to bear the yoke in youth, to sit alone in silence when the LORD has imposed it, to put one's mouth to the dust (there may yet be hope), to give one's cheek to the smiter, and be filled with insults. For the LORD will not reject forever. Although he causes grief, he will have compassion according to the abundance of his steadfast love; for he does not willingly afflict or grieve anyone.

A Reading (Lesson) from the First Letter of Peter [1:10–20]

Concerning this salvation, the prophets who prophesied of the grace that was to be yours made careful search and inquiry, inquiring about the person or time that the Spirit of Christ within them indicated when it testified in advance to the sufferings destined for Christ and the subsequent glory. It was revealed to them that they were serving not themselves but you, in regard to the things that have now been announced to you through those who brought you good news by the Holy Spirit sent from heaven—things into which angels long to look! Therefore prepare your minds for action; discipline yourselves; set all your hope on the grace that Jesus Christ will bring you when he is revealed. Like obedient children, do not be conformed to the desires that you formerly had in ignorance. Instead, as he who called you is holy, be holy yourselves in all your conduct; for it is written, "You shall be holy, for I am holy." If you invoke as Father the one who judges all people impartially according to their deeds, live in reverent fear during the time of your exile. You know that you were ransomed from the futile ways inherited from your ancestors, not with perishable things like silver or gold, but with the precious blood of Christ, like that of a lamb without defect or blemish. He was destined before the foundation of the world, but was revealed at the end of the ages for your sake.

A Reading (Lesson) from the Gospel according to John [13:36–38]

Intended for use in the morning

Simon Peter said to Jesus, "Lord, where are you going?" Jesus answered, "Where I am going, you cannot follow me now; but you will follow afterward." Peter said to him, "Lord, why can I not follow you now? I will lay down my life for you." Jesus answered, "Will you lay down your life for me? Very truly, I tell you, before the cock crows, you will have denied me three times."

A Reading (Lesson) from the Gospel according to John [19:38–42]

Intended for use in the evening

After Jesus had died on the cross, Joseph of Arimathea, who was a disciple of Jesus, though a secret one because of his fear of the Jews, asked

Pilate to let him take away the body of Jesus. Pilate gave him permission; so he came and removed his body. Nicodemus, who had at first come to Jesus by night, also came, bringing a mixture of myrrh and aloes, weighing about a hundred pounds. They took the body of Jesus and wrapped it with the spices in linen cloths, according to the burial custom of the Jews. Now there was a garden in the place where he was crucified, and in the garden there was a new tomb in which no one had ever been laid. And so, because it was the Jewish day of Preparation, and the tomb was nearby, they laid Jesus there.

Holy Saturday

A Reading (Lesson) from the Book of Lamentations [3:37–58]

Who can command and have it done, if the LORD has not ordained it? Is it not from the mouth of the Most High that good and bad come? Why should any who draw breath complain about the punishment of their sins? Let us test and examine our ways, and return to the LORD. Let us lift up our hearts as well as our hands to God in heaven. We have transgressed and rebelled, and you have not forgiven. You have wrapped yourself with anger and pursued us, killing without pity; you have wrapped yourself with a cloud so that no prayer can pass through. You have made us filth and rubbish among the peoples. All our enemies have opened their mouths against us; panic and pitfall have come upon us, devastation and destruction. My eyes flow with rivers of tears because of the destruction of my people. My eyes will flow without ceasing, without respite, until the LORD from heaven looks down and sees. My eyes cause me grief at the fate of all the young women in my city. Those who were my enemies without cause have hunted me like a bird; they flung me alive into a pit and hurled stones on me; water closed over my head; I said, "I am lost." I called on your name, O LORD, from the depths of the pit; you heard my plea, "Do not close your ear to my cry for help, but give me relief!" You came near when I called on you; you said, "Do not fear!" You have taken up my cause, O LORD, you have redeemed my life.

A Reading (Lesson) from the Letter to the Hebrews [4:1–16]

Intended for use in the morning

While the promise of entering his rest is still open, let us take care that none of you should seem to have failed to reach it. For indeed the good news came to us just as to them; but the message they heard did not benefit them, because they were not united by faith with those who listened. For we who have believed enter that rest, just as God has said,

"As in my anger I swore, 'They shall not enter my rest,'" though his works were finished at the foundation of the world. For in one place it speaks about the seventh day as follows, "And God rested on the seventh day from all his works." And again in this place it says, "They shall not enter my rest." Since therefore it remains open for some to enter it, and those who formerly received the good news failed to enter because of disobedience, again he sets a certain day—"today"— saying through David much later, in the words already quoted, "Today, if you hear his voice, do not harden your hearts." For if Joshua had given them rest, God would not speak later about another day. So then, a sabbath rest still remains for the people of God; for those who enter God's rest also cease from their labors as God did from his. Let us therefore make every effort to enter that rest, so that no one may fall through such disobedience as theirs. Indeed, the word of God is living and active, sharper than any two-edged sword, piercing until it divides soul from spirit, joints from marrow; it is able to judge the thoughts and intentions of the heart. And before him no creature is hidden, but all are naked and laid bare to the eyes of the one to whom we must render an account. Since, then, we have a great high priest who has passed through the heavens, Jesus, the Son of God, let us hold fast to our confession. For we do not have a high priest who is unable to sympathize with our weaknesses, but we have one who in every respect has been tested as we are, yet without sin. Let us therefore approach the throne of grace with boldness, so that we may receive mercy and find grace to help in time of need.

A Reading (Lesson) from the Letter of Paul to the Romans [8:1–11]

Intended for use in the evening

There is therefore now no condemnation for those who are in Christ Jesus. For the law of the Spirit of life in Christ Jesus has set you free from the law of sin and of death. For God has done what the law, weakened by the flesh, could not do: by sending his own Son in the likeness of sinful flesh, and to deal with sin, he condemned sin in the flesh, so that the just requirement of the law might be fulfilled in us, who walk not according to the flesh but according to the Spirit. For those who live according to the flesh set their minds on the things of the flesh, but those who live according to the Spirit set their minds on the things of the Spirit. To set the mind on the flesh is death, but to set the mind on the Spirit is life and peace. For this reason the mind that is set on the flesh is hostile to God; it does not submit to God's law— indeed it cannot, and those who are in the flesh cannot please God. But you are not in the flesh; you are in the Spirit, since the Spirit of God dwells in you. Anyone who does not have the Spirit of Christ does not belong to him. But if Christ is in you, though the body is dead because of sin, the Spirit is life because of righteousness. If the Spirit of him who raised Jesus from the dead dwells in you, he who raised Christ from the dead will give life to your mortal bodies also through his Spirit that dwells in you.

St. Joseph (March 19)
MORNING PRAYER

A Reading (Lesson) from the Book of Isaiah [63:7–16]

I will recount the gracious deeds of the LORD, the praiseworthy acts of the LORD, because of all that the LORD has done for us, and the great favor to the house of Israel that he has shown them according to his mercy, according to the abundance of his steadfast love. For he said, "Surely they are my people, children who will not deal falsely;" and he became their savior in all their distress. It was no messenger or angel but his presence that saved them; in his love and in his pity he redeemed them; he lifted them up and carried them all the days of old. But they rebelled and grieved his holy spirit; therefore he became their enemy; he himself fought against them. Then they remembered the days of old, of Moses his servant. Where is the one who brought them up out of the sea with the shepherds of his flock? Where is the one who put within them his holy spirit, who caused his glorious arm to march at the right hand of Moses, who divided the waters before them to make for himself an everlasting name, who led them through the depths? Like a horse in the desert, they did not stumble. Like cattle that go down into the valley, the spirit of the LORD gave them rest. Thus you led your people, to make for yourself a glorious name. Look down from heaven and see, from your holy and glorious habitation. Where are your zeal and your might? The yearning of your heart and your compassion? They are withheld from me. For you are our father, though Abraham does not know us and Israel does not acknowledge us; you, O LORD, are our father; our Redeemer from of old is your name.

A Reading (Lesson) from the Gospel according to Matthew [1:18–25]

Now the birth of Jesus the Messiah took place in this way. When his mother Mary had been engaged to Joseph, but before they lived together, she was found to be with child from the Holy Spirit. Her husband Joseph, being a righteous man and unwilling to expose her to public disgrace, planned to dismiss her quietly. But just when he had resolved to do this, an angel of the Lord appeared to him in a dream and said, "Joseph, son of David, do not be afraid to take Mary as your wife, for the child conceived in her is from the Holy Spirit. She will bear a son, and you are to name him Jesus, for he will save his people from their sins." All this took place to fulfill what had been spoken by the Lord through the prophet: "Look, the virgin shall conceive and bear a son, and they shall name him Emmanuel," which means, "God is with us." When Joseph awoke from sleep, he did as the angel of the Lord commanded him; he took her as his wife, but had no marital relations with her until she had borne a son; and he named him Jesus.

EVENING PRAYER

A Reading (Lesson) from the Second Book of Chronicles [6:12–17]

Solomon stood before the altar of the LORD in the presence of the whole assembly of Israel, and spread out his hands. Solomon had made a bronze platform five cubits long, five cubits wide, and three cubits high, and had set it in the court; and he stood on it. Then he knelt on his knees in the presence of the whole assembly of Israel, and spread out his hands toward heaven. He said, "O LORD, God of Israel, there is no God like you, in heaven or on earth, keeping covenant in steadfast love with your servants who walk before you with all their heart—you who have kept for your servant, my father David, what you promised to him. Indeed, you promised with your mouth and this day have fulfilled with your hand. Therefore, O LORD, God of Israel, keep for your servant, my father David, that which you promised him, saying, 'There shall never fail you a successor before me to sit on the throne of Israel, if only your children keep to their way, to walk in my law as you have walked before me.' Therefore, O LORD, God of Israel, let your word be confirmed, which you promised to your servant David."

A Reading (Lesson) from the Letter of Paul to the Ephesians [3:14–21]

For the sake of the gospel I bow my knees before the Father, from whom every family in heaven and on earth takes its name. I pray that, according to the riches of his glory, he may grant that you may be strengthened in your inner being with power through his Spirit, and that Christ may dwell in your hearts through faith, as you are being rooted and grounded in love. I pray that you may have the power to comprehend, with all the saints, what is the breadth and length and height and depth, and to know the love of Christ that surpasses knowledge, so that you may be filled with all the fullness of God. Now to him who by the power at work within us is able to accomplish abundantly far more than all we can ask or imagine, to him be glory in the church and in Christ Jesus to all generations, forever and ever. Amen.

Eve of the Annunciation (March 24)
EVENING PRAYER

A Reading (Lesson) from the Book of Genesis [3:1–15]

The serpent was more crafty than any other wild animal that the LORD God had made. He said to the woman, "Did God say, 'You shall not eat from any tree in the garden'?" The woman said to the serpent, "We may eat of the fruit of the trees in the garden; but God said, 'You shall not eat of the fruit of the tree that is in the middle of the garden, nor shall you touch it, or you shall die.'" But the serpent said to the woman, "You will not die; for God knows that when you eat of it your eyes will be opened, and you will be like God, knowing good and evil." So when the woman saw that the tree was good for food, and that it was a delight to the eyes, and that the tree was to be desired to make one wise, she took of its fruit and ate; and she also gave some to her husband, who was with her, and he ate. Then the eyes of both were opened, and they knew that they were naked; and they sewed fig leaves together and made loincloths for themselves. They heard the sound of the LORD God walking in the garden at the time of the evening breeze, and the man and his wife hid themselves from the presence of the LORD God among the trees of the garden. But the LORD God called to the man, and said to him, "Where are you?" He said, "I heard the sound of you in the garden, and I was afraid, because I was naked; and I hid myself." He said, "Who told you that you were naked? Have you eaten from the tree of which I commanded you not to eat?" The man said, "The woman whom you gave to be with me, she gave me fruit from the tree, and I ate." Then the LORD God said to the woman, "What is this that you have done?" The woman said, "The serpent tricked me, and I ate." The LORD God said to the serpent, "Because you have done this, cursed are you among all animals and among all wild creatures; upon your belly you shall go, and dust you shall eat all the days of your life. I will put enmity between you and the woman, and between your offspring and hers; he will strike your head, and you will strike his heel."

A Reading (Lesson) from the Letter of Paul to the Romans [5:12–21]

Therefore, just as sin came into the world through one man, and death came through sin, and so death spread to all because all have sinned—sin was indeed in the world before the law, but sin is not reckoned when there is no law. Yet death exercised dominion from Adam to Moses, even over those whose sins were not like the transgression of Adam, who is a type of the one who was to come. But the free gift is not like the trespass. For if the many died through the one man's trespass, much more surely have the grace of God and the free gift in the grace of the one man, Jesus Christ, abounded for the many. And the free gift is not like the effect of the one man's sin. For the judgment following one trespass brought condemnation, but the free gift following many trespasses brings justification. If, because of the one man's trespass, death exercised dominion through that one, much more surely will those who receive the abundance of grace and the free gift of righteousness exercise dominion in life through the one man, Jesus Christ. Therefore just as one man's trespass led to condemnation for all, so one man's act of righteousness leads to justification and life for all. For just as by the one man's disobedience the many were made sinners, so by the one man's obedience the many will be made righteous. But law came in, with the result that the trespass multiplied; but where sin increased, grace abounded all the more, so that, just as sin exercised dominion in death, so grace might also exercise dominion through justification leading to eternal life through Jesus Christ our Lord.

or this

A Reading (Lesson) from the Letter of Paul to the Galatians [4:1–7]

My point is this: heirs, as long as they are minors, are no better than slaves, though they are the owners of all the property; but they remain under guardians and trustees until the date set by the father. So with us; while we were minors, we were enslaved to the elemental spirits of the world. But when the fullness of time had come, God sent his Son, born of a woman, born under the law, in order to redeem those who were under the law, so that we might receive adoption as children. And because you are children, God has sent the Spirit of his Son into our hearts, crying, "Abba! Father!" So you are no longer a slave but a child, and if a child then also an heir, through God.

The Annunciation (March 25)
MORNING PRAYER

A Reading (Lesson) from the Book of Isaiah [52:7–12]

How beautiful upon the mountains are the feet of the messenger who announces peace, who brings good news, who announces salvation, who says to Zion, "Your God reigns." Listen! Your sentinels lift up their voices, together they sing for joy; for in plain sight they see the return of the LORD to Zion. Break forth together into singing, you ruins of Jerusalem; for the LORD has comforted his people, he has redeemed Jerusalem. The LORD has bared his holy arm before the eyes of all the nations; and all the ends of the earth shall see the salvation of our God.

226   Eve of the Annunciation

Depart, depart, go out from there! Touch no unclean thing; go out from the midst of it, purify yourselves, you who carry the vessels of the LORD. For you shall not go out in haste, and you shall not go in flight; for the LORD will go before you, and the God of Israel will be your rear guard.

A Reading (Lesson) from the Letter to the Hebrews [2:5–10]

God did not subject the coming world, about which we are speaking, to angels. But someone has testified somewhere, "What are human beings that you are mindful of them, or mortals, that you care for them? You have made them for a little while lower than the angels; you have crowned them with glory and honor, subjecting all things under their feet." Now in subjecting all things to them, God left nothing outside their control. As it is, we do not yet see everything in subjection to them, but we do see Jesus, who for a little while was made lower than the angels, now crowned with glory and honor because of the suffering of death, so that by the grace of God he might taste death for everyone. It was fitting that God, for whom and through whom all things exist, in bringing many children to glory, should make the pioneer of their salvation perfect through sufferings.

EVENING PRAYER

A Reading (Lesson) from the Book of Wisdom [9:1–12]

With my whole heart I said: "O God of my ancestors and LORD of mercy, who have made all things by your word, and by your wisdom have formed humankind to have dominion over the creatures you have made, and rule the world in holiness and righteousness, and pronounce judgment in uprightness of soul, give me the wisdom that sits by your throne, and do not reject me from among your servants. For I am your servant the son of your serving girl, a man who is weak and short-lived, with little understanding of judgment and laws, for even one who is perfect among human beings will be regarded as nothing without the wisdom that comes from you. You have chosen me to be king of your people and to be judge over your sons and daughters. You have given command to build a temple on your holy mountain, and an altar in the city of your habitation, a copy of the holy tent that you prepared from the beginning. With you is wisdom, she who knows your works and was present when you made the world; she understands what is pleasing in your sight and what is right according to your commandments. Send her forth from the holy heavens, and from the throne of your glory send her, that she may labor at my side, and that I may learn what is pleasing to you. For she knows and understands all things, and she will guide me wisely in my actions and guard me with her glory. Then my works will be acceptable, and I shall judge your people justly, and shall be worthy of the throne of my father."

A Reading (Lesson) from the Gospel according to John [1:9–14]

The true light, which enlightens everyone, was coming into the world. He was in the world, and the world came into being through him; yet the world did not know him. He came to what was his own, and his own people did not accept him. But to all who received him, who believed in his name, he gave power to become children of God, who were born, not of blood or of the will of the flesh or of the will of man, but of God. And the Word became flesh and lived among us, and we have seen his glory, the glory as of a father's only son, full of grace and truth.

The Psalter

For the Invitatory

95   *Venite, exultemus*

1 Come, let us sing to the Lord;*
   let us shout for joy to the Rock of our salvation.

2 Let us come before his presence with thanksgiving*
   and raise a loud shout to him with psalms.

3 For the Lord is a great God, *
   and a great King above all gods.

4 In his hand are the caverns of the earth, *
   and the heights of the hills are his also.

5 The sea is his, for he made it, *
   and his hands have molded the dry land.

6 Come, let us bow down, and bend the knee,*
   and kneel before the Lord our Maker.

7 For he is our God,
   and we are the people of his pasture and the sheep of his hand.*
   Oh, that today you would hearken to his voice!

8 Harden not your hearts,
   as your forebears did in the wilderness,*
   at Meribah, and on that day at Massah,
   when they tempted me.

9 They put me to the test, *
   though they had seen my works.

10 Forty years long I detested that generation and said,*
   "This people are wayward in their hearts;
   they do not know my ways."

11 So I swore in my wrath,*
   "They shall not enter into my rest."

32 *Beati quorum*

1 Happy are they whose transgressions are forgiven, *
     and whose sin is put away!

2 Happy are they to whom the LORD imputes no guilt,*
     and in whose spirit there is no guile!

3 While I held my tongue, my bones withered away, *
     because of my groaning all day long.

4 For your hand was heavy upon me day and night; *
     my moisture was dried up as in the heat of summer.

5 Then I acknowledged my sin to you, *
     and did not conceal my guilt.

6 I said, "I will confess my transgressions to the LORD." *
     Then you forgave me the guilt of my sin.

7 Therefore all the faithful will make their prayers to you in
       time of trouble;*
     when the great waters overflow, they shall not reach them.

8 You are my hiding-place;
     you preserve me from trouble; *
     you surround me with shouts of deliverance.

9 "I will instruct you and teach you in the way that you
       should go; *
     I will guide you with my eye.

10 Do not be like horse or mule, which have no understanding;*
     who must be fitted with bit and bridle,
     or else they will not stay near you."

11 Great are the tribulations of the wicked;*
     but mercy embraces those who trust in the Lord.

12 Be glad, you righteous, and rejoice in the Lord;*
     shout for joy, all who are true of heart.

143 *Domine, exaudi*

1 Lord, hear my prayer,
     and in your faithfulness heed my supplications;*
     answer me in your righteousness.

2 Enter not into judgment with your servant,*
   for in your sight shall no one living be justified.

3 For my enemy has sought my life;
   he has crushed me to the ground; *
      he has made me live in dark places like those who
         are long dead.

4 My spirit faints within me; *
   my heart within me is desolate.

5 I remember the time past;
   I muse upon all your deeds; *
      I consider the works of your hands.

6 I spread out my hands to you; *
   my soul gasps to you like a thirsty land.

7 O Lord, make haste to answer me; my spirit fails me;*
   do not hide your face from me
   or I shall be like those who go down to the Pit.

8 Let me hear of your loving-kindness in the morning,
   for I put my trust in you;*
      show me the road that I must walk,
      for I lift up my soul to you.

9 Deliver me from my enemies, O Lord, *
   for I flee to you for refuge.

10 Teach me to do what pleases you, for you are my God;*
   let your good Spirit lead me on level ground.

11 Revive me, O Lord, for your Name's sake;*
   for your righteousness' sake, bring me out of trouble.

12 Of your goodness, destroy my enemies
   and bring all my foes to naught, *
      for truly I am your servant.

Evening

102 *Domine, exaudi*

1 Lord, hear my prayer, and let my cry come before you;*
   hide not your face from me in the day of my trouble.

2 Incline your ear to me; *
   when I call, make haste to answer me,

3 For my days drift away like smoke, *
   and my bones are hot as burning coals.

4 My heart is smitten like grass and withered, *
   so that I forget to eat my bread.

5 Because of the voice of my groaning *
   I am but skin and bones.

6 I have become like a vulture in the wilderness, *
   like an owl among the ruins.

7 I lie awake and groan; *
   I am like a sparrow, lonely on a house-top.

8 My enemies revile me all day long,*
   and those who scoff at me have taken an oath against me.

9 For I have eaten ashes for bread *
   and mingled my drink with weeping.

10 Because of your indignation and wrath*
    you have lifted me up and thrown me away.

11 My days pass away like a shadow,*
    and I wither like the grass.

12 But you, O Lord, endure for ever,*
    and your Name from age to age.

13 You will arise and have compassion on Zion,
    for it is time to have mercy upon her;*
       indeed, the appointed time has come.

14 For your servants love her very rubble,*
    and are moved to pity even for her dust.

15 The nations shall fear your Name, O Lord,*
    and all the kings of the earth your glory.

16 For the Lord will build up Zion,*
    and his glory will appear.

17 He will look with favor on the prayer of the homeless;*
    he will not despise their plea.

18 Let this be written for a future generation,*
    so that a people yet unborn may praise the Lord.

19 For the Lord looked down from his holy place on high;*
    from the heavens he beheld the earth;

20   That he might hear the groan of the captive*
        and set free those condemned to die;

21   That they may declare in Zion the Name of the Lord,*
        and his praise in Jerusalem;

22   When the peoples are gathered together,*
        and the kingdoms also, to serve the Lord.

23   He has brought down my strength before my time;*
        he has shortened the number of my days;

24   And I said, "O my God,
     do not take me away in the midst of my days;*
        your years endure throughout all generations.

25   In the beginning, O Lord, you laid the foundations
            of the earth,*
        and the heavens are the work of your hands;

26   They shall perish, but you will endure;
     they all shall wear out like a garment; *
        as clothing you will change them,
        and they shall be changed;

27   But you are always the same, *
        and your years will never end.

28   The children of your servants shall continue, *
        and their offspring shall stand fast in your sight."

   130 *De profundis*
1   Out of the depths have I called to you, O Lord;
    Lord, hear my voice;*
        let your ears consider well the voice of my supplication.

2   If you, Lord, were to note what is done amiss,*
        O Lord, who could stand?

3   For there is forgiveness with you;*
        therefore you shall be feared.

4   I wait for the Lord; my soul waits for him;*
        in his word is my hope.

5   My soul waits for the Lord,
    more than watchmen for the morning,*
        more than watchmen for the morning.

6 O Israel, wait for the Lord,*
    for with the Lord there is mercy;

7 With him there is plenteous redemption,*
    and he shall redeem Israel from all their sins.

Thursday

Morning

37

Part I   *Noli æmulari*

1 Do not fret yourself because of evildoers;*
    do not be jealous of those who do wrong.

2 For they shall soon wither like the grass, *
    and like the green grass fade away.

3 Put your trust in the Lord and do good; *
    dwell in the land and feed on its riches.

4 Take delight in the Lord, *
    and he shall give you your heart's desire.

5 Commit your way to the Lord and put your trust in him,*
    and he will bring it to pass.

6 He will make your righteousness as clear as the light *
    and your just dealing as the noonday.

7 Be still before the Lord *
    and wait patiently for him.

8 Do not fret yourself over the one who prospers, *
    the one who succeeds in evil schemes.

9 Refrain from anger, leave rage alone; *
    do not fret yourself; it leads only to evil.

10 For evildoers shall be cut off,*
    but those who wait upon the Lord shall possess the land.

11 In a little while the wicked shall be no more;*
    you shall search out their place, but they will not be there.

12 But the lowly shall possess the land;*
    they will delight in abundance of peace.

13 The wicked plot against the righteous*
    and gnash at them with their teeth.

14 The Lord laughs at the wicked,*
    because he sees that their day will come.

15 The wicked draw their sword and bend their bow
    to strike down the poor and needy,*
    to slaughter those who are upright in their ways.

16 Their sword shall go through their own heart,*
    and their bow shall be broken.

17 The little that the righteous has*
    is better than great riches of the wicked.

18 For the power of the wicked shall be broken,*
    but the Lord upholds the righteous.

Evening

37

Part II *Novit Dominus*

19 The Lord cares for the lives of the godly,*
    and their inheritance shall last for ever.

20 They shall not be ashamed in bad times,*
    and in days of famine they shall have enough.

21 As for the wicked, they shall perish,*
    and the enemies of the Lord, like the glory of
                    the meadows, shall vanish;
    they shall vanish like smoke.

22 The wicked borrow and do not repay,*
    but the righteous are generous in giving.

23 Those who are blessed by God shall possess the land,*
    but those who are cursed by him shall be destroyed.

24 Our steps are directed by the Lord;*
    he strengthens those in whose way he delights.

25 If they stumble, they shall not fall headlong,*
    for the Lord holds them by the hand.

26 I have been young and now I am old,*
    but never have I seen the righteous forsaken,
    or their children begging bread.

27 The righteous are always generous in their lending,*
and their children shall be a blessing.

28 Turn from evil, and do good,*
and dwell in the land for ever.

29 For the Lord loves justice;*
he does not forsake his faithful ones.

30 They shall be kept safe for ever,*
but the offspring of the wicked shall be destroyed.

31 The righteous shall possess the land*
and dwell in it for ever.

32 The mouth of the righteous utters wisdom,*
and their tongue speaks what is right.

33 The law of their God is in their heart,*
and their footsteps shall not falter.

34 The wicked spy on the righteous*
and seek occasion to kill them.

35 The Lord will not abandon them to their hand,*
nor let them be found guilty when brought to trial.

36 Wait upon the Lord and keep his way; *
he will raise you up to possess the land,
and when the wicked are cut off, you will see it.

37 I have seen the wicked in their arrogance,*
flourishing like a tree in full leaf.

38 I went by, and behold, they were not there;*
I searched for them, but they could not be found.

39 Mark those who are honest; observe the upright;*
for there is a future for the peaceable.

40 Transgressors shall be destroyed, one and all;*
the future of the wicked is cut off.

41 But the deliverance of the righteous comes from the Lord;*
he is their stronghold in time of trouble.

42 The Lord will help them and rescue them; *
he will rescue them from the wicked and deliver them,
because they seek refuge in him.

Friday

Morning

For the Invitatory

95   *Venite, exultemus*

1 Come, let us sing to the Lord;*
    let us shout for joy to the Rock of our salvation.

2 Let us come before his presence with thanksgiving*
    and raise a loud shout to him with psalms.

3 For the Lord is a great God, *
    and a great King above all gods.

4 In his hand are the caverns of the earth, *
    and the heights of the hills are his also.

5 The sea is his, for he made it, *
    and his hands have molded the dry land.

6 Come, let us bow down, and bend the knee,*
    and kneel before the Lord our Maker.

7 For he is our God,
    and we are the people of his pasture and the sheep of his hand.*
    Oh, that today you would hearken to his voice!

8 Harden not your hearts,
    as your forebears did in the wilderness,*
    at Meribah, and on that day at Massah,
    when they tempted me.

9 They put me to the test, *
    though they had seen my works.

10 Forty years long I detested that generation and said,*
    "This people are wayward in their hearts;
    they do not know my ways."

11 So I swore in my wrath,*
    "They shall not enter into my rest."

31   *In te, Domine, speravi*

1 In you, O Lord, have I taken refuge;
    let me never be put to shame; *
    deliver me in your righteousness.

2 Incline your ear to me; *
    make haste to deliver me.

3 Be my strong rock, a castle to keep me safe,
    for you are my crag and my stronghold; *
      for the sake of your Name, lead me and guide me.

4 Take me out of the net that they have secretly set for me,*
    for you are my tower of strength.

5 Into your hands I commend my spirit, *
    for you have redeemed me,
    O Lord, O God of truth.

6 I hate those who cling to worthless idols,*
    and I put my trust in the Lord.

7 I will rejoice and be glad because of your mercy; *
    for you have seen my affliction;
    you know my distress.

8 You have not shut me up in the power of the enemy;*
    you have set my feet in an open place.

9 Have mercy on me, O Lord, for I am in trouble; *
    my eye is consumed with sorrow,
    and also my throat and my belly.

10 For my life is wasted with grief, and my years with sighing;*
    my strength fails me because of affliction,
    and my bones are consumed.

11 I have become a reproach to all my enemies and
        even to my neighbors,
    a dismay to those of my acquaintance;*
      when they see me in the street they avoid me.

12 I am forgotten like a dead man, out of mind;*
    I am as useless as a broken pot.

13 For I have heard the whispering of the crowd;
    fear is all around;*
      they put their heads together against me;
      they plot to take my life.

14 But as for me, I have trusted in you, O Lord.*
    I have said, "You are my God.

15 My times are in your hand;*
       rescue me from the hand of my enemies,
       and from those who persecute me.

16 Make your face to shine upon your servant,*
       and in your loving-kindness save me."

17 Lord, let me not be ashamed for having called upon you;*
       rather, let the wicked be put to shame;
       let them be silent in the grave.

18 Let the lying lips be silenced which speak against
           the righteous,*
       haughtily, disdainfully, and with contempt.

19 How great is your goodness, O Lord!
       which you have laid up for those who fear you;*
       which you have done in the sight of all
       for those who put their trust in you.

20 You hide them in the covert of your presence from those who
           slander them;*
       you keep them in your shelter from the strife of tongues.

21 Blessed be the Lord!*
       for he has shown me the wonders of his love in a besieged city.

22 Yet I said in my alarm,
       "I have been cut off from the sight of your eyes."*
       Nevertheless, you heard the sound of my entreaty
       when I cried out to you.

23 Love the Lord, all you who worship him;*
       the Lord protects the faithful,
       but repays to the full those who act haughtily.

24 Be strong and let your heart take courage,*
       all you who wait for the Lord.

Evening

35 *Judica, Domine*

1 Fight those who fight me, O Lord;*
       attack those who are attacking me.

2 Take up shield and armor *
       and rise up to help me.

3 Draw the sword and bar the way against those who pursue me; *
   say to my soul, "I am your salvation."

4 Let those who seek after my life be shamed and humbled,*
   let those who plot my ruin fall back and be dismayed.

5 Let them be like chaff before the wind, *
   and let the angel of the Lord drive them away.

6 Let their way be dark and slippery,*
   and let the angel of the Lord pursue them.

7 For they have secretly spread a net for me without a cause; *
   without a cause they have dug a pit to take me alive.

8 Let ruin come upon them unawares; *
   let them be caught in the net they hid;
   let them fall into the pit they dug.

9 Then I will be joyful in the Lord; *
   I will glory in his victory.

10 My very bones will say, "Lord, who is like you?*
   You deliver the poor from those who are too strong for them,
   the poor and needy from those who rob them."

11 Malicious witnesses rise up against me;*
   they charge me with matters I know nothing about.

12 They pay me evil in exchange for good;*
   my soul is full of despair.

13 But when they were sick I dressed in sack-cloth*
   and humbled myself by fasting;

14 I prayed with my whole heart,
   as one would for a friend or a brother;*
   I behaved like one who mourns for his mother,
   bowed down and grieving.

15 But when I stumbled, they were glad and gathered together;
   they gathered against me;*
   strangers whom I did not know tore me to pieces and would not
   stop.

16 They put me to the test and mocked me;*
   they gnashed at me with their teeth.

17 O Lord, how long will you look on?*
   rescue me from the roaring beasts,
   and my life from the young lions.

18 I will give you thanks in the great congregation;*
      I will praise you in the mighty throng.

19 Do not let my treacherous foes rejoice over me,*
      nor let those who hate me without a cause wink at each other.

20 For they do not plan for peace,*
      but invent deceitful schemes against the quiet in the land.

21 They opened their mouths at me and said,*
      "Aha! we saw it with our own eyes."

22 You saw it, O Lord; do not be silent;*
      O Lord, be not far from me.

23 Awake, arise, to my cause!*
      to my defense, my God and my Lord!

24 Give me justice, O Lord my God,
    according to your righteousness;*
      do not let them triumph over me.

25 Do not let them say in their hearts,
    "Aha! just what we want!"*
      Do not let them say, "We have swallowed him up."

26 Let all who rejoice at my ruin be ashamed and disgraced;*
      let those who boast against me be clothed with
            dismay and shame.

27 Let those who favor my cause sing out with joy and be glad;*
      let them say always, "Great is the Lord,
        who desires the prosperity of his servant."

28 And my tongue shall be talking of your righteousness*
      and of your praise all the day long.

Saturday
Morning

30 *Exaltabo te, Domine*

1 I will exalt you, O Lord,
   because you have lifted me up *
     and have not let my enemies triumph over me.

2 O Lord my God, I cried out to you, *
     and you restored me to health.

3   You brought me up, O Lord, from the dead; *
       you restored my life as I was going down to the grave.

4   Sing to the Lord, you servants of his; *
       give thanks for the remembrance of his holiness.

5   For his wrath endures but the twinkling of an eye, *
       his favor for a lifetime.

6   Weeping may spend the night, *
       but joy comes in the morning.

7   While I felt secure, I said,
       "I shall never be disturbed. *
       You, Lord, with your favor, made me as strong as
                   the mountains."

8   Then you hid your face, *
       and I was filled with fear.

9   I cried to you, O Lord; *
       I pleaded with the Lord, saying,

10 "What profit is there in my blood, if I go down to the Pit? *
       will the dust praise you or declare your faithfulness?

11 Hear, O Lord, and have mercy upon me;*
       O Lord, be my helper."

12 You have turned my wailing into dancing;*
       you have put off my sack-cloth and clothed me with joy.

13 Therefore my heart sings to you without ceasing;*
       O Lord my God, I will give you thanks for ever.

32   *Beati quorum*

1   Happy are they whose transgressions are forgiven, *
       and whose sin is put away!

2   Happy are they to whom the Lord imputes no guilt,*
       and in whose spirit there is no guile!

3   While I held my tongue, my bones withered away, *
       because of my groaning all day long.

4   For your hand was heavy upon me day and night; *
       my moisture was dried up as in the heat of summer.

5   Then I acknowledged my sin to you, *
       and did not conceal my guilt.

6 I said, "I will confess my transgressions to the Lord." *
   Then you forgave me the guilt of my sin.

7 Therefore all the faithful will make their prayers to you in
         time of trouble;*
   when the great waters overflow, they shall not reach them.

8 You are my hiding-place;
   you preserve me from trouble; *
   you surround me with shouts of deliverance.

9 "I will instruct you and teach you in the way that you should go; *
   I will guide you with my eye.

10 Do not be like horse or mule, which have no understanding;*
   who must be fitted with bit and bridle,
      or else they will not stay near you."

11 Great are the tribulations of the wicked;*
   but mercy embraces those who trust in the Lord.

12 Be glad, you righteous, and rejoice in the Lord;*
   shout for joy, all who are true of heart.

Evening

42 *Quemadmodum*

1 As the deer longs for the water-brooks,*
   so longs my soul for you, O God.

2 My soul is athirst for God, athirst for the living God; *
   when shall I come to appear before the presence of God?

3 My tears have been my food day and night, *
   while all day long they say to me,
   "Where now is your God?"

4 I pour out my soul when I think on these things: *
   how I went with the multitude and led them into the
         house of God,

5 With the voice of praise and thanksgiving, *
   among those who keep holy-day.

6 Why are you so full of heaviness, O my soul? *
   and why are you so disquieted within me?

7 Put your trust in God; *
    for I will yet give thanks to him,
    who is the help of my countenance, and my God.

8 My soul is heavy within me;*
    therefore I will remember you from the land of Jordan, and
    from the peak of Mizar among the heights of Hermon.

9 One deep calls to another in the noise of your cataracts; *
    all your rapids and floods have gone over me.

10 The Lord grants his loving-kindness in the daytime;*
    in the night season his song is with me,
    a prayer to the God of my life.

11 I will say to the God of my strength,
    "Why have you forgotten me?*
    and why do I go so heavily while the enemy oppresses me?"

12 While my bones are being broken,*
    my enemies mock me to my face;

13 All day long they mock me*
    and say to me, "Where now is your God?"

14 Why are you so full of heaviness, O my soul?*
    and why are you so disquieted within me?

15 Put your trust in God;*
    for I will yet give thanks to him,
    who is the help of my countenance, and my God.

43   *Judica me, Deus*

1 Give judgment for me, O God,
    and defend my cause against an ungodly people; *
    deliver me from the deceitful and the wicked.

2 For you are the God of my strength;
    why have you put me from you? *
    and why do I go so heavily while the enemy oppresses me?

3 Send out your light and your truth, that they may lead me,*
    and bring me to your holy hill
    and to your dwelling;

4 That I may go to the altar of God,
    to the God of my joy and gladness;*
    and on the harp I will give thanks to you, O God my God.

5   Why are you so full of heaviness, O my soul? *
      and why are you so disquieted within me?

6   Put your trust in God; *
      for I will yet give thanks to him,
      who is the help of my countenance, and my God.

Week of 1 Lent

Sunday

Morning

63 *Deus, Deus meus*

1   O God, you are my God; eagerly I seek you;*
      my soul thirsts for you, my flesh faints for you,
      as in a barren and dry land where there is no water.

2   Therefore I have gazed upon you in your holy place,*
      that I might behold your power and your glory.

3   For your loving-kindness is better than life itself; *
      my lips shall give you praise.

4   So will I bless you as long as I live *
      and lift up my hands in your Name.

5   My soul is content, as with marrow and fatness, *
      and my mouth praises you with joyful lips,

6   When I remember you upon my bed, *
      and meditate on you in the night watches.

7   For you have been my helper,*
      and under the shadow of your wings I will rejoice.

8   My soul clings to you; *
      your right hand holds me fast.

9   May those who seek my life to destroy it*
      go down into the depths of the earth;

10   Let them fall upon the edge of the sword,*
      and let them be food for jackals.

11   But the king will rejoice in God;
      all those who swear by him will be glad;*
      for the mouth of those who speak lies shall be stopped.

98 *Cantate Domino*

1 Sing to the Lord a new song, *
  for he has done marvelous things.

2 With his right hand and his holy arm*
  has he won for himself the victory.

3 The Lord has made known his victory; *
  his righteousness has he openly shown in the sight of the
  nations.

4 He remembers his mercy and faithfulness to the house of Israel, *
  and all the ends of the earth have seen the victory of our God.

5 Shout with joy to the Lord, all you lands; *
  lift up your voice, rejoice, and sing.

6 Sing to the Lord with the harp, *
  with the harp and the voice of song.

7 With trumpets and the sound of the horn *
  shout with joy before the King, the Lord.

8 Let the sea make a noise and all that is in it, *
  the lands and those who dwell therein.

9 Let the rivers clap their hands,*
  and let the hills ring out with joy before the Lord,
  when he comes to judge the earth.

10 In righteousness shall he judge the world*
  and the peoples with equity.

Evening

103 *Benedic, anima mea*

1 Bless the Lord, O my soul, *
  and all that is within me, bless his holy Name.

2 Bless the Lord, O my soul, *
  and forget not all his benefits.

3 He forgives all your sins *
  and heals all your infirmities;

4 He redeems your life from the grave *
  and crowns you with mercy and loving-kindness;

5　He satisfies you with good things, *
　　　and your youth is renewed like an eagle's.

6　The Lord executes righteousness *
　　　and judgment for all who are oppressed.

7　He made his ways known to Moses *
　　　and his works to the children of Israel.

8　The Lord is full of compassion and mercy, *
　　　slow to anger and of great kindness.

9　He will not always accuse us, *
　　　nor will he keep his anger for ever.

10　He has not dealt with us according to our sins,*
　　　nor rewarded us according to our wickedness.

11　For as the heavens are high above the earth,*
　　　so is his mercy great upon those who fear him.

12　As far as the east is from the west,*
　　　so far has he removed our sins from us.

13　As a father cares for his children,*
　　　so does the Lord care for those who fear him.

14　For he himself knows whereof we are made;*
　　　he remembers that we are but dust.

15　Our days are like the grass;*
　　　we flourish like a flower of the field;

16　When the wind goes over it, it is gone,*
　　　and its place shall know it no more.

17　But the merciful goodness of the Lord endures for ever on those
　　　　　　who fear him,*
　　　and his righteousness on children's children;

18　On those who keep his covenant*
　　　and remember his commandments and do them.

19　The Lord has set his throne in heaven,*
　　　and his kingship has dominion over all.

20　Bless the Lord, you angels of his,
　　　you mighty ones who do his bidding,*
　　　and hearken to the voice of his word.

21　Bless the Lord, all you his hosts,*
　　　you ministers of his who do his will.

22 Bless the Lord, all you works of his,
in all places of his dominion;*
bless the Lord, O my soul.

Monday

Morning

41 *Beatus qui intelligit*

1 Happy are they who consider the poor and needy! *
the Lord will deliver them in the time of trouble.

2 The Lord preserves them and keeps them alive,
so that they may be happy in the land;*
he does not hand them over to the will of their enemies.

3 The Lord sustains them on their sickbed *
and ministers to them in their illness.

4 I said, "Lord, be merciful to me; *
heal me, for I have sinned against you."

5 My enemies are saying wicked things about me: *
"When will he die, and his name perish?"

6 Even if they come to see me, they speak empty words; *
their heart collects false rumors;
they go outside and spread them.

7 All my enemies whisper together about me *
and devise evil against me.

8 "A deadly thing," they say, "has fastened on him; *
he has taken to his bed and will never get up again."

9 Even my best friend, whom I trusted,
who broke bread with me, *
has lifted up his heel and turned against me.

10 But you, O Lord, be merciful to me and raise me up,*
and I shall repay them.

11 By this I know you are pleased with me,*
that my enemy does not triumph over me.

12 In my integrity you hold me fast,*
and shall set me before your face for ever.

13 Blessed be the Lord God of Israel,*
from age to age. Amen. Amen.

52 *Quid gloriaris?*

1 You tyrant, why do you boast of wickedness *
  against the godly all day long?

2 You plot ruin; your tongue is like a sharpened razor, *
  O worker of deception.

3 You love evil more than good*
  and lying more than speaking the truth.

4 You love all words that hurt, *
  O you deceitful tongue.

5 Oh, that God would demolish you utterly, *
  topple you, and snatch you from your dwelling,
  and root you out of the land of the living!

6 The righteous shall see and tremble, *
  and they shall laugh at him, saying,

7 "This is the one who did not take God for a refuge, *
  but trusted in great wealth
  and relied upon wickedness."

8 But I am like a green olive tree in the house of God; *
  I trust in the mercy of God for ever and ever.

9 I will give you thanks for what you have done*
  and declare the goodness of your Name in the presence
        of the godly.

Evening

44 *Deus, auribus*

1 We have heard with our ears, O God,
  our forefathers have told us, *
  the deeds you did in their days, in the days of old.

2 How with your hand you drove the peoples out
  and planted our forefathers in the land; *
  how you destroyed nations and made your people flourish.

3 For they did not take the land by their sword,
  nor did their arm win the victory for them; *
  but your right hand, your arm, and the light of your
        countenance, because you favored them.

4 You are my King and my God; *
    you command victories for Jacob.

5 Through you we pushed back our adversaries; *
    through your Name we trampled on those who
    rose up against us.

6 For I do not rely on my bow, *
    and my sword does not give me the victory.

7 Surely, you gave us victory over our adversaries *
    and put those who hate us to shame.

8 Every day we gloried in God,*
    and we will praise your Name for ever.

9 Nevertheless, you have rejected and humbled us *
    and do not go forth with our armies.

10 You have made us fall back before our adversary,*
    and our enemies have plundered us.

11 You have made us like sheep to be eaten*
    and have scattered us among the nations.

12 You are selling your people for a trifle*
    and are making no profit on the sale of them.

13 You have made us the scorn of our neighbors,*
    a mockery and derision to those around us.

14 You have made us a byword among the nations,*
    a laughing-stock among the peoples.

15 My humiliation is daily before me,*
    and shame has covered my face;

16 Because of the taunts of the mockers and blasphemers,*
    because of the enemy and avenger.

17 All this has come upon us;*
    yet we have not forgotten you,
    nor have we betrayed your covenant.

18 Our heart never turned back,*
    nor did our footsteps stray from your path;

19 Though you thrust us down into a place of misery,*
    and covered us over with deep darkness.

20 If we have forgotten the Name of our God,*
    or stretched out our hands to some strange god,

21 Will not God find it out?*
　　for he knows the secrets of the heart.

22 Indeed, for your sake we are killed all the day long;*
　　we are accounted as sheep for the slaughter.

23 Awake, O Lord! why are you sleeping?*
　　Arise! do not reject us for ever.

24 Why have you hidden your face*
　　and forgotten our affliction and oppression?

25 We sink down into the dust;*
　　our body cleaves to the ground.

26 Rise up, and help us,*
　　and save us, for the sake of your steadfast love.

Tuesday

Morning

45　*Eructavit cor meum*

1 My heart is stirring with a noble song;
　　let me recite what I have fashioned for the king; *
　　　my tongue shall be the pen of a skilled writer.

2 You are the fairest of men; *
　　grace flows from your lips,
　　　because God has blessed you for ever.

3 Strap your sword upon your thigh, O mighty warrior,*
　　in your pride and in your majesty.

4 Ride out and conquer in the cause of truth *
　　and for the sake of justice.

5 Your right hand will show you marvelous things; *
　　your arrows are very sharp, O mighty warrior.

6 The peoples are falling at your feet, *
　　and the king's enemies are losing heart.

7 Your throne, O God, endures for ever and ever,*
　　a scepter of righteousness is the scepter of your kingdom;
　　　you love righteousness and hate iniquity.

8 Therefore God, your God, has anointed you *
   with the oil of gladness above your fellows.

9 All your garments are fragrant with myrrh, aloes, and cassia,*
   and the music of strings from ivory palaces makes you glad.

10 Kings' daughters stand among the ladies of the court; *
   on your right hand is the queen,
   adorned with the gold of Ophir.

11 "Hear, O daughter; consider and listen closely;*
   forget your people and your father's house.

12 The king will have pleasure in your beauty;*
   he is your master; therefore do him honor.

13 The people of Tyre are here with a gift;*
   the rich among the people seek your favor."

14 All glorious is the princess as she enters;*
   her gown is cloth-of-gold.

15 In embroidered apparel she is brought to the king;*
   after her the bridesmaids follow in procession.

16 With joy and gladness they are brought,*
   and enter into the palace of the king.

17 "In place of fathers, O king, you shall have sons;*
   you shall make them princes over all the earth.

18 I will make your name to be remembered
   from one generation to another;*
   therefore nations will praise you for ever and ever."

Evening

47 *Omnes gentes, plaudite*

1 Clap your hands, all you peoples;*
   shout to God with a cry of joy.

2 For the Lord Most High is to be feared; *
   he is the great King over all the earth.

3 He subdues the peoples under us, *
   and the nations under our feet.

4 He chooses our inheritance for us, *
   the pride of Jacob whom he loves.

5 God has gone up with a shout, *
   the Lord with the sound of the ram's-horn.

6 Sing praises to God, sing praises; *
   sing praises to our King, sing praises.

7 For God is King of all the earth; *
   sing praises with all your skill.

8 God reigns over the nations; *
   God sits upon his holy throne.

9 The nobles of the peoples have gathered together*
   with the people of the God of Abraham.

10 The rulers of the earth belong to God,*
   and he is highly exalted.

48 *Magnus Dominus*

1 Great is the Lord, and highly to be praised; *
   in the city of our God is his holy hill.

2 Beautiful and lofty, the joy of all the earth, is the hill of Zion, *
   the very center of the world and the city of the great King.

3 God is in her citadels; *
   he is known to be her sure refuge.

4 Behold, the kings of the earth assembled *
   and marched forward together.

5 They looked and were astounded; *
   they retreated and fled in terror.

6 Trembling seized them there; *
   they writhed like a woman in childbirth,
   like ships of the sea when the east wind shatters them.

7 As we have heard, so have we seen,
   in the city of the Lord of hosts, in the city of our God; *
   God has established her for ever.

8 We have waited in silence on your loving-kindness, O God, *
   in the midst of your temple.

9 Your praise, like your Name, O God, reaches to the world's end; *
   your right hand is full of justice.

10 Let Mount Zion be glad
     and the cities of Judah rejoice, *
     because of your judgments.

11 Make the circuit of Zion;
     walk round about her; *
     count the number of her towers.

12 Consider well her bulwarks; examine her strongholds;*
     that you may tell those who come after.

13 This God is our God for ever and ever;*
     he shall be our guide for evermore.

Wednesday
Morning

119

Zayin   *Memor esto verbi tui*

49 Remember your word to your servant,*
     because you have given me hope.

50 This is my comfort in my trouble,*
     that your promise gives me life.

51 The proud have derided me cruelly,*
     but I have not turned from your law.

52 When I remember your judgments of old,*
     O Lord, I take great comfort.

53 I am filled with a burning rage,*
     because of the wicked who forsake your law.

54 Your statutes have been like songs to me*
     wherever I have lived as a stranger.

55 I remember your Name in the night, O Lord,*
     and dwell upon your law.

56 This is how it has been with me,*
     because I have kept your commandments.

Heth   *Portio mea, Domine*

57 You only are my portion, O Lord;*
     I have promised to keep your words.

58 I entreat you with all my heart,*
   be merciful to me according to your promise.

59 I have considered my ways*
   and turned my feet toward your decrees.

60 I hasten and do not tarry*
   to keep your commandments.

61 Though the cords of the wicked entangle me,*
   I do not forget your law.

62 At midnight I will rise to give you thanks,*
   because of your righteous judgments.

63 I am a companion of all who fear you;*
   and of those who keep your commandments.

64 The earth, O Lord, is full of your love;*
   instruct me in your statutes.

Teth   *Bonitatem fecisti*

65 O Lord, you have dealt graciously with your servant,*
   according to your word.

66 Teach me discernment and knowledge,*
   for I have believed in your commandments.

67 Before I was afflicted I went astray,*
   but now I keep your word.

68 You are good and you bring forth good;*
   instruct me in your statutes.

69 The proud have smeared me with lies,*
   but I will keep your commandments with my whole heart.

70 Their heart is gross and fat,*
   but my delight is in your law.

71 It is good for me that I have been afflicted,*
   that I might learn your statutes.

72 The law of your mouth is dearer to me*
   than thousands in gold and silver.

49   *Audite hæc, omnes*

1   Hear this, all you peoples;
hearken, all you who dwell in the world, *
you of high degree and low, rich and poor together.

2   My mouth shall speak of wisdom, *
and my heart shall meditate on understanding.

3   I will incline my ear to a proverb *
and set forth my riddle upon the harp.

4   Why should I be afraid in evil days,*
when the wickedness of those at my heels surrounds me,

5   The wickedness of those who put their trust in their goods,*
and boast of their great riches?

6   We can never ransom ourselves, *
or deliver to God the price of our life;

7   For the ransom of our life is so great, *
that we should never have enough to pay it,

8   In order to live for ever and ever, *
and never see the grave.

9   For we see that the wise die also;
like the dull and stupid they perish *
and leave their wealth to those who come after them.

10   Their graves shall be their homes for ever,
their dwelling places from generation to generation,*
though they call the lands after their own names.

11   Even though honored, they cannot live for ever;*
they are like the beasts that perish.

12   Such is the way of those who foolishly trust in themselves,*
and the end of those who delight in their own words.

13   Like a flock of sheep they are destined to die;
Death is their shepherd;*
they go down straightway to the grave.

14   Their form shall waste away,*
and the land of the dead shall be their home.

15 But God will ransom my life;*
     he will snatch me from the grasp of death.

16 Do not be envious when some become rich,*
     or when the grandeur of their house increases;

17 For they will carry nothing away at their death,*
     nor will their grandeur follow them.

18 Though they thought highly of themselves while they lived,*
     and were praised for their success,

19 They shall join the company of their forebears,*
     who will never see the light again.

20 Those who are honored, but have no understanding,*
     are like the beasts that perish.

53 *Dixit insipiens*

1 The fool has said in his heart, "There is no God."*
    All are corrupt and commit abominable acts;
    there is none who does any good.

2 God looks down from heaven upon us all, *
    to see if there is any who is wise,
    if there is one who seeks after God.

3 Every one has proved faithless;
    all alike have turned bad; *
    there is none who does good; no, not one.

4 Have they no knowledge, those evildoers *
    who eat up my people like bread
    and do not call upon God?

5 See how greatly they tremble,
    such trembling as never was; *
    for God has scattered the bones of the enemy;
    they are put to shame, because God has rejected them.

6 Oh, that Israel's deliverance would come out of Zion! *
    when God restores the fortunes of his people
    Jacob will rejoice and Israel be glad.

Thursday

Morning

50   *Deus deorum*

1 The Lord, the God of gods, has spoken;*
    he has called the earth from the rising of the sun to its setting.

2 Out of Zion, perfect in its beauty, *
    God reveals himself in glory.

3 Our God will come and will not keep silence; *
    before him there is a consuming flame,
    and round about him a raging storm.

4 He calls the heavens and the earth from above *
    to witness the judgment of his people.

5 "Gather before me my loyal followers, *
    those who have made a covenant with me
    and sealed it with sacrifice."

6 Let the heavens declare the rightness of his cause; *
    for God himself is judge.

7 Hear, O my people, and I will speak:
    "O Israel, I will bear witness against you; *
    for I am God, your God.

8 I do not accuse you because of your sacrifices; *
    your offerings are always before me.

9 I will take no bull-calf from your stalls, *
    nor he-goats out of your pens;

10 For all the beasts of the forest are mine,*
    the herds in their thousands upon the hills.

11 I know every bird in the sky, *
    and the creatures of the fields are in my sight.

12 If I were hungry, I would not tell you, *
    for the whole world is mine and all that is in it.

13 Do you think I eat the flesh of bulls, *
    or drink the blood of goats?

14 Offer to God a sacrifice of thanksgiving *
    and make good your vows to the Most High.

15 Call upon me in the day of trouble; *
    I will deliver you, and you shall honor me."

16 But to the wicked God says: *
    "Why do you recite my statutes,
    and take my covenant upon your lips;

17 Since you refuse discipline, *
    and toss my words behind your back?

18 When you see a thief, you make him your friend, *
    and you cast in your lot with adulterers.

19 You have loosed your lips for evil, *
    and harnessed your tongue to a lie.

20 You are always speaking evil of your brother *
    and slandering your own mother's son.

21 These things you have done, and I kept still, *
    and you thought that I am like you."

22 "I have made my accusation; *
    I have put my case in order before your eyes.

23 Consider this well, you who forget God, *
    lest I rend you and there be none to deliver you.

24 Whoever offers me the sacrifice of thanksgiving honors me;*
    but to those who keep in my way will I show the
        salvation of God."

Evening

59 *Eripe me de inimicis*

1 Rescue me from my enemies, O God;*
    protect me from those who rise up against me.

2 Rescue me from evildoers *
    and save me from those who thirst for my blood.

3 See how they lie in wait for my life,
    how the mighty gather together against me; *
    not for any offense or fault of mine, O Lord.

4 Not because of any guilt of mine*
    they run and prepare themselves for battle.

5 Rouse yourself, come to my side, and see; *
    for you, Lord God of hosts, are Israel's God.

6 Awake, and punish all the ungodly;*
    show no mercy to those who are faithless and evil.

7 They go to and fro in the evening; *
    they snarl like dogs and run about the city.

8 Behold, they boast with their mouths,
    and taunts are on their lips; *
      "For who," they say, "will hear us?"

9 But you, O Lord, you laugh at them; *
    you laugh all the ungodly to scorn.

10 My eyes are fixed on you, O my Strength;*
    for you, O God, are my stronghold.

11 My merciful God comes to meet me;*
    God will let me look in triumph on my enemies.

12 Slay them, O God, lest my people forget;*
    send them reeling by your might
    and put them down, O Lord our shield.

13 For the sins of their mouths, for the words of their lips,
    for the cursing and lies that they utter,*
      let them be caught in their pride.

14 Make an end of them in your wrath;*
    make an end of them, and they shall be no more.

15 Let everyone know that God rules in Jacob,*
    and to the ends of the earth.

16 They go to and fro in the evening;*
    they snarl like dogs and run about the city.

17 They forage for food,*
    and if they are not filled, they howl.

18 For my part, I will sing of your strength;*
    I will celebrate your love in the morning;

19 For you have become my stronghold,*
    a refuge in the day of my trouble.

20 To you, O my Strength, will I sing;*
    for you, O God, are my stronghold and my merciful God.

60 *Deus, repulisti nos*

1 O God, you have cast us off and broken us;*
   you have been angry;
   oh, take us back to you again.

2 You have shaken the earth and split it open; *
   repair the cracks in it, for it totters.

3 You have made your people know hardship; *
   you have given us wine that makes us stagger.

4 You have set up a banner for those who fear you, *
   to be a refuge from the power of the bow.

5 Save us by your right hand and answer us, *
   that those who are dear to you may be delivered.

6 God spoke from his holy place and said:*
   "I will exult and parcel out Shechem;
   I will divide the valley of Succoth.

7 Gilead is mine and Manasseh is mine; *
   Ephraim is my helmet and Judah my scepter.

8 Moab is my wash-basin,
   on Edom I throw down my sandal to claim it, *
   and over Philistia will I shout in triumph."

9 Who will lead me into the strong city? *
   who will bring me into Edom?

10 Have you not cast us off, O God?*
   you no longer go out, O God, with our armies.

11 Grant us your help against the enemy,*
   for vain is the help of man.

12 With God we will do valiant deeds,*
   and he shall tread our enemies under foot.

or

19 *Cœli enarrant*

1 The heavens declare the glory of God,*
   and the firmament shows his handiwork.

2 One day tells its tale to another, *
   and one night imparts knowledge to another.

3 Although they have no words or language, *
    and their voices are not heard,

4 Their sound has gone out into all lands, *
    and their message to the ends of the world.

5 In the deep has he set a pavilion for the sun;*
    it comes forth like a bridegroom out of his chamber;
    it rejoices like a champion to run its course.

6 It goes forth from the uttermost edge of the heavens
    and runs about to the end of it again; *
    nothing is hidden from its burning heat.

7 The law of the Lord is perfect and revives the soul;*
    the testimony of the Lord is sure and gives wisdom to
          the innocent.

8 The statutes of the Lord are just and rejoice the heart; *
    the commandment of the Lord is clear and gives light to the
    eyes.

9 The fear of the Lord is clean and endures for ever; *
    the judgments of the Lord are true and righteous altogether.

10 More to be desired are they than gold, more than much fine gold,*
    sweeter far than honey, than honey in the comb.

11 By them also is your servant enlightened,*
    and in keeping them there is great reward.

12 Who can tell how often he offends?*
    cleanse me from my secret faults.

13 Above all, keep your servant from presumptuous sins;
    let them not get dominion over me;*
        then shall I be whole and sound,
        and innocent of a great offense.

14 Let the words of my mouth and the meditation of my heart be
        acceptable in your sight,*
    O Lord, my strength and my redeemer.

46   *Deus noster refugium*

1 God is our refuge and strength,*
    a very present help in trouble.

2 Therefore we will not fear, though the earth be moved, *
    and though the mountains be toppled into the depths of the sea;

3 Though its waters rage and foam, *
  and though the mountains tremble at its tumult.

4 The Lord of hosts is with us; *
  the God of Jacob is our stronghold.

5 There is a river whose streams make glad the city of God,*
  the holy habitation of the Most High.

6 God is in the midst of her;
  she shall not be overthrown; *
  God shall help her at the break of day.

7 The nations make much ado, and the kingdoms are shaken;*
  God has spoken, and the earth shall melt away.

8 The Lord of hosts is with us; *
  the God of Jacob is our stronghold.

9 Come now and look upon the works of the Lord,*
  what awesome things he has done on earth.

10 It is he who makes war to cease in all the world;*
  he breaks the bow, and shatters the spear,
  and burns the shields with fire.

11 "Be still, then, and know that I am God;*
  I will be exalted among the nations;
  I will be exalted in the earth."

12 The Lord of hosts is with us;*
  the God of Jacob is our stronghold.

Friday

Morning

For the Invitatory

95 *Venite, exultemus*

1 Come, let us sing to the Lord;*
  let us shout for joy to the Rock of our salvation.

2 Let us come before his presence with thanksgiving*
  and raise a loud shout to him with psalms.

3 For the Lord is a great God, *
  and a great King above all gods.

4 In his hand are the caverns of the earth, *
  and the heights of the hills are his also.

5 The sea is his, for he made it, *
   and his hands have molded the dry land.

6 Come, let us bow down, and bend the knee,*
   and kneel before the Lord our Maker.

7 For he is our God,
   and we are the people of his pasture and the sheep of his hand. *
     Oh, that today you would hearken to his voice!

8 Harden not your hearts,
   as your forebears did in the wilderness,*
     at Meribah, and on that day at Massah,
     when they tempted me.

9 They put me to the test, *
   though they had seen my works.

10 Forty years long I detested that generation and said,*
      "This people are wayward in their hearts;
      they do not know my ways."

11 So I swore in my wrath,*
      "They shall not enter into my rest."

   40   *Expectans, expectavi*

1 I waited patiently upon the Lord;*
   he stooped to me and heard my cry.

2 He lifted me out of the desolate pit, out of the mire and clay;*
   he set my feet upon a high cliff and made my footing sure.

3 He put a new song in my mouth,
   a song of praise to our God;*
     many shall see, and stand in awe,
     and put their trust in the Lord.

4 Happy are they who trust in the Lord! *
   they do not resort to evil spirits or turn to false gods.

5 Great things are they that you have done, O Lord my God!
   how great your wonders and your plans for us! *
     there is none who can be compared with you.

6 Oh, that I could make them known and tell them! *
   but they are more than I can count.

7 In sacrifice and offering you take no pleasure *
     (you have given me ears to hear you);

8 Burnt-offering and sin-offering you have not required, *
     and so I said, "Behold, I come.

9 In the roll of the book it is written concerning me: *
     'I love to do your will, O my God;
     your law is deep in my heart.'"

10 I proclaimed righteousness in the great congregation;*
     behold, I did not restrain my lips;
     and that, O Lord, you know.

11 I Your righteousness have I not hidden in my heart;
     I have spoken of your faithfulness and your deliverance;*
       I have not concealed your love and faithfulness from
         the great congregation.

12 You are the Lord;
     do not withhold your compassion from me;*
       let your love and your faithfulness keep me safe for ever,

13 For innumerable troubles have crowded upon me;
     my sins have overtaken me, and I cannot see;*
       they are more in number than the hairs of my head,
       and my heart fails me.

14 Be pleased, O Lord, to deliver me;*
     O Lord, make haste to help me.

15 Let them be ashamed and altogether dismayed
     who seek after my life to destroy it;*
       let them draw back and be disgraced
       who take pleasure in my misfortune.

16 Let those who say "Aha!" and gloat over me be confounded,
     because they are ashamed.

17 Let all who seek you rejoice in you and be glad;*
     let those who love your salvation continually say,
     "Great is the Lord!"

18 Though I am poor and afflicted,*
     the Lord will have regard for me.

19 You are my helper and my deliverer;*
     do not tarry, O my God.

54 *Deus, in nomine*

1 Save me, O God, by your Name; *
   in your might, defend my cause.

2 Hear my prayer, O God; *
   give ear to the words of my mouth.

3 For the arrogant have risen up against me,
   and the ruthless have sought my life, *
   those who have no regard for God.

4 Behold, God is my helper; *
   it is the Lord who sustains my life.

5 Render evil to those who spy on me; *
   in your faithfulness, destroy them.

6 I will offer you a freewill sacrifice*
   and praise your Name, O Lord, for it is good.

7 For you have rescued me from every trouble, *
   and my eye has seen the ruin of my foes.

Evening

51 *Miserere mei, Deus*

1 Have mercy on me, O God, according to your loving-kindness; *
   in your great compassion blot out my offenses.

2 Wash me through and through from my wickedness*
   and cleanse me from my sin.

3 For I know my transgressions, *
   and my sin is ever before me.

4 Against you only have I sinned *
   and done what is evil in your sight.

5 And so you are justified when you speak *
   and upright in your judgment.

6 Indeed, I have been wicked from my birth, *
   a sinner from my mother's womb.

7 For behold, you look for truth deep within me, *
   and will make me understand wisdom secretly.

8 Purge me from my sin, and I shall be pure; *
     wash me, and I shall be clean indeed.

9 Make me hear of joy and gladness, *
     that the body you have broken may rejoice.

10 Hide your face from my sins*
     and blot out all my iniquities.

11 Create in me a clean heart, O God,*
     and renew a right spirit within me.

12 Cast me not away from your presence*
     and take not your holy Spirit from me.

13 Give me the joy of your saving help again*
     and sustain me with your bountiful Spirit.

14 I shall teach your ways to the wicked,*
     and sinners shall return to you.

15 Deliver me from death, O God,*
     and my tongue shall sing of your righteousness,
     O God of my salvation.

16 Open my lips, O Lord,*
     and my mouth shall proclaim your praise.

17 Had you desired it, I would have offered sacrifice,*
     but you take no delight in burnt-offerings.

18 The sacrifice of God is a troubled spirit;*
     a broken and contrite heart, O God, you will not despise.

19 Be favorable and gracious to Zion,*
     and rebuild the walls of Jerusalem.

20 Then you will be pleased with the appointed sacrifices,
     with burnt-offerings and oblations;*
     then shall they offer young bullocks upon your altar.

Saturday
Morning

55 *Exaudi, Deus*

1 Hear my prayer, O God;*
     do not hide yourself from my petition.

2   Listen to me and answer me; *
     I have no peace, because of my cares.

3   I am shaken by the noise of the enemy *
     and by the pressure of the wicked;

4   For they have cast an evil spell upon me *
     and are set against me in fury.

5   My heart quakes within me,*
     and the terrors of death have fallen upon me.

6   Fear and trembling have come over me, *
     and horror overwhelms me.

7   And I said, "Oh, that I had wings like a dove!*
     I would fly away and be at rest.

8   I would flee to a far-off place *
     and make my lodging in the wilderness.

9   I would hasten to escape *
     from the stormy wind and tempest."

10   Swallow them up, O Lord;
    confound their speech;*
     for I have seen violence and strife in the city.

11   Day and night the watchmen make their rounds upon her walls,*
     but trouble and misery are in the midst of her.

12   There is corruption at her heart;*
     her streets are never free of oppression and deceit.

13   For had it been an adversary who taunted me,
    then I could have borne it;*
     or had it been an enemy who vaunted himself against me,
    then I could have hidden from him.

14   But it was you, a man after my own heart,*
     my companion, my own familiar friend.

15   We took sweet counsel together,*
     and walked with the throng in the house of God.

16   Let death come upon them suddenly;
    let them go down alive into the grave;*
     for wickedness is in their dwellings, in their very midst.

17   But I will call upon God,*
     and the Lord will deliver me.

18 In the evening, in the morning, and at noonday,
   I will complain and lament,*
      and he will hear my voice.

19 He will bring me safely back from the battle waged against me;*
      for there are many who fight me.

20 God, who is enthroned of old, will hear me and bring them down;*
      they never change; they do not fear God.

21 My companion stretched forth his hand against his comrade;*
      he has broken his covenant.

22 His speech is softer than butter,*
      but war is in his heart.

23 His words are smoother than oil,*
      but they are drawn swords.

24 Cast your burden upon the Lord, and he will sustain you;*
      he will never let the righteous stumble.

25 For you will bring the bloodthirsty and deceitful*
      down to the pit of destruction, O God.

26 They shall not live out half their days,*
      but I will put my trust in you.

Evening

138 *Confitebor tibi*

1 I will give thanks to you, O Lord, with my whole heart;*
      before the gods I will sing your praise.

2 I will bow down toward your holy temple
   and praise your Name,*
      because of your love and faithfulness;

3 For you have glorified your Name*
      and your word above all things.

4 When I called, you answered me;*
      you increased my strength within me.

5 All the kings of the earth will praise you, O Lord,*
      when they have heard the words of your mouth.

6 They will sing of the ways of the Lord,*
      that great is the glory of the Lord.

7   Though the Lord be high, he cares for the lowly;*
     he perceives the haughty from afar.

8   Though I walk in the midst of trouble, you keep me safe;*
     you stretch forth your hand against the fury of my enemies;
     your right hand shall save me.

9   The Lord will make good his purpose for me;*
     O Lord, your love endures for ever;
     do not abandon the works of your hands.

139 *Domine, probasti*

1   Lord, you have searched me out and known me;*
     you know my sitting down and my rising up;
     you discern my thoughts from afar.

2   You trace my journeys and my resting-places *
     and are acquainted with all my ways.

3   Indeed, there is not a word on my lips, *
     but you, O Lord, know it altogether.

4   You press upon me behind and before *
     and lay your hand upon me.

5   Such knowledge is too wonderful for me; *
     it is so high that I cannot attain to it.

6   Where can I go then from your Spirit? *
     where can I flee from your presence?

7   If I climb up to heaven, you are there;*
     if I make the grave my bed, you are there also.

8   If I take the wings of the morning *
     and dwell in the uttermost parts of the sea,

9   Even there your hand will lead me *
     and your right hand hold me fast.

10   If I say, "Surely the darkness will cover me,*
     and the light around me turn to night,"

11   Darkness is not dark to you;
     the night is as bright as the day;*
     darkness and light to you are both alike.

12   For you yourself created my inmost parts;*
     you knit me together in my mother's womb.

13 I will thank you because I am marvelously made;*
   your works are wonderful, and I know it well.

14 My body was not hidden from you,*
   while I was being made in secret
   and woven in the depths of the earth.

15 Your eyes beheld my limbs, yet unfinished in the womb;
   all of them were written in your book;*
      they were fashioned day by day,
      when as yet there was none of them.

16 How deep I find your thoughts, O God!*
   how great is the sum of them!

17 If I were to count them, they would be more in number
         than the sand;*
   to count them all, my life span would need to be like yours.

18 Oh, that you would slay the wicked, O God!*
   You that thirst for blood, depart from me.

19 They speak despitefully against you;*
   your enemies take your Name in vain.

20 Do I not hate those, O Lord, who hate you?*
   and do I not loathe those who rise up against you?

21 I hate them with a perfect hatred;*
   they have become my own enemies.

22 Search me out, O God, and know my heart;*
   try me and know my restless thoughts.

23 Look well whether there be any wickedness in me*
   and lead me in the way that is everlasting.

Week of 2 Lent

Sunday
Morning

24   *Domini est terra*

1 The earth is the Lord's and all that is in it, *
   the world and all who dwell therein.

2 For it is he who founded it upon the seas *
 and made it firm upon the rivers of the deep.

3 "Who can ascend the hill of the Lord? *
 and who can stand in his holy place?"

4 "Those who have clean hands and a pure heart, *
 who have not pledged themselves to falsehood,
 nor sworn by what is a fraud.

5 They shall receive a blessing from the Lord *
 and a just reward from the God of their salvation."

6 Such is the generation of those who seek him, *
 of those who seek your face, O God of Jacob.

7 Lift up your heads, O gates;
 lift them high, O everlasting doors; *
 and the King of glory shall come in.

8 "Who is this King of glory?" *
 "The Lord, strong and mighty,
 the Lord, mighty in battle."

9 Lift up your heads, O gates;
 lift them high, O everlasting doors; *
 and the King of glory shall come in.

10 "Who is he, this King of glory?"
 "The Lord of hosts,
 he is the King of glory."

29 *Afferte Domino*

1 Ascribe to the Lord, you gods,*
 ascribe to the Lord glory and strength.

2 Ascribe to the Lord the glory due his Name; *
 worship the Lord in the beauty of holiness.

3 The voice of the Lord is upon the waters;
 the God of glory thunders; *
 the Lord is upon the mighty waters.

4 The voice of the Lord is a powerful voice; *
 the voice of the Lord is a voice of splendor.

5 The voice of the Lord breaks the cedar trees; *
 the Lord breaks the cedars of Lebanon;

6 He makes Lebanon skip like a calf, *
and Mount Hermon like a young wild ox.

7 The voice of the Lord splits the flames of fire;
the voice of the Lord shakes the wilderness; *
the Lord shakes the wilderness of Kadesh.

8 The voice of the Lord makes the oak trees writhe*
and strips the forests bare.

9 And in the temple of the Lord *
all are crying, "Glory!"

10 The Lord sits enthroned above the flood;*
the Lord sits enthroned as King for evermore.

11 The Lord shall give strength to his people; *
the Lord shall give his people the blessing of peace.

Evening

8 *Domine, Dominus noster*

1 O Lord our Governor,*
how exalted is your Name in all the world!

2 Out of the mouths of infants and children *
your majesty is praised above the heavens.

3 You have set up a stronghold against your adversaries,*
to quell the enemy and the avenger.

4 When I consider your heavens, the work of your fingers,*
the moon and the stars you have set in their courses,

5 What is man that you should be mindful of him? *
the son of man that you should seek him out?

6 You have made him but little lower than the angels; *
you adorn him with glory and honor;

7 You give him mastery over the works of your hands; *
you put all things under his feet:

8 All sheep and oxen, *
even the wild beasts of the field,

9 The birds of the air, the fish of the sea, *
and whatsoever walks in the paths of the sea.

10 O Lord our Governor,*
how exalted is your Name in all the world!

84 *Quam dilecta!*

1 How dear to me is your dwelling, O Lord of hosts!*
   My soul has a desire and longing for the courts of the Lord;
   my heart and my flesh rejoice in the living God.

2 The sparrow has found her a house
   and the swallow a nest where she may lay her young;*
   by the side of your altars, O Lord of hosts,
   my King and my God.

3 Happy are they who dwell in your house! *
   they will always be praising you.

4 Happy are the people whose strength is in you! *
   whose hearts are set on the pilgrims' way.

5 Those who go through the desolate valley will find it a
                   place of springs,*
   for the early rains have covered it with pools of water.

6 They will climb from height to height, *
   and the God of gods will reveal himself in Zion.

7 Lord God of hosts, hear my prayer; *
   hearken, O God of Jacob.

8 Behold our defender, O God; *
   and look upon the face of your Anointed.

9 For one day in your courts is better than a thousand in
                   my own room,*
   and to stand at the threshold of the house of my God
   than to dwell in the tents of the wicked.

10 For the Lord God is both sun and shield;*
   he will give grace and glory;

11 No good thing will the Lord withhold*
   from those who walk with integrity.

12 O Lord of hosts,*
   happy are they who put their trust in you!

Monday

Morning

56 *Miserere mei, Deus*

1 Have mercy on me, O God,
   for my enemies are hounding me; *
     all day long they assault and oppress me.

2 They hound me all the day long;*
     truly there are many who fight against me, O Most High.

3 Whenever I am afraid, *
     I will put my trust in you.

4 In God, whose word I praise,
   in God I trust and will not be afraid, *
     for what can flesh do to me?

5 All day long they damage my cause; *
     their only thought is to do me evil.

6 They band together; they lie in wait;*
   they spy upon my footsteps;
     because they seek my life.

7 Shall they escape despite their wickedness? *
     O God, in your anger, cast down the peoples.

8 You have noted my lamentation;
   put my tears into your bottle; *
     are they not recorded in your book?

9 Whenever I call upon you, my enemies will be put to flight;*
     this I know, for God is on my side.

10 In God the Lord, whose word I praise,
   in God I trust and will not be afraid,*
     for what can mortals do to me?

11 I am bound by the vow I made to you, O God;*
     I will present to you thank-offerings;

12 For you have rescued my soul from death and my feet
       from stumbling,*
     that I may walk before God in the light of the living.

57 *Miserere mei, Deus*

1 Be merciful to me, O God, be merciful,
  for I have taken refuge in you;*
    in the shadow of your wings will I take refuge
    until this time of trouble has gone by.

2 I will call upon the Most High God, *
    the God who maintains my cause.

3 He will send from heaven and save me;
  he will confound those who trample upon me; *
    God will send forth his love and his faithfulness.

4 I lie in the midst of lions that devour the people;*
    their teeth are spears and arrows,
    their tongue a sharp sword.

5 They have laid a net for my feet, and I am bowed low; *
    they have dug a pit before me,
    but have fallen into it themselves.

6 Exalt yourself above the heavens, O God,*
    and your glory over all the earth.

7 My heart is firmly fixed, O God, my heart is fixed; *
    I will sing and make melody.

8 Wake up, my spirit;
  awake, lute and harp; *
    I myself will waken the dawn.

9 I will confess you among the peoples, O Lord; *
    I will sing praise to you among the nations.

10 For your loving-kindness is greater than the heavens,*
    and your faithfulness reaches to the clouds.

11 Exalt yourself above the heavens, O God,*
    and your glory over all the earth.

58 *Si vere utique*

1 Do you indeed decree righteousness, you rulers?*
    do you judge the peoples with equity?

2 No; you devise evil in your hearts, *
    and your hands deal out violence in the land.

3   The wicked are perverse from the womb; *
      liars go astray from their birth.

4   They are as venomous as a serpent,*
      they are like the deaf adder which stops its ears,

5   Which does not heed the voice of the charmer, *
      no matter how skillful his charming.

6   O God, break their teeth in their mouths; *
      pull the fangs of the young lions, O Lord.

7   Let them vanish like water that runs off; *
      let them wither like trodden grass.

8   Let them be like the snail that melts away, *
      like a stillborn child that never sees the sun.

9   Before they bear fruit, let them be cut down like a brier;*
      like thorns and thistles let them be swept away.

10 The righteous will be glad when they see the vengeance;*
      they will bathe their feet in the blood of the wicked.

11 And they will say,
      "Surely, there is a reward for the righteous;*
      surely, there is a God who rules in the earth."

Evening

64   *Exaudi, Deus*

1   Hear my voice, O God, when I complain;*
      protect my life from fear of the enemy.

2   Hide me from the conspiracy of the wicked, *
      from the mob of evildoers.

3   They sharpen their tongue like a sword, *
      and aim their bitter words like arrows,

4   That they may shoot down the blameless from ambush;*
      they shoot without warning and are not afraid.

5   They hold fast to their evil course; *
      they plan how they may hide their snares.

6   They say, "Who will see us? who will find out our crimes? *
      we have thought out a perfect plot."

7 The human mind and heart are a mystery; *
    but God will loose an arrow at them,
    and suddenly they will be wounded.

8 He will make them trip over their tongues,*
    and all who see them will shake their heads.

9 Everyone will stand in awe and declare God's deeds; *
    they will recognize his works.

10 The righteous will rejoice in the Lord and put their trust in him,*
    and all who are true of heart will glory.

65 *Te decet hymnus*

1 You are to be praised, O God, in Zion;*
    to you shall vows be performed in Jerusalem.

2 To you that hear prayer shall all flesh come, *
    because of their transgressions.

3 Our sins are stronger than we are, *
    but you will blot them out.

4 Happy are they whom you choose
    and draw to your courts to dwell there!*
        they will be satisfied by the beauty of your house,
        by the holiness of your temple.

5 Awesome things will you show us in your righteousness,
    O God of our salvation,*
        O Hope of all the ends of the earth
        and of the seas that are far away.

6 You make fast the mountains by your power; *
    they are girded about with might.

7 You still the roaring of the seas, *
    the roaring of their waves,
    and the clamor of the peoples.

8 Those who dwell at the ends of the earth will tremble at your
                    marvelous signs;*
    you make the dawn and the dusk to sing for joy.

9 You visit the earth and water it abundantly;
    you make it very plenteous; *
        the river of God is full of water.

10 You prepare the grain,*
      for so you provide for the earth.

11 I You drench the furrows and smooth out the ridges;*
      with heavy rain you soften the ground and bless its increase.

12 You crown the year with your goodness,*
      and your paths overflow with plenty.

13 May the fields of the wilderness be rich for grazing,*
      and the hills be clothed with joy.

14 May the meadows cover themselves with flocks,
      and the valleys cloak themselves with grain;*
      let them shout for joy and sing.

Tuesday

Morning

61 *Exaudi, Deus*

1 Hear my cry, O God,*
      and listen to my prayer.

2 I call upon you from the ends of the earth
      with heaviness in my heart; *
      set me upon the rock that is higher than I.

3 For you have been my refuge, *
      a strong tower against the enemy.

4 I will dwell in your house for ever;*
      I will take refuge under the cover of your wings.

5 For you, O God, have heard my vows; *
      you have granted me the heritage of those who fear your Name.

6 Add length of days to the king's life; *
      let his years extend over many generations.

7 Let him sit enthroned before God for ever;*
      bid love and faithfulness watch over him.

8 So will I always sing the praise of your Name,*
      and day by day I will fulfill my vows.

62 *Nonne Deo?*

1 For God alone my soul in silence waits;*
   from him comes my salvation.

2 He alone is my rock and my salvation,*
   my stronghold, so that I shall not be greatly shaken.

3 How long will you assail me to crush me,
 all of you together,*
   as if you were a leaning fence, a toppling wall?

4 They seek only to bring me down from my place of honor;*
   lies are their chief delight.

5 They bless with their lips,*
   but in their hearts they curse.

6 For God alone my soul in silence waits;*
   truly, my hope is in him.

7 He alone is my rock and my salvation,*
   my stronghold, so that I shall not be shaken.

8 In God is my safety and my honor;*
   God is my strong rock and my refuge.

9 Put your trust in him always, O people,*
   pour out your hearts before him, for God is our refuge.

10 Those of high degree are but a fleeting breath,*
   even those of low estate cannot be trusted.

11 On the scales they are lighter than a breath,*
   all of them together.

12 Put no trust in extortion; in robbery take no empty pride;*
   though wealth increase, set not your heart upon it.

13 God has spoken once, twice have I heard it,*
   that power belongs to God.

14 Steadfast love is yours, O Lord,*
   for you repay everyone according to his deeds.

68   *Exsurgat Deus*

1 Let God arise, and let his enemies be scattered;*
    let those who hate him flee before him.

2 Let them vanish like smoke when the wind drives it away;*
    as the wax melts at the fire, so let the wicked perish at the
        presence of God.

3 But let the righteous be glad and rejoice before God; *
    let them also be merry and joyful.

4 Sing to God, sing praises to his Name;
    exalt him who rides upon the heavens; *
    Yahweh is his Name, rejoice before him!

5 Father of orphans, defender of widows, *
    God in his holy habitation!

6 God gives the solitary a home and brings forth prisoners
        into freedom; *
    but the rebels shall live in dry places.

7 O God, when you went forth before your people, *
    when you marched through the wilderness,

8 The earth shook, and the skies poured down rain,
    at the presence of God, the God of Sinai, *
    at the presence of God, the God of Israel.

9 You sent a gracious rain, O God, upon your inheritance;*
    you refreshed the land when it was weary.

10 Your people found their home in it;*
    in your goodness, O God, you have made provision for the
        poor.

11 The Lord gave the word;*
    great was the company of women who bore the tidings:

12 "Kings with their armies are fleeing away;*
    the women at home are dividing the spoils."

13 Though you lingered among the sheepfolds,*
    you shall be like a dove whose wings are covered with silver,
    whose feathers are like green gold.

14 When the Almighty scattered kings,*
   it was like snow falling in Zalmon.

15 O mighty mountain, O hill of Bashan!*
   O rugged mountain, O hill of Bashan!

16 Why do you look with envy, O rugged mountain,
   at the hill which God chose for his resting place?*
      truly, the Lord will dwell there for ever.

17 The chariots of God are twenty thousand,
   even thousands of thousands;*
      the Lord comes in holiness from Sinai.

18 You have gone up on high and led captivity captive;
   you have received gifts even from your enemies,*
      that the Lord God might dwell among them.

19 Blessed be the Lord day by day,*
   the God of our salvation, who bears our burdens.

20 He is our God, the God of our salvation;*
   God is the Lord, by whom we escape death.

21 God shall crush the heads of his enemies,*
   and the hairy scalp of those who go on still in their wickedness.

22 The Lord has said, "I will bring them back from Bashan;*
   I will bring them back from the depths of the sea;

23 That your foot may be dipped in blood,*
   the tongues of your dogs in the blood of your enemies."

24 They see your procession, O God,*
   your procession into the sanctuary, my God and my King.

25 The singers go before, musicians follow after,*
   in the midst of maidens playing upon the hand-drums.

26 Bless God in the congregation;*
   bless the Lord, you that are of the fountain of Israel.

27 There is Benjamin, least of the tribes, at the head;
   the princes of Judah in a company;*
      and the princes of Zebulon and Naphtali.

28 Send forth your strength, O God;*
   establish, O God, what you have wrought for us.

29 Kings shall bring gifts to you,*
   for your temple's sake at Jerusalem.

30 Rebuke the wild beast of the reeds,*
    and the peoples, a herd of wild bulls with its calves.

31 Trample down those who lust after silver;*
    scatter the peoples that delight in war.

32 Let tribute be brought out of Egypt;*
    let Ethiopia stretch out her hands to God.

33 Sing to God, O kingdoms of the earth;*
    sing praises to the Lord.

34 He rides in the heavens, the ancient heavens;*
    he sends forth his voice, his mighty voice.

35 Ascribe power to God;*
    his majesty is over Israel; his strength is in the skies.

36 How wonderful is God in his holy places!*
    the God of Israel giving strength and power to his people!
    Blessed be God!

Wednesday
Morning

72 *Deus, judicium*

1 Give the King your justice, O God,*
    and your righteousness to the King's Son;

2 That he may rule your people righteously *
    and the poor with justice;

3 That the mountains may bring prosperity to the people,*
    and the little hills bring righteousness.

4 He shall defend the needy among the people; *
    he shall rescue the poor and crush the oppressor.

5 He shall live as long as the sun and moon endure, *
    from one generation to another.

6 He shall come down like rain upon the mown field, *
    like showers that water the earth.

7 In his time shall the righteous flourish; *
    there shall be abundance of peace till the moon shall be no
    more.

8 He shall rule from sea to sea, *
and from the River to the ends of the earth.

9 His foes shall bow down before him,*
and his enemies lick the dust.

10 The kings of Tarshish and of the isles shall pay tribute,*
and the kings of Arabia and Saba offer gifts.

11 All kings shall bow down before him,*
and all the nations do him service.

12 For he shall deliver the poor who cries out in distress,*
and the oppressed who has no helper.

13 He shall have pity on the lowly and poor;*
he shall preserve the lives of the needy.

14 He shall redeem their lives from oppression and violence,*
and dear shall their blood be in his sight.

15 Long may he live!
and may there be given to him gold from Arabia;*
may prayer be made for him always,
and may they bless him all the day long.

16 May there be abundance of grain on the earth,
growing thick even on the hilltops;*
may its fruit flourish like Lebanon,
and its grain like grass upon the earth.

17 May his Name remain for ever
and be established as long as the sun endures;*
may all the nations bless themselves in him and call him blessed.

18 Blessed be the Lord God, the God of Israel,*
who alone does wondrous deeds!

19 And blessed be his glorious Name for ever!*
and may all the earth be filled with his glory. Amen. Amen.

Evening

119

Yodh *Manus tuœ fecerunt me*

73 Your hands have made me and fashioned me;*
give me understanding, that I may learn your commandments.

74 Those who fear you will be glad when they see me,*
    because I trust in your word.

75 I know, O Lord, that your judgments are right*
    and that in faithfulness you have afflicted me.

76 Let your loving-kindness be my comfort,*
    as you have promised to your servant.

77 Let your compassion come to me, that I may live,*
    for your law is my delight.

78 Let the arrogant be put to shame, for they wrong me with lies;*
    but I will meditate on your commandments.

79 Let those who fear you turn to me,*
    and also those who know your decrees.

80 Let my heart be sound in your statutes,*
    that I may not be put to shame.

Kaph   *Defecit in salutare*

81 My soul has longed for your salvation;*
    I have put my hope in your word.

82 My eyes have failed from watching for your promise,*
    and I say, "When will you comfort me?"

83 I have become like a leather flask in the smoke,*
    but I have not forgotten your statutes.

84 How much longer must I wait?*
    when will you give judgment against those who persecute me?

85 The proud have dug pits for me;*
    they do not keep your law.

86 All your commandments are true;*
    help me, for they persecute me with lies.

87 They had almost made an end of me on earth,*
    but I have not forsaken your commandments.

88 In your loving-kindness, revive me,*
    that I may keep the decrees of your mouth.

Lamedh   *In æternum, Domine*

89 O Lord, your word is everlasting;*
    it stands firm in the heavens.

90 Your faithfulness remains from one generation to another;*
    you established the earth, and it abides.

91 By your decree these continue to this day, *
    for all things are your servants.

92 If my delight had not been in your law, *
    I should have perished in my affliction.

93 I will never forget your commandments, *
    because by them you give me life.

94 I am yours; oh, that you would save me! *
    for I study your commandments.

95 Though the wicked lie in wait for me to destroy me, *
    I will apply my mind to your decrees.

96 I see that all things come to an end, *
    but your commandment has no bounds.

Thursday

Morning

70 *Deus, in adjutorium*

1 Be pleased, O God, to deliver me;*
    O Lord, make haste to help me.

2 Let those who seek my life be ashamed
and altogether dismayed;*
    let those who take pleasure in my misfortune
    draw back and be disgraced.

3 Let those who say to me "Aha!" and gloat over me turn back,*
    because they are ashamed.

4 Let all who seek you rejoice and be glad in you; *
    let those who love your salvation say for ever,
    "Great is the Lord!"

5 But as for me, I am poor and needy; *
    come to me speedily, O God.

6 You are my helper and my deliverer; *
    O Lord, do not tarry.

71 *In te, Domine, speravi*

1 In you, O Lord, have I taken refuge;*
   let me never be ashamed.

2 In your righteousness, deliver me and set me free; *
   incline your ear to me and save me.

3 Be my strong rock, a castle to keep me safe; *
   you are my crag and my stronghold.

4 Deliver me, my God, from the hand of the wicked, *
   from the clutches of the evildoer and the oppressor.

5 For you are my hope, O Lord God, *
   my confidence since I was young.

6 I have been sustained by you ever since I was born;
   from my mother's womb you have been my strength; *
   my praise shall be always of you.

7 I have become a portent to many; *
   but you are my refuge and my strength.

8 Let my mouth be full of your praise *
   and your glory all the day long.

9 Do not cast me off in my old age; *
   forsake me not when my strength fails.

10 For my enemies are talking against me,*
    and those who lie in wait for my life take counsel together.

11 They say, "God has forsaken him;
    go after him and seize him;*
    because there is none who will save."

12 O God, be not far from me;*
    come quickly to help me, O my God.

13 Let those who set themselves against me be put to shame and
                be disgraced;*
    let those who seek to do me evil be covered with scorn
                and reproach.

14 But I shall always wait in patience,*
    and shall praise you more and more.

15 My mouth shall recount your mighty acts
    and saving deeds all day long;*
    though I cannot know the number of them.

16 I will begin with the mighty works of the Lord God*
    I will recall your righteousness, yours alone.

17 O God, you have taught me since I was young,*
    and to this day I tell of your wonderful works.

18 And now that I am old and gray-headed, O God, do not
                    forsake me,*
    till I make known your strength to this generation
    and your power to all who are to come.

19 Your righteousness, O God, reaches to the heavens;*
    you have done great things; who is like you, O God?

20 You have showed me great troubles and adversities,*
    but you will restore my life and bring me up again from the
    deep places of the earth.

21 You strengthen me more and more;
    you enfold and comfort me,

22 Therefore I will praise you upon the lyre for your
                    faithfulness, O my God;*
    I will sing to you with the harp, O Holy One of Israel.

23 My lips will sing with joy when I play to you,*
    and so will my soul, which you have redeemed.

24 My tongue will proclaim your righteousness all day long, *
    for they are ashamed and disgraced who sought to do me harm.

Evening

74   *Ut quid, Deus?*

1   O God, why have you utterly cast us off?*
    why is your wrath so hot against the sheep of your pasture?

2   Remember your congregation that you purchased long ago,*
    the tribe you redeemed to be your inheritance,
    and Mount Zion where you dwell.

3   Turn your steps toward the endless ruins; *
    the enemy has laid waste everything in your sanctuary.

4   Your adversaries roared in your holy place; *
    they set up their banners as tokens of victory.

5   They were like men coming up with axes to a grove of trees;*
    they broke down all your carved work with hatchets
                    and hammers.

6 They set fire to your holy place; *
   they defiled the dwelling-place of your Name
   and razed it to the ground.

7 They said to themselves, "Let us destroy them altogether." *
   They burned down all the meeting-places of God in the land.

8 There are no signs for us to see; there is no prophet left; *
   there is not one among us who knows how long.

9 How long, O God, will the adversary scoff? *
   will the enemy blaspheme your Name for ever?

10 Why do you draw back your hand? *
   why is your right hand hidden in your bosom?

11 Yet God is my King from ancient times, *
   victorious in the midst of the earth.

12 You divided the sea by your might *
   and shattered the heads of the dragons upon the waters;

13 You crushed the heads of Leviathan *
   and gave him to the people of the desert for food.

14 You split open spring and torrent; *
   you dried up ever-flowing rivers.

15 Yours is the day, yours also the night; *
   you established the moon and the sun.

16 You fixed all the boundaries of the earth; *
   you made both summer and winter.

17 Remember, O Lord, how the enemy scoffed, *
   how a foolish people despised your Name.

18 Do not hand over the life of your dove to wild beasts; *
   never forget the lives of your poor.

19 Look upon your covenant; *
   the dark places of the earth are haunts of violence.

20 Let not the oppressed turn away ashamed; *
   let the poor and needy praise your Name.

21 Arise, O God, maintain your cause; *
   remember how fools revile you all day long.

22 Forget not the clamor of your adversaries, *
   the unending tumult of those who rise up against you.

Friday

Morning

For the Invitatory

95 *Venite, exultemus*

1 Come, let us sing to the Lord;*
   let us shout for joy to the Rock of our salvation.

2 Let us come before his presence with thanksgiving*
   and raise a loud shout to him with psalms.

3 For the Lord is a great God, *
   and a great King above all gods.

4 In his hand are the caverns of the earth, *
   and the heights of the hills are his also.

5 The sea is his, for he made it, *
   and his hands have molded the dry land.

6 Come, let us bow down, and bend the knee,*
   and kneel before the Lord our Maker.

7 For he is our God,
   and we are the people of his pasture and the sheep of his hand.*
   Oh, that today you would hearken to his voice!

8 Harden not your hearts,
   as your forebears did in the wilderness,*
   at Meribah, and on that day at Massah,
   when they tempted me.

9 They put me to the test, *
   though they had seen my works.

10 Forty years long I detested that generation and said,*
   "This people are wayward in their hearts;
   they do not know my ways."

11 So I swore in my wrath,*
   "They shall not enter into my rest."

69 *Salvum me fac*

1 Save me, O God,*
   for the waters have risen up to my neck.

2 I am sinking in deep mire, *
   and there is no firm ground for my feet.

3 I have come into deep waters, *
    and the torrent washes over me.

4 I have grown weary with my crying;
    my throat is inflamed; *
    my eyes have failed from looking for my God.

5 Those who hate me without a cause are more than the hairs
        of my head;
    my lying foes who would destroy me are mighty.*
    Must I then give back what I never stole?

6 O God, you know my foolishness, *
    and my faults are not hidden from you.

7 Let not those who hope in you be put to shame through me,
        Lord God of hosts;*
    let not those who seek you be disgraced because of me,
        O God of Israel.

8 Surely, for your sake have I suffered reproach,*
    and shame has covered my face.

9 I have become a stranger to my own kindred, *
    an alien to my mother's children.

10 Zeal for your house has eaten me up;*
    the scorn of those who scorn you has fallen upon me.

11 I humbled myself with fasting,*
    but that was turned to my reproach.

12 I put on sack-cloth also,*
    and became a byword among them.

13 Those who sit at the gate murmur against me,*
    and the drunkards make songs about me.

14 But as for me, this is my prayer to you,*
    at the time you have set, O Lord:

15 "In your great mercy, O God,*
    answer me with your unfailing help.

16 Save me from the mire; do not let me sink;*
    let me be rescued from those who hate me
    and out of the deep waters.

17 Let not the torrent of waters wash over me,
    neither let the deep swallow me up;*
    do not let the Pit shut its mouth upon me.

18 Answer me, O Lord, for your love is kind;*
   in your great compassion, turn to me.'

19 "Hide not your face from your servant;*
   be swift and answer me, for I am in distress.

20 Draw near to me and redeem me;*
   because of my enemies deliver me.

21 You know my reproach, my shame, and my dishonor; *
   my adversaries are all in your sight."

22 Reproach has broken my heart, and it cannot be healed; *
   I looked for sympathy, but there was none,
   for comforters, but I could find no one.

23 They gave me gall to eat, *
   and when I was thirsty, they gave me vinegar to drink.

24 Let the table before them be a trap *
   and their sacred feasts a snare.

25 Let their eyes be darkened, that they may not see, *
   and give them continual trembling in their loins.

26 Pour out your indignation upon them, *
   and let the fierceness of your anger overtake them.

27 Let their camp be desolate, *
   and let there be none to dwell in their tents.

28 For they persecute him whom you have stricken *
   and add to the pain of those whom you have pierced.

29 Lay to their charge guilt upon guilt, *
   and let them not receive your vindication.

30 Let them be wiped out of the book of the living *
   and not be written among the righteous.

31 As for me, I am afflicted and in pain; *
   your help, O God, will lift me up on high.

32 I will praise the Name of God in song; *
   I will proclaim his greatness with thanksgiving.

33 This will please the Lord more than an offering of oxen, *
   more than bullocks with horns and hoofs.

34 The afflicted shall see and be glad;*
   you who seek God, your heart shall live.

35 For the Lord listens to the needy,*
   and his prisoners he does not despise.

36 Let the heavens and the earth praise him,*
   the seas and all that moves in them;

37 For God will save Zion and rebuild the cities of Judah;*
   they shall live there and have it in possession.

38 The children of his servants will inherit it,*
   and those who love his Name will dwell therein.

Evening

73   *Quam bonus Israel!*

1 Truly, God is good to Israel,*
   to those who are pure in heart.

2 But as for me, my feet had nearly slipped; *
   I had almost tripped and fallen;

3 Because I envied the proud *
   and saw the prosperity of the wicked:

4 For they suffer no pain, *
   and their bodies are sleek and sound;

5 In the misfortunes of others they have no share;*
   they are not afflicted as others are;

6 Therefore they wear their pride like a necklace*
   and wrap their violence about them like a cloak.

7 Their iniquity comes from gross minds,*
   and their hearts overflow with wicked thoughts.

8 They scoff and speak maliciously; *
   out of their haughtiness they plan oppression.

9 They set their mouths against the heavens, *
   and their evil speech runs through the world.

10 And so the people turn to them*
   and find in them no fault.

11 They say, "How should God know?*
   is there knowledge in the Most High?"

12 So then, these are the wicked;*
   always at ease, they increase their wealth.

13 In vain have I kept my heart clean,*
   and washed my hands in innocence.

14 I have been afflicted all day long,*
   and punished every morning.

15 Had I gone on speaking this way,*
   I should have betrayed the generation of your children.

16 When I tried to understand these things,*
   it was too hard for me;

17 Until I entered the sanctuary of God*
   and discerned the end of the wicked.

18 Surely, you set them in slippery places;*
   you cast them down in ruin.

19 Oh, how suddenly do they come to destruction,*
   come to an end, and perish from terror!

20 Like a dream when one awakens, O Lord,*
   when you arise you will make their image vanish.

21 When my mind became embittered,*
   I was sorely wounded in my heart.

22 I was stupid and had no understanding;*
   I was like a brute beast in your presence.

23 Yet I am always with you;*
   you hold me by my right hand.

24 You will guide me by your counsel,*
   and afterwards receive me with glory.

25 Whom have I in heaven but you?*
   and having you I desire nothing upon earth.

26 Though my flesh and my heart should waste away,*
   God is the strength of my heart and my portion for ever.

27 Truly, those who forsake you will perish;*
   you destroy all who are unfaithful.

28 But it is good for me to be near God;*
   I have made the Lord God my refuge.

29 I will speak of all your works*
   in the gates of the city of Zion.

Saturday

Morning

75 *Confitebimur tibi*

1 We give you thanks, O God, we give you thanks, *
   calling upon your Name and declaring all your wonderful deeds.

2 "I will appoint a time," says God; *
   "I will judge with equity.

3 Though the earth and all its inhabitants are quaking, *
   I will make its pillars fast.

4 I will say to the boasters, 'Boast no more,' *
   and to the wicked, 'Do not toss your horns;

5 Do not toss your horns so high, *
   nor speak with a proud neck.'"

6 For judgment is neither from the east nor from the west, *
   nor yet from the wilderness or the mountains.

7 It is God who judges; *
   he puts down one and lifts up another.

8 For in the Lord's hand there is a cup,
   full of spiced and foaming wine, which he pours out, *
   and all the wicked of the earth shall drink and drain the dregs.

9 But I will rejoice for ever; *
   I will sing praises to the God of Jacob.

10 He shall break off all the horns of the wicked; *
   but the horns of the righteous shall be exalted.

76 *Notus in Judœa*

1 In Judah is God known;*
   his Name is great in Israel.

2 At Salem is his tabernacle, *
   and his dwelling is in Zion.

3 There he broke the flashing arrows, *
   the shield, the sword, and the weapons of battle.

4 How glorious you are! *
   more splendid than the everlasting mountains!

5 The strong of heart have been despoiled; they sink into sleep; *
   none of the warriors can lift a hand.

6 At your rebuke, O God of Jacob, *
   both horse and rider lie stunned.

7 What terror you inspire! *
   who can stand before you when you are angry?

8 From heaven you pronounced judgment; *
   the earth was afraid and was still;

9 When God rose up to judgment *
   and to save all the oppressed of the earth.

10 Truly, wrathful Edom will give you thanks,*
   and the remnant of Hamath will keep your feasts.

11 Make a vow to the Lord your God and keep it;*
   let all around him bring gifts to him who is worthy to be feared.

12 He breaks the spirit of princes,*
   and strikes terror in the kings of the earth.

Evening

23   *Dominus regit me*

1 The Lord is my shepherd;*
   I shall not be in want.

2 He makes me lie down in green pastures *
   and leads me beside still waters.

3 He revives my soul *
   and guides me along right pathways for his Name's sake.

4 Though I walk through the valley of the shadow of death,
  I shall fear no evil; *
   for you are with me;
   your rod and your staff, they comfort me.

5 You spread a table before me in the presence of those who
         trouble me; *
   you have anointed my head with oil,
   and my cup is running over.

6 Surely your goodness and mercy shall follow me all the days
         of my life, *
   and I will dwell in the house of the Lord for ever.

27 *Dominus illuminatio*

1   The Lord is my light and my salvation;
whom then shall I fear?*
   the Lord is the strength of my life;
   of whom then shall I be afraid?

2   When evildoers came upon me to eat up my flesh, *
   it was they, my foes and my adversaries, who stumbled and fell.

3   Though an army should encamp against me, *
   yet my heart shall not be afraid;

4   And though war should rise up against me, *
   yet will I put my trust in him.

5   One thing have I asked of the Lord;
one thing I seek;*
   that I may dwell in the house of the Lord all the days of my life;

6   To behold the fair beauty of the Lord *
   and to seek him in his temple.

7   For in the day of trouble he shall keep me safe in his shelter;*
   he shall hide me in the secrecy of his dwelling
   and set me high upon a rock.

8   Even now he lifts up my head *
   above my enemies round about me.

9   Therefore I will offer in his dwelling an oblation
with sounds of great gladness; *
   I will sing and make music to the Lord.

10   Hearken to my voice, O Lord, when I call;*
   have mercy on me and answer me.

11   You speak in my heart and say, "Seek my face."*
   Your face, Lord, will I seek.

12   Hide not your face from me,*
   nor turn away your servant in displeasure.

13   You have been my helper; cast me not away;*
   do not forsake me, O God of my salvation.

14   Though my father and my mother forsake me,*
   the Lord will sustain me.

15   Show me your way, O Lord;*
   lead me on a level path, because of my enemies.

16   Deliver me not into the hand of my adversaries,*
     for false witnesses have risen up against me,
     and also those who speak malice.

17   What if I had not believed
     that I should see the goodness of the Lord*
     in the land of the living!

18   O tarry and await the Lord's pleasure;
     be strong, and he shall comfort your heart;*
     wait patiently for the Lord.

Week of 3 Lent

Sunday

Morning

93   *Dominus regnavit*

1   The Lord is King;
     he has put on splendid apparel;*
     the Lord has put on his apparel
     and girded himself with strength.

2   He has made the whole world so sure*
     that it cannot be moved;

3   Ever since the world began, your throne has been established;*
     you are from everlasting.

4   The waters have lifted up, O Lord,
     the waters have lifted up their voice;*
     the waters have lifted up their pounding waves.

5   Mightier than the sound of many waters,
     mightier than the breakers of the sea,*
     mightier is the Lord who dwells on high.

6   Your testimonies are very sure,*
     and holiness adorns your house, O Lord,
     for ever and for evermore.

96 *Cantate Domino*

1 Sing to the Lord a new song;*
    sing to the Lord, all the whole earth.

2 Sing to the Lord and bless his Name; *
    proclaim the good news of his salvation from day to day.

3 Declare his glory among the nations *
    and his wonders among all peoples.

4 For great is the Lord and greatly to be praised; *
    he is more to be feared than all gods.

5 As for all the gods of the nations, they are but idols;*
    but it is the Lord who made the heavens.

6 Oh, the majesty and magnificence of his presence! *
    Oh, the power and the splendor of his sanctuary!

7 Ascribe to the Lord, you families of the peoples; *
    ascribe to the Lord honor and power.

8 Ascribe to the Lord the honor due his Name; *
    bring offerings and come into his courts.

9 Worship the Lord in the beauty of holiness; *
    let the whole earth tremble before him.

10 Tell it out among the nations: "The Lord is King!*
    he has made the world so firm that it cannot be moved;

    he will judge the peoples with equity."

11 Let the heavens rejoice, and let the earth be glad;
    let the sea thunder and all that is in it;*
    let the field be joyful and all that is therein.

12 Then shall all the trees of the wood shout for joy
    before the Lord when he comes,*
    when he comes to judge the earth.

13 He will judge the world with righteousness*
    and the peoples with his truth.

34 *Benedicam Dominum*

1 I will bless the Lord at all times; *
   his praise shall ever be in my mouth.

2 I will glory in the Lord; *
   let the humble hear and rejoice.

3 Proclaim with me the greatness of the Lord;
   let us exalt his Name together.

4 I sought the Lord, and he answered me*
   and delivered me out of all my terror.

5 Look upon him and be radiant, *
   and let not your faces be ashamed.

6 I called in my affliction and the Lord heard me *
   and saved me from all my troubles.

7 The angel of the Lord encompasses those who fear him,*
   and he will deliver them.

8 Taste and see that the Lord is good; *
   happy are they who trust in him!

9 Fear the Lord, you that are his saints,*
   for those who fear him lack nothing.

10 The young lions lack and suffer hunger,*
    but those who seek the Lord lack nothing that is good.

11 Come, children, and listen to me;*
    I will teach you the fear of the Lord.

12 Who among you loves life*
    and desires long life to enjoy prosperity?

13 Keep your tongue from evil-speaking*
    and your lips from lying words.

14 Turn from evil and do good;*
    seek peace and pursue it.

15 The eyes of the Lord are upon the righteous,*
    and his ears are open to their cry.

16 The face of the Lord is against those who do evil,*
    to root out the remembrance of them from the earth.

17 The righteous cry, and the Lord hears them*
   and delivers them from all their troubles.

18 The Lord is near to the brokenhearted*
   and will save those whose spirits are crushed.

19 Many are the troubles of the righteous,*
   but the Lord will deliver him out of them all.

20 He will keep safe all his bones;*
   not one of them shall be broken.

21 Evil shall slay the wicked,*
   and those who hate the righteous will be punished.

22 The Lord ransoms the life of his servants,*
   and none will be punished who trust in him.

Monday

Morning

80   *Qui regis Israel*

1 Hear, O Shepherd of Israel, leading Joseph like a flock;*
   shine forth, you that are enthroned upon the cherubim.

2 In the presence of Ephraim, Benjamin, and Manasseh, *
   stir up your strength and come to help us.

3 Restore us, O God of hosts;*
   show the light of your countenance, and we shall be saved.

4 O Lord God of hosts,*
   how long will you be angered

   despite the prayers of your people?

5 You have fed them with the bread of tears; *
   you have given them bowls of tears to drink.

6 You have made us the derision of our neighbors, *
   and our enemies laugh us to scorn.

7 Restore us, O God of hosts;*
   show the light of your countenance, and we shall be saved.

8 You have brought a vine out of Egypt;*
   you cast out the nations and planted it.

9   You prepared the ground for it; *
     it took root and filled the land.

10   The mountains were covered by its shadow*
     and the towering cedar trees by its boughs.

11   You stretched out its tendrils to the Sea*
     and its branches to the River.

12   Why have you broken down its wall,*
     so that all who pass by pluck off its grapes?

13   The wild boar of the forest has ravaged it,*
     and the beasts of the field have grazed upon it.

14   Turn now, O God of hosts, look down from heaven;
     behold and tend this vine;*
     preserve what your right hand has planted.

15   They burn it with fire like rubbish;*
     at the rebuke of your countenance let them perish.

16   Let your hand be upon the man of your right hand,*
     the son of man you have made so strong for yourself.

17   And so will we never turn away from you;*
     give us life, that we may call upon your Name.

18   Restore us, O Lord God of hosts;*
     show the light of your countenance, and we shall be saved.

Evening

77   *Voce mea ad Dominum*

1 I will cry aloud to God; *
   I will cry aloud, and he will hear me.

2 In the day of my trouble I sought the Lord; *
   my hands were stretched out by night and did not tire;
   I refused to be comforted.

3 I think of God, I am restless, *
   I ponder, and my spirit faints.

4 You will not let my eyelids close; *
   I am troubled and I cannot speak.

5 I consider the days of old; *
   I remember the years long past;

6   I commune with my heart in the night; *
       I ponder and search my mind.

7   Will the Lord cast me off for ever? *
       will he no more show his favor?

8   Has his loving-kindness come to an end for ever? *
       has his promise failed for evermore?

9   Has God forgotten to be gracious? *
       has he, in his anger, withheld his compassion?

10   And I said, "My grief is this: *
       the right hand of the Most High has lost its power."

11   I will remember the works of the Lord, *
       and call to mind your wonders of old time.

12   I will meditate on all your acts *
       and ponder your mighty deeds.

13   Your way, O God, is holy; *
       who is so great a god as our God?

14   You are the God who works wonders*
       and have declared your power among the peoples.

15   By your strength you have redeemed your people,*
       the children of Jacob and Joseph.

16   The waters saw you, O God; the waters saw you and trembled;*
       the very depths were shaken.

17   The clouds poured out water;
     the skies thundered;*
       your arrows flashed to and fro;

18   The sound of your thunder was in the whirlwind;
     your lightnings lit up the world;*
       the earth trembled and shook.

19   Your way was in the sea, and
     your paths in the great waters,*
       yet your footsteps were not seen.

20   You led your people like a flock*
       by the hand of Moses and Aaron.

79 *Deus, venerunt*

1 O God, the heathen have come into your inheritance;
they have profaned your holy temple;*
   they have made Jerusalem a heap of rubble.

2 They have given the bodies of your servants as food for the
     birds of the air,*
   and the flesh of your faithful ones to the beasts of the field.

3 They have shed their blood like water on every side of
     Jerusalem,*
   and there was no one to bury them.

4 We have become a reproach to our neighbors,*
   an object of scorn and derision to those around us.

5 How long will you be angry, O Lord?*
   will your fury blaze like fire for ever?

6 Pour out your wrath upon the heathen who have not known you*
   and upon the kingdoms that have not called upon your Name.

7 For they have devoured Jacob*
   and made his dwelling a ruin.

8 Remember not our past sins;
let your compassion be swift to meet us;*
   for we have been brought very low.

9 Help us, O God our Savior, for the glory of your Name;*
   deliver us and forgive us our sins, for your Name's sake.

10 Why should the heathen say, "Where is their God?"*
Let it be known among the heathen and in our sight
   that you avenge the shedding of your servants' blood.

11 Let the sorrowful sighing of the prisoners come before you,*
   and by your great might spare those who are condemned to die.

12 May the revilings with which they reviled you, O Lord,*
   return seven-fold into their bosoms.

13 For we are your people and the sheep of your pasture;*
we will give you thanks for ever
   and show forth your praise from age to age.

Tuesday

Morning

78

Part I *Attendite, popule*

1 Hear my teaching, O my people;*
incline your ears to the words of my mouth.

2 I will open my mouth in a parable; *
I will declare the mysteries of ancient times.

3 That which we have heard and known,
and what our forefathers have told us, *
we will not hide from their children.

4 We will recount to generations to come
the praiseworthy deeds and the power of the Lord, *
and the wonderful works he has done.

5 He gave his decrees to Jacob
and established a law for Israel, *
which he commanded them to teach their children;

6 That the generations to come might know,
and the children yet unborn; *
that they in their turn might tell it to their children;

7 So that they might put their trust in God, *
and not forget the deeds of God,
but keep his commandments;

8 And not be like their forefathers,
a stubborn and rebellious generation, *
a generation whose heart was not steadfast,
and whose spirit was not faithful to God.

9 The people of Ephraim, armed with the bow, *
turned back in the day of battle;

10 They did not keep the covenant of God, *
and refused to walk in his law;

11 They forgot what he had done, *
and the wonders he had shown them.

12 He worked marvels in the sight of their forefathers, *
in the land of Egypt, in the field of Zoan.

13 He split open the sea and let them pass through; *
        he made the waters stand up like walls.

14 He led them with a cloud by day,*
        and all the night through with a glow of fire.

15 He split the hard rocks in the wilderness*
        and gave them drink as from the great deep.

16 He brought streams out of the cliff,*
        and the waters gushed out like rivers.

17 But they went on sinning against him,*
        rebelling in the desert against the Most High.

18 They tested God in their hearts,*
        demanding food for their craving.

19 They railed against God and said,*
        "Can God set a table in the wilderness?

20 True, he struck the rock, the waters gushed out, and the
                gullies overflowed;*
        but is he able to give bread
        or to provide meat for his people?"

21 When the Lord heard this, he was full of wrath;*
        a fire was kindled against Jacob,
        and his anger mounted against Israel;

22 For they had no faith in God,*
        nor did they put their trust in his saving power.

23 So he commanded the clouds above*
        and opened the doors of heaven.

24 He rained down manna upon them to eat*
        and gave them grain from heaven.

25 So mortals ate the bread of angels;*
        he provided for them food enough.

26 He caused the east wind to blow in the heavens*
        and led out the south wind by his might.

27 He rained down flesh upon them like dust*
        and wingéd birds like the sand of the sea.

28 He let it fall in the midst of their camp*
        and round about their dwellings.

29 So they ate and were well filled,*
        for he gave them what they craved.

30 But they did not stop their craving,*
   though the food was still in their mouths.

31 So God's anger mounted against them; *
   he slew their strongest men
   and laid low the youth of Israel.

32 In spite of all this, they went on sinning*
   and had no faith in his wonderful works.

33 So he brought their days to an end like a breath*
   and their years in sudden terror.

34 Whenever he slew them, they would seek him,*
   and repent, and diligently search for God.

35 They would remember that God was their rock,*
   and the Most High God their redeemer.

36 But they flattered him with their mouths*
   and lied to him with their tongues.

37 Their heart was not steadfast toward him,*
   and they were not faithful to his covenant.

38 But he was so merciful that he forgave their sins
   and did not destroy them; *
   many times he held back his anger
   and did not permit his wrath to be roused.

39 For he remembered that they were but flesh,*
   a breath that goes forth and does not return.

Evening

78

Part II *Quoties exacerbaverunt*

40 How often the people disobeyed him in the wilderness*
   and offended him in the desert!

41 Again and again they tempted God*
   and provoked the Holy One of Israel.

42 They did not remember his power*
   in the day when he ransomed them from the enemy;

43 How he wrought his signs in Egypt*
   and his omens in the field of Zoan.

44 He turned their rivers into blood,*
   so that they could not drink of their streams.

45 He sent swarms of flies among them, which ate them up,*
   and frogs, which destroyed them.

46 He gave their crops to the caterpillar,*
   the fruit of their toil to the locust.

47 He killed their vines with hail*
   and their sycamores with frost.

48 He delivered their cattle to hailstones*
   and their livestock to hot thunderbolts.

49 He poured out upon them his blazing anger:*
   fury, indignation, and distress, a troop of destroying angels.

50 He gave full rein to his anger;
   he did not spare their souls from death;*
   but delivered their lives to the plague.

51 He struck down all the firstborn of Egypt,*
   the flower of manhood in the dwellings of Ham.

52 He led out his people like sheep*
   and guided them in the wilderness like a flock.

53 He led them to safety, and they were not afraid;*
   but the sea overwhelmed their enemies.

54 He brought them to his holy land,*
   the mountain his right hand had won.

55 He drove out the Canaanites before them
   and apportioned an inheritance to them by lot;*
   he made the tribes of Israel to dwell in their tents.

56 But they tested the Most High God, and defied him,*
   and did not keep his commandments.

57 They turned away and were disloyal like their fathers;*
   they were undependable like a warped bow.

58 They grieved him with their hill-altars*
   and provoked his displeasure with their idols.

59 When God heard this, he was angry*
   and utterly rejected Israel.

60 He forsook the shrine at Shiloh,*
   the tabernacle where he had lived among his people.

61 He delivered the ark into captivity,*
    his glory into the adversary's hand.

62 He gave his people to the sword*
    and was angered against his inheritance.

63 The fire consumed their young men;*
    there were no wedding songs for their maidens.

64 Their priests fell by the sword,*
    and their widows made no lamentation.

65 Then the Lord woke as though from sleep,*
    like a warrior refreshed with wine.

66 He struck his enemies on the backside*
    and put them to perpetual shame.

67 He rejected the tent of Joseph*
    and did not choose the tribe of Ephraim;

68 He chose instead the tribe of Judah*
    and Mount Zion, which he loved.

69 He built his sanctuary like the heights of heaven,*
    like the earth which he founded for ever.

70 He chose David his servant,*
    and took him away from the sheepfolds.

71 He brought him from following the ewes,*
    to be a shepherd over Jacob his people
    and over Israel his inheritance.

72 So he shepherded them with a faithful and true heart*
    and guided them with the skillfulness of his hands.

Wednesday
Morning

119

Mem   *Quomodo dilexi!*

97 Oh, how I love your law! *
    all the day long it is in my mind.

98 Your commandment has made me wiser than my enemies, *
    and it is always with me.

99 I have more understanding than all my teachers, *
    for your decrees are my study.

100 I am wiser than the elders, *
    because I observe your commandments.

101 I restrain my feet from every evil way, *
    that I may keep your word.

102 I do not shrink from your judgments, *
    because you yourself have taught me.

103 How sweet are your words to my taste! *
    they are sweeter than honey to my mouth.

104 Through your commandments I gain understanding;*
    therefore I hate every lying way.

Nun   *Lucerna pedibus meis*

105 Your word is a lantern to my feet*
    and a light upon my path.

106 I have sworn and am determined*
    to keep your righteous judgments.

107 I am deeply troubled;*
    preserve my life, O Lord, according to your word.

108 Accept, O Lord, the willing tribute of my lips,*
    and teach me your judgments.

109 My life is always in my hand,*
    yet I do not forget your law.

110 The wicked have set a trap for me,*
    but I have not strayed from your commandments.

111 Your decrees are my inheritance for ever;*
    truly, they are the joy of my heart.

112 I have applied my heart to fulfill your statutes*
    for ever and to the end.

Samekh   *Iniquos odio habui*

113 I hate those who have a divided heart,*
    but your law do I love.

114 You are my refuge and shield; *
    my hope is in your word.

115 Away from me, you wicked! *
    I will keep the commandments of my God.

116 Sustain me according to your promise, that I may live, *
    and let me not be disappointed in my hope.

117 Hold me up, and I shall be safe, *
    and my delight shall be ever in your statutes.

118 You spurn all who stray from your statutes; *
    their deceitfulness is in vain.

119 In your sight all the wicked of the earth are but dross; *
    therefore I love your decrees.

120 My flesh trembles with dread of you; *
    I am afraid of your judgments.

Evening

81   *Exultate Deo*

1 Sing with joy to God our strength*
    and raise a loud shout to the God of Jacob.

2 Raise a song and sound the timbrel, *
    the merry harp, and the lyre.

3 Blow the ram's-horn at the new moon, *
    and at the full moon, the day of our feast.

4 For this is a statute for Israel, *
    a law of the God of Jacob.

5 He laid it as a solemn charge upon Joseph, *
    when he came out of the land of Egypt.

6 I heard an unfamiliar voice saying *
    "I eased his shoulder from the burden;
    his hands were set free from bearing the load."

7 You called on me in trouble, and I saved you; *
    I answered you from the secret place of thunder
    and tested you at the waters of Meribah.

8 Hear, O my people, and I will admonish you: *
    O Israel, if you would but listen to me!

9 There shall be no strange god among you; *
    you shall not worship a foreign god.

10 I am the Lord your God,
    who brought you out of the land of Egypt and said,*
    "Open your mouth wide, and I will fill it."

11 And yet my people did not hear my voice,*
    and Israel would not obey me.

12 So I gave them over to the stubbornness of their hearts,*
    to follow their own devices.

13 Oh, that my people would listen to me!*
    that Israel would walk in my ways!

14 I should soon subdue their enemies*
    and turn my hand against their foes.

15 Those who hate the Lord would cringe before him,*
    and their punishment would last for ever.

16 But Israel would I feed with the finest wheat*
    and satisfy him with honey from the rock.

82 *Deus stetit*

1 God takes his stand in the council of heaven;*
   he gives judgment in the midst of the gods:

2 "How long will you judge unjustly, *
   and show favor to the wicked?

3 Save the weak and the orphan; *
   defend the humble and needy;

4 Rescue the weak and the poor; *
   deliver them from the power of the wicked.

5 They do not know, neither do they understand;
   they go about in darkness; *
   all the foundations of the earth are shaken.

6 Now I say to you, 'You are gods, *
   and all of you children of the Most High;

7 Nevertheless, you shall die like mortals, *
   and fall like any prince.'"

8 Arise, O God, and rule the earth, *
   for you shall take all nations for your own.

Thursday
Morning

83   *Deus, quis similis?*

1   O God, do not be silent;*
    do not keep still nor hold your peace, O God;

2   For your enemies are in tumult, *
    and those who hate you have lifted up their heads.

3   They take secret counsel against your people *
    and plot against those whom you protect.

4   They have said, "Come, let us wipe them out from among
        the nations;*
    let the name of Israel be remembered no more."

5   They have conspired together; *
    they have made an alliance against you:

6   The tents of Edom and the Ishmaelites; *
    the Moabites and the Hagarenes;

7   Gebal, and Ammon, and Amalek; *
    the Philistines and those who dwell in Tyre.

8   The Assyrians also have joined them, *
    and have come to help the people of Lot.

9   Do to them as you did to Midian, *
    to Sisera, and to Jabin at the river of Kishon:

10   They were destroyed at Endor;*
     they became like dung upon the ground.

11   Make their leaders like Oreb and Zeëb,*
     and all their commanders like Zebah and Zalmunna,

12   Who said, "Let us take for ourselves*
     the fields of God as our possession."

13   O my God, make them like whirling dust*
     and like chaff before the wind;

14   Like fire that burns down a forest,*
     like the flame that sets mountains ablaze.

15   Drive them with your tempest*
     and terrify them with your storm;

16 Cover their faces with shame, O Lord,
    that they may seek your Name.

17 Let them be disgraced and terrified for ever;
    let them be put to confusion and perish.

18 Let them know that you, whose Name is Yahweh,*
    you alone are the Most High over all the earth.

or

42   *Quemadmodum*

1 As the deer longs for the water-brooks,*
    so longs my soul for you, O God.

2 My soul is athirst for God, athirst for the living God; *
    when shall I come to appear before the presence of God?

3 My tears have been my food day and night, *
    while all day long they say to me,
    "Where now is your God?"

4 I pour out my soul when I think on these things: *
    how I went with the multitude and led them into the
        house of God,

5 With the voice of praise and thanksgiving, *
    among those who keep holy-day.

6 Why are you so full of heaviness, O my soul? *
    and why are you so disquieted within me?

7 Put your trust in God; *
    for I will yet give thanks to him,

    who is the help of my countenance, and my God.

8 My soul is heavy within me;*
    therefore I will remember you from the land of Jordan, and
    from the peak of Mizar among the heights of Hermon.

9 One deep calls to another in the noise of your cataracts; *
    all your rapids and floods have gone over me.

10 The Lord grants his loving-kindness in the daytime;*
    in the night season his song is with me,
    a prayer to the God of my life.

11 I will say to the God of my strength,
    "Why have you forgotten me?*
    and why do I go so heavily while the enemy oppresses me?"

12 While my bones are being broken,*
    my enemies mock me to my face;

13 All day long they mock me*
    and say to me, "Where now is your God?"

14 Why are you so full of heaviness, O my soul?*
    and why are you so disquieted within me?

15 Put your trust in God;*
    for I will yet give thanks to him,
    who is the help of my countenance, and my God.

43   *Judica me, Deus*

1 Give judgment for me, O God,
    and defend my cause against an ungodly people; *
    deliver me from the deceitful and the wicked.

2 For you are the God of my strength;
    why have you put me from you? *
    and why do I go so heavily while the enemy oppresses me?

3 Send out your light and your truth, that they may lead me,*
    and bring me to your holy hill
    and to your dwelling;

4 That I may go to the altar of God,
    to the God of my joy and gladness;*
    and on the harp I will give thanks to you, O God my God.

5 Why are you so full of heaviness, O my soul? *
    and why are you so disquieted within me?

6 Put your trust in God; *
    for I will yet give thanks to him,
    who is the help of my countenance, and my God.

Evening

85   *Benedixisti, Domine*

1 You have been gracious to your land, O Lord,*
    you have restored the good fortune of Jacob.

2 You have forgiven the iniquity of your people *
    and blotted out all their sins.

3 You have withdrawn all your fury*
   and turned yourself from your wrathful indignation.

4 Restore us then, O God our Savior;*
   let your anger depart from us.

5 Will you be displeased with us for ever? *
   will you prolong your anger from age to age?

6 Will you not give us life again, *
   that your people may rejoice in you?

7 Show us your mercy, O Lord,*
   and grant us your salvation.

8 I will listen to what the Lord God is saying, *
   for he is speaking peace to his faithful people
   and to those who turn their hearts to him.

9 Truly, his salvation is very near to those who fear him,*
   that his glory may dwell in our land.

10 Mercy and truth have met together;*
   righteousness and peace have kissed each other.

11 Truth shall spring up from the earth,*
   and righteousness shall look down from heaven.

12 The Lord will indeed grant prosperity,*
   and our land will yield its increase.

13 Righteousness shall go before him,*
   and peace shall be a pathway for his feet.

86   *Inclina, Domine*

1 Bow down your ear, O Lord, and answer me, *
   for I am poor and in misery.

2 Keep watch over my life, for I am faithful;*
   save your servant who puts his trust in you.

3 Be merciful to me, O Lord, for you are my God; *
   I call upon you all the day long.

4 Gladden the soul of your servant, *
   for to you, O Lord, I lift up my soul.

5 For you, O Lord, are good and forgiving,*
   and great is your love toward all who call upon you.

6 Give ear, O Lord, to my prayer, *
   and attend to the voice of my supplications.

7 In the time of my trouble I will call upon you, *
   for you will answer me.

8 Among the gods there is none like you, O Lord, *
   nor anything like your works.

9 All nations you have made will come and worship you, O Lord, *
   and glorify your Name.

10 For you are great;
   you do wondrous things;*
      and you alone are God.

11 Teach me your way, O Lord,
   and I will walk in your truth;*
      knit my heart to you that I may fear your Name.

12 I will thank you, O Lord my God, with all my heart,*
   and glorify your Name for evermore.

13 For great is your love toward me;*
   you have delivered me from the nethermost Pit.

14 The arrogant rise up against me, O God,
   and a band of violent men seeks my life;*
      they have not set you before their eyes.

15 But you, O Lord, are gracious and full of compassion,*
   slow to anger, and full of kindness and truth.

16 Turn to me and have mercy upon me;*
   give your strength to your servant;
   and save the child of your handmaid.

17 Show me a sign of your favor,
   so that those who hate me may see it and be ashamed;*
      because you, O Lord, have helped me and comforted me.

Friday

Morning

For the Invitatory

95 *Venite, exultemus*

1 Come, let us sing to the Lord;*
   let us shout for joy to the Rock of our salvation.

2 Let us come before his presence with thanksgiving*
    and raise a loud shout to him with psalms.

3 For the Lord is a great God, *
    and a great King above all gods.

4 In his hand are the caverns of the earth, *
    and the heights of the hills are his also.

5 The sea is his, for he made it, *
    and his hands have molded the dry land.

6 Come, let us bow down, and bend the knee,*
    and kneel before the Lord our Maker.

7 For he is our God,
    and we are the people of his pasture and the sheep of his hand.*
        Oh, that today you would hearken to his voice!

8 Harden not your hearts,
    as your forebears did in the wilderness,*
        at Meribah, and on that day at Massah,
        when they tempted me.

9 They put me to the test, *
    though they had seen my works.

10 Forty years long I detested that generation and said,*
    "This people are wayward in their hearts;
    they do not know my ways."

11 So I swore in my wrath,*
    "They shall not enter into my rest."

88 *Domine, Deus*

1 O Lord, my God, my Savior,*
    by day and night I cry to you.

2 Let my prayer enter into your presence; *
    incline your ear to my lamentation.

3 For I am full of trouble; *
    my life is at the brink of the grave.

4 I am counted among those who go down to the Pit; *
    I have become like one who has no strength;

5 Lost among the dead, *
    like the slain who lie in the grave,

6   Whom you remember no more, *
    for they are cut off from your hand.

7   You have laid me in the depths of the Pit, *
    in dark places, and in the abyss.

8   Your anger weighs upon me heavily, *
    and all your great waves overwhelm me.

9   You have put my friends far from me;
    you have made me to be abhorred by them; *
    I am in prison and cannot get free.

10 My sight has failed me because of trouble;*
    Lord, I have called upon you daily;
    I have stretched out my hands to you.

11 Do you work wonders for the dead?*
    will those who have died stand up and give you thanks?

12 Will your loving-kindness be declared in the grave?*
    your faithfulness in the land of destruction?

13 Will your wonders be known in the dark?*
    or your righteousness in the country where all is forgotten?

14 But as for me, O Lord, I cry to you for help;*
    in the morning my prayer comes before you.

15 Lord, why have you rejected me?*
    why have you hidden your face from me?

16 Ever since my youth, I have been wretched and at the
      point of death;*
    I have borne your terrors with a troubled mind.

17 Your blazing anger has swept over me;*
    your terrors have destroyed me;

18 They surround me all day long like a flood;*
    they encompass me on every side.

19 My friend and my neighbor you have put away from me,*
    and darkness is my only companion.

Evening

91   *Qui habitat*

1   He who dwells in the shelter of the Most High,*
    abides under the shadow of the Almighty.

2 He shall say to the Lord,
   "You are my refuge and my stronghold, *
   my God in whom I put my trust."

3 He shall deliver you from the snare of the hunter *
   and from the deadly pestilence.

4 He shall cover you with his pinions,
   and you shall find refuge under his wings; *
   his faithfulness shall be a shield and buckler.

5 You shall not be afraid of any terror by night, *
   nor of the arrow that flies by day;

6 Of the plague that stalks in the darkness, *
   nor of the sickness that lays waste at mid-day.

7 A thousand shall fall at your side
   and ten thousand at your right hand, *
   but it shall not come near you.

8 Your eyes have only to behold*
   to see the reward of the wicked.

9 Because you have made the Lord your refuge, *
   and the Most High your habitation,

10 There shall no evil happen to you,*
   neither shall any plague come near your dwelling.

11 For he shall give his angels charge over you,*
   to keep you in all your ways.

12 They shall bear you in their hands,*
   lest you dash your foot against a stone.

13 You shall tread upon the lion and adder;*
   you shall trample the young lion and the serpent
                        under your feet.

14 Because he is bound to me in love,
   therefore will I deliver him;*
   I will protect him, because he knows my Name.

15 He shall call upon me, and I will answer him;*
   I am with him in trouble;
   I will rescue him and bring him to honor.

16 With long life will I satisfy him,*
   and show him my salvation.

92 *Bonum est confiteri*

1 It is a good thing to give thanks to the Lord,*
and to sing praises to your Name, O Most High;

2 To tell of your loving-kindness early in the morning*
and of your faithfulness in the night season;

3 On the psaltery, and on the lyre,*
and to the melody of the harp.

4 For you have made me glad by your acts, O Lord;*
and I shout for joy because of the works of your hands.

5 Lord, how great are your works! *
your thoughts are very deep.

6 The dullard does not know,
nor does the fool understand,*
that though the wicked grow like weeds,
and all the workers of iniquity flourish,

7 They flourish only to be destroyed for ever; *
but you, O Lord, are exalted for evermore.

8 For lo, your enemies, O Lord,
lo, your enemies shall perish, *
and all the workers of iniquity shall be scattered.

9 But my horn you have exalted like the horns of wild bulls;*
I am anointed with fresh oil.

10 My eyes also gloat over my enemies,*
and my ears rejoice to hear the doom of the wicked who
rise up against me.

11 The righteous shall flourish like a palm tree,*
and shall spread abroad like a cedar of Lebanon.

12 Those who are planted in the house of the Lord*
shall flourish in the courts of our God;

13 They shall still bear fruit in old age;*
they shall be green and succulent;

14 That they may show how upright the Lord is,*
my Rock, in whom there is no fault.

Saturday

Morning

87 *Fundamenta ejus*

1 On the holy mountain stands the city he has founded;*
  the Lord loves the gates of Zion
  more than all the dwellings of Jacob.

2 Glorious things are spoken of you, *
  O city of our God.

3 I count Egypt and Babylon among those who know me; *
  behold Philistia, Tyre, and Ethiopia:
  in Zion were they born.

4 Of Zion it shall be said, "Everyone was born in her, *
  and the Most High himself shall sustain her."

5 The Lord will record as he enrolls the peoples, *
  "These also were born there."

6 The singers and the dancers will say, *
  "All my fresh springs are in you."

90 *Domine, refugium*

1 Lord, you have been our refuge *
  from one generation to another.

2 Before the mountains were brought forth,
  or the land and the earth were born, *
  from age to age you are God.

3 You turn us back to the dust and say, *
  "Go back, O child of earth."

4 For a thousand years in your sight are like yesterday
                when it is past *
  and like a watch in the night.

5 You sweep us away like a dream; *
  we fade away suddenly like the grass.

6 In the morning it is green and flourishes; *
  in the evening it is dried up and withered.

7 For we consume away in your displeasure;*
  we are afraid because of your wrathful indignation.

8　Our iniquities you have set before you,*
　　and our secret sins in the light of your countenance.

9　When you are angry, all our days are gone; *
　　we bring our years to an end like a sigh.

10　The span of our life is seventy years,
　　perhaps in strength even eighty;*
　　　yet the sum of them is but labor and sorrow,
　　　for they pass away quickly and we are gone.

11　Who regards the power of your wrath?*
　　who rightly fears your indignation?

12　So teach us to number our days*
　　that we may apply our hearts to wisdom.

13　Return, O Lord; how long will you tarry?*
　　be gracious to your servants.

14　Satisfy us by your loving-kindness in the morning;*
　　so shall we rejoice and be glad all the days of our life.

15　Make us glad by the measure of the days that you afflicted us*
　　and the years in which we suffered adversity.

16　Show your servants your works*
　　and your splendor to their children.

17　May the graciousness of the Lord our God be upon us;*
　　prosper the work of our hands;
　　prosper our handiwork.

Evening

136 *Confitemini*

1　Give thanks to the Lord, for he is good,*
　　for his mercy endures for ever.

2　Give thanks to the God of gods, *
　　for his mercy endures for ever.

3　Give thanks to the Lord of Lords, *
　　for his mercy endures for ever.

4　Who only does great wonders,*
　　for his mercy endures for ever;

5 Who by wisdom made the heavens, *
   for his mercy endures for ever;

6 Who spread out the earth upon the waters, *
   for his mercy endures for ever;

7 Who created great lights, *
   for his mercy endures for ever;

8 The sun to rule the day, *
   for his mercy endures for ever;

9 The moon and the stars to govern the night, *
   for his mercy endures for ever.

10 Who struck down the firstborn of Egypt,*
   for his mercy endures for ever;

11 And brought out Israel from among them,*
   for his mercy endures for ever;

12 With a mighty hand and a stretched-out arm,*
   for his mercy endures for ever;

13 Who divided the Red Sea in two,*
   for his mercy endures for ever;

14 And made Israel to pass through the midst of it,*
   for his mercy endures for ever;

15 But swept Pharaoh and his army into the Red Sea,*
   for his mercy endures for ever;

16 Who led his people through the wilderness,*
   for his mercy endures for ever.

17 Who struck down great kings,*
   for his mercy endures for ever;

18 And slew mighty kings,*
   for his mercy endures for ever;

19 Sihon, king of the Amorites,*
   for his mercy endures for ever;

20 And Og, the king of Bashan,*
   for his mercy endures for ever;

21 And gave away their lands for an inheritance,*
   for his mercy endures for ever;

22 An inheritance for Israel his servant,*
    for his mercy endures for ever.

23 Who remembered us in our low estate,*
    for his mercy endures for ever;

24 And delivered us from our enemies,*
    for his mercy endures for ever;

25 Who gives food to all creatures,*
    for his mercy endures for ever.

26 Give thanks to the God of heaven,*
    for his mercy endures for ever.

Week of 4 Lent

Sunday
Morning

66 *Jubilate Deo*

1 Be joyful in God, all you lands;*
    sing the glory of his Name;
    sing the glory of his praise.

2 Say to God, "How awesome are your deeds! *
    because of your great strength your enemies
    cringe before you.

3 All the earth bows down before you, *
    sings to you, sings out your Name."

4 Come now and see the works of God,*
    how wonderful he is in his doing toward all people.

5 He turned the sea into dry land,
    so that they went through the water on foot, *
    and there we rejoiced in him.

6 In his might he rules for ever;
    his eyes keep watch over the nations; *
    let no rebel rise up against him.

7 Bless our God, you peoples; *
    make the voice of his praise to be heard;

8 Who holds our souls in life, *
    and will not allow our feet to slip.

9 For you, O God, have proved us; *
    you have tried us just as silver is tried.

10 You brought us into the snare;*
    you laid heavy burdens upon our backs.

11 You let enemies ride over our heads;
    we went through fire and water;*
      but you brought us out into a place of refreshment.

12 I will enter your house with burnt-offerings
    and will pay you my vows,*
      which I promised with my lips
      and spoke with my mouth when I was in trouble.

13 I will offer you sacrifices of fat beasts
    with the smoke of rams;*
      I will give you oxen and goats.

14 Come and listen, all you who fear God,*
    and I will tell you what he has done for me.

15 I called out to him with my mouth,*
    and his praise was on my tongue.

16 If I had found evil in my heart,*
    the Lord would not have heard me;

17 But in truth God has heard me;*
    he has attended to the voice of my prayer.

18 Blessed be God, who has not rejected my prayer,*
    nor withheld his love from me.

67   *Deus misereatur*

1 May God be merciful to us and bless us,*
    show us the light of his countenance and come to us.

2 Let your ways be known upon earth, *
    your saving health among all nations.

3 Let the peoples praise you, O God; *
    let all the peoples praise you.

4 Let the nations be glad and sing for joy, *
    for you judge the peoples with equity
    and guide all the nations upon earth.

5 Let the peoples praise you, O God; *
   let all the peoples praise you.

6 The earth has brought forth her increase; *
   may God, our own God, give us his blessing.

7 May God give us his blessing,*
   and may all the ends of the earth stand in awe of him.

Evening

19 *Cœli enarrant*

1 The heavens declare the glory of God,*
   and the firmament shows his handiwork.

2 One day tells its tale to another, *
   and one night imparts knowledge to another.

3 Although they have no words or language, *
   and their voices are not heard,

4 Their sound has gone out into all lands, *
   and their message to the ends of the world.

5 In the deep has he set a pavilion for the sun;*
   it comes forth like a bridegroom out of his chamber;
   it rejoices like a champion to run its course.

6 It goes forth from the uttermost edge of the heavens
   and runs about to the end of it again; *
   nothing is hidden from its burning heat.

7 The law of the Lord is perfect and revives the soul;*
   the testimony of the Lord is sure and gives wisdom
               to the innocent.

8 The statutes of the Lord are just and rejoice the heart; *
   the commandment of the Lord is clear and gives light to
               the eyes.

9 The fear of the Lord is clean and endures for ever; *
   the judgments of the Lord are true and righteous altogether.

10 More to be desired are they than gold,
        more than much fine gold,*
    sweeter far than honey, than honey in the comb.

11 By them also is your servant enlightened,*
    and in keeping them there is great reward.

12 Who can tell how often he offends?*
    cleanse me from my secret faults.

13 Above all, keep your servant from presumptuous sins;
    let them not get dominion over me;*
        then shall I be whole and sound,
        and innocent of a great offense.

14 Let the words of my mouth and the meditation of my heart be
        acceptable in your sight,*
    O Lord, my strength and my redeemer.

46   *Deus noster refugium*

1 God is our refuge and strength,*
    a very present help in trouble.

2 Therefore we will not fear, though the earth be moved, *
    and though the mountains be toppled into the depths of the sea;

3 Though its waters rage and foam, *
    and though the mountains tremble at its tumult.

4 The Lord of hosts is with us; *
    the God of Jacob is our stronghold.

5 There is a river whose streams make glad the city of God,*
    the holy habitation of the Most High.

6 God is in the midst of her;
    she shall not be overthrown; *
        God shall help her at the break of day.

7 The nations make much ado, and the kingdoms are shaken;*
    God has spoken, and the earth shall melt away.

8 The Lord of hosts is with us; *
    the God of Jacob is our stronghold.

9 Come now and look upon the works of the Lord,*
    what awesome things he has done on earth.

10 It is he who makes war to cease in all the world;*
    he breaks the bow, and shatters the spear,
    and burns the shields with fire.

11 "Be still, then, and know that I am God;*
    I will be exalted among the nations;
    I will be exalted in the earth."

12 The Lord of hosts is with us;*
    the God of Jacob is our stronghold.

Monday
Morning

89

Part I *Misericordias Domini*

1 Your love, O Lord, for ever will I sing;*
  from age to age my mouth will proclaim your faithfulness.

2 For I am persuaded that your love is established for ever; *
  you have set your faithfulness firmly in the heavens.

3 "I have made a covenant with my chosen one; *
  I have sworn an oath to David my servant:

4 'I will establish your line for ever,*
  and preserve your throne for all generations.'"

5 The heavens bear witness to your wonders, O Lord, *
  and to your faithfulness in the assembly of the holy ones;

6 For who in the skies can be compared to the Lord? *
  who is like the Lord among the gods?

7 God is much to be feared in the council of the holy ones, *
  great and terrible to all those round about him.

8 Who is like you, Lord God of hosts? *
  O mighty Lord, your faithfulness is all around you.

9 You rule the raging of the sea *
  and still the surging of its waves.

10 You have crushed Rahab of the deep with a deadly wound;*
   you have scattered your enemies with your mighty arm.

11 Yours are the heavens; the earth also is yours;*
   you laid the foundations of the world and all that is in it.

12 You have made the north and the south;*
   Tabor and Hermon rejoice in your Name.

13 You have a mighty arm;*
   strong is your hand and high is your right hand.

14 Righteousness and justice are the foundations of your throne;*
   love and truth go before your face.

15 Happy are the people who know the festal shout!*
   they walk, O Lord, in the light of your presence.

16 They rejoice daily in your Name;*
     they are jubilant in your righteousness.

17 For you are the glory of their strength,*
     and by your favor our might is exalted.

18 Truly, the Lord is our ruler;*
     the Holy One of Israel is our King.

Evening

89

Part II *Tunc locutus es*

19 You spoke once in a vision and said to your faithful people:*
     "I have set the crown upon a warrior
     and have exalted one chosen out of the people.

20 I have found David my servant;*
     with my holy oil have I anointed him.

21 My hand will hold him fast*
     and my arm will make him strong.

22 No enemy shall deceive him,*
     nor any wicked man bring him down.

23 I will crush his foes before him*
     and strike down those who hate him.

24 My faithfulness and love shall be with him,*
     and he shall be victorious through my Name.

25 I shall make his dominion extend*
     from the Great Sea to the River.

26 He will say to me, 'You are my Father,*
     my God, and the rock of my salvation.'

27 I will make him my firstborn*
     and higher than the kings of the earth.

28 I will keep my love for him for ever,*
     and my covenant will stand firm for him.

29 I will establish his line for ever*
     and his throne as the days of heaven."

30 "If his children forsake my law*
   and do not walk according to my judgments;

31 If they break my statutes*
   and do not keep my commandments;

32 I will punish their transgressions with a rod*
   and their iniquities with the lash;

33 But I will not take my love from him,*
   nor let my faithfulness prove false.

34 I will not break my covenant,*
   nor change what has gone out of my lips.

35 Once for all I have sworn by my holiness:*
   'I will not lie to David.

36 His line shall endure for ever*
   and his throne as the sun before me;

37 It shall stand fast for evermore like the moon,*
   the abiding witness in the sky.'"

38 But you have cast off and rejected your anointed;*
   you have become enraged at him.

39 You have broken your covenant with your servant,*
   defiled his crown, and hurled it to the ground.

40 You have breached all his walls*
   and laid his strongholds in ruins.

41 All who pass by despoil him;*
   he has become the scorn of his neighbors.

42 You have exalted the right hand of his foes*
   and made all his enemies rejoice.

43 You have turned back the edge of his sword*
   and have not sustained him in battle.

44 You have put an end to his splendor*
   and cast his throne to the ground.

45 You have cut short the days of his youth*
   and have covered him with shame.

46 How long will you hide yourself, O Lord?
   will you hide yourself for ever?*
   how long will your anger burn like fire?

47 Remember, Lord, how short life is,*
how frail you have made all flesh.

48 Who can live and not see death?*
who can save himself from the power of the grave?

49 Where, Lord, are your loving-kindnesses of old,*
which you promised David in your faithfulness?

50 Remember, Lord, how your servant is mocked,*
how I carry in my bosom the taunts of many peoples,

51 The taunts your enemies have hurled, O Lord,*
which they hurled at the heels of your anointed.

52 Blessed be the Lord for evermore!*
Amen, I say, Amen.

Tuesday

Morning

97 *Dominus regnavit*

1 The Lord is King;
let the earth rejoice; *
let the multitude of the isles be glad.

2 Clouds and darkness are round about him,*
righteousness and justice are the foundations of his throne.

3 A fire goes before him *
and burns up his enemies on every side.

4 His lightnings light up the world; *
the earth sees it and is afraid.

5 The mountains melt like wax at the presence of the Lord, *
at the presence of the Lord of the whole earth.

6 The heavens declare his righteousness, *
and all the peoples see his glory.

7 Confounded be all who worship carved images
and delight in false gods! *
Bow down before him, all you gods.

8 Zion hears and is glad, and the cities of Judah rejoice, *
because of your judgments, O Lord.

9 For you are the Lord,
    most high over all the earth; *
      you are exalted far above all gods.

10 The Lord loves those who hate evil; *
    he preserves the lives of his saints
    and delivers them from the hand of the wicked.

11 Light has sprung up for the righteous, *
    and joyful gladness for those who are truehearted.

12 Rejoice in the Lord, you righteous, *
    and give thanks to his holy Name.

99 *Dominus regnavit*

1 The Lord is King;
   let the people tremble; *
     he is enthroned upon the cherubim;
     let the earth shake.

2 The Lord is great in Zion; *
    he is high above all peoples.

3 Let them confess his Name, which is great and awesome; *
    he is the Holy One.

4 "O mighty King, lover of justice,
   you have established equity; *
     you have executed justice and righteousness in Jacob."

5 Proclaim the greatness of the Lord our God
   and fall down before his footstool; *
     he is the Holy One.

6 Moses and Aaron among his priests,
   and Samuel among those who call upon his Name, *
     they called upon the Lord, and he answered them.

7 He spoke to them out of the pillar of cloud; *
    they kept his testimonies and the decree that he gave them.

8 "O Lord our God, you answered them indeed; *
    you were a God who forgave them,
    yet punished them for their evil deeds."

9 Proclaim the greatness of the Lord our God
   and worship him upon his holy hill; *
     for the Lord our God is the Holy One.

IOO *Jubilate Deo*

1 Be joyful in the Lord, all you lands; *
    serve the Lord with gladness
    and come before his presence with a song.

2 Know this: The Lord himself is God; *
    he himself has made us, and we are his;
    we are his people and the sheep of his pasture.

3 Enter his gates with thanksgiving;
    go into his courts with praise;*
    give thanks to him and call upon his Name.

4 For the Lord is good;
    his mercy is everlasting;*
    and his faithfulness endures from age to age.

Evening

94   *Deus ultionum*

1 O Lord God of vengeance,*
    O God of vengeance, show yourself

2 Rise up, O Judge of the world;*
    give the arrogant their just deserts.

3 How long shall the wicked, O Lord,*
    how long shall the wicked triumph?

4 They bluster in their insolence;*
    all evildoers are full of boasting.

5 They crush your people, O Lord, *
    and afflict your chosen nation.

6 They murder the widow and the stranger *
    and put the orphans to death.

7 Yet they say, "The Lord does not see, *
    the God of Jacob takes no notice."

8 Consider well, you dullards among the people; *
    when will you fools understand?

9 He that planted the ear, does he not hear? *
    he that formed the eye, does he not see?

10 He who admonishes the nations, will he not punish?*
    he who teaches all the world, has he no knowledge?

11 The Lord knows our human thoughts;*
    how like a puff of wind they are.

12 Happy are they whom you instruct, O Lord!*
    whom you teach out of your law;

13 To give them rest in evil days,*
    until a pit is dug for the wicked.

14 For the Lord will not abandon his people,*
    nor will he forsake his own.

15 For judgment will again be just,*
    and all the true of heart will follow it.

16 Who rose up for me against the wicked?*
    who took my part against the evildoers?

17 If the Lord had not come to my help,*
    I should soon have dwelt in the land of silence.

18 As often as I said, "My foot has slipped,"*
    your love, O Lord, upheld me.

19 When many cares fill my mind,*
    your consolations cheer my soul.

20 Can a corrupt tribunal have any part with you,*
    one which frames evil into law?

21 They conspire against the life of the just*
    and condemn the innocent to death.

22 But the Lord has become my stronghold,*
    and my God the rock of my trust.

23 He will turn their wickedness back upon them
    and destroy them in their own malice;*
    the Lord our God will destroy them.

95 *Venite, exultemus*

1 Come, let us sing to the Lord;*
   let us shout for joy to the Rock of our salvation.

2 Let us come before his presence with thanksgiving*
   and raise a loud shout to him with psalms.

3   For the Lord is a great God, *
    and a great King above all gods.

4   In his hand are the caverns of the earth, *
    and the heights of the hills are his also.

5   The sea is his, for he made it, *
    and his hands have molded the dry land.

6   Come, let us bow down, and bend the knee,*
    and kneel before the Lord our Maker.

7   For he is our God,
    and we are the people of his pasture and the sheep of his hand.*
      Oh, that today you would hearken to his voice!

8   Harden not your hearts,
    as your forebears did in the wilderness,*
      at Meribah, and on that day at Massah,
      when they tempted me.

9   They put me to the test, *
    though they had seen my works.

10   Forty years long I detested that generation and said,*
    "This people are wayward in their hearts;
    they do not know my ways."

11   So I swore in my wrath,*
    "They shall not enter into my rest."

Wednesday

Morning

IOI *Misericordiam et judicium*

1   I will sing of mercy and justice;*
    to you, O Lord, will I sing praises.

2   I will strive to follow a blameless course;
    oh, when will you come to me?*
      I will walk with sincerity of heart within my house.

3   I will set no worthless thing before my eyes;*
    I hate the doers of evil deeds;
    they shall not remain with me.

4   A crooked heart shall be far from me;*
    I will not know evil.

5   Those who in secret slander their neighbors I will destroy;*
    those who have a haughty look and a proud heart I
        cannot abide.

6   My eyes are upon the faithful in the land, that they may
        dwell with me,*
    and only those who lead a blameless life shall be my servants.

7   Those who act deceitfully shall not dwell in my house,*
    and those who tell lies shall not continue in my sight.

8   I will soon destroy all the wicked in the land,*
    that I may root out all evildoers from the city of the Lord.

109 *Deus, laudem*

1   Hold not your tongue, O God of my praise; *
    for the mouth of the wicked,
    the mouth of the deceitful, is opened against me.

2   They speak to me with a lying tongue; *
    they encompass me with hateful words
    and fight against me without a cause.

3   Despite my love, they accuse me; *
    but as for me, I pray for them.

4   They repay evil for good, *
    and hatred for my love.

5   Set a wicked man against him, *
    and let an accuser stand at his right hand.

6   When he is judged, let him be found guilty, *
    and let his appeal be in vain.

7   Let his days be few, *
    and let another take his office.

8   Let his children be fatherless, *
    and his wife become a widow.

9   Let his children be waifs and beggars; *
    let them be driven from the ruins of their homes.

10 Let the creditor seize everything he has; *
    let strangers plunder his gains.

11 Let there be no one to show him kindness, *
    and none to pity his fatherless children.

12 Let his descendants be destroyed, *
    and his name be blotted out in the next generation.

13 Let the wickedness of his fathers be remembered before
        the Lord, *
    and his mother's sin not be blotted out;

14 Let their sin be always before the Lord; *
    but let him root out their names from the earth;

15 Because he did not remember to show mercy,*
    but persecuted the poor and needy
    and sought to kill the brokenhearted.

16 He loved cursing,
    let it come upon him;*
    he took no delight in blessing,
    let it depart from him.

17 He put on cursing like a garment,*
    let it soak into his body like water
    and into his bones like oil;

18 Let it be to him like the cloak which he wraps around himself,*
    and like the belt that he wears continually.

19 Let this be the recompense from the Lord to my accusers,*
    and to those who speak evil against me.

20 But you, O Lord my God,
    oh, deal with me according to your Name;*
    for your tender mercy's sake, deliver me.

21 For I am poor and needy,*
    and my heart is wounded within me.

22 I have faded away like a shadow when it lengthens;*
    I am shaken off like a locust.

23 My knees are weak through fasting,*
    and my flesh is wasted and gaunt.

24 I have become a reproach to them;*
    they see and shake their heads.

25 Help me, O Lord my God;*
    save me for your mercy's sake.

26 Let them know that this is your hand,*
    that you, O Lord, have done it.

27 They may curse, but you will bless;*
    let those who rise up against me be put to shame,
    and your servant will rejoice.

28 Let my accusers be clothed with disgrace*
    and wrap themselves in their shame as in a cloak.

29 I will give great thanks to the Lord with my mouth;*
    in the midst of the multitude will I praise him;

30 Because he stands at the right hand of the needy,*
    to save his life from those who would condemn him.

Evening

119

Ayin   *Feci judicium*

121 I have done what is just and right; *
    do not deliver me to my oppressors.

122 Be surety for your servant's good; *
    let not the proud oppress me.

123 My eyes have failed from watching for your salvation *
    and for your righteous promise.

124 Deal with your servant according to your loving-kindness *
    and teach me your statutes.

125 I am your servant; grant me understanding, *
    that I may know your decrees.

126 It is time for you to act, O Lord, *
    for they have broken your law.

127 Truly, I love your commandments*
    more than gold and precious stones.

128 I hold all your commandments to be right for me;*
    all paths of falsehood I abhor.

Pe   *Mirabilia*

129 Your decrees are wonderful;*
    therefore I obey them with all my heart.

130 When your word goes forth it gives light;*
    it gives understanding to the simple.

131 I open my mouth and pant;*
    I long for your commandments.

132 Turn to me in mercy,*
    as you always do to those who love your Name.

133 Steady my footsteps in your word;*
    let no iniquity have dominion over me.

134 Rescue me from those who oppress me,*
    and I will keep your commandments.

135 Let your countenance shine upon your servant*
    and teach me your statutes.

136 My eyes shed streams of tears,*
    because people do not keep your law.

Sadhe *Justus es, Domine*

137 You are righteous, O Lord,*
    and upright are your judgments.

138 You have issued your decrees*
    with justice and in perfect faithfulness.

139 My indignation has consumed me,*
    because my enemies forget your words.

140 Your word has been tested to the uttermost,*
    and your servant holds it dear.

141 I am small and of little account,*
    yet I do not forget your commandments.

142 Your justice is an everlasting justice*
    and your law is the truth.

143 Trouble and distress have come upon me,*
    yet your commandments are my delight.

144 The righteousness of your decrees is everlasting;*
    grant me understanding, that I may live.

Thursday

Morning

69   *Salvum me fac*

1 Save me, O God,*
    for the waters have risen up to my neck.

2 I am sinking in deep mire, *
    and there is no firm ground for my feet.

3 I have come into deep waters, *
    and the torrent washes over me.

4 I have grown weary with my crying;
    my throat is inflamed; *
    my eyes have failed from looking for my God.

5 Those who hate me without a cause are more than the hairs
        of my head;
    my lying foes who would destroy me are mighty.*
    Must I then give back what I never stole?

6 O God, you know my foolishness, *
    and my faults are not hidden from you.

7 Let not those who hope in you be put to shame through me,
        Lord God of hosts;*
    let not those who seek you be disgraced because of me,
        O God of Israel.

8 Surely, for your sake have I suffered reproach,*
    and shame has covered my face.

9 I have become a stranger to my own kindred, *
    an alien to my mother's children.

10 Zeal for your house has eaten me up;*
    the scorn of those who scorn you has fallen upon me.

11 I humbled myself with fasting,*
    but that was turned to my reproach.

12 I put on sack-cloth also,*
    and became a byword among them.

13 Those who sit at the gate murmur against me,*
    and the drunkards make songs about me.

14 But as for me, this is my prayer to you,*
    at the time you have set, O Lord:

15 "In your great mercy, O God,*
    answer me with your unfailing help.

16 Save me from the mire; do not let me sink;*
    let me be rescued from those who hate me
    and out of the deep waters.

17 Let not the torrent of waters wash over me,
    neither let the deep swallow me up;*
    do not let the Pit shut its mouth upon me.

18 Answer me, O Lord, for your love is kind;*
    in your great compassion, turn to me.'

19 "Hide not your face from your servant;*
    be swift and answer me, for I am in distress.

20 Draw near to me and redeem me;*
    because of my enemies deliver me.

21 You know my reproach, my shame, and my dishonor; *
    my adversaries are all in your sight."

22 Reproach has broken my heart, and it cannot be healed; *
    I looked for sympathy, but there was none,
    for comforters, but I could find no one.

23 They gave me gall to eat, *
    and when I was thirsty, they gave me vinegar to drink.

24 Let the table before them be a trap *
    and their sacred feasts a snare.

25 Let their eyes be darkened, that they may not see, *
    and give them continual trembling in their loins.

26 Pour out your indignation upon them, *
    and let the fierceness of your anger overtake them.

27 Let their camp be desolate, *
    and let there be none to dwell in their tents.

28 For they persecute him whom you have stricken *
    and add to the pain of those whom you have pierced.

29 Lay to their charge guilt upon guilt, *
    and let them not receive your vindication.

30 Let them be wiped out of the book of the living *
and not be written among the righteous.

31 As for me, I am afflicted and in pain; *
your help, O God, will lift me up on high.

32 I will praise the Name of God in song; *
I will proclaim his greatness with thanksgiving.

33 This will please the Lord more than an offering of oxen, *
more than bullocks with horns and hoofs.

34 The afflicted shall see and be glad;*
you who seek God, your heart shall live.

35 For the Lord listens to the needy,*
and his prisoners he does not despise.

36 Let the heavens and the earth praise him,*
the seas and all that moves in them;

37 For God will save Zion and rebuild the cities of Judah;*
they shall live there and have it in possession.

38 The children of his servants will inherit it,*
and those who love his Name will dwell therein.

Evening

73 *Quam bonus Israel!*

1 Truly, God is good to Israel,*
to those who are pure in heart.

2 But as for me, my feet had nearly slipped; *
I had almost tripped and fallen;

3 Because I envied the proud *
and saw the prosperity of the wicked:

4 For they suffer no pain, *
and their bodies are sleek and sound;

5 In the misfortunes of others they have no share;*
they are not afflicted as others are;

6 Therefore they wear their pride like a necklace*
and wrap their violence about them like a cloak.

7 Their iniquity comes from gross minds,*
    and their hearts overflow with wicked thoughts.

8 They scoff and speak maliciously; *
    out of their haughtiness they plan oppression.

9 They set their mouths against the heavens, *
    and their evil speech runs through the world.

10 And so the people turn to them*
    and find in them no fault.

11 They say, "How should God know?*
    is there knowledge in the Most High?"

12 So then, these are the wicked;*
    always at ease, they increase their wealth.

13 In vain have I kept my heart clean,*
    and washed my hands in innocence.

14 I have been afflicted all day long,*
    and punished every morning.

15 Had I gone on speaking this way,*
    I should have betrayed the generation of your children.

16 When I tried to understand these things,*
    it was too hard for me;

17 Until I entered the sanctuary of God*
    and discerned the end of the wicked.

18 Surely, you set them in slippery places;*
    you cast them down in ruin.

19 Oh, how suddenly do they come to destruction,*
    come to an end, and perish from terror!

20 Like a dream when one awakens, O Lord,*
    when you arise you will make their image vanish.

21 When my mind became embittered,*
    I was sorely wounded in my heart.

22 I was stupid and had no understanding;*
    I was like a brute beast in your presence.

23 Yet I am always with you;*
    you hold me by my right hand.

24 You will guide me by your counsel,*
    and afterwards receive me with glory.

25 Whom have I in heaven but you?*
   and having you I desire nothing upon earth.

26 Though my flesh and my heart should waste away,*
   God is the strength of my heart and my portion for ever.

27 Truly, those who forsake you will perish;*
   you destroy all who are unfaithful.

28 But it is good for me to be near God;*
   I have made the Lord God my refuge.

29 I will speak of all your works*
   in the gates of the city of Zion.

Friday

Morning

For the Invitatory

95   *Venite, exultemus*

1 Come, let us sing to the Lord;*
   let us shout for joy to the Rock of our salvation.

2 Let us come before his presence with thanksgiving*
   and raise a loud shout to him with psalms.

3 For the Lord is a great God, *
   and a great King above all gods.

4 In his hand are the caverns of the earth, *
   and the heights of the hills are his also.

5 The sea is his, for he made it, *
   and his hands have molded the dry land.

6 Come, let us bow down, and bend the knee,*
   and kneel before the Lord our Maker.

7 For he is our God,
   and we are the people of his pasture and the sheep of his hand.*
      Oh, that today you would hearken to his voice!

8 Harden not your hearts,
   as your forebears did in the wilderness,*
      at Meribah, and on that day at Massah,
      when they tempted me.

9 They put me to the test, *
   though they had seen my works.

10 Forty years long I detested that generation and said,*
   "This people are wayward in their hearts;
   they do not know my ways."

11 So I swore in my wrath,*
   "They shall not enter into my rest."

102 *Domine, exaudi*

1 Lord, hear my prayer, and let my cry come before you;*
   hide not your face from me in the day of my trouble.

2 Incline your ear to me; *
   when I call, make haste to answer me,

3 For my days drift away like smoke, *
   and my bones are hot as burning coals.

4 My heart is smitten like grass and withered, *
   so that I forget to eat my bread.

5 Because of the voice of my groaning *
   I am but skin and bones.

6 I have become like a vulture in the wilderness, *
   like an owl among the ruins.

7 I lie awake and groan; *
   I am like a sparrow, lonely on a house-top.

8 My enemies revile me all day long,*
   and those who scoff at me have taken an oath against me.

9 For I have eaten ashes for bread *
   and mingled my drink with weeping.

10 Because of your indignation and wrath*
   you have lifted me up and thrown me away.

11 My days pass away like a shadow,*
   and I wither like the grass.

12 But you, O Lord, endure for ever,*
   and your Name from age to age.

13 You will arise and have compassion on Zion,
   for it is time to have mercy upon her;*
   indeed, the appointed time has come.

14 For your servants love her very rubble,*
    and are moved to pity even for her dust.

15 The nations shall fear your Name, O Lord,*
    and all the kings of the earth your glory.

16 For the Lord will build up Zion,*
    and his glory will appear.

17 He will look with favor on the prayer of the homeless;*
    he will not despise their plea.

18 Let this be written for a future generation,*
    so that a people yet unborn may praise the Lord.

19 For the Lord looked down from his holy place on high;*
    from the heavens he beheld the earth;

20 That he might hear the groan of the captive*
    and set free those condemned to die;

21 That they may declare in Zion the Name of the Lord,*
    and his praise in Jerusalem;

22 When the peoples are gathered together,*
    and the kingdoms also, to serve the Lord.

23 He has brought down my strength before my time;*
    he has shortened the number of my days;

24 And I said, "O my God,
    do not take me away in the midst of my days;*
    your years endure throughout all generations.

25 In the beginning, O Lord, you laid the foundations
                    of the earth,*
    and the heavens are the work of your hands;

26 They shall perish, but you will endure;
    they all shall wear out like a garment; *
        as clothing you will change them,
        and they shall be changed;

27 But you are always the same, *
    and your years will never end.

28 The children of your servants shall continue, *
    and their offspring shall stand fast in your sight."

107

Part I *Confitemini Domino*

1 Give thanks to the Lord, for he is good,*
   and his mercy endures for ever.

2 Let all those whom the Lord has redeemed proclaim*
   that he redeemed them from the hand of the foe.

3 He gathered them out of the lands;*
   from the east and from the west,
   from the north and from the south.

4 Some wandered in desert wastes;*
   they found no way to a city where they might dwell.

5 They were hungry and thirsty;*
   their spirits languished within them.

6 Then they cried to the Lord in their trouble,*
   and he delivered them from their distress.

7 He put their feet on a straight path*
   to go to a city where they might dwell.

8 Let them give thanks to the Lord for his mercy*
   and the wonders he does for his children.

9 For he satisfies the thirsty*
   and fills the hungry with good things.

10 Some sat in darkness and deep gloom,*
   bound fast in misery and iron;

11 Because they rebelled against the words of God*
   and despised the counsel of the Most High.

12 So he humbled their spirits with hard labor;*
   they stumbled, and there was none to help.

13 Then they cried to the Lord in their trouble,*
   and he delivered them from their distress.

14 He led them out of darkness and deep gloom*
   and broke their bonds asunder.

15 Let them give thanks to the Lord for his mercy*
   and the wonders he does for his children.

16 For he shatters the doors of bronze*
     and breaks in two the iron bars.

17 Some were fools and took to rebellious ways;*
     they were afflicted because of their sins.

18 They abhorred all manner of food*
     and drew near to death's door.

19 Then they cried to the Lord in their trouble,*
     and he delivered them from their distress.

20 He sent forth his word and healed them*
     and saved them from the grave.

21 Let them give thanks to the Lord for his mercy*
     and the wonders he does for his children.

22 Let them offer a sacrifice of thanksgiving*
     and tell of his acts with shouts of joy.

23 Some went down to the sea in ships*
     and plied their trade in deep waters;

24 They beheld the works of the Lord*
     and his wonders in the deep.

25 Then he spoke, and a stormy wind arose,*
     which tossed high the waves of the sea.

26 They mounted up to the heavens and fell back to the depths;*
     their hearts melted because of their peril.

27 They reeled and staggered like drunkards*
     and were at their wits' end.

28 Then they cried to the Lord in their trouble,
     and he delivered them from their distress.

29 He stilled the storm to a whisper*
     and quieted the waves of the sea.

30 Then were they glad because of the calm,*
     and he brought them to the harbor they were bound for.

31 Let them give thanks to the Lord for his mercy*
     and the wonders he does for his children.

32 Let them exalt him in the congregation of the people*
     and praise him in the council of the elders.

Saturday

Morning

107

Part II *Posuit flumina*

33 The Lord changed rivers into deserts,*
   and water-springs into thirsty ground,

34 A fruitful land into salt flats,*
   because of the wickedness of those who dwell there.

35 He changed deserts into pools of water*
   and dry land into water-springs.

36 He settled the hungry there,*
   and they founded a city to dwell in.

37 They sowed fields, and planted vineyards,*
   and brought in a fruitful harvest.

38 He blessed them, so that they increased greatly;*
   he did not let their herds decrease.

39 Yet when they were diminished and brought low,*
   through stress of adversity and sorrow,

40 (He pours contempt on princes*
   and makes them wander in trackless wastes)

41 He lifted up the poor out of misery*
   and multiplied their families like flocks of sheep.

42 The upright will see this and rejoice,*
   but all wickedness will shut its mouth.

43 Whoever is wise will ponder these things,*
   and consider well the mercies of the Lord.

108 *Paratum cor meum*

1 My heart is firmly fixed, O God, my heart is fixed;*
   I will sing and make melody.

2 Wake up, my spirit;
   awake, lute and harp; *
   I myself will waken the dawn.

3   I will confess you among the peoples, O Lord; *
     I will sing praises to you among the nations.

4   For your loving-kindness is greater than the heavens,*
     and your faithfulness reaches to the clouds.

5   Exalt yourself above the heavens, O God, *
     and your glory over all the earth.

6   So that those who are dear to you may be delivered,*
     save with your right hand and answer me.

7   God spoke from his holy place and said,*
     "I will exult and parcel out Shechem;
     I will divide the valley of Succoth.

8   Gilead is mine and Manasseh is mine; *
     Ephraim is my helmet and Judah my scepter.

9   Moab is my washbasin,
     on Edom I throw down my sandal to claim it, *
     and over Philistia will I shout in triumph."

10   Who will lead me into the strong city?*
     who will bring me into Edom?

11   Have you not cast us off, O God?*
     you no longer go out, O God, with our armies.

12   Grant us your help against the enemy,*
     for vain is the help of man.

13   With God we will do valiant deeds,*
     and he shall tread our enemies under foot.

Evening

33   *Exultate, justi*

1   Rejoice in the Lord, you righteous;*
     it is good for the just to sing praises.

2   Praise the Lord with the harp; *
     play to him upon the psaltery and lyre.

3   Sing for him a new song; *
     sound a fanfare with all your skill upon the trumpet.

4   For the word of the Lord is right, *
     and all his works are sure.

5 He loves righteousness and justice;*
   the loving-kindness of the Lord fills the whole earth.

6 By the word of the Lord were the heavens made, *
   by the breath of his mouth all the heavenly hosts.

7 He gathers up the waters of the ocean as in a water-skin*
   and stores up the depths of the sea.

8 Let all the earth fear the Lord; *
   let all who dwell in the world stand in awe of him.

9 For he spoke, and it came to pass; *
   he commanded, and it stood fast.

10 The Lord brings the will of the nations to naught;*
   he thwarts the designs of the peoples.

11 But the Lord's will stands fast for ever,*
   and the designs of his heart from age to age.

12 Happy is the nation whose God is the Lord!*
   happy the people he has chosen to be his own!

13 The Lord looks down from heaven, *
   and beholds all the people in the world.

14 From where he sits enthroned he turns his gaze *
   on all who dwell on the earth.

15 He fashions all the hearts of them *
   and understands all their works.

16 There is no king that can be saved by a mighty army;
   a strong man is not delivered by his great strength.

17 The horse is a vain hope for deliverance; *
   for all its strength it cannot save.

18 Behold, the eye of the Lord is upon those who fear him, *
   on those who wait upon his love,

19 To pluck their lives from death, *
   and to feed them in time of famine.

20 Our soul waits for the Lord; *
   he is our help and our shield.

21 Indeed, our heart rejoices in him, *
   for in his holy Name we put our trust.

22 Let your loving-kindness, O Lord, be upon us, *
   as we have put our trust in you.

Week of 5 Lent

Sunday
Morning

118 *Confitemini Domino*

1 Give thanks to the Lord, for he is good;*
   his mercy endures for ever.

2 Let Israel now proclaim, *
   "His mercy endures for ever."

3 Let the house of Aaron now proclaim,*
   "His mercy endures for ever."

4 Let those who fear the Lord now proclaim, *
   "His mercy endures for ever."

5 I called to the Lord in my distress; *
   the Lord answered by setting me free.

6 The Lord is at my side, therefore I will not fear;*
   what can anyone do to me?

7 The Lord is at my side to help me; *
   I will triumph over those who hate me.

8 It is better to rely on the Lord *
   than to put any trust in flesh.

9 It is better to rely on the Lord *
   than to put any trust in rulers.

10 All the ungodly encompass me;*
   in the name of the Lord I will repel them.

11 They hem me in, they hem me in on every side;*
   in the name of the Lord I will repel them.

12 They swarm about me like bees;
   they blaze like a fire of thorns;*
   in the name of the Lord I will repel them.

13 I was pressed so hard that I almost fell,*
   but the Lord came to my help.

14 The Lord is my strength and my song,*
   and he has become my salvation.

15 There is a sound of exultation and victory*
   in the tents of the righteous:

16 "The right hand of the Lord has triumphed!*
   the right hand of the Lord is exalted!
   the right hand of the Lord has triumphed!"

17 I shall not die, but live,*
   and declare the works of the Lord.

18 The Lord has punished me sorely,*
   but he did not hand me over to death.

19 Open for me the gates of righteousness;*
   I will enter them; I will offer thanks to the Lord.

20 "This is the gate of the Lord;*
   he who is righteous may enter."

21 I will give thanks to you, for you answered me*
   and have become my salvation.

22 The same stone which the builders rejected*
   has become the chief cornerstone.

23 This is the Lord's doing,*
   and it is marvelous in our eyes.

24 On this day the Lord has acted;*
   we will rejoice and be glad in it.

25 Hosannah, Lord, hosannah!*
   Lord, send us now success.

26 Blessed is he who comes in the name of the Lord;*
   we bless you from the house of the Lord.

27 God is the Lord; he has shined upon us;*
   form a procession with branches up to the horns of the altar.

28 "You are my God, and I will thank you;*
   you are my God, and I will exalt you."

29 Give thanks to the Lord, for he is good;*
   his mercy endures for ever.

145 *Exaltabo te, Deus*

1 I will exalt you, O God my King,*
    and bless your Name for ever and ever.

2 Every day will I bless you *
    and praise your Name for ever and ever.

3 Great is the Lord and greatly to be praised; *
    there is no end to his greatness.

4 One generation shall praise your works to another *
    and shall declare your power.

5 I will ponder the glorious splendor of your majesty *
    and all your marvelous works.

6 They shall speak of the might of your wondrous acts, *
    and I will tell of your greatness.

7 They shall publish the remembrance of your great goodness;*
    they shall sing of your righteous deeds.

8 The Lord is gracious and full of compassion,*
    slow to anger and of great kindness.

9 The Lord is loving to everyone *
    and his compassion is over all his works.

10 All your works praise you, O Lord,*
     and your faithful servants bless you.

11 They make known the glory of your kingdom*
     and speak of your power;

12 That the peoples may know of your power*
     and the glorious splendor of your kingdom.

13 Your kingdom is an everlasting kingdom;*
     your dominion endures throughout all ages.

14 The Lord is faithful in all his words*
     and merciful in all his deeds.

15 The Lord upholds all those who fall;*
     he lifts up those who are bowed down.

16 The eyes of all wait upon you, O Lord,*
     and you give them their food in due season.

17 You open wide your hand*
  and satisfy the needs of every living creature.

18 The Lord is righteous in all his ways*
  and loving in all his works.

19 The Lord is near to those who call upon him,*
  to all who call upon him faithfully.

20 He fulfills the desire of those who fear him;*
  he hears their cry and helps them.

21 The Lord preserves all those who love him,*
  but he destroys all the wicked.

22 My mouth shall speak the praise of the Lord;*
  let all flesh bless his holy Name for ever and ever.

Monday

Morning

31   *In te, Domine, speravi*

1 In you, O Lord, have I taken refuge;
  let me never be put to shame; *
    deliver me in your righteousness.

2 Incline your ear to me; *
  make haste to deliver me.

3 Be my strong rock, a castle to keep me safe,
  for you are my crag and my stronghold; *
    for the sake of your Name, lead me and guide me.

4 Take me out of the net that they have secretly set for me,*
  for you are my tower of strength.

5 Into your hands I commend my spirit, *
  for you have redeemed me,
    O Lord, O God of truth.

6 I hate those who cling to worthless idols,*
  and I put my trust in the Lord.

7 I will rejoice and be glad because of your mercy; *
  for you have seen my affliction;
    you know my distress.

8 You have not shut me up in the power of the enemy;*
  you have set my feet in an open place.

9 Have mercy on me, O Lord, for I am in trouble; *
  my eye is consumed with sorrow,

  and also my throat and my belly.

10 For my life is wasted with grief, and my years with sighing;*
  my strength fails me because of affliction,

  and my bones are consumed.

11 I have become a reproach to all my enemies and
                even to my neighbors,
  a dismay to those of my acquaintance;*
  when they see me in the street they avoid me.

12 I am forgotten like a dead man, out of mind;*
  I am as useless as a broken pot.

13 For I have heard the whispering of the crowd;
  fear is all around;*
    they put their heads together against me;
    they plot to take my life.

14 But as for me, I have trusted in you, O Lord.*
  I have said, "You are my God.

15 My times are in your hand;*
    rescue me from the hand of my enemies,
    and from those who persecute me.

16 Make your face to shine upon your servant,*
  and in your loving-kindness save me."

17 Lord, let me not be ashamed for having called upon you;*
    rather, let the wicked be put to shame;
    let them be silent in the grave.

18 Let the lying lips be silenced which speak against
        the righteous,*
  haughtily, disdainfully, and with contempt.

19 How great is your goodness, O Lord!
  which you have laid up for those who fear you;*
    which you have done in the sight of all
    for those who put their trust in you.

20 You hide them in the covert of your presence from those who
            slander them;*
        you keep them in your shelter from the strife of tongues.

21 Blessed be the Lord!*
        for he has shown me the wonders of his love in a besieged city.

22 Yet I said in my alarm,
        "I have been cut off from the sight of your eyes."*
        Nevertheless, you heard the sound of my entreaty
        when I cried out to you.

23 Love the Lord, all you who worship him;*
        the Lord protects the faithful,
        but repays to the full those who act haughtily.

24 Be strong and let your heart take courage,*
        all you who wait for the Lord.

Evening

35   *Judica, Domine*

1 Fight those who fight me, O Lord;*
        attack those who are attacking me.

2 Take up shield and armor *
        and rise up to help me.

3 Draw the sword and bar the way against those who pursue me; *
        say to my soul, "I am your salvation."

4 Let those who seek after my life be shamed and humbled,*
        let those who plot my ruin fall back and be dismayed.

5 Let them be like chaff before the wind, *
        and let the angel of the Lord drive them away.

6 Let their way be dark and slippery,*
        and let the angel of the Lord pursue them.

7 For they have secretly spread a net for me without a cause; *
        without a cause they have dug a pit to take me alive.

8 Let ruin come upon them unawares; *
        let them be caught in the net they hid;
        let them fall into the pit they dug.

9   Then I will be joyful in the Lord; *
     I will glory in his victory.

10   My very bones will say, "Lord, who is like you?*
     You deliver the poor from those who are too strong for them,
     the poor and needy from those who rob them."

11   Malicious witnesses rise up against me;*
     they charge me with matters I know nothing about.

12   They pay me evil in exchange for good;*
     my soul is full of despair.

13   But when they were sick I dressed in sack-cloth*
     and humbled myself by fasting;

14   I prayed with my whole heart,
     as one would for a friend or a brother;*
     I behaved like one who mourns for his mother,
     bowed down and grieving.

15   But when I stumbled, they were glad and gathered together;
     they gathered against me;*
     strangers whom I did not know tore me to pieces and would not
     stop.

16   They put me to the test and mocked me;*
     they gnashed at me with their teeth.

17   O Lord, how long will you look on?*
     rescue me from the roaring beasts,
     and my life from the young lions.

18   I will give you thanks in the great congregation;*
     I will praise you in the mighty throng.

19   Do not let my treacherous foes rejoice over me,*
     nor let those who hate me without a cause wink at each other.

20   For they do not plan for peace,*
     but invent deceitful schemes against the quiet in the land.

21   They opened their mouths at me and said,*
     "Aha! we saw it with our own eyes."

22   You saw it, O Lord; do not be silent;*
     O Lord, be not far from me.

23   Awake, arise, to my cause!*
     to my defense, my God and my Lord!

24 Give me justice, O Lord my God,
 according to your righteousness;*
  do not let them triumph over me.

25 Do not let them say in their hearts,
 "Aha! just what we want!"*
  Do not let them say, "We have swallowed him up."

26 Let all who rejoice at my ruin be ashamed and disgraced;*
 let those who boast against me be clothed with
  dismay and shame.

27 Let those who favor my cause sing out with joy and be glad;*
 let them say always, "Great is the Lord,
  who desires the prosperity of his servant."

28 And my tongue shall be talking of your righteousness*
 and of your praise all the day long.

Tuesday

Morning

120 *Ad ominum*

1 When I was in trouble, I called to the Lord;*
 I called to the Lord, and he answered me.

2 Deliver me, O Lord, from lying lips *
 and from the deceitful tongue.

3 What shall be done to you, and what more besides,*
 O you deceitful tongue?

4 The sharpened arrows of a warrior, *
 along with hot glowing coals.

5 How hateful it is that I must lodge in Meshech *
 and dwell among the tents of Kedar!

6 Too long have I had to live; *
 among the enemies of peace.

7 I am on the side of peace, *
 but when I speak of it, they are for war.

121 *Levavi oculos*

1 I lift up my eyes to the hills;*
 from where is my help to come?

2 My help comes from the Lord,*
  the maker of heaven and earth.

3 He will not let your foot be moved*
  and he who watches over you will not fall asleep.

4 Behold, he who keeps watch over Israel*
  shall neither slumber nor sleep;

5 The Lord himself watches over you;*
  the Lord is your shade at your right hand,

6 So that the sun shall not strike you by day,*
  nor the moon by night.

7 The Lord shall preserve you from all evil;*
  it is he who shall keep you safe.

8 The Lord shall watch over your going out and your coming in,*
  from this time forth for evermore.

122 *Lœtatus sum*

1 I was glad when they said to me,*
  "Let us go to the house of the Lord."

2 Now our feet are standing*
  within your gates, O Jerusalem.

3 Jerusalem is built as a city*
  that is at unity with itself;

4 To which the tribes go up,
  the tribes of the Lord,*
    the assembly of Israel,
    to praise the Name of the Lord.

5 For there are the thrones of judgment,*
  the thrones of the house of David.

6 Pray for the peace of Jerusalem:*
  "May they prosper who love you.

7 Peace be within your walls*
  and quietness within your towers.

8 For my brethren and companions' sake,*
  I pray for your prosperity.

9 Because of the house of the Lord our God,*
  I will seek to do you good."

123 *Ad te levavi oculos meos*

1 To you I lift up my eyes,*
    to you enthroned in the heavens.

2 As the eyes of servants look to the hand of their masters,*
    and the eyes of a maid to the hand of her mistress,

3 So our eyes look to the Lord our God,*
    until he show us his mercy.

4 Have mercy upon us, O Lord, have mercy,*
    for we have had more than enough of contempt,

5 Too much of the scorn of the indolent rich,*
    and of the derision of the proud.

Evening

124 *Nisi quia Dominus*

1 If the Lord had not been on our side, *
    let Israel now say;

2 If the Lord had not been on our side, *
    when enemies rose up against us;

3 Then would they have swallowed us up alive *
    in their fierce anger toward us;

4 Then would the waters have overwhelmed us *
    and the torrent gone over us;

5 Then would the raging waters *
    have gone right over us.

6 Blessed be the Lord! *
    he has not given us over to be a prey for their teeth.

7 We have escaped like a bird from the snare of the fowler; *
    the snare is broken, and we have escaped.

8 Our help is in the Name of the Lord, *
    the maker of heaven and earth.

125 *Qui confidunt*

1 Those who trust in the Lord are like Mount Zion, *
    which cannot be moved, but stands fast for ever.

2 The hills stand about Jerusalem; *
    so does the Lord stand round about his people,
    from this time forth for evermore.

3 The scepter of the wicked shall not hold sway over the
    land allotted to the just, *
    so that the just shall not put their hands to evil.

4 Show your goodness, O Lord, to those who are good*
    and to those who are true of heart.

5 As for those who turn aside to crooked ways,
    the Lord will lead them away with the evildoers;*
    but peace be upon Israel.

126 *In convertendo*

1 When the Lord restored the fortunes of Zion,*
    then were we like those who dream.

2 Then was our mouth filled with laughter,*
    and our tongue with shouts of joy.

3 Then they said among the nations,*
    "The Lord has done great things for them."

4 The Lord has done great things for us,*
    and we are glad indeed.

5 Restore our fortunes, O Lord,*
    like the watercourses of the Negev.

6 Those who sowed with tears*
    will reap with songs of joy.

7 Those who go out weeping, carrying the seed,*
    will come again with joy, shouldering their sheaves.

127 *Nisi Dominus*

1 Unless the Lord builds the house,*
    their labor is in vain who build it.

2 Unless the Lord watches over the city,*
    in vain the watchman keeps his vigil.

3 It is in vain that you rise so early and go to bed so late; *
    vain, too, to eat the bread of toil,
    for he gives to his beloved sleep.

4 Children are a heritage from the Lord,*
    and the fruit of the womb is a gift.

5 Like arrows in the hand of a warrior*
    are the children of one's youth.

6 Happy is the man who has his quiver full of them! *
    he shall not be put to shame
    when he contends with his enemies in the gate.

Wednesday
Morning

119

Qoph *Clamavi in toto corde meo*

145 I call with my whole heart;*
    answer me, O Lord, that I may keep your statutes.

146 I call to you;
    oh, that you would save me!*
    I will keep your decrees.

147 Early in the morning I cry out to you,*
    for in your word is my trust.

148 My eyes are open in the night watches,*
    that I may meditate upon your promise.

149 Hear my voice, O Lord, according to your loving-kindness;*
    according to your judgments, give me life.

150 They draw near who in malice persecute me;*
    they are very far from your law.

151 You, O Lord, are near at hand,*
    and all your commandments are true.

152 Long have I known from your decrees*
    that you have established them for ever.

Resh *Vide humilitatem*

153 Behold my affliction and deliver me,*
    for I do not forget your law.

154 Plead my cause and redeem me;*
    according to your promise, give me life.

155 Deliverance is far from the wicked,*
　　for they do not study your statutes.

156 Great is your compassion, O Lord;*
　　preserve my life, according to your judgments.

157 There are many who persecute and oppress me,*
　　yet I have not swerved from your decrees.

158 I look with loathing at the faithless,*
　　for they have not kept your word.

159 See how I love your commandments!*
　　O Lord, in your mercy, preserve me.

160 The heart of your word is truth;*
　　all your righteous judgments endure for evermore.

Shin　*Principes persecuti sunt*

161 Rulers have persecuted me without a cause,*
　　but my heart stands in awe of your word.

162 I am as glad because of your promise*
　　as one who finds great spoils.

163 As for lies, I hate and abhor them,*
　　but your law is my love.

164 Seven times a day do I praise you,*
　　because of your righteous judgments.

165 Great peace have they who love your law;*
　　for them there is no stumbling block.

166 I have hoped for your salvation, O Lord,*
　　and I have fulfilled your commandments.

167 I have kept your decrees*
　　and I have loved them deeply.

168 I have kept your commandments and decrees,*
　　for all my ways are before you.

Taw　*Appropinquet deprecatio*

169 Let my cry come before you, O Lord;*
　　give me understanding, according to your word.

170 Let my supplication come before you;*
　　deliver me, according to your promise.

171 My lips shall pour forth your praise,*
    when you teach me your statutes.

172 My tongue shall sing of your promise,*
    for all your commandments are righteous.

173 Let your hand be ready to help me,*
    for I have chosen your commandments.

174 I long for your salvation, O Lord,*
    and your law is my delight.

175 Let me live, and I will praise you,*
    and let your judgments help me.

176 I have gone astray like a sheep that is lost;*
    search for your servant,
    for I do not forget your commandments.

Evening

128 *Beati omnes*

1 Happy are they all who fear the Lord,*
    and who follow in his ways!

2 You shall eat the fruit of your labor;*
    happiness and prosperity shall be yours.

3 Your wife shall be like a fruitful vine within your house,*
    your children like olive shoots round about your table.

4 The man who fears the Lord*
    shall thus indeed be blessed.

5 The Lord bless you from Zion,*
    and may you see the prosperity of Jerusalem all the days
        of your life.

6 May you live to see your children's children;*
    may peace be upon Israel.

129 *Sæpe expugnaverunt*

1 "Greatly have they oppressed me since my youth,"*
    let Israel now say;

2 "Greatly have they oppressed me since my youth,*
  but they have not prevailed against me."

3 The plowmen plowed upon my back*
  and made their furrows long.

4 The Lord, the Righteous One,*
  has cut the cords of the wicked.

5 Let them be put to shame and thrown back,*
  all those who are enemies of Zion.

6 Let them be like grass upon the housetops,*
  which withers before it can be plucked;

7 Which does not fill the hand of the reaper,*
  nor the bosom of him who binds the sheaves;

8 So that those who go by say not so much as,
  "The Lord prosper you.*
  We wish you well in the Name of the Lord."

130 *De profundis*

1 Out of the depths have I called to you, O Lord;
  Lord, hear my voice;*
    let your ears consider well the voice of my supplication.

2 If you, Lord, were to note what is done amiss,*
  O Lord, who could stand?

3 For there is forgiveness with you;*
  therefore you shall be feared.

4 I wait for the Lord; my soul waits for him;*
  in his word is my hope.

5 My soul waits for the Lord,
  more than watchmen for the morning,*
    more than watchmen for the morning.

6 O Israel, wait for the Lord,*
  for with the Lord there is mercy;

7 With him there is plenteous redemption,*
  and he shall redeem Israel from all their sins.

Thursday

Morning

131 *Domine, non est*

1 O Lord, I am not proud;*
    I have no haughty looks.

2 I do not occupy myself with great matters,*
    or with things that are too hard for me.

3 But I still my soul and make it quiet,
    like a child upon its mother's breast;*
    my soul is quieted within me.

4 O Israel, wait upon the Lord,*
    from this time forth for evermore.

132 *Memento, Domine*

1 Lord, remember David,*
    and all the hardships he endured;

2 How he swore an oath to the Lord*
    and vowed a vow to the Mighty One of Jacob:

3 "I will not come under the roof of my house," *
    nor climb up into my bed;

4 I will not allow my eyes to sleep, *
    nor let my eyelids slumber;

5 Until I find a place for the Lord, *
    a dwelling for the Mighty One of Jacob."

6 "The ark! We heard it was in Ephratah; *
    we found it in the fields of Jearim.

7 Let us go to God's dwelling place; *
    let us fall upon our knees before his footstool."

8 Arise, O Lord, into your resting-place, *
    you and the ark of your strength.

9 Let your priests be clothed with righteousness; *
    let your faithful people sing with joy.

10 For your servant David's sake,*
    do not turn away the face of your Anointed.

11 The Lord has sworn an oath to David;*
   in truth, he will not break it:

12 "A son, the fruit of your body*
   will I set upon your throne.

13 If your children keep my covenant
   and my testimonies that I shall teach them,*
      their children will sit upon your throne for evermore."

14 For the Lord has chosen Zion;*
   he has desired her for his habitation:

15 "This shall be my resting-place for ever;*
   here will I dwell, for I delight in her.

16 I will surely bless her provisions, *
   and satisfy her poor with bread.

17 I will clothe her priests with salvation, *
   and her faithful people will rejoice and sing.

18 There will I make the horn of David flourish; *
   I have prepared a lamp for my Anointed.

19 As for his enemies, I will clothe them with shame; *
   but as for him, his crown will shine."

133 *Ecce, quam bonum!*

1 Oh, how good and pleasant it is, *
   when brethren live together in unity!

2 It is like fine oil upon the head *
   that runs down upon the beard,

3 Upon the beard of Aaron, *
   and runs down upon the collar of his robe.

4 It is like the dew of Hermon *
   that falls upon the hills of Zion.

5 For there the Lord has ordained the blessing: *
   life for evermore.

140 *Eripe me, Domine*

1 Deliver me, O Lord, from evildoers;*
   protect me from the violent,

2 Who devise evil in their hearts *
   and stir up strife all day long.

3 They have sharpened their tongues like a serpent; *
   adder's poison is under their lips.

4 Keep me, O Lord, from the hands of the wicked; *
   protect me from the violent,
   who are determined to trip me up.

5 The proud have hidden a snare for me
   and stretched out a net of cords; *
   they have set traps for me along the path.

6 I have said to the Lord, "You are my God; *
   listen, O Lord, to my supplication.

7 O Lord God, the strength of my salvation, *
   you have covered my head in the day of battle.

8 Do not grant the desires of the wicked, O Lord, *
   Nor let their evil plans prosper.

9 Let not those who surround me lift up their heads; *
   let the evil of their lips overwhelm them.

10 Let hot burning coals fall upon them;*
    let them be cast into the mire, never to rise up again."

11 A slanderer shall not be established on the earth,*
    and evil shall hunt down the lawless.

12 I know that the Lord will maintain the cause of the poor*
    and render justice to the needy.

13 Surely, the righteous will give thanks to your Name, *
    and the upright shall continue in your sight.

142 *Voce mea ad Dominum*

1 I cry to the Lord with my voice;*
   to the Lord I make loud supplication.

2 I pour out my complaint before him*
   and tell him all my trouble.

3 When my spirit languishes within me, you know my path;*
   in the way wherein I walk they have hidden a trap for me.

4 I look to my right hand and find no one who knows me;*
   I have no place to flee to, and no one cares for me.

5 I cry out to you, O Lord;*
   I say, "You are my refuge,
   my portion in the land of the living."

6 Listen to my cry for help, for I have been brought very low;*
   save me from those who pursue me,
   for they are too strong for me.

7 Bring me out of prison, that I may give thanks to your Name;*
   when you have dealt bountifully with me,
   the righteous will gather around me.

Friday
Morning

For the Invitatory

95 *Venite, exultemus*

1 Come, let us sing to the Lord;*
   let us shout for joy to the Rock of our salvation.

2 Let us come before his presence with thanksgiving*
   and raise a loud shout to him with psalms.

3 For the Lord is a great God, *
   and a great King above all gods.

4 In his hand are the caverns of the earth, *
   and the heights of the hills are his also.

5 The sea is his, for he made it, *
   and his hands have molded the dry land.

6 Come, let us bow down, and bend the knee,*
   and kneel before the Lord our Maker.

7 For he is our God,
   and we are the people of his pasture and the sheep of his hand.*
   Oh, that today you would hearken to his voice!

8 Harden not your hearts,
    as your forebears did in the wilderness,*
      at Meribah, and on that day at Massah,
      when they tempted me.

9 They put me to the test, *
    though they had seen my works.

10 Forty years long I detested that generation and said,*
    "This people are wayward in their hearts;
    they do not know my ways."

11 So I swore in my wrath,*
    "They shall not enter into my rest."

22   *Deus, Deus meus*

1 My God, my God, why have you forsaken me?*
    and are so far from my cry
    and from the words of my distress?

2 O my God, I cry in the daytime, but you do not answer;*
    by night as well, but I find no rest.

3 Yet you are the Holy One, *
    enthroned upon the praises of Israel.

4 Our forefathers put their trust in you; *
    they trusted, and you delivered them.

5 They cried out to you and were delivered; *
    they trusted in you and were not put to shame.

6 But as for me, I am a worm and no man, *
    scorned by all and despised by the people.

7 All who see me laugh me to scorn; *
    they curl their lips and wag their heads, saying,

8 "He trusted in the Lord; let him deliver him; *
    let him rescue him, if he delights in him."

9 Yet you are he who took me out of the womb, *
    and kept me safe upon my mother's breast.

10 I have been entrusted to you ever since I was born;*
    you were my God when I was still in my mother's womb.

11 Be not far from me, for trouble is near,*
    and there is none to help.

12 Many young bulls encircle me;*
   strong bulls of Bashan surround me.

13 They open wide their jaws at me,*
   like a ravening and a roaring lion.

14 I am poured out like water;
   all my bones are out of joint;*
   my heart within my breast is melting wax.

15 My mouth is dried out like a pot-sherd;
   my tongue sticks to the roof of my mouth;*
   and you have laid me in the dust of the grave.

16 Packs of dogs close me in,
   and gangs of evildoers circle around me;*
   they pierce my hands and my feet;
   I can count all my bones.

17 They stare and gloat over me;*
   they divide my garments among them;
   they cast lots for my clothing.

18 Be not far away, O Lord;*
   you are my strength; hasten to help me.

19 Save me from the sword,*
   my life from the power of the dog.

20 Save me from the lion's mouth,*
   my wretched body from the horns of wild bulls.

21 I will declare your Name to my brethren;*
   in the midst of the congregation I will praise you.

22 Praise the Lord, you that fear him;*
   stand in awe of him, O offspring of Israel;
   all you of Jacob's line, give glory.

23 For he does not despise nor abhor the poor in their poverty;
   neither does he hide his face from them;*
   but when they cry to him he hears them.

24 My praise is of him in the great assembly;*
   I will perform my vows in the presence of those who
      worship him.

25 The poor shall eat and be satisfied,
   and those who seek the Lord shall praise him:*
   "May your heart live for ever!"

26 All the ends of the earth shall remember and turn to the Lord, *
   and all the families of the nations shall bow before him.

27 For kingship belongs to the Lord; *
   he rules over the nations.

28 To him alone all who sleep in the earth bow down in worship; *
   all who go down to the dust fall before him.

29 My soul shall live for him;
   my descendants shall serve him; *
   they shall be known as the Lord's for ever.

30 They shall come and make known to a people yet unborn *
   the saving deeds that he has done.

Evening

141 *Domine, clamavi*

1 O Lord, I call to you; come to me quickly; *
   hear my voice when I cry to you.

2 Let my prayer be set forth in your sight as incense, *
   the lifting up of my hands as the evening sacrifice.

3 Set a watch before my mouth, O Lord,
   and guard the door of my lips; *
   let not my heart incline to any evil thing.

4 Let me not be occupied in wickedness with evildoers, *
   nor eat of their choice foods.

5 Let the righteous smite me in friendly rebuke;
   let not the oil of the unrighteous anoint my head; *
   for my prayer is continually against their wicked deeds.

6 Let their rulers be overthrown in stony places, *
   that they may know my words are true.

7 As when a plowman turns over the earth in furrows, *
   let their bones be scattered at the mouth of the grave.

8 But my eyes are turned to you, Lord God; *
   in you I take refuge;
   do not strip me of my life.

9 Protect me from the snare which they have laid for me *
   and from the traps of the evildoers.

10 Let the wicked fall into their own nets, *
       while I myself escape.

143 *Domine, exaudi*

1 Lord, hear my prayer,
     and in your faithfulness heed my supplications;*
       answer me in your righteousness.

2 Enter not into judgment with your servant,*
       for in your sight shall no one living be justified.

3 For my enemy has sought my life;
     he has crushed me to the ground; *
       he has made me live in dark places like those who
              are long dead.

4 My spirit faints within me; *
       my heart within me is desolate.

5 I remember the time past;
     I muse upon all your deeds; *
       I consider the works of your hands.

6 I spread out my hands to you; *
       my soul gasps to you like a thirsty land.

7 O Lord, make haste to answer me; my spirit fails me;*
     do not hide your face from me
     or I shall be like those who go down to the Pit.

8 Let me hear of your loving-kindness in the morning,
     for I put my trust in you;*
       show me the road that I must walk,
       for I lift up my soul to you.

9 Deliver me from my enemies, O Lord, *
       for I flee to you for refuge.

10 Teach me to do what pleases you, for you are my God;*
       let your good Spirit lead me on level ground.

11 Revive me, O Lord, for your Name's sake;*
       for your righteousness' sake, bring me out of trouble.

12 Of your goodness, destroy my enemies
     and bring all my foes to naught, *
       for truly I am your servant.

Saturday

Morning

137 *Super flumina*

1 By the waters of Babylon we sat down and wept,*
    when we remembered you, O Zion.

2 As for our harps, we hung them up*
    on the trees in the midst of that land.

3 For those who led us away captive asked us for a song,
  and our oppressors called for mirth:*
    "Sing us one of the songs of Zion."

4 How shall we sing the Lord's song*
    upon an alien soil?

5 If I forget you, O Jerusalem,*
    let my right hand forget its skill.

6 Let my tongue cleave to the roof of my mouth
  if I do not remember you,*
    if I do not set Jerusalem above my highest joy.

7 Remember the day of Jerusalem, O Lord,
  against the people of Edom,*
    who said, "Down with it! down with it!
    even to the ground!"

8 O Daughter of Babylon, doomed to destruction,*
  happy the one who pays you back
  for what you have done to us!

9 Happy shall he be who takes your little ones,*
  and dashes them against the rock!

144 *Benedictus Dominus*

1 Blessed be the Lord my rock!*
    who trains my hands to fight and my fingers to battle;

2 My help and my fortress, my stronghold and my deliverer,*
  my shield in whom I trust,
  who subdues the peoples under me.

3 O Lord, what are we that you should care for us? *
  mere mortals that you should think of us?

4 We are like a puff of wind; *
 our days are like a passing shadow.

5 Bow your heavens, O Lord, and come down; *
 touch the mountains, and they shall smoke.

6 Hurl the lightning and scatter them; *
 shoot out your arrows and rout them.

7 Stretch out your hand from on high; *
 rescue me and deliver me from the great waters,
 from the hand of foreign peoples,

8 Whose mouths speak deceitfully *
 and whose right hand is raised in falsehood.

9 O God, I will sing to you a new song; *
 I will play to you on a ten-stringed lyre.

10 You give victory to kings*
 and have rescued David your servant.

11 Rescue me from the hurtful sword*
 and deliver me from the hand of foreign peoples,

12 Whose mouths speak deceitfully*
 and whose right hand is raised in falsehood.

13 May our sons be like plants well nurtured from their youth,*
 and our daughters like sculptured corners of a palace.

14 May our barns be filled to overflowing with all manner of crops;*
 may the flocks in our pastures increase by thousands
 and tens of thousands;
 may our cattle be fat and sleek.

15 May there be no breaching of the walls,
 no going into exile, no wailing in the public squares.

16 Happy are the people of whom this is so!*
 happy are the people whose God is the Lord!

Evening

42 *Quemadmodum*

1 As the deer longs for the water-brooks,*
 so longs my soul for you, O God.

2 My soul is athirst for God, athirst for the living God; *
    when shall I come to appear before the presence of God?

3 My tears have been my food day and night, *
    while all day long they say to me,
    "Where now is your God?"

4 I pour out my soul when I think on these things: *
    how I went with the multitude and led them into the
        house of God,

5 With the voice of praise and thanksgiving, *
    among those who keep holy-day.

6 Why are you so full of heaviness, O my soul? *
    and why are you so disquieted within me?

7 Put your trust in God; *
    for I will yet give thanks to him,

    who is the help of my countenance, and my God.

8 My soul is heavy within me;*
    therefore I will remember you from the land of Jordan, and
    from the peak of Mizar among the heights of Hermon.

9 One deep calls to another in the noise of your cataracts; *
    all your rapids and floods have gone over me.

10 The Lord grants his loving-kindness in the daytime;*
    in the night season his song is with me,
    a prayer to the God of my life.

11 I will say to the God of my strength,
    "Why have you forgotten me?*
    and why do I go so heavily while the enemy oppresses me?"

12 While my bones are being broken,*
    my enemies mock me to my face;

13 All day long they mock me*
    and say to me, "Where now is your God?"

14 Why are you so full of heaviness, O my soul?*
    and why are you so disquieted within me?

15 Put your trust in God;*
    for I will yet give thanks to him,
    who is the help of my countenance, and my God.

43 *Judica me, Deus*

1 Give judgment for me, O God,
and defend my cause against an ungodly people; *
    deliver me from the deceitful and the wicked.

2 For you are the God of my strength;
why have you put me from you? *
    and why do I go so heavily while the enemy oppresses me?

3 Send out your light and your truth, that they may lead me,*
    and bring me to your holy hill
    and to your dwelling;

4 That I may go to the altar of God,
to the God of my joy and gladness;*
    and on the harp I will give thanks to you, O God my God.

5 Why are you so full of heaviness, O my soul? *
    and why are you so disquieted within me?

6 Put your trust in God; *
    for I will yet give thanks to him,
    who is the help of my countenance, and my God.

Holy Week

Palm Sunday
Morning

24 *Domini est terra*

1 The earth is the Lord's and all that is in it, *
    the world and all who dwell therein.

2 For it is he who founded it upon the seas *
    and made it firm upon the rivers of the deep.

3 "Who can ascend the hill of the Lord? *
    and who can stand in his holy place?"

4 "Those who have clean hands and a pure heart, *
    who have not pledged themselves to falsehood,
    nor sworn by what is a fraud.

5 They shall receive a blessing from the Lord *
    and a just reward from the God of their salvation."

6 Such is the generation of those who seek him, *
    of those who seek your face, O God of Jacob.

7 Lift up your heads, O gates; lift them high, O everlasting doors; *
    and the King of glory shall come in.

8 "Who is this King of glory?" *
    "The Lord, strong and mighty,
    the Lord, mighty in battle."

9 Lift up your heads, O gates;
    lift them high, O everlasting doors; *
    and the King of glory shall come in.

10 "Who is he, this King of glory?"
    "The Lord of hosts,
    he is the King of glory."

29   *Afferte Domino*

1 Ascribe to the Lord, you gods, *
    ascribe to the Lord glory and strength.

2 Ascribe to the Lord the glory due his Name; *
    worship the Lord in the beauty of holiness.

3 The voice of the Lord is upon the waters;
    the God of glory thunders; *
    the Lord is upon the mighty waters.

4 The voice of the Lord is a powerful voice; *
    the voice of the Lord is a voice of splendor.

5 The voice of the Lord breaks the cedar trees; *
    the Lord breaks the cedars of Lebanon;

6 He makes Lebanon skip like a calf, *
    and Mount Hermon like a young wild ox.

7 The voice of the Lord splits the flames of fire;
    the voice of the Lord shakes the wilderness; *
    the Lord shakes the wilderness of Kadesh.

8 The voice of the Lord makes the oak trees writhe *
    and strips the forests bare.

9 And in the temple of the Lord *
   all are crying, "Glory!"

10 The Lord sits enthroned above the flood;*
   the Lord sits enthroned as King for evermore.

11 The Lord shall give strength to his people; *
   the Lord shall give his people the blessing of peace.

Evening

103 *Benedic, anima mea*

1 Bless the Lord, O my soul, *
   and all that is within me, bless his holy Name.

2 Bless the Lord, O my soul, *
   and forget not all his benefits.

3 He forgives all your sins *
   and heals all your infirmities;

4 He redeems your life from the grave *
   and crowns you with mercy and loving-kindness;

5 He satisfies you with good things, *
   and your youth is renewed like an eagle's.

6 The Lord executes righteousness *
   and judgment for all who are oppressed.

7 He made his ways known to Moses *
   and his works to the children of Israel.

8 The Lord is full of compassion and mercy, *
   slow to anger and of great kindness.

9 He will not always accuse us, *
   nor will he keep his anger for ever.

10 He has not dealt with us according to our sins,*
   nor rewarded us according to our wickedness.

11 For as the heavens are high above the earth,*
   so is his mercy great upon those who fear him.

12 As far as the east is from the west,*
   so far has he removed our sins from us.

13 As a father cares for his children,*
    so does the Lord care for those who fear him.

14 For he himself knows whereof we are made;*
    he remembers that we are but dust.

15 Our days are like the grass;*
    we flourish like a flower of the field;

16 When the wind goes over it, it is gone,*
    and its place shall know it no more.

17 But the merciful goodness of the Lord endures for ever on those
        who fear him,*
    and his righteousness on children's children;

18 On those who keep his covenant*
    and remember his commandments and do them.

19 The Lord has set his throne in heaven,*
    and his kingship has dominion over all.

20 Bless the Lord, you angels of his,
    you mighty ones who do his bidding,*
        and hearken to the voice of his word.

21 Bless the Lord, all you his hosts,*
    you ministers of his who do his will.

22 Bless the Lord, all you works of his,
    in all places of his dominion;*
        bless the Lord, O my soul.

Monday

Morning

51 *Miserere mei, Deus*

1 Have mercy on me, O God, according to your loving-kindness; *
    in your great compassion blot out my offenses.

2 Wash me through and through from my wickedness*
    and cleanse me from my sin.

3 For I know my transgressions, *
    and my sin is ever before me.

4 Against you only have I sinned *
   and done what is evil in your sight.

5 And so you are justified when you speak *
   and upright in your judgment.

6 Indeed, I have been wicked from my birth, *
   a sinner from my mother's womb.

7 For behold, you look for truth deep within me, *
   and will make me understand wisdom secretly.

8 Purge me from my sin, and I shall be pure; *
   wash me, and I shall be clean indeed.

9 Make me hear of joy and gladness, *
   that the body you have broken may rejoice.

10 Hide your face from my sins*
   and blot out all my iniquities.

11 Create in me a clean heart, O God,*
   and renew a right spirit within me.

12 Cast me not away from your presence*
   and take not your holy Spirit from me.

13 Give me the joy of your saving help again*
   and sustain me with your bountiful Spirit.

14 I shall teach your ways to the wicked,*
   and sinners shall return to you.

15 Deliver me from death, O God,*
   and my tongue shall sing of your righteousness,
   O God of my salvation.

16 Open my lips, O Lord,*
   and my mouth shall proclaim your praise.

17 Had you desired it, I would have offered sacrifice,*
   but you take no delight in burnt-offerings.

18 The sacrifice of God is a troubled spirit;*
   a broken and contrite heart, O God, you will not despise.

19 Be favorable and gracious to Zion,*
   and rebuild the walls of Jerusalem.

20 Then you will be pleased with the appointed sacrifices,
   with burnt-offerings and oblations;*
   then shall they offer young bullocks upon your altar.

69   *Salvum me fac*

1 Save me, O God,*
     for the waters have risen up to my neck.

2 I am sinking in deep mire, *
     and there is no firm ground for my feet.

3 I have come into deep waters, *
     and the torrent washes over me.

4 I have grown weary with my crying;
     my throat is inflamed; *
     my eyes have failed from looking for my God.

5 Those who hate me without a cause are more than the hairs
                           of my head;
     my lying foes who would destroy me are mighty.*
     Must I then give back what I never stole?

6 O God, you know my foolishness, *
     and my faults are not hidden from you.

7 Let not those who hope in you be put to shame through me,
                           Lord God of hosts;*
     let not those who seek you be disgraced because of me,
                           O God of Israel.

8 Surely, for your sake have I suffered reproach,*
     and shame has covered my face.

9 I have become a stranger to my own kindred, *
     an alien to my mother's children.

10 Zeal for your house has eaten me up;*
     the scorn of those who scorn you has fallen upon me.

11 I humbled myself with fasting,*
     but that was turned to my reproach.

12 I put on sack-cloth also,*
     and became a byword among them.

13 Those who sit at the gate murmur against me,*
     and the drunkards make songs about me.

14 But as for me, this is my prayer to you,*
     at the time you have set, O Lord:

15 "In your great mercy, O God,*
     answer me with your unfailing help.

16 Save me from the mire; do not let me sink;*
    let me be rescued from those who hate me
    and out of the deep waters.

17 Let not the torrent of waters wash over me,
    neither let the deep swallow me up;*
    do not let the Pit shut its mouth upon me.

18 Answer me, O Lord, for your love is kind;*
    in your great compassion, turn to me.'

19 "Hide not your face from your servant;*
    be swift and answer me, for I am in distress.

20 Draw near to me and redeem me;*
    because of my enemies deliver me.

21 You know my reproach, my shame, and my dishonor; *
    my adversaries are all in your sight."

22 Reproach has broken my heart, and it cannot be healed; *
    I looked for sympathy, but there was none,
    for comforters, but I could find no one.

23 They gave me gall to eat, *
    and when I was thirsty, they gave me vinegar to drink.

Tuesday

Morning

6   *Domine, ne in furore*

1 Lord, do not rebuke me in your anger; *
    do not punish me in your wrath.

2 Have pity on me, Lord, for I am weak;*
    heal me, Lord, for my bones are racked.

3 My spirit shakes with terror; *
    how long, O Lord, how long?

4 Turn, O Lord, and deliver me; *
    save me for your mercy's sake.

5 For in death no one remembers you; *
    and who will give you thanks in the grave?

6 I grow weary because of my groaning; *
    every night I drench my bed and flood my couch with tears.

7 My eyes are wasted with grief *
   and worn away because of all my enemies.

8 Depart from me, all evildoers, *
   for the Lord has heard the sound of my weeping.

9 The Lord has heard my supplication; *
   the Lord accepts my prayer.

10 All my enemies shall be confounded and quake with fear;*
   they shall turn back and suddenly be put to shame.

12   *Salvum me fac*

1 Help me, Lord, for there is no godly one left;*
   the faithful have vanished from among us.

2 Everyone speaks falsely with his neighbor;*
   with a smooth tongue they speak from a double heart.

3 Oh, that the Lord would cut off all smooth tongues,*
   and close the lips that utter proud boasts!

4 Those who say, "With our tongue will we prevail;*
   our lips are our own; who is lord over us?"

5 "Because the needy are oppressed,
 and the poor cry out in misery,*
   I will rise up," says the Lord,
   "and give them the help they long for."

6 The words of the Lord are pure words,*
   like silver refined from ore
   and purified seven times in the fire.

7 O Lord, watch over us*
   and save us from this generation for ever.

8 The wicked prowl on every side,*
   and that which is worthless is highly prized by everyone.

Evening

94   *Deus ultionum*

1 O Lord God of vengeance,*
   O God of vengeance, show yourself

2 Rise up, O Judge of the world;*
   give the arrogant their just deserts.

3 How long shall the wicked, O Lord,*
   how long shall the wicked triumph?

4 They bluster in their insolence;*
   all evildoers are full of boasting.

5 They crush your people, O Lord, *
   and afflict your chosen nation.

6 They murder the widow and the stranger *
   and put the orphans to death.

7 Yet they say, "The Lord does not see, *
   the God of Jacob takes no notice."

8 Consider well, you dullards among the people; *
   when will you fools understand?

9 He that planted the ear, does he not hear? *
   he that formed the eye, does he not see?

10 He who admonishes the nations, will he not punish?*
   he who teaches all the world, has he no knowledge?

11 The Lord knows our human thoughts;*
   how like a puff of wind they are.

12 Happy are they whom you instruct, O Lord!*
   whom you teach out of your law;

13 To give them rest in evil days,*
   until a pit is dug for the wicked.

14 For the Lord will not abandon his people,*
   nor will he forsake his own.

15 For judgment will again be just,*
   and all the true of heart will follow it.

16 Who rose up for me against the wicked?*
   who took my part against the evildoers?

17 If the Lord had not come to my help,*
   I should soon have dwelt in the land of silence.

18 As often as I said, "My foot has slipped,"*
   your love, O Lord, upheld me.

19 When many cares fill my mind,*
  your consolations cheer my soul.

20 Can a corrupt tribunal have any part with you,*
  one which frames evil into law?

21 They conspire against the life of the just*
  and condemn the innocent to death.

22 But the Lord has become my stronghold,*
  and my God the rock of my trust.

23 He will turn their wickedness back upon them
  and destroy them in their own malice;*
  the Lord our God will destroy them.

Wednesday

Morning

55 *Exaudi, Deus*

1 Hear my prayer, O God;*
  do not hide yourself from my petition.

2 Listen to me and answer me; *
  I have no peace, because of my cares.

3 I am shaken by the noise of the enemy *
  and by the pressure of the wicked;

4 For they have cast an evil spell upon me *
  and are set against me in fury.

5 My heart quakes within me,*
  and the terrors of death have fallen upon me.

6 Fear and trembling have come over me, *
  and horror overwhelms me.

7 And I said, "Oh, that I had wings like a dove!*
  I would fly away and be at rest.

8 I would flee to a far-off place *
  and make my lodging in the wilderness.

9 I would hasten to escape *
  from the stormy wind and tempest."

10 Swallow them up, O Lord;
 confound their speech;*
  for I have seen violence and strife in the city.

11 Day and night the watchmen make their rounds upon her walls,*
  but trouble and misery are in the midst of her.

12 There is corruption at her heart;*
  her streets are never free of oppression and deceit.

13 For had it been an adversary who taunted me,
 then I could have borne it;*
  or had it been an enemy who vaunted himself against me,
  then I could have hidden from him.

14 But it was you, a man after my own heart,*
  my companion, my own familiar friend.

15 We took sweet counsel together,*
  and walked with the throng in the house of God.

16 Let death come upon them suddenly;
 let them go down alive into the grave;*
  for wickedness is in their dwellings, in their very midst.

17 But I will call upon God,*
  and the Lord will deliver me.

18 In the evening, in the morning, and at noonday,
 I will complain and lament,*
  and he will hear my voice.

19 He will bring me safely back from the battle waged against me;*
  for there are many who fight me.

20 God, who is enthroned of old, will hear me and bring them
                down;*
  they never change; they do not fear God.

21 My companion stretched forth his hand against his comrade;*
  he has broken his covenant.

22 His speech is softer than butter,*
  but war is in his heart.

23 His words are smoother than oil,*
  but they are drawn swords.

24 Cast your burden upon the Lord, and he will sustain you;*
  he will never let the righteous stumble.

25 For you will bring the bloodthirsty and deceitful*
    down to the pit of destruction, O God.

26 They shall not live out half their days,*
    but I will put my trust in you.

Evening

74 *Ut quid, Deus?*

1 O God, why have you utterly cast us off?*
    why is your wrath so hot against the sheep of your pasture?

2 Remember your congregation that you purchased long ago,*
    the tribe you redeemed to be your inheritance,
    and Mount Zion where you dwell.

3 Turn your steps toward the endless ruins; *
    the enemy has laid waste everything in your sanctuary.

4 Your adversaries roared in your holy place; *
    they set up their banners as tokens of victory.

5 They were like men coming up with axes to a grove of trees;*
    they broke down all your carved work with hatchets
        and hammers.

6 They set fire to your holy place; *
    they defiled the dwelling-place of your Name
    and razed it to the ground.

7 They said to themselves, "Let us destroy them altogether." *
    They burned down all the meeting-places of God in the land.

8 There are no signs for us to see; there is no prophet left; *
    there is not one among us who knows how long.

9 How long, O God, will the adversary scoff? *
    will the enemy blaspheme your Name for ever?

10 Why do you draw back your hand?*
    why is your right hand hidden in your bosom?

11 Yet God is my King from ancient times,*
    victorious in the midst of the earth.

12 You divided the sea by your might*
    and shattered the heads of the dragons upon the waters;

13 You crushed the heads of Leviathan*
    and gave him to the people of the desert for food.

14 You split open spring and torrent;*
    you dried up ever-flowing rivers.

15 Yours is the day, yours also the night;*
    you established the moon and the sun.

16 You fixed all the boundaries of the earth;*
    you made both summer and winter.

17 Remember, O Lord, how the enemy scoffed,*
    how a foolish people despised your Name.

18 Do not hand over the life of your dove to wild beasts;*
    never forget the lives of your poor.

19 Look upon your covenant;*
    the dark places of the earth are haunts of violence.

20 Let not the oppressed turn away ashamed;*
    let the poor and needy praise your Name.

21 Arise, O God, maintain your cause;*
    remember how fools revile you all day long.

22 Forget not the clamor of your adversaries, *
    the unending tumult of those who rise up against you.

Maundy Thursday
Morning

102 *Domine, exaudi*

1 Lord, hear my prayer, and let my cry come before you;*
   hide not your face from me in the day of my trouble.

2 Incline your ear to me; *
   when I call, make haste to answer me,

3 For my days drift away like smoke, *
   and my bones are hot as burning coals.

4 My heart is smitten like grass and withered, *
   so that I forget to eat my bread.

5 Because of the voice of my groaning *
   I am but skin and bones.

6   I have become like a vulture in the wilderness, *
      like an owl among the ruins.

7   I lie awake and groan; *
      I am like a sparrow, lonely on a house-top.

8   My enemies revile me all day long,*
      and those who scoff at me have taken an oath against me.

9   For I have eaten ashes for bread *
      and mingled my drink with weeping.

10   Because of your indignation and wrath*
      you have lifted me up and thrown me away.

11   My days pass away like a shadow,*
      and I wither like the grass.

12   But you, O Lord, endure for ever,*
      and your Name from age to age.

13   You will arise and have compassion on Zion,
      for it is time to have mercy upon her;*
      indeed, the appointed time has come.

14   For your servants love her very rubble,*
      and are moved to pity even for her dust.

15   The nations shall fear your Name, O Lord,*
      and all the kings of the earth your glory.

16   For the Lord will build up Zion,*
      and his glory will appear.

17   He will look with favor on the prayer of the homeless;*
      he will not despise their plea.

18   Let this be written for a future generation,*
      so that a people yet unborn may praise the Lord.

19   For the Lord looked down from his holy place on high;*
      from the heavens he beheld the earth;

20   That he might hear the groan of the captive*
      and set free those condemned to die;

21   That they may declare in Zion the Name of the Lord,*
      and his praise in Jerusalem;

22   When the peoples are gathered together,*
      and the kingdoms also, to serve the Lord.

23 He has brought down my strength before my time;*
    he has shortened the number of my days;

24 And I said, "O my God,
    do not take me away in the midst of my days;*
    your years endure throughout all generations.

25 In the beginning, O Lord, you laid the foundations
       of the earth,*
    and the heavens are the work of your hands;

26 They shall perish, but you will endure;
    they all shall wear out like a garment; *
    as clothing you will change them,
    and they shall be changed;

27 But you are always the same, *
    and your years will never end.

28 The children of your servants shall continue, *
    and their offspring shall stand fast in your sight."

Evening

142 *Voce mea ad Dominum*

1 I cry to the Lord with my voice;*
    to the Lord I make loud supplication.

2 I pour out my complaint before him*
    and tell him all my trouble.

3 When my spirit languishes within me, you know my path;*
    in the way wherein I walk they have hidden a trap for me.

4 I look to my right hand and find no one who knows me;*
    I have no place to flee to, and no one cares for me.

5 I cry out to you, O Lord;*
    I say, "You are my refuge,
    my portion in the land of the living."

6 Listen to my cry for help, for I have been brought very low;*
    save me from those who pursue me,
    for they are too strong for me.

7 Bring me out of prison, that I may give thanks to your Name;*
    when you have dealt bountifully with me,
    the righteous will gather around me.

143 *Domine, exaudi*

1 Lord, hear my prayer,
and in your faithfulness heed my supplications;*
answer me in your righteousness.

2 Enter not into judgment with your servant,*
for in your sight shall no one living be justified.

3 For my enemy has sought my life;
he has crushed me to the ground; *
he has made me live in dark places like those who
are long dead.

4 My spirit faints within me; *
my heart within me is desolate.

5 I remember the time past;
I muse upon all your deeds; *
I consider the works of your hands.

6 I spread out my hands to you; *
my soul gasps to you like a thirsty land.

7 O Lord, make haste to answer me; my spirit fails me;*
do not hide your face from me
or I shall be like those who go down to the Pit.

8 Let me hear of your loving-kindness in the morning,
for I put my trust in you;*
show me the road that I must walk,
for I lift up my soul to you.

9 Deliver me from my enemies, O Lord, *
for I flee to you for refuge.

10 Teach me to do what pleases you, for you are my God;*
let your good Spirit lead me on level ground.

11 Revive me, O Lord, for your Name's sake;*
for your righteousness' sake, bring me out of trouble.

12 Of your goodness, destroy my enemies
and bring all my foes to naught, *
for truly I am your servant.

Good Friday

Morning

For the Invitatory

95   *Venite, exultemus*

1 Come, let us sing to the Lord;*
   let us shout for joy to the Rock of our salvation.

2 Let us come before his presence with thanksgiving*
   and raise a loud shout to him with psalms.

3 For the Lord is a great God, *
   and a great King above all gods.

4 In his hand are the caverns of the earth, *
   and the heights of the hills are his also.

5 The sea is his, for he made it, *
   and his hands have molded the dry land.

6 Come, let us bow down, and bend the knee,*
   and kneel before the Lord our Maker.

7 For he is our God,
   and we are the people of his pasture and the sheep of his hand.*
   Oh, that today you would hearken to his voice!

8 Harden not your hearts,
   as your forebears did in the wilderness,*
   at Meribah, and on that day at Massah,
   when they tempted me.

9 They put me to the test, *
   though they had seen my works.

10 Forty years long I detested that generation and said,*
   "This people are wayward in their hearts;
   they do not know my ways."

11 So I swore in my wrath,*
   "They shall not enter into my rest."

22   *Deus, Deus meus*

1 My God, my God, why have you forsaken me?*
   and are so far from my cry
   and from the words of my distress?

2 O my God, I cry in the daytime, but you do not answer;*
   by night as well, but I find no rest.

3 Yet you are the Holy One, *
   enthroned upon the praises of Israel.

4 Our forefathers put their trust in you; *
   they trusted, and you delivered them.

5 They cried out to you and were delivered; *
   they trusted in you and were not put to shame.

6 But as for me, I am a worm and no man, *
   scorned by all and despised by the people.

7 All who see me laugh me to scorn; *
   they curl their lips and wag their heads, saying,

8 "He trusted in the Lord; let him deliver him; *
   let him rescue him, if he delights in him."

9 Yet you are he who took me out of the womb, *
   and kept me safe upon my mother's breast.

10 I have been entrusted to you ever since I was born;*
   you were my God when I was still in my mother's womb.

11 Be not far from me, for trouble is near,*
   and there is none to help.

12 Many young bulls encircle me;*
   strong bulls of Bashan surround me.

13 They open wide their jaws at me,*
   like a ravening and a roaring lion.

14 I am poured out like water;
   all my bones are out of joint;*
   my heart within my breast is melting wax.

15 My mouth is dried out like a pot-sherd;
   my tongue sticks to the roof of my mouth;*
   and you have laid me in the dust of the grave.

16 Packs of dogs close me in,
   and gangs of evildoers circle around me;*
   they pierce my hands and my feet;
   I can count all my bones.

17 They stare and gloat over me;*
   they divide my garments among them;
   they cast lots for my clothing.

18 Be not far away, O Lord;*
   you are my strength; hasten to help me.

19 Save me from the sword,*
   my life from the power of the dog.

20 Save me from the lion's mouth,*
   my wretched body from the horns of wild bulls.

21 I will declare your Name to my brethren;*
   in the midst of the congregation I will praise you.

22 Praise the Lord, you that fear him;*
   stand in awe of him, O offspring of Israel;
   all you of Jacob's line, give glory.

23 For he does not despise nor abhor the poor in their poverty;
   neither does he hide his face from them;*
   but when they cry to him he hears them.

24 My praise is of him in the great assembly;*
   I will perform my vows in the presence of those who
      worship him.

25 The poor shall eat and be satisfied,
   and those who seek the Lord shall praise him:*
   "May your heart live for ever!"

26 All the ends of the earth shall remember and turn to the Lord,*
   and all the families of the nations shall bow before him.

27 For kingship belongs to the Lord;*
   he rules over the nations.

28 To him alone all who sleep in the earth bow down in worship;*
   all who go down to the dust fall before him.

29 My soul shall live for him;
   my descendants shall serve him;*
   they shall be known as the Lord's for ever.

30 They shall come and make known to a people yet unborn*
   the saving deeds that he has done.

40   *Expectans, expectavi*

1 I waited patiently upon the Lord;*
   he stooped to me and heard my cry.

2 He lifted me out of the desolate pit, out of the mire and clay;*
   he set my feet upon a high cliff and made my footing sure.

3 He put a new song in my mouth,
   a song of praise to our God;*
      many shall see, and stand in awe,
      and put their trust in the Lord.

4 Happy are they who trust in the Lord! *
   they do not resort to evil spirits or turn to false gods.

5 Great things are they that you have done, O Lord my God!
   how great your wonders and your plans for us! *
      there is none who can be compared with you.

6 Oh, that I could make them known and tell them! *
   but they are more than I can count.

7 In sacrifice and offering you take no pleasure *
   (you have given me ears to hear you);

8 Burnt-offering and sin-offering you have not required, *
   and so I said, "Behold, I come.

9 In the roll of the book it is written concerning me: *
   'I love to do your will, O my God;
      your law is deep in my heart.'"

10 I proclaimed righteousness in the great congregation;*
    behold, I did not restrain my lips;
    and that, O Lord, you know.

11 I Your righteousness have I not hidden in my heart;
    I have spoken of your faithfulness and your deliverance;*
    I have not concealed your love and faithfulness from
                      the great congregation.

12 You are the Lord;
    do not withhold your compassion from me;*
       let your love and your faithfulness keep me safe for ever,

13 For innumerable troubles have crowded upon me;
my sins have overtaken me, and I cannot see;*
they are more in number than the hairs of my head,
and my heart fails me.

14 Be pleased, O Lord, to deliver me;*
O Lord, make haste to help me.

15 Let them be ashamed and altogether dismayed
who seek after my life to destroy it;*
let them draw back and be disgraced
who take pleasure in my misfortune.

16 Let those who say "Aha!" and gloat over me be confounded,
because they are ashamed.

17 Let all who seek you rejoice in you and be glad;*
let those who love your salvation continually say,
"Great is the Lord!"

18 Though I am poor and afflicted,*
the Lord will have regard for me.

19 You are my helper and my deliverer;*
do not tarry, O my God.

54 *Deus, in nomine*

1 Save me, O God, by your Name; *
in your might, defend my cause.

2 Hear my prayer, O God; *
give ear to the words of my mouth.

3 For the arrogant have risen up against me,
and the ruthless have sought my life, *
those who have no regard for God.

4 Behold, God is my helper; *
it is the Lord who sustains my life.

5 Render evil to those who spy on me; *
in your faithfulness, destroy them.

6 I will offer you a freewill sacrifice*
and praise your Name, O Lord, for it is good.

7 For you have rescued me from every trouble, *
and my eye has seen the ruin of my foes.

Holy Saturday
Morning

For the Invitatory

95   *Venite, exultemus*

1   Come, let us sing to the Lord;*
    let us shout for joy to the Rock of our salvation.

2   Let us come before his presence with thanksgiving*
    and raise a loud shout to him with psalms.

3   For the Lord is a great God, *
    and a great King above all gods.

4   In his hand are the caverns of the earth, *
    and the heights of the hills are his also.

5   The sea is his, for he made it, *
    and his hands have molded the dry land.

6   Come, let us bow down, and bend the knee,*
    and kneel before the Lord our Maker.

7   For he is our God,
    and we are the people of his pasture and the sheep of his hand.*
    Oh, that today you would hearken to his voice!

8   Harden not your hearts,
    as your forebears did in the wilderness,*
    at Meribah, and on that day at Massah,
    when they tempted me.

9   They put me to the test, *
    though they had seen my works.

10 Forty years long I detested that generation and said,*
    "This people are wayward in their hearts;
    they do not know my ways."

11 So I swore in my wrath,*
    "They shall not enter into my rest."

88   *Domine, Deus*

1   O Lord, my God, my Savior,*
    by day and night I cry to you.

2 Let my prayer enter into your presence; *
   incline your ear to my lamentation.

3 For I am full of trouble; *
   my life is at the brink of the grave.

4 I am counted among those who go down to the Pit; *
   I have become like one who has no strength;

5 Lost among the dead, *
   like the slain who lie in the grave,

6 Whom you remember no more, *
   for they are cut off from your hand.

7 You have laid me in the depths of the Pit, *
   in dark places, and in the abyss.

8 Your anger weighs upon me heavily, *
   and all your great waves overwhelm me.

9 You have put my friends far from me;
   you have made me to be abhorred by them; *
   I am in prison and cannot get free.

10 My sight has failed me because of trouble;*
   Lord, I have called upon you daily;
   I have stretched out my hands to you.

11 Do you work wonders for the dead?*
   will those who have died stand up and give you thanks?

12 Will your loving-kindness be declared in the grave?*
   your faithfulness in the land of destruction?

13 Will your wonders be known in the dark?*
   or your righteousness in the country where all is forgotten?

14 But as for me, O Lord, I cry to you for help;*
   in the morning my prayer comes before you.

15 Lord, why have you rejected me?*
   why have you hidden your face from me?

16 Ever since my youth, I have been wretched and at the
                  point of death;*
   I have borne your terrors with a troubled mind.

17 Your blazing anger has swept over me;*
   your terrors have destroyed me;

18 They surround me all day long like a flood;*
   they encompass me on every side.

19 My friend and my neighbor you have put away from me,*
   and darkness is my only companion.

Evening

27   *Dominus illuminatio*

1 The Lord is my light and my salvation;
  whom then shall I fear?*
     the Lord is the strength of my life;
     of whom then shall I be afraid?

2 When evildoers came upon me to eat up my flesh, *
     it was they, my foes and my adversaries, who stumbled and fell.

3 Though an army should encamp against me, *
     yet my heart shall not be afraid;

4 And though war should rise up against me, *
     yet will I put my trust in him.

5 One thing have I asked of the Lord;
  one thing I seek;*
     that I may dwell in the house of the Lord all the days of my life;

6 To behold the fair beauty of the Lord *
     and to seek him in his temple.

7 For in the day of trouble he shall keep me safe in his shelter;*
     he shall hide me in the secrecy of his dwelling
     and set me high upon a rock.

8 Even now he lifts up my head *
     above my enemies round about me.

9 Therefore I will offer in his dwelling an oblation
  with sounds of great gladness; *
     I will sing and make music to the Lord.

10 Hearken to my voice, O Lord, when I call;*
     have mercy on me and answer me.

11 You speak in my heart and say, "Seek my face."*
     Your face, Lord, will I seek.

12 Hide not your face from me,*
    nor turn away your servant in displeasure.

13 You have been my helper; cast me not away;*
    do not forsake me, O God of my salvation.

14 Though my father and my mother forsake me,*
    the Lord will sustain me.

15 Show me your way, O Lord;*
    lead me on a level path, because of my enemies.

16 Deliver me not into the hand of my adversaries,*
    for false witnesses have risen up against me,
    and also those who speak malice.

17 What if I had not believed
    that I should see the goodness of the Lord*
    in the land of the living!

18 O tarry and await the Lord's pleasure;
    be strong, and he shall comfort your heart;*
    wait patiently for the Lord.

St. Joseph (March 19)
Morning

132 *Memento, Domine*

1 Lord, remember David,*
   and all the hardships he endured;

2 How he swore an oath to the Lord*
   and vowed a vow to the Mighty One of Jacob:

3 "I will not come under the roof of my house," *
   nor climb up into my bed;

4 I will not allow my eyes to sleep, *
   nor let my eyelids slumber;

5 Until I find a place for the Lord, *
   a dwelling for the Mighty One of Jacob."

6 "The ark! We heard it was in Ephratah; *
   we found it in the fields of Jearim.

7 Let us go to God's dwelling place; *
  let us fall upon our knees before his footstool.";

8 Arise, O Lord, into your resting-place, *
  you and the ark of your strength.

9 Let your priests be clothed with righteousness; *
  let your faithful people sing with joy.

10 For your servant David's sake,*
   do not turn away the face of your Anointed.

11 The Lord has sworn an oath to David;*
   in truth, he will not break it:

12 "A son, the fruit of your body*
   will I set upon your throne.

13 If your children keep my covenant
   and my testimonies that I shall teach them,*
     their children will sit upon your throne for evermore."

14 For the Lord has chosen Zion;*
   he has desired her for his habitation:

15 "This shall be my resting-place for ever;*
   here will I dwell, for I delight in her.

16 I will surely bless her provisions, *
   and satisfy her poor with bread.

17 I will clothe her priests with salvation, *
   and her faithful people will rejoice and sing.

18 There will I make the horn of David flourish; *
   I have prepared a lamp for my Anointed.

19 As for his enemies, I will clothe them with shame; *
   but as for him, his crown will shine."

Evening

34 *Benedicam Dominum*

1 I will bless the Lord at all times; *
  his praise shall ever be in my mouth.

2 I will glory in the Lord; *
  let the humble hear and rejoice.

3　Proclaim with me the greatness of the Lord;
　　let us exalt his Name together.

4　I sought the Lord, and he answered me*
　　and delivered me out of all my terror.

5　Look upon him and be radiant, *
　　and let not your faces be ashamed.

6　I called in my affliction and the Lord heard me *
　　and saved me from all my troubles.

7　The angel of the Lord encompasses those who fear him,*
　　and he will deliver them.

8　Taste and see that the Lord is good; *
　　happy are they who trust in him!

9　Fear the Lord, you that are his saints,*
　　for those who fear him lack nothing.

10　The young lions lack and suffer hunger,*
　　but those who seek the Lord lack nothing that is good.

11　Come, children, and listen to me;*
　　I will teach you the fear of the Lord.

12　Who among you loves life*
　　and desires long life to enjoy prosperity?

13　Keep your tongue from evil-speaking*
　　and your lips from lying words.

14　Turn from evil and do good;*
　　seek peace and pursue it.

15　The eyes of the Lord are upon the righteous,*
　　and his ears are open to their cry.

16　The face of the Lord is against those who do evil,*
　　to root out the remembrance of them from the earth.

17　The righteous cry, and the Lord hears them*
　　and delivers them from all their troubles.

18　The Lord is near to the brokenhearted*
　　and will save those whose spirits are crushed.

19　Many are the troubles of the righteous,*
　　but the Lord will deliver him out of them all.

20 He will keep safe all his bones;*
   not one of them shall be broken.

21 Evil shall slay the wicked,*
   and those who hate the righteous will be punished.

22 The Lord ransoms the life of his servants,*
   and none will be punished who trust in him.

Eve of the Annunciation (March 24)

8 *Domine, Dominus noster*

1 O Lord our Governor,*
   how exalted is your Name in all the world!

2 Out of the mouths of infants and children *
   your majesty is praised above the heavens.

3 You have set up a stronghold against your adversaries,*
   to quell the enemy and the avenger.

4 When I consider your heavens, the work of your fingers,*
   the moon and the stars you have set in their courses,

5 What is man that you should be mindful of him? *
   the son of man that you should seek him out?

6 You have made him but little lower than the angels; *
   you adorn him with glory and honor;

7 You give him mastery over the works of your hands; *
   you put all things under his feet:

8 All sheep and oxen, *
   even the wild beasts of the field,

9 The birds of the air, the fish of the sea, *
   and whatsoever walks in the paths of the sea.

10 O Lord our Governor,*
   how exalted is your Name in all the world!

138 *Confitebor tibi*

1 I will give thanks to you, O Lord, with my whole heart;*
   before the gods I will sing your praise.

2 I will bow down toward your holy temple
and praise your Name,*
    because of your love and faithfulness;

3 For you have glorified your Name*
    and your word above all things.

4 When I called, you answered me;*
    you increased my strength within me.

5 All the kings of the earth will praise you, O Lord,*
    when they have heard the words of your mouth.

6 They will sing of the ways of the Lord,*
    that great is the glory of the Lord.

7 Though the Lord be high, he cares for the lowly;*
    he perceives the haughty from afar.

8 Though I walk in the midst of trouble, you keep me safe;*
    you stretch forth your hand against the fury of my enemies;
    your right hand shall save me.

9 The Lord will make good his purpose for me;*
    O Lord, your love endures for ever;
    do not abandon the works of your hands.

The Annunciation (March 25)

Morning

85 *Benedixisti, Domine*

1 You have been gracious to your land, O Lord,*
    you have restored the good fortune of Jacob.

2 You have forgiven the iniquity of your people *
    and blotted out all their sins.

3 You have withdrawn all your fury*
    and turned yourself from your wrathful indignation.

4 Restore us then, O God our Savior;*
    let your anger depart from us.

5 Will you be displeased with us for ever? *
    will you prolong your anger from age to age?

6 Will you not give us life again, *
    that your people may rejoice in you?

7 Show us your mercy, O Lord,*
    and grant us your salvation.

8 I will listen to what the Lord God is saying, *
    for he is speaking peace to his faithful people
    and to those who turn their hearts to him.

9 Truly, his salvation is very near to those who fear him,*
    that his glory may dwell in our land.

10 Mercy and truth have met together;*
    righteousness and peace have kissed each other.

11 Truth shall spring up from the earth,*
    and righteousness shall look down from heaven.

12 The Lord will indeed grant prosperity,*
    and our land will yield its increase.

13 Righteousness shall go before him,*
    and peace shall be a pathway for his feet.

87 *Fundamenta ejus*

1 On the holy mountain stands the city he has founded;*
    the Lord loves the gates of Zion
    more than all the dwellings of Jacob.

2 Glorious things are spoken of you, *
    O city of our God.

3 I count Egypt and Babylon among those who know me; *
    behold Philistia, Tyre, and Ethiopia:
    in Zion were they born.

4 Of Zion it shall be said, "Everyone was born in her, *
    and the Most High himself shall sustain her."

5 The Lord will record as he enrolls the peoples, *
    "These also were born there."

6 The singers and the dancers will say, *
    "All my fresh springs are in you."

110 *Dixit Dominus*

1 The Lord said to my Lord, "Sit at my right hand,*
  until I make your enemies your footstool."

2 The Lord will send the scepter of your power out of Zion,*
  saying, ";Rule over your enemies round about you.

3 Princely state has been yours from the day of your birth; *
  in the beauty of holiness have I begotten you,
  like dew from the womb of the morning."

4 The Lord has sworn and he will not recant:*
  "You are a priest for ever after the order of Melchizedek."

5 The Lord who is at your right hand
  will smite kings in the day of his wrath; *
  he will rule over the nations.

6 He will heap high the corpses;*
  he will smash heads over the wide earth.

7 He will drink from the brook beside the road;*
  therefore he will lift high his head.

132 *Memento, Domine*

1 Lord, remember David,*
  and all the hardships he endured;

2 How he swore an oath to the Lord*
  and vowed a vow to the Mighty One of Jacob:

3 "I will not come under the roof of my house," *
  nor climb up into my bed;

4 I will not allow my eyes to sleep, *
  nor let my eyelids slumber;

5 Until I find a place for the Lord, *
  a dwelling for the Mighty One of Jacob."

6 "The ark! We heard it was in Ephratah; *
  we found it in the fields of Jearim.

7 Let us go to God's dwelling place; *
  let us fall upon our knees before his footstool."

8 Arise, O Lord, into your resting-place, *
  you and the ark of your strength.

9 Let your priests be clothed with righteousness; *
  let your faithful people sing with joy.

10 For your servant David's sake,*
   do not turn away the face of your Anointed.

11 The Lord has sworn an oath to David;*
   in truth, he will not break it:

12 "A son, the fruit of your body*
   will I set upon your throne.

13 If your children keep my covenant
   and my testimonies that I shall teach them,*
     their children will sit upon your throne for evermore."

14 For the Lord has chosen Zion;*
   he has desired her for his habitation:

15 "This shall be my resting-place for ever;*
   here will I dwell, for I delight in her.

16 I will surely bless her provisions, *
   and satisfy her poor with bread.

17 I will clothe her priests with salvation, *
   and her faithful people will rejoice and sing.

18 There will I make the horn of David flourish; *
   I have prepared a lamp for my Anointed.

19 As for his enemies, I will clothe them with shame; *
   but as for him, his crown will shine."